An Empire of Regions

★★★★★★★★★★★★

A BRIEF HISTORY OF COLONIAL
BRITISH AMERICA

An Empire of Regions

★ ★ ★ ★ ★ ★ ★ ★ ★ ★ ★ ★ ★

A BRIEF HISTORY OF COLONIAL
BRITISH AMERICA

by Eric Nellis

UNIVERSITY OF TORONTO PRESS

Copyright © University of Toronto Press Incorporated 2010

www.utphighereducation.com

LIBRARY AND ARCHIVES CANADA CATALOGUING IN PUBLICATION

Nellis, Eric Guest, 1938–

    An empire of regions : a brief history of colonial British America / by Eric Nellis.

Includes bibliographical references and index.

ISBN 978-1-4426-0139-0 (bound).—ISBN 978-1-4426-0140-6 (pbk.)

    1. United States—History—Colonial period, ca. 1600–1775. 2. United States—History—16th century. I. Title.

E188.N44 2009   973.2   C2009-906226-7

We welcome comments and suggestions regarding any aspect of our publications—please feel free to contact us at news@utphighereducation.com or visit our Internet site at www.utphighereducation.com.

North America
5201 Dufferin Street
North York, Ontario, Canada, M3H 5T8

2250 Military Road
Tonawanda, New York, USA, 14150
ORDERS PHONE: 1-800-565-9523
ORDERS FAX: 1-800-221-9985
ORDERS E-MAIL: utpbooks@utpress.utoronto.ca

UK, Ireland, and continental Europe
NBN International
Estover Road, Plymouth, PL6 7PY, UK
TEL: 44 (0) 1752 202301
FAX ORDER LINE: 44 (0) 1752 202333
enquiries@nbninternational.com

The University of Toronto Press acknowledges the financial support for its publishing activities of the Government of Canada through the Book Publishing Industry Development Program (BPIDP).

Interior design by Jennifer Blais; cover design by Michel Vrána, blackeye.com

To my family

CONTENTS

* * * * * ★ ★ * * * * *

List of Maps and Tables

* * * * * ★ ★ ★ * * * *

Maps

Tables

Acknowledgements

I thank the colleagues and students who, over the years, have enriched my understanding of the first British Empire. I owe a debt to the archivists and librarians who have guided me through the records of the seventeenth and eighteenth century American colonies. As with any survey or synthesis, this book reflects the research and interpretations of the many scholars whose names appear in the references in this book. The editorial experts at Broadview Press and The University of Toronto Press have been a pleasure to work with. I thank Eric Leinberger of the University of British Columbia for his skill in producing the maps and his patience with my changes. Karen Taylor edited the final version of the text by refining the composition and correcting my errors of fact or citation. Among her many talents are cheerfulness and efficiency. My wife Vicky's assistance and support has made this a happy project.

A Note on Usage

America. The terms "Americas" and "America" are used to describe the entire continental mass and the Caribbean. Otherwise, "America" will be preceded by a qualifier, as in "French America" or "British America." Toward the end of the colonial period, the use of "America" to describe the colonies and "Americans" to describe colonists in British North America reflects the way the term was used contemporaneously.

Charters. The English colonies were created by a type of *patent* or license generally referred to as a charter. These were, in effect, *monopolies* with defined territorial boundaries (Virginia) or control over particular economic ventures in the case of trading companies (the Royal African Company for the slave trade, for example). They were granted under the Monarch's authority to groups of colonizers, to "companies" such as the Virginia Company or the Massachusetts Bay Company or the Hudson's Bay Company (the latter held both a territorial and a commodity monopoly—on furs), and even to individuals, to "proprietors" (William Penn, for example, or Lord Baltimore in Maryland) and groups of proprietors. A third type of charter was the "royal" charter, in effect a grant by the Crown to the Crown. These allowed the Crown to appoint governors and control administrative councils. But all charters eventually allowed for representative legislatures. That legislative component gave each North American colony a shared model for governance, even as each colony developed distinct social and economic personalities. There were strings attached to charters, including trade regulations and the acknowledgement of English (British) law. In all cases, the supremacy of the Crown's sovereignty was assumed. Nevertheless, the charter system allowed for a great deal of local authority that was seldom supervised by the Crown, so it enabled the residents to develop in their distinctive ways. The charter system was uniquely English and compares only slightly to the French and Spanish colonization models.

Colonies and Provinces. The term "colony" was the normal usage for the North American jurisdictions. In the late seventeenth century, the term "province" appeared in formal designation and informal usage. Thus, for example, the new 1691 Massachusetts charter referred to the "Province of Massachusetts Bay." In the present book, the term colony will normally be used throughout the time period. The use of "state" to refer to any of the "thirteen colonies" is anachronistic. Only after the Declaration of Independence in 1776 did the term "state" take on any official or specific meaning in America.

Counties and Towns. The colonies (provinces) used the common English system of "counties" to define local authority. The functions of the counties varied from colony to colony. The county unit in Virginia, for example, had greater political authority than it did in Massachusetts, where it was mostly a unit of jurisprudence, that is, for court and legal functions. The "town" was the fount of local political power in New England and although parishes, districts, townships, hundreds, manors, and cities could be found in various parts of colonial America, they were not always interchangeable or even similar in function. All references to local jurisdictions in this text will be identified by place and function. The term "city" will be used in a generalized way to refer to any, some, or all of the handful of ports that contained populations of several thousand or more people. These were not cities except in a relative sense. Boston, for example, was formally a town under the authority of the General Court of Massachusetts, like hundreds of other towns in New England. It was simply the largest and most important town in Massachusetts.

Dates. Much of the period covered in this book took place while adjustments to the English calendar were being made. Until 1752, the Anglo-American calendar was derived from the early medieval calendar, which marked the new year as beginning on March 25 (Annunciation Day) so that what we might think of as February 1691 was often expressed as either February 1690 or February 1690/91. Pope Gregory XIII issued a decree in 1582 to improve the leap-year calculations of the Julian calendar (named for Julius Caesar) and to reinstate that calendar's designation of January 1 as the start of the year. But the Protestant states were slow to accept these improvements. When Great Britain and her colonies belatedly adopted the Gregorian calendar in 1752,there was an adjustment of 11 days made in September of 1752 when the day after September 2, 1752 became September 14, to the confusion of much of the British population, which assumed it had "lost" 11 days. The terms "Old Style" and "New Style" were used by contemporaries for reference. George Washington, for example, was born on February 11, 1731 Old Style and that became February 22, 1732 New Style. The latter is the date always used to mark his birth. The dates given in this text are adjusted to New Style and assume the year beginning on January 1, even for years before 1752. The older terms BC (before Christ) and AD (*anno Domini*) are replaced here by BCE (before the common era) and CE (common era).

English and British. The colonies were English in terms of political sovereignty until 1707 when the parliaments of Scotland and England were joined to create Great Britain. Thereafter, it is proper to refer to the colonies as "British America" and the colonists as British or British Americans, although terms such as Scottish, Scotch-Irish (Northern Ireland), Welsh, or Irish can be used today to define the ethnic subdivisions of the British Isles just as those distinctions were used in the seventeenth and eighteenth centuries. The term "Anglo America" is a useful one given the persistence of the English language, the original English charters, and the overall structure of the English legal system and political institutions and principles, even though, by the time of the Revolution, approximately one-third of the white colonial population was not ethnic English. In the text, the term Britain will be used specifically to refer to Great Britain after 1707, and Scotland, Ireland, and England will be used to denote more specific subdivisions.

Farm and Plantation. Over 90 per cent of the colonial population was rural as late as the end of the eighteenth century, and the vast majority was engaged directly in agricultural production. The term "farm" in this text refers to family operations of limited scale, with all or most of the labor being done by family members with occasional neighborly or servant help being used. Some farms in the northern colonies did employ more than a few servants and did produce foodstuffs for the market, but most farms in the colonies were at or near "subsistence" (near or at sufficiency). The term "plantation" in this text is used specifically to refer to operations that produced "cash crops" (tobacco, rice, and even grains) with the use of slave labor. Contemporaries used the terms "farm" and "plantation" interchangeably at times, and the word "plantation" originally referred to a settlement, but, in this text, "plantation" will have a narrower application for the sake of economic, cultural, social, and race-related purposes.

Indigenous Peoples. In Canada today, the original peoples of the Americas and their descendents are referred to as "First Nations" people. The terms "indigenous," "aboriginal," and "native" are also used but the term "Indian" is now seen as derisory. In the United States, however, "Indian" is still commonly used mostly without any negative or positive connotations attached to it, as is the phrase "Native American." The latter tends to confusion because all Americans can refer to themselves as native-born Americans. Colonists and their successors for generations simply used the term "Indian." This text will use the lower case "native" and, where appropriate, the more specific tribal or group name, "Algonquin" or "Huron," for example. See below for the enslavement of natives.

Militia. This word refers to the citizen defense system developed in England and taken to the colonies. It obliged each able-bodied man, usually between the ages of 16 and 60, to "muster" (gather) at regular intervals for military training.

The practice was initiated early in Jamestown after 1607 and repeated with the founding of each colony. These musters were weekly, monthly, or irregular, depending on time and place. In serious conflicts, campaigns against natives, or defense against native attacks, the militias often had to leave their homes for days or weeks at a time. When wars between Britain and France broke out in the eighteenth century, colonial militias formed the majority of combatants in some of the campaigns. The authority for militia codes and rules was with the colonial authority, but each town, parish, county, or district was responsible for maintaining a ready, well-armed, and trained contingent. The numbers mustered in Massachusetts, for example, during King William's, Queen Anne's and King George's wars and the French and Indian War (the Seven Years' War) numbered in the thousands. Militias took part in every major military event during the colonial period. Their role in the War for Independence after 1775 was crucial.

Numbers. This book relies on trade, population, land distribution, and price estimates to make some of its interpretations. Some numbers are more reliable than others. For example, surviving imperial trade figures and some local land records are quite reliable. Slave imports are generally dependable, given the necessity of recording invoices and bills of lading and the fact that many of those records have survived. Population numbers are drawn from scattered censuses and extrapolations. For the colonies, see in particular, the *Historical Statistics of the United States, Colonial Times to 1970* (Washington: Bureau of the Census, 1975). The estimates of European and native populations are drawn from sources that are identified in the "Suggested Reading" and "General Reference" bibliographies. Monetary references are given in pounds sterling for the most part. Wealth estimates are based on converting any local or convenient exchange mechanism into sterling value. For a sense of the complex varieties of exchange, from the value of a day's labor in eighteenth century Massachusetts to the cost of a slave, see Chapter 7 and 8, respectively. For an indispensable reference for "rates of exchange," see John J. McCusker, *Money and Exchange in Europe and America, 1600–1775: A Handbook* (Chapel Hill: University of North Carolina Press, 1978).

Parliament, Crown, and Royal. Parliament, that is, the Houses of Commons and Lords is the legislative branch of the English/British government and refers specifically to that institution. The term "Crown" is used to mean the combined apparatus and authority of the Monarchy (the queen or king as "executive") and Parliament. "Royal" is usually used as a specific reference to the Monarch or the Monarchy.

Quotation. The author of the quotation will be identified in the text. Where the spelling, syntax, and punctuation of English language quotations have been changed or modified from the original, the quotation will be identified as "modernized." All material originally in a language other than English has been quoted from translations into modern English.

Slave, black, African, African American. The term "slave" in the text will usually denote "black," "African," or "African American" (a person of African descent, born in the colonies). Here and there, especially in the earlier decades of colonization, natives were enslaved, and there was a "trade" in kidnapped natives in the Carolinas, for example, that fed into the slave market. Natives were often sold into slavery as punishment for crimes or after capture in war. But slavery came to be defined by the African origins of the great majority of slaves. Contemporaries mostly used "negro" and sometimes "colored" or "mulatto" and often referred to their own slaves as "my servant" or "my man" and so on. In this text, slave, black, African, and African American will be used in contextual terms. The term "free black" is self-explanatory.

War and Weapons. Europeans brought firearms to America. In the early sixteenth century, the Spanish came with crossbows, pikes, metal helmets, and body armor, along with the matchlock arquebus, a heavy, awkward musket that had to rest on a forked rod while the match was applied to the charge to fire the shot, usually a lead ball. In the decades following the arrival of the northern Europeans in the seventeenth century, the matchlock gave way to the flintlock, a design that had a striking mechanism on a flint fixture that ignited the charge. Musketeers could now hold the weapon in both arms and increase their rate of fire. Wooden ramrods gave way to metal ones, and, by 1700, a new musket design allowed for a bayonet to be attached to a barrel end. Pikes, breastplates, and helmets gradually disappeared. Standardized bores (barrel diameters) meant that shot and the molds to make them could also be standardized. Gunsmiths were among the earliest immigrants to North America, and the occupation was an important one in all the colonies. Gunpowder was difficult to make and expensive and usually imported. Larger rural communities and towns built facilities to store gunpowder and cache arms for the militia. Iron works provided the material for manufacturing or repairing weapons and specialized parts were imported into the colonies along with muskets.

The natives who greeted the Europeans were armed with arrows and strung bows and stone clubs. Trade and alliances with Europeans led to the widespread distribution of firearms among the native populations in North

America, almost from the earliest contact. Other metals made their way into native society, and steel knives and axes appeared in the native towns. The club gave way to the metal hatchet, the tomahawk, which was favored by natives and whites alike as a combined weapon and tool.

As Europeans waged war against each other in North America, quantities of muskets made their way into colonial armories. Also, during the eighteenth century, efficient field and siege artillery were used increasingly in Europe's colonial wars. Constant weapons' acquisition and use in war and hunting led to innovation in design. Colonists modified or adapted European models. One of the most notable adaptations was the eighteenth century evolution of the long-barreled rifle or "rifled musket"; the most famous of these were known either as the Pennsylvania or, later, the Kentucky rifle. In this case, the smooth inside of the barrel was grooved to create a higher velocity and greater range. It took skill to achieve accuracy at distance, and the rifle gave rise to expert marksmen. But the smoothbore musket dominated. Its effective range was 100 yards or so, but it loosed a half-inch or larger missile that could tear bodies apart at that range.

Cutlasses, swords, and pistols were used in the hand-to-hand fighting that went with naval warfare. But the ship's cannon was the decisive weapon on the high seas and in the naval sieges and blockades that occurred when the Europeans fought each other in North America. By the middle of the eighteenth century, the British Navy had built the HMS *Victory*, later Nelson's flagship. It bristled with 100 smoothbore cannons capable of firing a variety of shot (e.g., grape and canister) and balls of up to 68 pounds in weight.

PREFACE

* * * * * * ★ ★ * * * * *

The historian... must stand, as it were, on the shores of England and look across the ocean at the American colonies, and at the same time be able to place his feet in the Western Hemisphere and look back at the British Isles. Such a feat of mental gymnastics would give a sort of double-exposure view of... the actual nature of the colonial world.

—Leonard W. Labaree, foreword to *The Colonial Background to the American Revolution*, by Charles M. Andrews (New Haven: Yale University Press, 1961), x.

In the decades since that comment, historians' views of the "actual nature of the colonial world" have changed. Historians now recreate a colonial world that includes not only the broad cultural and political themes of the older history but also the roles of natives, slaves, women, and families in its development. There is a lingering temptation to look back from the Revolution and its unifying outcome to see the colonies as a nursery for the confederated Republic and not as the rather separated parts they were. These colonies certainly did not have the Revolution on their horizons. When John Winthrop in

1630 recited his striking "city on the hill" scriptural metaphor for the Christian experiment in Massachusetts, he was not thinking of Jefferson's, Lincoln's, or Obama's vision of the United States of America. The social objective of Winthrop and his group was at once more limited, measuring "community" in a narrower way than nationhood, and more strongly ecclesiastical, looking for a way to regenerate the Church of England in an American exile—their "errand into the wilderness." The term "Zion" (or "Sion") crops up in some of the Puritans' descriptions of their exclusive community. A recent and stimulating biography by Francis J. Bremer, *John Winthrop: America's Forgotten Founding Father* (2003), calls Winthrop a "founder" with a legacy that survives in the greater American community. Suffice to say that Winthrop is certainly a founder of colonial Massachusetts. He died in 1649, his deeply spiritual vision not quite realized. It is still not realized. One wonders what he might have thought of today's America and its use of his "city on the hill" image as a slogan for national identity and purpose. Winthrop of Massachusetts, John Smith of Virginia, and William Penn of Pennsylvania, along with the other colonial "founders," each had a separate vision for the future of their enterprises. However, they hardly saw what they were doing as building blocks to a colonial union let alone to a national collective in America.

We need to stand with a foot in any colony of Britain's mainland North American Empire and one in any other to see them as separate entities, as disparate in their social and economic characteristics as Massachusetts was from Virginia or Pennsylvania from South Carolina. To study the history of the North American mainland colonies without reference to their European imperial neighbors or their transatlantic connections makes no sense, but ignoring the differences among the thirteen colonies and in their regional settings also distorts the "actual nature" of Britain's American colonies. They shared much in common, to be sure, but it was their differences that ultimately defined colonial America. Moreover, although the colonies matured, they did so as peripheral extensions of a Britain that was itself changing in fundamental ways. It was British ambition and institutional reorganization rather than collective colonial ambition that brought on the crisis that led to the Revolution. The present book suggests an alternative to conventional colonial histories by seeing the colonies as units in a largely incoherent whole, the wider world of Britain's North American Empire. It also notes that Britain's evolution in the seventeenth and eighteenth centuries ran ahead of the various colonies' ability to grasp it. Britain's priorities were never based on the nurturing of colonial rights, as claimed by colonial spokesmen after the middle of the eighteenth century.

This study acknowledges the historians' new paths of enquiry in areas such as African American, native and gender studies, the role of the

Caribbean, and the changing standards of living in the colonies. Other specific aspects of colonial history, such as the roots of capitalism, consumerism, and nascent individualism, now help us see colonial life from a wider range of perspectives. We now have a better sense of how the growth and development of the colonies was sustained by the forced labor of servants and slaves or the hopes of ordinary farmers and families and the ambitions of artisans, planters, and merchants. Although this book acknowledges those refreshing new approaches to the study of the colonies, it also emphasizes the importance of how the colonies were formed, by whom, and for what purpose. The ultimate form of each colonial society derived from its original objectives and separate history. Some colonies were established and shaped by Protestant theologians such as Winthrop and Penn, as experimental refuges; some by commercial interests such as the Virginia Company, for shareholder profit; and others by the wealthy and the titled for personal aggrandizement, such as the first Carolinian proprietors.

Britain was but one of several European imperial powers in America, and its interests clashed with those of the others. North America was never isolated from international rivalries, and European conflicts usually made their way to North America and the Caribbean. We need to compare contemporaneous Europe and pre-Columbian America while we compare the Spanish, Portuguese, French, and Dutch empires with the British. In other words, the present book spends some time examining the European background to the age of exploration and conquest, with due reflection on the native American and African cultures that would be drawn into the great European transformation of the Americas. Europeans were products of their own environments in time and place, and the native Americans they encountered were as varied in their circumstances and cultures as were the Europeans who intruded.

Geography and climate affected every European colonization process, both in their formative years and in their later adaptations. In the case of the British American colonies, the physical environments of the early settlements certainly influenced the commercial, ideological, or spiritual intentions of the colonizers. Moreover, in British America, the term "colonists" should be seen as a synonym for "colonizers." The British settlers and their progeny did not so much colonize the resident native populations in the usual sense of a minority ruling over a majority; settlers displaced or assimilated the indigenous residents to *become* the majority.

The major part of the book is set in the period between the arrival of Columbus in the Caribbean in 1492 and the publication of the Declaration of Independence in 1776. It is intended as a companion to my survey of the American Revolution, *The Long Road to Change: America's Revolution, 1750–1820,* but can also be read as a self-contained study of the political, social, and cultural characteristics of the thirteen mainland British American colonies. The book's chronological narrative moves to the point at which those colonies began the process of separation from the British Empire and examines the way the colonies' uneven, dissimilar characteristics were shaped. In important and unexpected ways, each colony developed quite specific features that arose from the English method of founding and legitimizing each of them, that is, the charter system. This system bestowed a clearly stated local authority on the holders of the charters—the groups, companies, and proprietors who settled America. Each began as a self-conscious autonomous unit with the Crown's blessing. However, ultimately, each became *part* of Britain's eighteenth century American Empire.

The haphazard methods of colonization, the sporadic timing of settlement, and varied characteristics of the thirteen colonies as they evolved over many generations would, in some ways, belie their unprecedented collaboration when they began to resist the empire's new policies after 1763. What spurred that concert was a common assumption of threats to their shared British citizenship. A defense of those rights fused into a *collective* defense of them. Yet twelve British American colonies, including Newfoundland, Nova Scotia, the newly defined Quebec, and the West Indian islands did *not* revolt. Why not? The explanation lies in the more fully developed local institutions of the contiguous mainland colonies. Quebec, recently detached from the French Empire, stood to benefit from Britain's protection of its language and religion. The West Indian colonies were populated by up to 90 per cent black majorities governed by a few royal officials and a small minority of transient white landlords and managers. Nova Scotia was a new colony, thinly populated by British subjects, and Newfoundland was remote, its small resident population logistically dependent on its British connection.

The English adventurers, investors, companies, and religious experimenters who established permanent settlements on the North American mainland did so a century after Spain and Portugal had colonized parts of the Americas, Asia, and Africa. The French and Dutch were also a century behind the Spanish in the Caribbean and North America. Thus the founding of the British North American colonies occurred in an Atlantic world of which the British had some understanding, gleaned from a growing descriptive literature and the reports of fishers, explorers, and traders. Also, their Europe was not the one that produced the fifteenth and early sixteenth century Portuguese and Spanish expansionists. The first surviving English colony in America, the troubled settlement at Jamestown, Virginia, was clearly a product of its time. It reflected the self-assurance of an emergent entrepreneurial class in the aftermath of the buoyant Elizabethan era, but its managers turned out to be incompetent and quite naive in the ways of colonization.

The founders of Virginia had none of the swaggering conquest mentality of the Spanish a century earlier. Their successors survived by modifying and redefining the Virginia Company's objectives and, over time, created a distinct society. But, more to the point, Virginia's early confusion stands in sharp contrast to the orderly Puritan enterprise of a generation later.

The century between Columbus and the arrival of the northern Europeans gave the latecomers less of the Americas to exploit. There was room for them throughout the Caribbean, but their belated arrival meant that their mainland settlements skirted the established Iberian boundaries in Mexico and Florida and went north. The future Canada and the United States took root in what the Spanish had not been able to exploit.

Within a century of their arrival, the northern Europeans had obscured or transformed much of the aboriginal footprint. They also reshaped the human landscape by displacing, assimilating, or exterminating a majority of the mainland's native populations. They began the process of populating the Caribbean with African slaves, who were, by the middle of the eighteenth century, in the majority on the islands. The Spanish had eliminated almost all the indigenous peoples of the Caribbean during the first half of the sixteenth century. Substantial black minorities also appeared on the North American mainland, in some of the British colonies, by the middle of the eighteenth century. As slaves, Africans clearly helped define the societies in which they were held. With their labor, they produced wealth and political power for generations of politically and economically powerful white elites in the Chesapeake and south. As for native populations in the eastern regions of North America, one can find political and economic white-native cooperation dating from the Jamestown experiment all the way to the Revolution, but, for the most part, natives encountered whites in wars of resistance and were devastated by the invisible invaders, the microbes that came with European exploration and settlement. The future of the eastern woodland native nations was imperiled even before the English came to stay.

Like the other Europeans in the Americas, the British redefined their settled spaces by sending administrators, emigrants, slaves, capital, goods, literature, and political ideas into the colonies. They took familiar ideas and values with them and adapted them to what they found in America. Over time, successive generations in all parts of the colonial world balanced their British cultural heritage with their identities as Virginians or Rhode Islanders. Historians have long acknowledged the differences between Virginia and Massachusetts or between South Carolina and Pennsylvania, for example, or between the distinct regions defined by the New England colonies and the Chesapeake. Regional differences survived the Revolution. They yielded to a commonly agreed set of political principles and institutions but preserved characteristics that had been, in some cases, 150 years in the making. The "nation" was superimposed on a set of discrete societies. Slavery, for example, was preserved in the regions where it began, was confirmed (by the middle of the eighteenth century), and then flourished (in the first part of the nineteenth century), expanding along with the new nation's expansion. The outcome was the American Civil War. While the Latin motto *E pluribus unum* ("out of many, one") is now understood to refer to the harmonious consolidation of peoples, of individuals, it originally signified the pulling together of a set of separate colonial communities that had not been firmly bound to each other before the Revolution.

Many "new" worlds were encountered by restless and exploring Europeans in the fifteenth and sixteenth centuries. Those new worlds were almost immediately reshaped into African and Asian trading posts and then into colonies in the Atlantic islands, the Caribbean, and the mainland of Central, South, and North America. Because imperial Europe took shape beyond its frontiers, we need to understand that the carriers of these enterprises were products of the European Renaissance. The earliest Europeans to venture into Africa and America came from a European milieu that reflected the complex changes aroused by the Renaissance. They were also contemporaries of the Protestant Reformation, which challenged Catholic Rome's monolithic hold on Christian Europe and came to America with the English and the Dutch.

As the British colonies matured into the eighteenth century, their attachment to the empire and especially to the mother country itself, culturally and economically, was maintained and even strengthened. But as this book suggests, Britain was changing in ways that were not obvious to any but the most alert and probing colonist. The empire's objectives became more complex as the global competition with France and others intensified. By the middle of the eighteenth century, Britain was in the early stages of industrialization while the American colonies remained steadfastly agrarian. As British political affairs underwent substantive change from the middle of the seventeenth century to the late eighteenth century, the general colonial perception of the imperial relationship was, at times, out of step.

In dealing with the "parent-child metaphor," one of the major themes of this book is to modify the thesis that the colonies outgrew their dependence and attachment to Britain. Rather, it suggests that the empire and Britain itself had begun to outgrow the colonies. The British triumph in the Seven Years' War (1756–1763) cleared France from North America and stunted Spanish interests. Overnight, the British Empire's future had to be reconsidered and reordered. The war brought British troops and administrators and finally new imperial policies directly into the colonies to reveal colonial societies that were less supine than expected. Colonists discovered a new British system that was less nurturing than had been assumed, one that seemed intent on restructuring the American Empire. The end of the Seven Years' War spelled the beginning of the end of the old imperial order. The various colonies were, consequently, introduced to each other in ways that had not been necessary in the older, looser British Empire.

SUGGESTED READINGS

Charles M. Andrews, *The Colonial Background of the American Revolution* (New Haven: Yale University Press, 1924) is a durable and brief introduction to colonial society and politics that inspired greater scholarly interest in the way the colonies' development shaped the revolutionary generation's values. Three-quarters of a century later, Jon Butler, *Becoming America: The Revolution before 1776* (Cambridge, MA: Harvard University Press, 2000) offers a similar thesis using the findings of three generations of scholarly research. Andrews's book has the virtue of seeing colonial America in a wider imperial and Atlantic setting, but both books see the genesis of later American national virtues forming in the prerevolutionary era. The reference to Winthrop can be traced to Francis J. Bremer, *John Winthrop: America's Forgotten Founding Father* (New York: Oxford University Press, 2003). For a brief and eloquent approach to Winthrop, see Edmund S. Morgan, *The Puritan Dilemma: The Story of John Winthrop* (Boston: Little Brown, 1958). There are many ways to interpret the history of white-native relations in prerevolutionary North America and Ian Steele, *Warpaths: Invasions of North America* (New York: Oxford University Press, 1994) and Richard White, *The Middle Ground: Indians, Empires, and Republics in the Great Lakes Region* (Cambridge: Cambridge University Press, 1991) offer two quite distinct but stimulating theories on the nature of those relations. The former sees the history of British America up to the revolutionary era as being shaped by militarism, while White, dealing with the Great Lakes region, presents a version of white-native relations that were potentially peaceful, collaborative, and mutually sustaining. There is nothing new in theories of colonial regionalism, and David Hackett Fischer, *Albion's Seed: Four British Folkways in America* (New York: Oxford University Press, 1989) and Jack P. Greene, *Pursuits of Happiness: The Social Development of Early Modern British Colonies and the Formation of American Culture* (Chapel Hill: University of North Carolina Press, 1988) offer two interesting and different ways to see those differences. A recent and useful historiographical commentary on reconciling early American history with early modern history is Christopher Grasso and Karin Wulf, "Nothing Says 'Democracy' Like a Visit from the Queen: Reflections on Empire and Nation in Early American Histories," *Journal of American History*, 95 (December 2008): 764–781.

An Empire of Regions

★★★★★★★★★★★★

A BRIEF HISTORY OF COLONIAL
BRITISH AMERICA

Time Line

Circa 20,000 to 8,000 BCE	Estimated early settlement of the American continent by migrating peoples from the Asian land mass.
1340s and 1350s	Black Death in Europe (first outbreaks of the second pandemic).
14th and 15th centuries CE	The apogee of Aztec authority in Mexico.
Late 15th and early 16th centuries CE	Height of Inca domination in the Andes.
10th to 15th centuries CE	Norse exploration of North Atlantic.
Early 15th century	The Portuguese establish outposts on the west coast of Africa and colonize the Atlantic islands of the Madeira archipelago and the Azores.
1492	Final Christian reconquest (*reconquista*) of Iberia.
1492	Columbus reaches the Caribbean.

Introduction

* * * * * * ★ ★ * * * * *

Many
and
Varied
New Worlds

These new regions which we found and explored with the fleet... we may rightly call a New World... a continent more densely peopled and abounding in animals than our Europe or Asia or Africa; and, in addition, a climate milder than in any other region known to us.

—Amerigo Vespucci, *Mundus Novus*, 1503. Modernized translation quoted in James D. Kornwolf and Georgiana Wallis Kornwolf, *Architecture and Town Planning in Colonial North America* (Baltimore, MD: Johns Hopkins University Press, 2002), xi.

The Europeans' New World

Amerigo Vespucci (1451–1512) was but one of a great many European explorers to visit the *mundus novus*, the "New World," in the wake of Columbus. Among the many names available to christen Europe's New World, including Columbus's, Vespucci's name stuck, likely because of the map of the world published in 1507 by the German cartographer Martin Waldseemüller, who labeled the region with a modified version of Amerigo, "America." Even then, the continents were mostly referred to as the "Indies" (*las Indias* to the Spanish, who retained that usage well into the eighteenth century) or the "New World," until "America" began to be a common designation later in the sixteenth century. Vespucci's feats as a geographer-explorer have been eclipsed by those of other contemporary mariners, colonizers, and cartographers; still, although his respectable scientific accomplishments are usually ignored, posterity has served his *name* very well. Nevertheless, there was and is a clear recognition that it was Columbus who had paved the way. His voyage of 1492 opened a chapter in world history, and the phrases "Columbus" and "fourteen-ninety-two" together or singly, without any embellishment, are universally understood as signifying one of modern history's most pivotal events.

He was born Cristoforo Colombo in Genoa and was known to the Spanish as Cristoval Colon and to the English as Christopher Columbus (1451–1506). His observations of his "discovery" and those of Vespucci and so many other sailors read in part like promotional literature. They reported a world of wonders. It was also clear that it was a daunting wilderness. It was spectacular and exotic, to be sure, and its potential bounty appeared unlimited to the explorers, conquerors, traders, and settlers who crossed the Atlantic in that era. Even if they had not seen an ocean larger than the North Sea or the Mediterranean or been much beyond Europe, they were worldly men who knew of the steppes of central Asia and the tropical forests of Africa and Asia from written accounts that had long circulated in Europe. Before Columbus, however, what lay to the west had only vaguely registered in the European imagination. After 1492, it became a laboratory for European experiments in colonization. By the late seventeenth century, most of the continent's coastlines had been mapped and Spanish and then French explorers had seen much of the continent's interior long before the Europeans ventured far beyond the coastal zones of India, Africa, and China. Moreover, before Columbus, Europeans understood the wider world mostly in literary or abstract geometrical terms. America opened the way for an empirical vision of the world.

When Columbus left Spain, he had no inkling of what lay between him, the Atlantic islands, and the Orient. However, his familiarity with contemporary travel literature and his grasp of astronomy told him that he would eventually reach Cathay or India. He also trusted his seamanship, and it took him far, but what he reached was not India but islands in a tropical sea at the farthest reach of the Atlantic. What his successors found within a few years was a continent that, as a whole, was without a designation; its inhabitants had no comprehensive name for its totality. The later subdivisions, such as South, Central, or North America or Spanish, French, or English America, are generalized spatial coordinates or imperial claims superimposed on multiple and distinctive physical and cultural features. The broad concept of a "new world" suited Europeans, but it masked a contradiction. The whole was much more than a single geography, and its geological and human complexities were staggering. There happened to be a plurality of "worlds."

Map 0.1 The Atlantic World of the Early Modern Imperialists

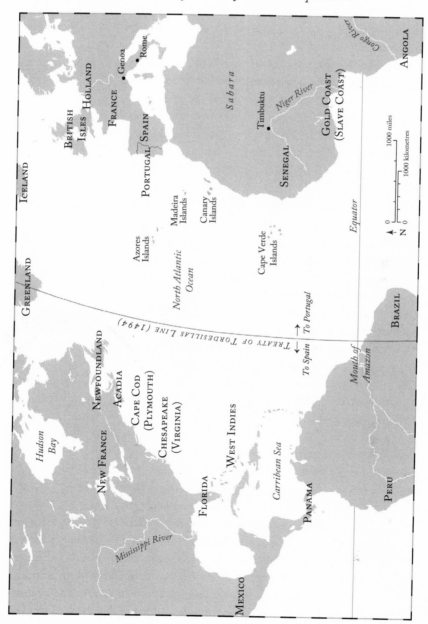

The Grand Geography of the Americas

The land mass of the western hemisphere runs from the high Arctic to the edges of the Antarctic Ocean, a distance on a rough longitudinal axis of some 8,500 miles, from 70 degrees north latitude to 55 degrees south latitude. At its narrowest east to west point on the Isthmus of Panama, the distance is a mere 30 miles, but it is over 3,000 miles wide between the Atlantic and Pacific Oceans at roughly latitude 6 degrees south and approximately 3,500 miles from east to west near latitude 55 degrees north. North, Central, and South America; the Caribbean; the Arctic; and the Atlantic and Pacific islands adjacent to these areas comprise about 16 million square miles, some 28 per cent of the land surface of the earth. The sheer size of the continent and its latitude-defying length have endowed it with physical characteristics that are as varied as those of any comparably sized portion of the earth. America comprises an awesome array of climates, geology, and soils. Its flora and fauna abound in varieties; some are versions of African, Asian, or European types but others are exclusive to the Americas. The age and scale of its mountains and the contours of its landforms resemble those found on other parts of the earth's surface, but isolation from Asia, Europe, and Africa has allowed for the evolution of distinctive biological variation. Geologically, the continent began as a part of Pangaea, but as the earth's tectonic plates moved, so did Pangaea. About 200 million years ago, what would be the Americas began to separate into two massive pieces, roughly the present North and South Americas. By 100 million years ago, the two parts had been rejoined in Central America.

Europeans encountered hotter summers and colder winters in America, more violent storms, and skies that seemed higher and wider than their own. Some landscapes were reminiscent of Europe or of those described in travelogues about Asia and Africa, but, for the most part, America was a tantalizing tactile and visual novelty. The mountain ranges of the Americas are among the most daunting in the world. Elsewhere are savannas that resemble those in Africa and arid regions that compare with the great deserts of Africa and Asia. For the first generations of Europeans, some of the woodlands and rivers, lakes and pastures, especially in the northern latitudes, may have seemed familiar, but, in most cases, the forests were deeper, the rivers greater, and the lakes gargantuan by comparison. Immense zones of year-round frigidity and apparent sterility exist in the far north, and glacial ice never melts in the great mountain ranges of both North and South America. The Atacama Desert of Chile is perhaps the driest place on earth, and, directly across the Andes from it is the Amazon rainforest, one of the planet's wettest and remotest regions. There are steppes and prairie grasslands comparable to those of central Asia. Some of the world's great river systems flow through the Americas into the Pacific, Atlantic, and Arctic Oceans, in the way that the Nile, the Ganges, and the Mekong flow into the Mediterranean, the Bay of Bengal and the South China Sea, respectively, supporting large human populations as they pass. The drainage basins of the Amazon and Mississippi are among the most extensive in the world.

The American continent straddles the equator. It is tropical as well as polar, so that, while the high Arctic experiences 20 hours of partial or full daylight in June and 20 hours of darkness and its graduations in late December, people at the mouth of the Amazon live in a perfectly calibrated diurnal-nocturnal sequence of two 12-hour blocks every day of their lives. South America lies farther east than North America, and its southernmost reach tapers to a point at Cape Horn. North America broadens to a wide northern span that includes islands in the Arctic that run from west of Greenland at 60 degrees to 170 degrees west longitude in the Bering Strait. The most easterly point in South America is closer to Africa than it is to the Pacific Ocean across the continent to the west.

Europe was compact by comparison, and European societies were more coherent as well, at least on one important level—Christianity. Written and spoken Latin linked scholars, monarchs, churchmen, and traders. Common economic, legal, and religious patterns survived as legacies of the Roman Empire. Polish noblemen and their English counterparts, Italian and French priests, or any educated European, for that matter, had some common knowledge of the geography and sociology of the European world of 1492. On the other hand, as the historian J.H. Elliott has noted, on the eve of the Spanish conquests, it is unlikely that the priests and rulers of the Inca Empire had any knowledge of the Aztec civilization to the north, and vice versa. They were separated by a great space, and the forests and mountains that lay between the Aztec capital at Tenochtitlan and the Inca centre at Cuzco barred contact. Other parts of the Americas did allow for mobility and close contact between peoples, but space, climate, and topography kept many of America's hundreds of "nations" distinct from each other.

None of this is to suggest that Europe was a harmonious whole. As Chapter 1 will show, it was not. The ecclesiastical, political, intellectual, and economic currents that surged through Europe in the late fifteenth and early sixteenth centuries were important markers of common links. On the other hand, Europe's linguistic and cultural diversity could be seen everywhere in a great patchwork of regional or local languages, dialects, and cultures. Nevertheless, there was a great deal of cross-cultural communication, across a great many borders, in the exchange of ideas and goods, peoples and technologies. Even as local custom thrived and national and regional rivalries fueled religious disputes, the scientific, intellectual, and literary currents were usually shared across boundaries. Columbus was a product of this milieu. By his time, navigational innovation, the power of the gun, and the reach of the printing press had promoted a rising European belief in its potential for mastering the natural world. Still, European colonizers had to adapt. Their American enterprises in the three centuries after Columbus were shaped in some considerable part by climate and terrain. It is worth emphasizing the combination of awe and optimism that Europeans felt in their extended introduction to the Americas. They spent much of the next three centuries dealing not only with its geographical magnificence but also with its impediments, as they continued with their presumed license to exploit it all.

But first, the size and shape of what they had found needed to be understood. In a letter to his royal sponsors after his third voyage to and through the Caribbean in 1498, writing when his ship was just beyond Trinidad, Columbus noted, "I have come to believe that this is a mighty continent that was hitherto unknown. I am greatly supported in this view by reason of this great river [the Orinoco Delta], and by the sea which is fresh." Columbus had rightly supposed that the landmass he had seen was part of a "mighty continent," part of what is now Venezuela. Still, he had no idea of the continent's scale. He went ashore on what is now the Paria Peninsula and named it *Isla de Gracia*. He was likely the first European since the Vikings to reach the American mainland, and, while he guessed that he had seen a continental landmass, he seemed unaware of the fact that he had actually stood on it.

A century later the Spanish had seen deserts, mountains, and forests of unexpected size. They had touched the Pacific by land across the Isthmus of Panama before Magellan had seen it by sea after going west around the southern tip of the continent. Before the end of the sixteenth century, an English expedition led by Martin Frobisher, seeking a northern route to the Orient, had witnessed the terrifying physical force of the ice and storms of the sub-Arctic waters. The French, too, in the following century, encountered and recorded their impressions of some of the continent's natural wonders, such as Niagara Falls, the Great Lakes, the Mississippi River, and the edges of the Rocky Mountains. They had stamped their own sense of Columbian irony on the rapids just west of Montreal by naming them "La Chine" (China) to mock La Salle's continued quest for a route through the continent to China. Still, the Europeans, within a few decades of Columbus's view of the South American mainland, were mapping and describing the continent with increasing accuracy.

It had taken a good deal longer for the original Americans to reach the continent's extremities. Beginning near the end of the last great ice age, some 20,000 or more years ago, Stone Age peoples began crossing the natural bridge between Asia and the American continent. That land bridge is gone, replaced by the Bering Strait, a waterway between the Arctic and Pacific Oceans (the Chukchi and Bering Seas). Those societies were far from static, yet they appeared to Europeans to be fixed in a timeless state of arrested progress. The environments that had influenced indigenous societies affected Europeans too but not as deeply. Europeans installed their crops, animals, social organization, and cultures in America even if the environment slowed, diverted, or modified them. There would never be a clean replication of any European society in the Americas, partly on purpose but also because geography, climate, and resident native cultures worked against it. However, there was one important distinction between pre-Columbian natives and Europeans in their relationships with their surroundings, the natives had been much more conservative, cooperative, and flexible, and, although indigenous peoples modified their surrounding to suit their needs, their impact on the land was much softer than that of the Europeans who displaced them.

In the end, Europe transformed the Americas, in physical and human terms that differ from their impact on Asia and Africa. For example, Europeans did not wholly redefine India or Africa but superimposed themselves on majority local populations and modified or managed local cultures. In America, the near elimination of the indigenous peoples and their replacement by Europeans and Africans constitutes change on a revolutionary scale. If at times the landscape and climate restrained European enterprise and limited ambitions in some places at other times, it also presented a welcoming, accessible, and potential cornucopia in others. European America was varied to be sure: New France in the seventeenth century was set in the forests and cold of the St. Lawrence, while early Spanish latifundia in New Spain took shape in both warmer and drier climates and tropical jungles. The French went after fur-bearing animals; the Spanish created agricultural estates and mined for silver. The English ended up by overwhelming the peoples and lands of the eastern seaboard of North America with their farms, towns, seaports, and distinctive political subdivisions. On the other hand, the English, French, and Spanish in the Caribbean shared identical climates and developed sugar plantations, of similar design, using slave labor.

The Native American Population at the Time of Columbus

By the time Europeans had overrun the continent, during the nineteenth century, the traditional structures and values of indigenous peoples had been obscured, and, in many cases, the people themselves had disappeared. The shattering of much of the rich substance of indigenous America stands as one of the great demographic tragedies of recorded history. Modern research methods and fresh perspectives have brought Columbus's legacy and the so-called contact between Europe and America into a new focus. Chroniclers and historians from the colonial period into the twentieth century saw Columbus as being in the vanguard of progress that brought "Western Civilization" to the "New World." That view is now being revised. In the early 1990s, the 500th anniversary of Columbus's voyages inspired hundreds of popular and scholarly books and articles. There was no longer a celebratory tone to the literature, and irony or even regret can be seen in many of the newer analyses. One revisionist, J. Fitzpatrick Sale, went so far as to describe Columbus's legacy as a "holocaust" in his provocatively titled *The Conquest of Paradise.*

The estimated native populations at the time of Columbus in aggregate and local densities are vitally important as indicators of the overall impact of Europe on America. If there were 50 million or more aboriginal peoples in the Americas in 1492, as some ethnographers, geographers, demographers, and historians now suggest, what happened to them? Regardless of when and where contact occurred, all native communities, large and small, suffered loss. Some communities offered military or political resistance, but many scattered or thin populations afforded Europeans a completely free hand to establish themselves.

More to the point, the size of specific native populations at the time of the European arrival helps us understand the ultimate human cost of the encounter. Only a few million independent native people, usually in the most remote corners of the Americas, survived into the nineteenth century. Disease epidemics, along with wars and miscegenation, hammered indigenous populations into dependency, demoralization, and often extinction or near extinction. Only the scale and rate of the devastation varied.

Until recently, estimates of the pre-Columbian population of the Americas were low. For example, Alfred Kroeber in the 1930s placed the total native population of the Americas in 1492 at 8.4 million. That number has more to do with apologetics than with rigorous scientific analysis or statistical common sense. His estimate for North America north of Mexico was 900,000. In other words, the half million Native Americans reported by the 1940 United States census suggested to Kroeber a decline of 50 per cent over the preceding 450 years. In itself, those numbers posed serious questions about the European impact on native populations. Perhaps lower birthrates, susceptibility to disease, a lower life expectancy, and racial mixing, assimilation, and under reporting could explain the outcome. But as the fields of ethnography, anthropology, and historical demography grew more sophisticated, estimates of the 1492 population rose dramatically to the point where figures of 50 million to as many as 112 million were being suggested for the Americas as a whole. By the 1990s, a pre-Columbian population estimate of about 50 million was beginning to seem acceptable to scholars. Estimates for the area north of Mexico now run from about 2 million to 4.4 million natives. The latter figure is more generally accepted, although the debate on numbers continues. The frequently revised and wide range of estimates should caution us about their imprecision. Still, the higher numbers now accepted add controversy when considered with the 1940 native population of a half million. Now, the United States and its predecessor, the British American colonies, are implicated in reducing from *four to eight times* as much of the native population as Kroeber's lighter figures had suggested.

Consequently, the apparent scale of the post-Columbian demographic disaster puts a new face on the meaning of Europe's America. Until recently, the history of the United States has marginalized or romanticized or, most often, ignored the native. So too, in many cases, did the colonists. Many of the colonial censuses that survive do not mention them. Those that do, tell a sorry tale. The Massachusetts census of 1764–1765, for example, lists only 1,681 "Indians" in a total provincial population of 223,841. Those 1,681 "Indians," less than 1 per cent of the population, were all that remained of the estimated 30,000 natives who were in Massachusetts when the Puritans arrived in 1630. Some estimates put the New England regional native population at 100,000 in the generation before the arrival of the English. Sounding a troubling note, the first United States federal census of 1790 did not list natives. As recently as the 1860 census, only 54,000 natives were recognized, surely an absurdly low number and perhaps the result of counting only natives identified in the general population. In a cruel and ironic twist, as native populations receded, the number of African Americans rose, reaching 4.4 million in the 1860 United States census.

Before the permanent settlement of the English colonies in the early seventeenth century, native depopulation had been underway in the vast Spanish colonies to the south. In the case of Mexico (New Spain), for example, an estimated 20 million natives in the early sixteenth century had dwindled to about 3.5 million by 1650, an astonishing decline, even allowing for errors in counting or identification. When one excludes the children born to native and European parents, the native population can be seen to have shrunk, in part, because of interracial mixing, but the loss, whatever the cause, is staggering. In all of Spanish America, the native population dropped to 8.5 million by 1570 and remained at that level in 1650. The *mestizo* (mixed Caucasian and native) population doubled during that period, but the Spanish military onslaught and the reorganization or elimination of indigenous political and economic systems contributed to high mortality rates in Mexico. So too did the diseases the Spanish brought with them, such as diphtheria, influenza, and, especially smallpox. Indigenous Americans, for the most part, had no resistance to the microbial invaders. The development of immunities in any gene pool requires generations or centuries of exposure. Most important, as the high rates of miscegenation ate into indigenous populations, war, malnutrition, disease, and displacement exacerbated the decline by curbing even modest natural increase. Ironically, this grim process merged with another problem that faced native populations even before Columbus. There is some evidence that, in the case of Central America, the huge growth in population in the generations before the Spanish invasions had put a great strain on the region's carrying capacity. The Spaniards may have encountered a weakened population headed toward collapse, with deteriorating dietary standards and a susceptibility to lethal infections. Although these erosions in Mexico and Honduras are striking, the natives of the Caribbean met an even more fearsome fate.

Within decades of contact with Europeans, the Caribbean's indigenous population had all but disappeared. It is little wonder that the so-called "black legend" has persisted, alleging not only Spanish military and microbial assaults on indigenous America but violence and cruelty too. The "black" in the "black legend" represents evil. Spain's enemies likely applied the term in the sixteenth century as a slur on the Spanish character, already damned for its treatment of the Jews and the horrors of the ever-expanding and punitive Catholic Inquisition. That formal "policing" branch of the Church was responsible for the often brutal persecution of heretics. This is not to suggest that pre-Columbian America was a happy paradise. Various forms of slavery were practiced, and cycles of famine and war meant that, in some areas, life expectancy, influenced by astronomical infant mortality rates, was as low as 20 years.

In any case, wherever Europeans went, even deadlier conditions prevailed. As noted, some remote populations were spared the sixteenth and seventeenth century onslaught of imported diseases, in the Amazon and parts of the Andes, for example, or in the Arctic and along the northwest coast of North America. Eventually, however, as the conquest of the Americas continued into the nineteenth century, the descendants of the pre-Columbian populations had become fractional minorities. Yet over the last several decades, the native populations have begun to recover. In North America, over two million people now claim native ancestry, and the birth rates are healthy and growing. In many parts of Canada and the United States, indigenous language, custom, and community are being restored, and the prospects are brightening for the recovery of some of what was lost after 1492.

William Denevan's 1992 summary of the total American population in 1492 is as reasonable as any scholarly hypothesis now available to us, but it must be qualified by noting, as he does, that we can never be sure of the accuracy of any estimate.

Table 0.1 The Aboriginal American Population, ca.1492

North America (including the Arctic)	4,400,000
Mexico (present-day boundaries)	21,400,000
Central America (south of today's Mexico)	5,560,000
Caribbean Islands	5,850,000
Andean Regions	11,500,000
Lowland South America	8,500,000
TOTAL	**57,300,000**

Source: Adapted from William M. Denevan, *The Native Population of the Americas in 1492*, 2nd ed. (Madison, WI: University of Wisconsin Press, 1992), 291.

To put Denevan's estimates into perspective, the 53 million natives he finds in Central and South America and the Caribbean in 1492 had shrunk to about 9 million in 1650, with fewer than a million in Portuguese Brazil. Whites, blacks, and mixed races made up less than 20 per cent of the Latin American population in 1650, which is now estimated to have been about 11 million *in total*. African slaves would radically reshape the demography of Brazil after 1650. Mixed race populations would grow, but it is clear that serious depopulation had occurred in Latin America by 1650. A very important contrast between the settlement patterns, practices, and outcomes of English America and Spanish America can be drawn from a simple statistic: after 150 years of settlement (in 1650), the white Spanish population in the Americas represented only 6.3 per cent of the whole; after 150 years of settlement (in 1760), the white British population in their colonies east of the Appalachians in North America represented over 70 per cent of the whole, with African Americans constituting another 20 per cent. Unlike the colonizers of Latin America, the British had largely removed a native population and replaced it. In the process, they took the region's historical levels of population to new heights. By the time of the Revolution, the population of the mainland British colonies was as much as five times what it had been when only natives occupied the same area.

Historical reconstruction of the pre-Columbian world has become more detailed with every advance in archeological and statistical technique and in the way biological science is applied to estimating past human societies. Still, the reconstruction appears at times to be an exercise in statistical theory or applied mathematics and an arcane debate among specialists. But recent findings are more plausible than most of the earlier estimates and certainly caution us to be wary of population estimates made by early observers.

Map 0.2 Major Native Groups in Eastern North America

For example, Columbus in Hispaniola and John Smith (1580–1631) a century later in Virginia simply miscalculated or deliberately inflated what they saw to suit their purposes. As noted, Columbus claimed incorrectly that Hispaniola was larger than either England or Spain. The Spanish missionary Bartolomé de Las Casas (1484–1566), of the Dominican order, was bent on converting the population to Christianity, and he criticized the Spanish imperial venture for its racism and brutality. To make his point about the scale of decimation, he claimed that Hispaniola had been home to three million natives.

European Perceptions

Two of the major population shifts in modern history occurred in the aftermath of Columbus's venture. They converge in the making of the modern Atlantic world. The decimation of the indigenous populations of the Americas corresponded with the forced migration of some 10 to 12 million Africans to the Americas in the period between 1500 and the early nineteenth century. As that was underway, it intersected with the movement to the Americas of several hundred thousand Europeans who brought along their cultural baggage. Everywhere, and especially in the Spanish and Portuguese colonies, miscegenation further complicated the human face of the Americas. The terms *mestizo* (Spanish), *mestiço* (Portuguese), and *métis* (French) appeared to explain a new phenomenon, the mixed white and native people. The English used the term "half breed." At the same time, permutations of racial mixing appeared with definitions such as *mulatto* for Caucasian and African mixtures or *zambo* or even *caboclo* for combinations of white, native, and African miscegenation. In Brazil, a bizarre and lengthy dictionary of racial permutations emerged by the nineteenth century that defined categories by not only color but also shadings.

Europeanization eroded, distorted, or erased, in some cases abruptly, the living pasts of millions of families and thousands of communities, along with centuries of artistic and religious habits. Words such as "Indian" or "savage" or "people" were used by the Spanish to describe Caribs or Aztecs, by the French to describe Hurons, by the English to identify Abenaki, or by the Portuguese to name the Tupinambá. Those generalizations reduced the European sense of pre-Columbian America to a misleading blandness. The continent contained a richer array of societies than did Europe. Undoubtedly, one of the tragedies of the transformation of the Americas into what we call the United States, Argentina, Jamaica, and the dozens of other designations was the general indifference to any serious scholarly consideration of America's rich multitude of cultures and their fates until the rise of anthropological studies in the late nineteenth century.

Stereotypes emerged early. Depending on who was doing the reporting, a conquistador, a friar, a government official, a Puritan minister, or a fur trader, the impressions transmitted by Europeans of natives were as varied as the reporter's values or expectations. At a notable level, however, most early European observations followed one of two conflicting lines: equally lavish descriptions of the inhabitants either as barbarous and incorrigible or as simple, gentle, and malleable peoples. In one of Columbus's letters to the Spanish sovereign, he comments on the natives of the Caribbean:

> And they know neither sect nor idolatry, with the exception that all believe that the source of all power and goodness is in the sky, and they believe very firmly that I, with these ships and people, came from the sky, and in this belief they everywhere received me, after they had overcome their fear.

> Quoted in Giles Gunn, *Early American Writing* (New York: Penguin Books, 1994), 28.

A recorded observation of Amerigo Vespucci catches the subjective nature of the European view. Here Vespucci describes natives somewhere on the Atlantic coast of South America in the early sixteenth century:

> They showed themselves very desirous of copulating with us Christians. While among these people we did not learn that they had any religion. They can be termed neither Moors nor Jews; and they are worse than heathen; because we did not see that they offered any sacrifice, nor did they have [any] house of prayer. I deem their way of life to be Epicurean.

> Quoted in Rosemary O'Day, *Culture and Belief in Europe, 1450–1600: An Anthology of Sources* (New York: Blackwell, 1990), 318.

Vespucci's reference to native spirituality and lasciviousness is a clear denigration of the character of the people he observed, but its tone of combined curiosity and prejudice informed and influenced European views of New World people for a very long time.

Columbus and Vespucci and so many thousands of others twisted the cultural significance of what they saw, heard, or experienced. For example, most of the native peoples of the Americas did have "religion." As animists, most assumed that their inner and outer worlds were linked to and revealed in every plant, animal, and physical feature in the natural world. Europeans found these spiritual practices to be "worse than heathen," which meant, literally, worse than Muslims and Jews whose practices were already contemptible to Christian Europeans. At a more prosaic level, Renaissance Europeans found native explanations of life, death, and nature perplexing. The different myths, oral traditions, and superstitions of each group reinforced European assumptions that natives (and, indeed, all non-Christians) were heathens.

Africa was a special case. To Europeans, Muslim North Africans were notably exotic and distrusted, but sub-Saharan Africans were stranger yet. The English, in particular, found them to be not only primitive but also singularly puzzling, especially in comparison to American natives. Sixteenth century observers were quick to associate the African "blackness without" with a "blackness within" as historian Winthrop Jordan has noted. Reports of Africans copulating with apes seemed plausible to English readers, and even favorable impressions of Africans still marked them off as a separate branch of humanity. Although longer historical exposure had made them appear less mysterious to the Spanish and Portuguese, Africans were still subject to pejoratives and to exploitation by the Iberians. The tendency to lump peoples together as "Africans" or "Indians" derived from an aggressive application of European subjectivity. The ethnocentric view of Africans and native Americans *was* racist in that it lumped entire peoples together as having both common and inferior assets. It is fair to say that we now know that all Africans share some common genetic characteristics, as do all native Americans and all Caucasian Europeans. However, these generalizations obscured the often complex cultural distinctions between one group of Africans and another. The same was true for native Americans.

A greater respect for cultural integrity has made today's interest in the Columbian encounter more sensitive than that of Vespucci or the rest who followed. For example, given his cultural background, worldview, moral values, and material objectives, how could the conquistador Hernando Cortés (1485–1547) fully understand or respect the validity of the multitude of new cultures he encountered? Renaissance Europeans were acutely tuned to European differences but were loath to ascribe any importance to non-Christian or non-white cultural differentiations unless it suited them.

Language is one of the ways a group, tribe, nation, or polity bonds. A common language transmits authority and helps organize economic, religious, legal, and familial relations. Languages evolve organically or are imposed from the outside by conquest or are borrowed for diplomatic or economic reasons. In Renaissance Europe, Latin was the language of international relations, trade, science, philosophy, and formal ecclesiastical matters. The so-called vernacular languages offered considerable range, and, by the fifteenth century, versions of all modern European languages were in use. Later, French and English would begin to replace Latin in international communications. The Indo-European languages of Europe—including the Romance languages of France, Italy, and Iberia; the Germanic and related hybrids of northern Europe; the Slavic of eastern Europe; and the Celtic of the western periphery—created a medley of distinct and often incompatible languages, all of them complicated by local dialects. But if a learned Genoese encountered a learned Swede or Scot, it was likely that they could share some written or oral Latin.

There was no such linguistic medium between the major language families of the Americas. That is not to say that there were immovable barriers between adjacent groups. The languages of Mesoamerica did overlap and fuse at certain points, and it defies logic to suppose that the several language groups of the North American plains were isolated from each other, given the borderless landscape and the mobility, social interaction, and political or military relations between tribes, clans, and confederations. So it was in most of the Americas, with clear exceptions in remote pockets of habitat such as Amazonia, Patagonia, or the Arctic or where major physical impediments limited interaction. Yet even in the latter case, ethnographers have seen linguistic and cultural linkages between the Dene of northern Canada and, farther north in the huge sweep from Alaska to Greenland, the Inuit.

If, as research suggests, there were 370 or more distinct languages in North America at the time of Columbus and perhaps 2,000 in all the Americas, that does not mean that each represented a unique culture. The calculations of the late anthropologist George Murdock and others have shown that the vast array of languages in pre-Columbian North America can be broken down into five major language families and fewer than 150 "linguistic stocks." According to linguistic theory, these languages appear to have developed in isolation from any other known global roots. In Mesoamerica, an estimated 24 linguistic stocks embraced myriad languages and hundreds of dialects. Caribbean influences and ancestries could also be found on the mainland. Over the centuries, many smaller native linguistic stocks in Mesoamerica converged or were absorbed or associated by proximity, war, or politics into larger systems such as those of the Olmec, Toltec, Maya, and Aztec.

Central and South America

In the Caribbean, Mexico, and Central America, the Spanish encountered millions of people in the throes of social, political, and economic change. The Aztec Empire that Cortés confronted is perhaps the best-recorded example of a pre-colonial era society in flux. The Aztecs had risen from obscurity from the aftermath of the Toltec civilization in the twelfth century Common Era (CE) to control an area extending from the Valley of Mexico to near present-day Guadalajara in the north and to Chiapas in the south, and from the Pacific to the Yucatán Peninsula on the Atlantic coast. Aztec trade and political links went beyond those boundaries and reached into the older Mayan areas of Yucatán and the forests of Guatemala. This great social web was essentially a system of enforced labor and material tributes. The Aztecan influence had slowly displaced the Toltecs who had surpassed the earlier "classic" era of Mayan civilization after about 900 CE.

The Spanish saw the signs of those and other civilizations in Mexico and South America, but their assessment of them was unfavorable. They saw what they considered peoples locked in a prolonged stage of underdevelopment. To the Spanish, the absence of the wheel indicated that the Aztecs were technologically backward, and the hieroglyphics they saw there or the Mayan pictographs elsewhere did not conform to what the Spanish supposed was literacy but rather suggested crudity and terminal cultural progress. Native people everywhere in the Americas did record their stories, usually in drawings, illustrated maps, and various images in stone and wood. The Aztec and Inca civilizations and their predecessors had long histories of developing urban and agricultural infrastructures and sophisticated esthetics and spiritual values. The Spanish inevitably saw art and architecture that objectively belied their negative judgements. But none of that meant a great deal to them. They and the later colonizers were not out to do scholarly research but were bent on conquest or negotiated settlement treaties.

The world south of Panama had even more various and numerous languages and societies. One need think only of the Jivaro and other small, isolated groups in the rainforests in contrast to the Quechua-speaking Incas of the Andes and Pacific strand and the great Tupi-Guarani of the Atlantic regions of present-day Brazil to get a sense of South America's human geography. Those living in what is now coastal Venezuela shared some of the Arawak and Carib language and culture of the Caribbean. The sophistication of the Andean civilizations were light years away from the remote and scattered Fuegians of the extreme south or the 1,500 or so Patagonians who seemed to have disappeared within decades of European contact. South America contained perhaps as many as 1,000 languages, about half those estimated to have existed in all the Americas when Columbus arrived.

The best known of the pre-Columbian South American populations constituted the Inca Empire, which embraced present-day Ecuador, Chile, Bolivia, and Peru. The Inca Empire was, in fact, an extended set of social and political alliances controlled by the economic power that emanated from Cuzco, in present-day Peru. The territorial range of the Incas ran some 2,000 miles from north to south. From tropical sea level to the temperate valleys of the Andean cordillera, some of which were inhabited at dizzying elevations of 12,000 feet and more, the Inca hierarchy governed the lives of several million diverse peoples. "Inca" (sometimes transliterated as "Inka") is best understood as defining a great civilization and not a single ethnicity. It more precisely applied to a ruling class of Quechua-speaking nobility who had earlier colonized the region and imposed authority over a great many kingdoms and communities about a century or so before the Spanish arrived. Inca success rested on superior administrative and agricultural organization. Even without a written language, this great civilization managed to communicate its authority. Without draft animals, it built cities and bridges in one of the world's most intimidating environments. The engineering feats of the Incas included terraced and irrigated land for crop farming in steep valleys. They raised some livestock, such as alpacas and llamas, for wool, transportation, and food, a rare practice among pre-Columbian peoples.

What, then, made Inca power vulnerable to relatively small numbers of Spanish invaders? For a start, like the Aztec Empire to the north, the Inca world was softened up by microbes after 1492. Some estimates suggest up to 50 per cent mortality rates in the decades before Francisco Pizarro (ca.1478–1541) arrived in the 1530s. Internal tensions or fragile connections among the congeries of groups associated with the Incas, compounded by withering disease rates, weakened the system. Remember that, as formidable as the Aztec and Inca empires were, they were also in transition. Their infrastructures succumbed very rapidly and hurried along the decline of Inca and Aztec political power. Social breakdown, including, perhaps, a crisis of food supply, clearly aided the Spanish conquests.

When the Portuguese came to Brazil, they found no empires comparable to those of the Inca or Aztecs of Peru or Mexico. Tupi-Guarani peoples dominated large areas without forming coherent imperial networks. The warlike Tupinambá of the area around present-day Rio de Janeiro kept slaves, as did the Aztecs of Tenochtitlan and perhaps as many as another fifteen smaller groups throughout pre-Columbian North and South America and the Caribbean. The Tupinambá system of slaveholding had little or no economic purpose. It appears that slaves were kept as a mark of prestige and for eventual ritualistic slaughter and food. Indeed, the early Portuguese colonists were horrified by the cannibalism practiced by the Tupinambá. The Spanish saw ritual cannibalism in the Caribbean and in Mexico, which confirmed their assumptions of native barbarism. Anthropologists have speculated that the eating of human flesh in some New World cultures was for dietary protein. To Europeans of the contact era, the practice was evidence of a disturbing paganism.

North America

Northern Europeans established themselves in America a full century after the Spanish and Portuguese. They settled north of the most northern Spanish settlements, in areas that were deemed "open" to Europeans. The English, French, Dutch, Swedes, and Danes did not encounter anything like the population densities or the grand imperial structures of the Aztecs or Incas. Moreover, two things preceded the northern European settlements: one was a set of images and assumptions about native Americans dating back to the early sixteenth century, acquired from Spanish accounts and from earlier French and English explorers. Another advance party consisted of microbes. In the early seventeenth century, when Samuel de Champlain and the Virginia Company established permanent outposts on the St. Lawrence and Chesapeake, respectively, eastern North America had already been visited by explorers, transient traders, and lethal bacteria and viruses.

The North American Atlantic coastal zone from the cold St. Lawrence Valley south to warmer Spanish Florida fused into a larger geographical region marked by dense pine and hardwood forests that stretched from the Atlantic across the Appalachians to the Mississippi and from the Great Lakes to the Gulf of Mexico. At the western reaches, the geography trailed off into prairies, plains, and deserts. In the east, the dominant linguistic form was Algonquian, with others, such as Iroquoian, Muskogean, and Siouan, embracing hundreds of languages and dialects. Tribal structure dominated, but not in islands of isolation. Politics, trade, war, and intermarriage made tribal relations flexible as well as competitive. There was a great deal of intertribal contact. Tribes defined themselves as communities of common ancestries in distinct spaces. But they were not static pods. Their composition and culture changed over time as they moved, expanded, divided, and allied themselves with others. The peoples who greeted Europeans in eastern North America lived in a variety of large and small settled communities and towns and depended on corn, fish, and game for diet. There were small groups with some autonomy within a larger group. Clans, extended kinship groups, tribes, and nations presented a complex pattern within the aboriginal world. Some sedentary groups had evolved sophisticated, long-lasting, and stable military, political, and trade structures.

Environment mattered a great deal to the cultural integrity of the small indigenous nations. Lowland and coastal peoples in northern New England, for example, occupied a landscape and climate quite unlike that of the Cherokee to the south or the Iroquois to the west. Yet, for most northern Europeans, their hosts merged into a pagan and primitive composite. Beyond the eastern woodlands, beyond the Mississippi, lay other major groups in quite different ecologies.

An obvious example was the way the buffalo-dependent plains people differed from those in the southwest deserts. Climate, intertribal contact, topography, and tradition spelled out the dietary, residential, and spiritual habits of the human presence in continental North America. The California intermountain societies were sociologically unique, as were the northwest coast and trans-mountain cultures. The latter were the least agricultural of all major regional groupings, deriving their sustenance from the abundant Pacific and the rivers that fed it. The most isolated of all native North Americans were the Arctic and sub-Arctic peoples. The Inuit, for example, hugged the coasts of Alaska and the islands of the Arctic Ocean, and their societies stretched as far east as Greenland. The peoples of the arid regions of the far southwest were linked to the peoples of the northern reaches of Mexico.

The histories of these civilizations stringing out across the continent lay in culture-specific symbols and oral traditions, and the French and Spanish experienced more of the variety of those cultures than did the English. The early decades of European contact in the western regions of this continent were dominated by French and Spanish traders, missionaries, and explorers, who probed the lands beyond the Appalachians, the Mississippi, and the Great Lakes. The English, on the other hand, although they eventually established the largest permanent colonies and populations in North America, confined themselves to the Atlantic side of the Appalachians until the era of the Revolution and had scant contact with the full range of native societies to the west.

Cultural Exchange and Conflict

The European contact period, the so-called clash of cultures, was marked by ethnocentrism, but in some cases, the relationship between newcomer, settler, traveler, and native was one of curiosity and respect. The case for "exchange" was made in 1972 most eloquently in Alfred Crosby's *The Columbian Exchange,* a thesis that influenced a generation of ethnographers and historians. Here and there natives did take part on roughly reciprocal terms with Europeans in trade. They often supported the newcomers with food and provided guides for hunting and settlement sites. In a later era, when rival European nations struggled with each other in North America over territory, natives were solicited as military allies. Native women became wives of Europeans, especially among the French, and acted as go-betweens in the expanding fur trade. Native terms for the natural world, the American flora and fauna, were adopted by all the European languages. Europeans brought back tobacco, potatoes, and other edibles and incorporated them into their own cultures.

They also left their mark on North American native societies with metal tools, guns, axes, and liquor.

In 1986 in *Ecological Imperialism,* Alfred Crosby noted that, over time, European livestock, crops, grasses, weeds, and agricultural and settlement infrastructures transformed the American environment in fundamental ways. As for "exchange," the European adoption of the potato does not compare in any way to the impact of wheat, cattle, sheep, and so much more on the original biology of the Americas. Some New World venereal diseases taken to Europe did little to balance the shattering costs of the smallpox and influenza that went the other way. While Europeans were stripping the natives of their lands and autonomy, there was, however, a fascination with some aspects of the "savage." But as exploration gave way to permanent settlements and then to a flood of newcomers, America's many older and smaller worlds were overrun. Hispaniola, New England, New France, Sao Paulo, Suriname, and hundreds of other places, represented "new worlds" superimposed on so many older worlds and their peoples. Europeans redefined America's physical, political, and ethnic norms through conquest, profit, settlement, and environmental reconstruction. The fear and fascination of the early sailors gave way to dominion. The impact of the potato on Europe, as significant as it later became, or of gonorrhea paled in the shadow of smallpox, guns, and alcohol and the economies of sugar, tobacco, and slavery.

The political, national, and religious rivalries that were forming in Europe in the early modern era were carried to the western hemisphere as part of the increasingly global outlooks of the major European powers. In that sense, the effects of the Columbian moment on Europe were immense, as they were on Africa. While the images and experiences of the American encounters stimulated Europeans' imaginations, the outcome of the conquest of the Americas led back across the Atlantic to a profound reordering of European politics, economics, and international relations. Within a century of Columbus, Europe, Africa, and America, moved by European power and purpose, were bound together in a great triangular enterprise that integrated the economics, politics, and cultures of the entire Atlantic world under the supervision of European nations. The great legacy of the Columbian transformation is a set of flattened cultural and linguistic zones, a Spanish America, a Portuguese America, a French America, and an English America, all of them superimposed on the remnants of viable and timeless cultures. The "New World" that took Vespucci's name was really many long established worlds. Europeans turned those worlds into many new worlds.

And who were these Europeans? They were racist and ethnocentric. They were class conscious and ambitious. They were *not* Europe's masses. Unless they came to America as servants, the colonizers were often associates of wealthy patrons or were part of a religious mission. They were products of the Renaissance who often juggled medieval values at the same time. They came to America bearing particular cultural, social, and political ideas and practices. But whether they were Spanish in the sixteenth century or French or English in the seventeenth, their Europe was a place of curiosity and creativity, of conflict, violence, and restlessness.

SUGGESTED READINGS

The pre-Columbian world of the Americas is surveyed in Charles C. Mann's accessible *1491: New Revelations of the Americas Before Columbus* (New York: Knopf, 2005) a large volume that is intended for a wide readership but has an immense and up-to-date scholarly bibliography. Bruce G. Trigger, Richard E. W. Adams, Wilcomb E. Washburn, eds., *The Cambridge History of the Native Peoples of the Americas*, 3 vols. in 6 (New York: Cambridge University Press, 1996–2000) reflects the scholarship and importance of the subject, and its range is impressive. The best single summary of the western hemisphere's pre-Columbian populations is William M. Denevan, *The Native Populations of the Americas in 1492*, 2nd ed. (Madison, WI: University of Wisconsin Press, 1992). Useful post-Columbian population figures for Central and South America can be found in Lyle N. McAlister, *Spain and Portugal in the New World, 1492–1700* (Minneapolis: University of Minnesota Press, 1984). Among the most useful sources dealing with the so-called contact of Europeans and native Americans is Alfred Crosby, *Columbian Exchange: Biological and Cultural Consequences of 1492*, 30th anniversary ed. (Westport, CT: Praeger, 2003). This is an original and influential model for the subject. See also Peter Mancall and James Merrell, eds., *American Encounters: Natives and Newcomers, 1500–1850*, 2nd ed. (New York: Routledge, 2006). For an example of the themes of "invasion" and "conquest" rather than "contact," see the provocative Francis Jennings, *The Invasion of America: Indians, Colonialism, and the Cant of Conquest* (1975; repr., New York: Norton, 1976). See also Karen O. Kupperman, *Indians and English: Facing off in Early America* (Ithaca, NY: Cornell University Press, 2000). Colin Calloway, ed., *The World Turned Upside Down: Indian Voices from Early America* (Boston: St. Martin's Press, 1994) is indispensable. A superb collection of the way the Americas were seen by early explorers and colonizers is Fredi Chiappelli, ed., *First Images of America: The Impact of the New World on the Old*, 2 vols. (Berkeley, CA: University of California Press, 1976). See also J.H. Elliott, *The Old World and the New: 1492–1650* (Cambridge: Cambridge University Press, 1970) and S.E. Morrison, *The Great Explorers: The European Discovery of America* (New York: Oxford, 1978). There is a growing literature, much of it interdisciplinary, on the subject of global cultural variation that touches on the way early modern history took shape. Much of the literature involves colonization, conquest, imperialism, and ethnocentricity. The anthropological essays in William W. Fitzhugh, ed., *Cultures in Contact: The Impact of European Contacts on Native American Cultural Institutions* (Washington: Smithsonian, 1985) are a good starting point. Similar themes are found in Alfred Crosby, *Ecological Imperialism: The Biological Expansion of Europe, 900–1900*, 2nd ed. (Cambridge: Cambridge University Press, 2004); Jared Diamond,

Guns, Germs, and Steel: The Fates of Human Societies (New York: Norton, 1997); William H. McNeill, *Plagues and Peoples* (Garden City, NY: Anchor Books, 1976). Hans Zinsser's *Rats, Lice, and History* (Boston: Little, Brown, 1935) is an original and provocative treatment. Norman Thrower, *Maps and Civilization: Cartography in Culture and Society* (Chicago: Chicago University Press, 2007) is a valuable addition to the study of the effects of spatial concepts. Kenneth Katzner, *The Languages of the World* (New York: Funk & Wagnall, 1975) is a very good introduction to global linguistic variation. J.H. Elliott, *Do the Americas Have a Common History?* (Providence, RI: John Carter Brown Library, 1998) is a lively set of ruminations offered originally as lectures, on comparative hemispheric history by one of the leading scholars in the field of early modern European imperialism.

Time Line

1340s	Black Death in Europe (first outbreaks of the second pandemic).
1394	Birth of Henry the Navigator.
1420s to 1440s	Portuguese establish colonies in the Azores and Madeira and trading posts in West Africa.
1492	Final Christian recovery of Spain and Portugal (*reconquista*).
1492	Columbus reaches the Caribbean.
1494	The Treaty of Tordesillas (based on Pope Alexander VI's bull of 4 May 1493).
1500	Cabral touches the Brazilian coast.
1517	Martin Luther attacks the selling of "indulgences" by the Catholic Church.
1519–1521	Hernando Cortés's invasion of Mexico.
1532–1533	Francisco Pizarro's Andean conquest.

＊＊＊＊＊★＊★＊★＊＊＊＊＊

Europe in the Age of Exploration: The Portuguese and Spanish Empires

...as if on a given signal, splendid talents are stirring. (26 February 1517)

This is the worst age of history. (1536)

—Desiderius Erasmus of Rotterdam, quoted by Jonathan W. Zophy, *A Short History of Renaissance and Reformation Europe*, 2nd ed. (Upper Saddle River, NJ: Prentice Hall, 1998).

The apparently contradictory remarks of Erasmus (1466–1536), the Dutch-born theologian and philosopher, define a Europe that seemed to be enjoying a glorious awakening of human ideas, skills, and energy but was also enduring seemingly endless wars, famine, plagues, poverty, and cruelty. Erasmus was a product of an age that was asking questions of itself.

The European Landscape

The earliest European observers of America noted that it resembled Europe in some minor ways. But most were just as quick to record its specific kinds of flora and fauna, its immense scale, and its range of climates that were benign in places and forbidding in others. The landscape, like the people, was unique. It was not Europe.

Europe is the western extremity of the immense Eurasian continental land mass and is bounded on the other three sides by the Arctic Ocean to the north, the Atlantic Ocean in the west, and the Mediterranean Sea to the south. The North Sea, the Baltic Sea, and a great many smaller seas are extensions of the major ones. The eastern limits of the continent are defined, often vaguely, by the Slavic and Balkan borderlands or by a distinctive landmark farther east, the Ural Mountains. The land area of Europe is only about half the size of North America. At the beginning of the sixteenth century, it contained large areas of crop and pasture lands, mountains and plains, and substantial forests remained in the north and east, despite centuries of deforestation in most areas. Two great river systems, the Rhine and the Danube traversed the continent, and many smaller river systems linked its parts. Europe lies entirely north of the 35th degree of latitude, and the climate reflects a south to north and west to east range of higher to lower temperatures. There are mountainous regions in Iberia, in the Caucasus of eastern Europe, and in northern Scotland, but only the Alps of south-central Europe can compare to the great cordillera of the Americas. Mountains represent only about 7 per cent of the land area, and the continent has a much lower average elevation than either America or Asia, a feature that had encouraged population mobility over the millennia. The wheel, the horse, and a network of river and coastal water routes, all available to Europeans for centuries, enabled not only the migrations of whole communities but also economic, diplomatic, and cultural exchange. By 1500, however, the vast majority of Europeans were sedentary, and it is reckoned that 75 per cent or more of Renaissance peoples never traveled more than a few miles from their birthplaces during their lifetimes. Mobility was the purview of artists, soldiers, merchants, scholars, and political emissaries and agents. The art and ideas of the Renaissance sustained transnational communities of artists and intellectuals, but there was no such bonding of the continent's masses. Their experiences were grounded in local, insular environments.

European global expansion was not a result of the Renaissance, literally, in English, "rebirth," but rather coincided with it. In fact, the era's international mariners, traders, and warriors actually contributed to Renaissance learning with their maps and chronicles. Even if America was a great unknown in Columbus's time, Europeans had a long-standing awareness of other worlds beyond their Christian one. The Crusades from the eleventh to thirteenth centuries took Europe into the Arab and Muslim worlds to the east, and, in the thirteenth century, Venetian merchants traveled the great trade routes of Central Asia. The legendary Venetian trader and traveler Marco Polo (1254–1324) reputedly reached China in 1275 and resided there before returning to Europe with detailed news of the splendid achievements of Chinese culture. Stories of his exploits and the exotic worlds he had seen had long circulated throughout medieval Europe. By the fifteenth century, educated Europeans and traders had established notions about a wider world beyond their own.

The Renaissance World of the Explorers

The Renaissance was a long bumpy epoch of heightened human curiosity and intellectual and artistic experimentation. The term itself is an awkward generalization and did not come into use until the nineteenth century as a scholarly convenience. There was no break with the past or sudden "recovery" of lost ideas; rather, the period was an accelerated phase of a longer era of change in politics, science, art, and literature. It was not a secular revolution by any means, even though it elevated the value of human endeavor in the divine design of things. The humanist strain in Renaissance thought was still a long way from what the English poet Alexander Pope suggested in his *Essay on Man* of 1734—that the "proper study of mankind is man." Christian values informed all issues. In Europe, Satan was as palpable to most as he was symbolic to others. Accused heretics and witches were tortured and executed until well into the seventeenth century for their questioning of Christian doctrine or worse, aligning with the devil. During his trial in 1633 for apparently violating a papal edict against promoting the theory of a heliocentric universe, the Italian physicist, astronomer, and mathematician Galileo Galilei (1564–1642) was at pains to argue that science and Christianity were not mutually exclusive but reinforced each other.

Galileo ran afoul of the Inquisition, the Roman Catholic Church's formal agency for monitoring the spiritual habits of the population, ferreting out heretics and dissenters, and enforcing orthodoxy. The Inquisition was less active in northern Europe but was a potent force in the Mediterranean world, especially in Spain. It was also busy in the Italian city-states. In Florence the Inquisition's prosecution of Galileo was a bit of an anomaly, given the way the church had encouraged scientific enquiry, especially in the universities. Still, he was placed under house arrest. Yet in spite of the reactionary behavior of the Church, the era was marked by vocal and aggressive intellectual and spiritual innovation. There was no rigid dichotomy between the secular and the profane but rather an apparent rise in interest in the role of mankind in God's universe. Importantly, the Church's domination was not threatened by any external secular movement but was challenged from within. The Protestant Reformation grew out of the Church of Rome's dominant place in all of Europe's civil, diplomatic, intellectual, and spiritual matters.

Pictorial Art in the Renaissance

Renaissance pictorial art drew its subject imagery from scriptural sources and also broadcast a growing affection for the history of classical civilization. At the same time, architectural style and design borrowed from ancient Greece and Rome. Andrea Palladio (1508–1580) took the designs of the Roman architect Vitruvius and introduced them to the world. The shapes of and materials used in his townhouses and villas in Italy reveal a giant step away from the Gothic style that we see in the great medieval cathedrals. What came to be known as classical or neoclassical architecture began with Palladio. It found its way to America in time, and can be seen in much public and private building of the mid- to late-eighteenth century. Planters in the Chesapeake and the south imitated the style in their manors, and Thomas Jefferson's celebrated home, Monticello ("little mountain"), is a fine example of Palladio's continuing influence.

Although architectural and sculptural evidence survives, the most familiar Renaissance legacy today is its pictorial art. From the fourteenth century on, painters worked with new materials, depicted three-dimensional perspectives, and chose subjects of increasing realism. The artists themselves reflect the influence of merchant or political patronage and civic consciousness. The body of Renaissance painting is vast and the familiar list of artists is long. The work of Giotto (1266–1337) provides an early example of the evolution of conceptual imagery that leads to the high Renaissance contributions of Leonardo da Vinci (1452–1519), Michelangelo (1475–1564), Raphael (1483–1520), Titian (ca. 1488–1576), and so many others in the Italian city-states. The Christian celebratory and sacred imagery, depictions of classical Roman and Greek history, contemporary portraiture that captured the new political and financial men and their families, and backdrops of fifteenth and sixteenth century landscapes give us a window into the Renaissance mentality. The art reflects a culture that is self-assured, creative, enquiring. In the Renaissance, artists presented gods in human form. Leonardo left behind visual studies of aeronautics, anatomy, military technology, and zoology. His *La Giaconda*, the

Mona Lisa of circa 1503, one of today's best-known portraits, reaches across the centuries with tantalizing speculations on the thoughts of the subject, who was the wife of a Florentine merchant. *La Giaconda* makes eye contact with the viewer. There is nothing like it in medieval art; it is a study of simple humanity, viewed objectively with a human eye.

Renaissance artists in northern Europe sought graphic realism in their work, and the technical genius of Albrecht Dürer (1471–1528) and the sometimes fanciful and extravagant social settings revealed by Hieronymus Bosch (ca.1450–1516) use detail and atmospherics in allegories that are also social commentaries. The Flemish master, Pieter Brueghel the Elder (ca.1525–1569), depicted scenes of peasant life with allegorical imagination. By the seventeenth century, Dutch and Flemish painters had taken pictorial art so far as to use images of ordinary people and everyday life in near photographic detail. The paintings of Rembrandt Harmensz van Rijn (1606–1669) and Jan Vermeer (1632–1675), for example, appeal to the modern mind on any number of levels. A cosmopolitan perspective runs through their work and reflects Holland's seventeenth century internationalism. Mapmakers, businessmen, and military images appear as self-conscious expressions of Dutch globalism.

Today, the art of the Renaissance is widely accessible in original or image form, but, during its creation, the work was not seen by Europe's masses but was the special purview of the ruling classes, the monarchs, princes, lords, merchants, and churches that owned and commissioned the paintings in the first place. Those artists let us *see* the Renaissance through the eyes of the generations of European adventurers and colonizers who saw in their own world a display of "civilized" Christian culture and who compared their refinements to the "primitive" expressions they found in most of the Americas and Africa. If visual art lets us see the Renaissance as it saw itself, then the scientists, philosophers, theologians, and technicians reveal the era's intellectual energy. That energy began with the slow recovery of ancient knowledge from the Arab world. Mathematics led the way. The work of the Greek mathematician, Euclid (fl.300 BCE) for example, became a guide to new possibilities in geometry and astronomy and allowed Renaissance scholars and scientists to measure the world and the universe in abstract terms. Moreover, the arrival of the mechanical printing press with movable type in the middle of the fifteenth century meant that the developing ideas and technologies of the Middle Ages, in metallurgy, waterpower, ship design, and architecture, were now more easily disseminated. The invention ascribed to Johann Gutenberg (ca.1398–1468) revolutionized communications, and, a half century after its introduction, it was being used to publish multiple copies of written descriptions of exploration and discovery and books on mathematics and astronomy. It is worth noting too that one of the first things that Gutenberg printed was a Bible. Although new knowledge seemed to invite boundless innovation, the Christian explanation for all existence remained central to human understanding.

Renaissance Ideas and Literature

The Europeans who went to America carried with them many of the Renaissance era's changing values, attitudes, and perceptions. But they also carried with them some older assumptions about the place of humans in God's scheme. A medieval metaphor, the taxonomy of all things, of creation itself, the *scala naturae* ("Chain of Being") put God and the angels at the top of an interlocking hierarchy. The chain resembled a ladder as the European concept of order in God's design. Christians were placed below the angels but above the animals, plants, and geology. Because native Americans and Africans were not Christian, their places in the chain were lower or even indeterminate.

Europeans embraced technologies to circumvent some of nature's limitations. The medieval weight-driven clock, for example, was already measuring time in a precise way that the sun, moon, and seasons could not. Then the invention of the coiled spring during the Renaissance brought about the concept of "clockwork" and stored motion. The idea of a universe centered by the sun, with planets moving around it, was proposed by the multitalented physician, educator, and astronomer Nicolaus Copernicus (1473–1543) in his studies of observable phenomena. He qualifies as a physicist, and yet, later in life, he settled as a church canon to remind us that the theory of a mechanical universe and the arcane language of mathematics were not at odds with Christian theology. Galileo later observed that "the universe…is written in the language of mathematics" but saw it as the work of the Christian God who was all knowing and all powerful. The influence of mathematics and its central place in the laws of physics encouraged experiment and observation. By the early seventeenth century, the telescope had pushed the bounds of observable space even farther. As scientific inquiry flourished, the great English thinker Francis Bacon could still write in Book 1 of his *The Advancement of Learning* (1605) that "[human knowledge] is a rich storehouse for the glory of the Creator and the relief [benefit] of man's estate." Science, that is, inquiry and observable testing, travel, discovery, and contemplation all tended to affirm God's great design.

By 1500, signs appeared of modern political theory, enhanced studies of Roman institutions, ideals, and history. Niccolò Machiavelli (1469–1527), a Florentine statesman, wrote treatises on civil authority, republicanism, the nation-state, and citizenship that survive as political models. On a broader plane, humanism appeared as a movement to bring newer approaches to learning by accommodating God's plan with humankind's place in earthly affairs. The universities prepared lawyers, theologians, statesmen, and teachers, and, as they did, they helped in the recovery of classical Roman, Greek, and Arab texts, ideas, and pedagogy. In short, they introduced the "humanities" into European life, that is, the study and investigation of history, politics, and ancient philosophies. The humanists saw the human role as an organic and self-directed one, while recognizing the omnipotence of the Christian God, the revelations in the scriptures, and the centrality of the Trinity: the Father, the Son, and the Holy Ghost. The poets, dramatists, and chroniclers of the age also reflected a growing sense of human self-awareness and identity.

The Renaissance produced a remarkable body of poetry, prose, and drama. From the ribald to the absurd, from romanticism to realism, the literature strikes chords with modern audiences. As early as the fourteenth century, Giovanni Boccaccio (1313–1375) produced in the *Decameron* a series of tales that drew together fiction and social commentary, all set in the midst of the Black Death. Previously, in an early form of Italian, Dante Alighieri (1265–1321) had written the *Divine Comedy*, an allegorical epic about sin and piety and human fate that is among the most profound in any literature. It reflects a medieval notion of a fixed universe, but it uses the theme of odyssey, of a pilgrimage, as a way for humans to *understand* God's will.

England's Geoffrey Chaucer (ca.1342–1400) has left us with the *Canterbury Tales*, which, in its timeless design and telling, sharply observes the class-consciousness and humor of vividly drawn everyday characters. When it was published, Chaucer's use of what we now see as "Middle English" was a sign of a rapidly evolving common tongue for the English. Boccaccio, Dante, and Chaucer composed their stories and poetry before the printing press appeared. Although all were known to the cognoscenti in their time, they achieved greater fame and influence after the middle of the fifteenth century when printed versions of their works circulated to expanding audiences. In France, François Rabelais (ca.1494–1553), the Benedictine monk, physician, and lawyer, produced great satire, *Pantagruel* (1532) and *Gargantua* (1534), works for the common man that attack the residue of medieval monastic organization and clericalism. His writings celebrate humanity's virtues in a fictional liberal monastery. Rabelais combined farce with editorial vigor and spoke to humans for humanity's sake. Miguel de Cervantes (1547–1616) produced what is still considered Spain's most durable piece of literature, *Don Quixote*. It is a masterpiece of wit, irony, and the picaresque, an odyssey in structure and a revelation of the often futile course of human endeavor. One of Cervantes's contemporaries, William Shakespeare (1563–1616), is the most durable and perhaps the most universal of the Renaissance writers. He refined the theater and left behind in his tragedies, romances, and comedies a poetic encyclopedia of humanity's pains and joys. In addition, Christianity was also well served. One of the greatest literary achievements of the English Renaissance was the publication in 1611 of the "authorized" Bible in English, the King James Version. Literature encouraged standardized languages, which, in turn, helped to further define national identities. As the major colonizing powers planted their religions, agriculture, and social structures in America, they also planted their languages.

Debate and theory bloomed. Two church-based theorists, the Dutch-born philosopher, theologian, and humanist Desiderius Erasmus of Rotterdam (1466–1536) and the German priest and reformer Martin Luther (1483–1546), suggested new ways of understanding Christian organization. Their speculations on the role of the Church of Rome underscore the inquiring temper of the age. They also initiated, especially in the case of Luther, a revolution in the spiritual and political direction of European society in the sixteenth century. Erasmus was the most eminent intellectual and among the most prolific writers of the age, a peripatetic and relentless reformer who lived all over Europe. He attacked contemporary scholars and churchmen whose values he saw as lodged in the Middle Ages, a period he saw as regressive. He wrote original treatises on abstract principles promoting toleration and moderation and published new editions of Greek and Roman classics. His much celebrated writings were couched in a refined and scholarly Latin. He sought a more enlightened and reformed clergy and an accessible New Testament translated into the vernacular. His ideas were presented in reasonable, modest, and always thoughtful tones. His place as a leading humanist is reflected in his desire to see humankind take a more progressive role in civil affairs while retaining its Christian ethic.

While Erasmus was more influential than earlier Christian philosophers in his approach to human understanding, he had predecessors. Nearly two centuries earlier, the Florentine writer Francesco Petrarch (1304–1374) had touched off what came to be the humanist proclivity of searching for new understanding by rummaging through classical texts and ideas. He and generations of thinkers brought to the Renaissance a way of seeing the world from a human perspective while adding to the glory of God. Erasmus was more reflective than tactical, even though he argued for a church that opened itself to popular needs. However, his editorial advice was superseded by that of Martin Luther, who made a direct and revolutionary attack on the Roman Church. It was Luther's denunciation of the Catholic Church's authority and the birth of the Protestant movement, rather than Erasmus's reasoning or that of other activist intellectuals, that opened up one of the most dynamic movements of early modern Europe, the Reformation. The breaking of the Church of Rome's control of Christian practices in Europe would eventually emerge in the North American colonies of the English and Dutch.

The Reformation

The movement to reform the Roman Catholic Church was a product of many minds over many decades. It raised issues that were both political and spiritual, and Martin Luther's contribution was central to its outcome. His life and legacy merge with the movement because he launched a direct challenge to the church's hegemony, demanding a "reformation" of it rather than a simple tweaking of the ecclesiastical order. The Reformation attacked the organization, political power, and rites of the Catholic Church, in short, the *way* the church presumed to be the exclusive earthly medium of God's will. The thrust of the Reformation suggested that ordinary people had a more active role to play in their own salvation. Luther was a seeker of genuine faith, a deeply committed Christian with an intense personal relation to God. He is best known for his 1517 attack on the practice of "indulgences," the church's habit of selling access to heaven from purgatory. His carefully listed "ninety-five theses" was the opening salvo in what would be a continuous assault on Catholic universalism, especially in northern Europe and North America. In his posthumously published *Table Talk* (1569) he is quoted as writing that "The Mass is the greatest blasphemy of God, and the highest idolatry upon earth, an abomination the like of which has never been in Christendom since the time of the Apostles." This angry riposte mixes theology with church practice and raises Luther's ideas to the highest level of importance in an age marked by intellectual innovation.

A fundamental tenet of Lutheran thought is the emphasis on faith and Luther's warning of the dangers of "reason" in spiritual matters. In *Table Talk* he claims, "Reason is the greatest enemy that faith has [and] struggles against the divine Word, treating with contempt all that emanates from God." Luther's theology runs counter to a world of priests and Christian rationalism, and it greatly influenced European and American spiritual matters in the seventeenth and eighteenth centuries. In his own time, he inspired common people to consider establishing a "universal priesthood of all believers" (a thesis and statement sometimes ascribed to him). There was more than a hint of Luther's anti-establishment thesis in the German Peasant Revolt and war of 1524–1526. Inevitably, some wanted to carry Lutheranism further than Luther himself. He came from poorer stock and appealed to the lower classes to think outside their roles. However, in 1525, he wrote a critique entitled *Against the Rioting Peasants*, appearing to side with the ruling classes. He was, in fact, a complicated man and turned against the Jews at one point.

Luther translated the Bible into a common German, breaking through the multitude of dialects in the German-speaking states in much the same way that Chaucer, Cervantes, and Rabelais encouraged standardized usage in their languages. The printing press was a boon to the dissemination of writings in the vernacular. An estimated 30,000 copies of Luther's *Ninety-Five Theses* were sold, overshadowed, perhaps, by as many as 9 million printed works, representing some 40,000 separate titles that were in circulation in Europe in the first half of the sixteenth century. The impact of this is difficult to judge, but, clearly, theological and philosophical works, assorted practical information, propaganda, advice, scientific treatises, and literature were crossing borders and finding their way into the minds of the educated and curious. Most of the publications were in Latin, and over half of all printed works were Christian themed, including Bibles, tracts, sermons, and instructions for priests and missionaries. But secular philosophy and scientific writing was in print at the same time. When we think of a revolution in ideas forming in the Renaissance, we should note also the revolution in the way ideas were circulated.

Calvinism and Protestant Pluralism

The Reformation hit Europe with sectarian strife, religious wars, and purges. Where Protestantism dominated, it usually attacked Catholics, and that inspired a "Counter-Reformation" in which Catholic majorities purged Protestants. Moreover, Protestantism itself was subject to fragmentation. The "predestination" doctrine of the French theologian Jean Calvin (1509–1564), for example, remains one of the most important of Protestant theologies. In his great work, *The Institutes of the Christian Religion*, Calvin claimed that the soul was predestined for either salvation or damnation because God had placed into the population only a small minority of "visible saints," that is, an "elect" of those with saving grace. In straightforward terms, Calvin described an omnipotent and determinist God:

> Predestination we call the eternal decree of God, by which He has determined in Himself what…would have to become of every individual of mankind. For they are not all created with a similar destiny, but *eternal life* is foreordained for some and *eternal damnation* for others. Every man, therefore, being created for one or the other of these two ends, we say he is predestined either to life or to death. (Emphasis added.)

Even though this is at odds with his own views, Luther saw the brilliance of the *Institutes*, which Calvin himself translated from Latin into French. The *Institutes* later found their way into the literary canon of New England Puritans. Calvin was the most impressive of a wave of theologians who took up the cause of Protestant reform. An extreme manifestation was Anabaptism, which eschewed all authority and formality in worship and devotion and which appeared to some to be a species of religious anarchy. Over time, Protestantism led to dozens of subdivisions, smaller sects, and denominational movements. Like most of the reform theories, Calvinism attacked both the pomp and trappings of the Church of Rome and its tangled association with civil authority. The predestination thesis was an original and sophisticated treatise, and, as such, one of its central tenets was the insistence on the separation of the church and the state. Calvinists practiced a form of contracted affiliation, a "covenant," to use the contemporary term, whereby congregation members bound themselves spiritually and socially. In this model, members made solemn pacts with each other, with the collective, that is, the community, and then with God. Calvin's model in Geneva practiced a severe, plain, unemotional form of worship that denounced finery, frivolity, and feeling. Calvinism spread throughout northern Europe in the sixteenth century and came to America with the Pilgrims and Puritans in the early seventeenth century. In Europe, it thrived in Holland and in Scotland, where it produced one of the greatest of all Protestant divines in John Knox (ca.1513–1572) who sought to make Calvinism Scotland's national church. The Presbyterian Church, which became a powerful force in Protestant America, is a legacy of Knox's mid-sixteenth century impact on Scottish Christianity. He preached a fiery hatred of Catholics and pushed the plain, stern approach of the Calvinist protocols.

Protestantism, in its many variants, became firmly settled in places like Scotland, Holland, Bohemia, Scandinavia, and England. By the end of the eighteenth century in Europe and North America, it had spawned Anglicans, Presbyterians, Separatists, Puritans, Baptists, Methodists, Quakers, Dutch and German Reformed, Dunkers, Shakers, Mennonites, and a plethora of smaller and evolving sects. It added breadth, variety, and energy to the ecclesiastical and theological underpinning of Christian culture. It also encouraged social and political innovation. Its mark on America is profound, and it stands as an important historical determinant in any comparison with the Catholic Spanish, Portuguese, and French presence. As for Luther, he left behind a huge published body of theological contemplation and advice and volumes of personal ruminations. It is not enough to say that he stands as a major figure in the history of the Christian religion; he is, in many ways, one of the most influential figures in the history of European thought. His impact on American history reverberates to the present.

Europe's Peoples

The Reformation found audiences at every cultural, economic, and national level in Europe and had a measurable social and political impact wherever it appeared. On the other hand, the arts and sciences associated with the Renaissance did not penetrate deeply into the mass of European society, and we should be cautious about its social effects. As noted, the Renaissance was a staggered series of "rebirths" and experimental ideas. Science and technology had been evolving for centuries before Copernicus, Gutenberg, and Da Vinci appeared and medieval monks, for example, had long experimented in optics, metallurgy, and astronomy. The medieval church not only coexisted with learning and inquiry but fostered both. People like Copernicus and Galileo did not come across their theories in the dark, or alone. Moreover, we need to keep in mind that the Renaissance did not bring about a period of unalloyed "progress." We have an image of a world of high culture and architectural grandeur. Popes and princes appear in ostentatious, even gaudy dress, and their poses speak to power and self-confidence. Although literature, scientific innovation, and philosophy did advance learning and stimulate enquiry, for the great majority of Europeans in 1500 or 1600, the Renaissance was unseen, unfelt, and irrelevant.

Most Europeans scrambled to sustain themselves with food and shelter. Religion and folk culture provided color, hope, and community, but the gulf between the rich and the poor, the tutored and illiterate, the powerful and the powerless, was immense. The earthly reality for most people lay in the crude simplicity of their ordinary dwelling places and the filth, smells, and sickness that prevailed in the rural stretches of agrarian Europe as well as in the dense alleys and tenements of the cities and towns. Urban artisans and craftsmen enjoyed unique status linked to the needs and economic infrastructures of artists and architects, merchants and manufacturers (weapons factories, for example), but most Europeans were peasants, tied to the land. For those masses, social and economic conditions retained their traditional rhythms. Life was a tenuous daily grind compounded by the specter of disease, periodic wars, extremes of drought or cold, and crops destroyed by blight. For families, there were often too many mouths to feed and not enough work to go around. The rich and the poor were in constant view of each other in intimate and structured hierarchies, but this strictly laddered social order did not preclude riots or even revolts by the poor.

In 1500, Europe's population had recovered to about 80 million. This was the approximate number on the eve of the great bubonic plagues of the 1340s, the "Black Death," which killed between a quarter and a third of Europeans. Recovery and growth was slow; it took until the late eighteenth

century for the population to double, when improved diets, the partial consequence of reliable and improved crop and livestock yields, allowed the
population to expand. In 1500, most scientific discourse and technological experimentation took place in urban settings, but the vast majority of
Europeans lived in hamlets, villages, and scattered farming communities.
The emergence of important towns, city-states, seaports, and land and water-
borne trade networks carved up a landscape that was otherwise dominated by
structured agricultural societies. Trade was important, and the river, sea, and
land routes that crisscrossed the continent spurred commercial enterprise and
accommodated greater mobility among the upper classes, even as the majority of the population remained sedentary.

Life expectancy was extremely short by twenty-first century standards
and was on average between 30 and 40 years. Infant mortality, that is death
before the first birthday, was as high in some places as 250 deaths per thousand births, dragging down the statistical average life span. The hardships
encountered by most adults meant that, even when one survived childhood,
life expectancy was short. While 75 per cent of the English population survived to age 15, only half the French population did. The survival rates for
many other parts of Europe were even lower. The common lot of adults was
hard work, precarious diet, and the prospect of infirmity if one did reach
old age. Reproduction was dangerous for women. Puerperal sepsis and other
obstetric infections carried away great numbers of mothers during and after
childbirth. Although the Renaissance opened the way to enquiry, travel, and
novel ideas, changes in medical science and practices were terribly slow in
following. Europeans of the sixteenth century were still attached to the medical theories of the ancient Greek Aristotle and those of Galen, the second
century CE theorist.

Infectious diseases ravaged European communities from time to time.
Among the more lethal of these were recurring outbreaks of typhus, a relatively
new louse- and flea-borne disease, bubonic plague, and cholera. Malnutrition
was more common than images of fat burghers would have us believe.
Undernourished and weakened people succumbed to influenza, common colds,
and pneumonia. An especially wet season or an early killer frost could wreak
havoc on food supply. Nevertheless, in a crucial way, the European population
over the millennia had developed immunities to a host of diseases, and healthy
Europeans had the means of resisting potentially fatal illnesses. However, the
smallpox epidemics that devastated native populations in the Americas for
three centuries after Columbus also wreaked havoc on white populations on
both sides of the Atlantic well into the eighteenth century.

Europe's population of 80 million in 1500 rose to 111 million in 1600,
125 million in 1700, and then to 195 million in 1800. The seventeenth century

growth rate was lower than that of the preceding century in part because of the slaughterhouse of the religious-inspired Thirty Years' War of 1618–1648 and its impact on agricultural planning and function. Among the colonizing nations, Spain's population rose from about 5 million to 7.4 million between 1500 and 1700; Portugal stayed at roughly 1 million; France's population was about 18 million in 1500 and reached 22.6 million in 1700. It took 300 years for the Netherlands' population of one million to double. England's 2.5 million rose to about 5 million in 1700 and to over 6 million in 1750. At that time, Scotland's population was about 1.2 million. The fastest rising population in Europe was Ireland's, which doubled in the eighteenth century to over 5 million, thanks in part to the potato, the variant of the American tuber that became a staple in many parts of Europe.

Europe's political structures included small city-states, duchies, and principalities as well as the emerging large nation-states. The Holy Roman Empire embraced the German-speaking small states of central Europe in a system held together by the common authority of the Church of Rome. The Vatican's influence was felt in direct ways throughout Europe, even in the larger, powerful monarchies. Local authority was determined by birthright and heredity entitlement. Aristocracy and the modified remnants of the feudal organization of lord, church, and serf determined social, economic, and even legal relations. Villages and towns and rural clusters were often harmonious and even egalitarian at a communal level, but all were subject to hereditary civil authority and the powerful agencies of the church. By 1500, the feudal system that had dominated Europe for most of the Middle Ages was breaking down. In the most generalized sense, feudalism had bound the rural masses to a particular place under a fixed system of obligation, hence the prefix "feu," a duty or tax. Feudal estates comprised a set of land tenures held in title by an aristocratic family and distributed to a range of farmers whose attachment to the land was defined by various tenures ranging from hereditary leasehold, lifetime tenancy rights, annual leases, rented plots, and direct servitude. In some European states, the fading away of feudalism removed some of the customary rights peasants had enjoyed and replaced them with a general application of Roman civil law.

Feudalism had not disappeared entirely by the sixteenth century, and, in fact, survived far into the nineteenth century in Russia and even later in parts of the Austro-Hungarian Empire. By 1500, the legacy of feudalism had put most usable land in the hands of a very small minority of European aristocrats. One estimate suggests, for example, that all the agricultural land of England not held by the monarch or the church was *owned* by 4 per cent of the nation's families. Even as some of the political power of the landed aristocracies was being aggregated, under the aegis of kings and princes, hereditary elites remained at the top of a social, economic, and local political pyramid. The peasant populations remained technically landless, even if they occupied a bit of land under tenancy, lease, or sharecropping contract. On the eve of the colonization of the Americas, the vast majority of Europeans were in long- or short-term servitude with little opportunity for improvement. The only geographic mobility for peasants occurred when they fled famine, war, or pestilence or when the enclosure of cropland for pasture forced them from their villages. Large-scale trans-European migrations were a thing of the past, the distant past. But peasants and urban servant classes enjoyed vibrant folk cultures as depicted in the popular scenes painted by Brueghel and Bosch. Life was precarious, but hardship was balanced in good times by music, festivals, and feasting. The landed classes and the coteries of elites in politics, commerce, and church were combining to create early versions of the centralized modern nation-state in the late fifteenth and early sixteenth centuries.

European Varieties

Europe's common features were offset by nationalities, climate zones, and local traditions, politics, and religious particulars. While there were substantial numbers of Muslims in southeastern Europe and Iberia and Jewish populations throughout the continent, the vast majority of Europeans were Christians. The Christian cultures that were established in the Americas reflect the variety of the donor cultures that brought their religious practices with them. The learned classes of Europe exchanged literary, philosophical, and theological ideas and tastes but national, regional, and local divisions were meaningful. Being a Spaniard, for example, was not defined by simply speaking a vernacular version of Spanish or a local dialect, or by the fact that Spaniards drank wine while Scots drank ale and whisky and Russians drank vodka. In fact, the Iberian Peninsula comprised another set of smaller subdivisions, of Basques, Catalans, Portuguese, and others. The differences between lowland Scots and Highlanders, between the Welsh and the Thames English, and between Swedes and Norwegians, Bavarians and Saxons, Poles and Silesians, and so on, illustrate the complexity of Europe's local societies and cultures.

The church could not fuse those localisms any more than Latin-based knowledge could. The ruling classes in each of Europe's many subsystems of manors, city-states, principalities, and nations might exhibit common habits and outlooks, but their *raison d'être* was the retention of local power even as they recognized their places in the emerging nation-states. Like the peasants or burghers who occupied the same space and shared the same language, the aristocratic leaders of Europe's many polities shared a firm attachment to locality, everywhere in Europe. The transient philosophers, traders, diplomats, and divines notwithstanding, Europe consisted mainly of smaller, parochial communities often at odds with their neighbors and rivals.

But change was underway. During the Renaissance, some smaller political and social units merged into larger ones. For example, the consolidation of Aragon and Castile in Spain allowed for more means and thus more potential for security and authority. On the other hand, the 30 or more culturally and politically advanced small German-speaking enclaves of the Holy Roman Empire all paid lip service to the emperor while retaining their independence in local affairs and avoiding any meaningful union. The great Renaissance city-states of Italy, including the powerful Kingdom of Naples, the Republic of Venice, and the heartbeat of the Renaissance in many ways, Florence, remained apart from each other. Genoa might have been the home of Columbus, Florence of Vespucci, and Venice the birthplace of Giovanni Caboto (ca.1450–ca.1498), John Cabot to the English, but it was foreign nation states that employed them. No Italian state ventured beyond the Mediterranean nor did any of the German principalities, duchies, and kingdoms leave the Baltic. The history of the European conquest of the Americas begins with the early shaping of the modern state.

Spain, Portugal, England, France, and Holland were major forces in the colonization of the Americas while Sweden and Denmark had minor roles. The important colonizers all had at least two things in common: first, they were maritime societies sitting at the western edge of Europe; second, they had coherent, unifying political institutions and cultural attributes. Even tiny Scotland made a vain attempt to establish a colony in Central America as late as 1701. The most common vernacular language in Europe was German in its several regional variants. But there was no extended German political community of any significance nor the means or incentives for a formal role outside Europe, except later, by large-scale immigration to the British colonies.

The trick in colonization was to get there first, fix a settlement, and then sustain it and that required the resources of a cohesive state apparatus or entrepreneurs with state backing. The Portuguese and Spanish established overseas colonies long before their neighbors to the north because of their will to act and their means to sustain the act. The first permanent French and English colonies were not set up in America until 1605 and 1607, respectively. The French and English were certainly technologically capable of fixing colonies in the Americas long before they did, but they were delayed by preoccupation with national or regional issues or, more likely, the absence of clearly defined incentives. French and English traders, adventures, and state-sponsored explorers scoured the Atlantic and made landfall in the Americas within years of the Spanish and the Portuguese but did not deem it worthwhile to settle permanently.

Europe and Africa

Decades before Columbus headed west, the Portuguese established colonies in the Atlantic by going south and west to the Madeira islands and then to the Azores, which are nearly 1,000 miles directly west of Portugal. Oddly, it was the west coast of Africa that drew them into the Atlantic in the first place in the early decades of the fifteenth century. The northern parts of Africa had long been familiar to southern Europeans. As long ago as the apex of its empire, Rome had spread itself along the entire southern Mediterranean coast and some distance inland. But the rest of Africa was largely *terra incognita*. Arabs had probed into the eastern sub-Saharan regions from the Indian Ocean, and Muslims from North Africa had reached south through the Sahara and west toward the Atlantic. For the most part, however, Africa's mass remained beyond the reach of both Europeans and Arabs. In fact, the interior, the so-called dark continent was not fully surveyed or traversed by Europeans until late in the nineteenth century. But in the early fifteenth century, Portuguese traders began to set up trading posts along the west coast. These early contacts grew over time and came to exploit what Europeans decided was the African continent's most precious commodity, its peoples, as slaves.

The entire African continent is roughly three times the size of Europe and lies between 35 degrees latitude north to 35 degrees latitude south; most of it is in the tropics. It is over 4,000 miles from east to west at its widest point at 15 degrees north and about 4,800 miles from the far north to the Cape of Good Hope in the south. In the north, at the Strait of Gibraltar, where the Mediterranean meets the Atlantic, Morocco is visible from the Spanish side. The Sahara Desert separates the fertile Mediterranean lands of the north from the bulk of the continent, which consists of savannah, rainforest, and highlands; more deserts in the southwest; and great stretches of grasslands in the far south.

When the Portuguese first landed on the northwestern coast in the 1430s, Africa's population was about 40 million people comprising a great many cultures. For Renaissance Europeans, however, the common distinguishing features of the continent's millions, south of the Sahara, were the genetic pigmentation and physiognomic characteristics that were often translated into a single African stereotype. In fact, variety rather than uniformity distinguished the continent's social and cultural characteristics. For example, five major language families and hundreds of variants within them made for a rich complexity, as did regional art and cultural habits. The very tall Masai people and the very short Pygmy people, the Bushmen of the southwest, the pastoralists of the plains and savannahs, and the nomadic tribes of the rainforest were a small part of the rich diversity of Africa's peoples, societies, and cultures.

Ironworking societies, sedentary agrarian communities, hunters and gatherers, nomadic game herders and traders, warriors, lake and river fishers, and urban traders made for a rich multicultural quilt. The Bantu peoples were the largest linguistic and population group south of the Sahara. Great numbers of them would end up as slaves in the Americas. Today, they have spread into the farthest southern reaches of the continent. Empires, including the great Mali Empire of West Africa, rose and fell in the continent's shifting politics. The Songhai Empire and the several Hausa city-states stretched inland from the coastlines of Sierra Leone and Senegal on the farthest western extension of the continent. On the other side of the continent, as noted, Arab traders had by 1450 established trading posts all along Africa's Indian Ocean coast.

Africa's fringes, then, were known to Europeans and Arabs. In fact, in geological terms, Africa was a contiguous part of the Eurasian land mass. The Levant, the membrane of land that joined Africa to Asia and thus to Europe, was not severed until the opening of the Suez Canal in the late nineteenth century. From the western Mediterranean to the Persian Gulf, traders and slavers had long operated south of the Sahara, which, although it presented a physical obstacle, was not a complete barrier to movement from North Africa into Timbuktu and the sub-Saharan nations.

When the Portuguese did touch on the coast of West Africa in the 1430s, they encountered African converts to Islam, slaves and slave traders, and North African Muslims who had penetrated into the sub-Saharan hinterland. Once the Portuguese had made regular contact, they and other Europeans became permanently involved in Africa over the next few generations without settling into colonies. The Portuguese learned that gold had long been mined in some regions; they knew of the value of African spices and other commodities, but it was the gathering of slaves, ultimately in the millions, as labor-producing commodities that drew Africa into the web of European expansion. The interior was ignored except insofar as it could provide slaves through intermediaries. As the Portuguese began their transit south along the Atlantic coast, they slowly but surely pulled unwilling Africans into the colonization of America, and that trade eventually encouraged the other European expansionists to seek treasure in Africa's human stocks.

Iberia Stirs: Portugal

Europe's American enterprise began with Columbus, acting for the Spanish, but it was the Portuguese and, in particular, the initiatives of Prince Henry the Navigator (1394–1460), the third son of John I of Portugal, that pulled Europe into the Atlantic. The Kingdom of Portugal had been established during the Christian recovery of that area of Iberia in the twelfth century, the *reconquista*, and then was ruled under the House of Burgundy until the late fourteenth century when the House of Avis was founded. Portugal was a thoroughgoing maritime nation, but it had no access to the Mediterranean; the Atlantic was its ocean. Prince Henry had an intellectual disposition but eschewed abstract matters for practical ones. He was an ambitious, devout Christian whose main objectives were profit, national security, and international respect. Still, after 1415, he instituted what might be called a school for sailors and navigators at Sagres in southwestern Portugal, and, before that, he had helped to establish the first European foothold in North Africa, at Ceuta in present-day Morocco.

Henry made the exploration of the Atlantic coast of Africa a priority, and, before he died in 1460, his *marinheiros* had traced the coastline south of the Cape Verde Islands, which itself is about 1,800 miles south and west of the European-African and Mediterranean-Atlantic junction at Gibraltar. His school went on to produce outstanding sailors such as Vasco da Gama and Ferdinand Magellan. By the 1440s, the Portuguese were exploiting African slaves as well as the seals off the coast and the profits from gold and other materials. Before he died, Henry denounced slavery in a belated plea for atonement, but, by then, African slaves had been hard at work in the Portuguese Atlantic islands of the Azores, Madeira, and Cape Verde. The Portuguese had tapped into an apparently secure supply of slaves, organized a method of acquiring them, and found a way of exploiting them as labor for the sugar and grape crops of the Atlantic islands.

Henry's title, "navigator," applies to his vision rather than to any personal, significant nautical experience. But that vision did lead to remarkable "navigations." By the end of the fifteenth century, three great voyagers had extended the Portuguese maritime world. In the 1480s, first Diogo Cão and then Bartolomeu Dias pushed to the very tip of South Africa at the Cape of Good Hope. Then, in 1497–1498, Vasco da Gama (ca.1469–1524) sailed several hundred miles out into the Atlantic south of the equator. He then swung back east to round the Cape of Good Hope, sailed up the eastern side of the continent, and crossed the Indian Ocean to Calicut. This feat can be compared fairly with Columbus's Atlantic crossing as a signal event in the history of European expansion. It established Portugal as the first European presence on African coasts and the Indian subcontinent. Columbus and Vasco da Gama made their momentous voyages within a few years of each other, but Columbus "found" a new continent.

Iberia Stirs: Spain

In 1492, Spain was an aggregation of regional Christian communities overlaying the remnants of earlier Roman and then Moorish societies. Galicia in the north, Catalonia in the east, and Granada in the south had been formally joined to the Aragon-Castile alliance of 1476 in the waning days of the *reconquista*. By 1492, all of Spain was under the joint control of King Ferdinand of Aragon and Queen Isabella of Castile. The long Christian recovery of Iberia from centuries of Muslim rule was completed at the end of the fifteenth century with the conquest of Granada, the last Moorish enclave in Spain. During the long recovery of Iberia, the Catholic Church had become a powerful force in Spanish public life. As a measure of a growing collectivism, the church oversaw the formal expulsion of the Jews in the same year that Columbus sailed west. By the time the Habsburgs came to power, after 1504 with the death of Isabella, Spain's "golden" age had begun.

The nation that opened up the Americas to Europe was by no means "advanced," even by contemporary European standards. As much as 25 per cent of its arable land was owned by the church with most of the remainder in the hands of the secular hereditary aristocratic minority. The majority of the population was rural, dependant, and poor. Some parts of Spain were little more than wilderness, quite remote from the centers of learning or power, and thinly populated, as was much of Iberia's lengthy coastline. The development of great fishing fleets and their ports still lay ahead. In the fifteenth century, it was expensive to salt and preserve and then transport the Atlantic and Mediterranean fish stocks. Much of Spain's and Portugal's population subsisted on grains and whatever beef, mutton, and pork could be fed and raised. There was considerable regional disparity, and the relative fecundity and prosperity of parts of Catalonia or Andalusia were offset by the impoverishment of areas like Estremadura on the edges of Castile in west central Portugal. What Spain did have was a powerful alliance between Castile-Aragon and the Catholic Church. A 1479 treaty with Portugal had secured for Spain control of the Canary Islands, a small archipelago stretching between 100 and 250 miles off the Atlantic coast of what is now Morocco. Those islands, which had been known to Romans, Arab traders, and medieval Europeans, were taken over by the Spanish. In the process, the native population, the Guanches, was decimated.

The decision to fund and commission Columbus was certainly a sign of Castilian ambition, but some of the credit must go to the persistence of Columbus the entrepreneur. He had shopped his proposal to other Europeans, including the crown heads of Portugal and England. In fact, Henry VII of England had considered funding the mission. Before Queen Isabella, who had earlier rejected his plan, and King Ferdinand were moved to finance the project, Columbus had also canvassed Venice and his native Genoa. Like other maritime entrepreneurs of the era, Columbus had already visited Lisbon, Bristol, Ireland, and possibly Iceland. His seamanship came from long experience. He knew how to sail by "dead reckoning," the skill of navigating in the open sea, away from the sight of land, by calculating speed, elapsed time, and the direction of the ship. These calculations were done with an hourglass, perhaps, and a crude compass and an astrolabe to set the ship's position according to the noonday sun at known latitudes. Competent sailors could head into the ocean along a line of latitude using "dead reckoning." It is a measure of Columbus's talents that he could retrace his route back to Spain from the Caribbean after his initial voyage. Before long, of course, Renaissance mariners produced oceanic charts showing longitude, adding to the accelerating development of geometrically accurate cartography. Columbus's writings reveal some lingering notions of medieval Christian morality, and it has been supposed that his desire to reach the Indies was as much to initiate a Christian crusade as it was to enrich himself and his patrons or expand the fund of human knowledge. Columbus was also a man of his time, and his cosmopolitanism reflected Renaissance values in the way he described things by experience and experiment. He also knew his way around the courts of western Europe.

When Columbus left Palos in southeastern Spain, he took the counterintuitive route of going west to get to the east. He believed the world was smaller than it actually was and that the Atlantic extended uninterrupted to Asia. His knowledge of the occupied Atlantic islands was offset by his and his crews' genuine apprehension of the unknown waters beyond the Portuguese Azores. Moreover, the expedition's vessels were merely improved versions of the type that the Portuguese had used in the previous half century, and which were common in the Mediterranean. The *Pinta* and the *Niña* were caravels, fast ships less than 100 feet long and lighter than 100 tons deadweight, using triangular (lateen) mainsails. The flagship, *Santa Maria*, was a *nao*, a larger, sturdier, and more advanced ocean-going vessel than the caravels with a more effective square mainsail. In an important way, Columbus and his crews showed the potential for transoceanic voyages using contemporary vessels and navigational techniques.

Within decades, the Atlantic and then the Indian and Pacific Oceans became busy highways. The precedents set by Prince Henry, Columbus, Vasco da Gama, and others led the way to more exploration and more distant objectives. Voyages increased in frequency and distance so that, in 1521, Ferdinand Magellan (ca.1480–1521) completed the first recorded circumnavigation of the world. Like Columbus, Magellan was an explorer-entrepreneur and, in his case, ironically, a Portuguese working for the Spanish. He died on the way back to Europe, and the triumph was completed by his crew. Although the physical world was revealed to be larger than Columbus had predicted, it would, figuratively, shrink as Europe's ships and peoples flowed into its farthest reaches establishing a web of contacts. Within a generation of Columbus's speculative expedition, hundreds of calculated and predictable routes were being described and charted.

The Treaty of Tordesillas and the Founding of the Spanish Empire in America

At the closing of the fifteenth century, the Spanish reached the Americas and the Portuguese rounded Africa—with a surfeit of audacity and, to modern eyes, the most rudimentary and flimsiest of sea craft. Still, they can hardly be counted as the first to venture out into the world's oceans; the Chinese had previously visited the east coast of Africa, and the Vikings much earlier had likely spent some time on the east coast of continental North America. If we think more carefully about the "west" from the European perspective, we note that Iceland, just below the Arctic Circle (66 degrees north latitude) and 600 miles west of the Norwegian coast was settled by Scandinavians in the ninth century and was known to traders and fishers. But that was as far as western settlement had gone. Archaeologists have confirmed the existence of a Norse settlement from about 1000 CE at L'Anse aux Meadows in Newfoundland, and the great Norse sagas hint at even more extensive contact with North America. Other travelers and migrants in earlier times had doubtless traversed the world's oceans without plausible verbal records of the results. What changed at the end of the fifteenth century was that permanent settlements, and the emphasis is on "permanent," were made far beyond the shores of Atlantic Europe.

Columbus was immediately rewarded for his deeds. On his return to Spain, he was elevated to "admiral of the ocean seas" and made governor of the lands he had found, in accordance with his commission. His ego was satisfied, but he had also reached the peak of his personal relevance. He made three return voyages to the Caribbean, establishing small settlements, and he sailed as far south as the mouth of the Orinoco River on the South American mainland. His vanity, however, drove him to a false sense of importance. Regardless of his other talents, he was a poor administrator, and his reputation had faded before he retired to Spain where he died in 1506, fully aware of his precedent-setting voyage but unaware that the world he had revealed was ready to explode in ways he could not have imagined.

Some time before Columbus had set out, the Portuguese sought to have their claims to the Atlantic islands endorsed by the Church of Rome. Pope Sixtus IV had heard their claims in 1481. After 1492, the Portuguese challenged Spanish rights to territorial exclusivity. Pope Alexander VI, a Spaniard, issued a "bull" (an order) that fixed a line some 900 miles west of Cape Verde in the Atlantic, defining Africa to the east as Portuguese and America to the west as Spanish. In 1494, a more streamlined and satisfactory treaty was devised; the Treaty of Tordesillas set the western mark a little farther west than the earlier line at what would be longitude 39 degrees and 53 minutes west. That line happens to run through the great eastern bulge of South America and so afforded Portugal a foothold in the Americas. Brazil would be the result, and, after 1500, the two Iberian nations began colonizing America in earnest. After Magellan's circumnavigation of 1521, another treaty, signed at Zaragosa in 1529, took the 1494 line and divided the world into hemispheres at the "anti-meridian." Magellan had reached islands that later were named for Philip II of Spain, the Philippines. The Portuguese held on to the nearby Moluccas, the storied Spice Islands. Spain's claim ran from the mid-Atlantic west, across America and the Pacific to the Philippines. The Portuguese claim ran east from the mid-Atlantic across Africa to India and to southern China. The pope had conveniently divided the world into hemispheres, one for Portugal and one for Spain. Early in the sixteenth century, Spain began to colonize America in a burst of extraordinary violence.

The Conquest of Mexico and Peru

The *conquistador* Hernando Cortés was commissioned to take an expedition from the Caribbean to the mainland in 1519. He landed near present-day Vera Cruz and within two years had laid waste to the Aztec Empire. Cortés secured for himself a prominent place in the annals of imperial and military history. His success in Mexico was due in part to his military prowess and the technological superiority of his small Spanish army. He brought 500 soldiers and 100 sailors to Mexico on 11 ships, which he later scuttled in order to preclude any alternative to his expedition to Tenochtitlan. His entourage included 32 crossbowmen also equipped with *arquebuses,* heavy and difficult to use muskets whose noise and smoke intimidated some natives even though the weapons were inferior to crossbows in their ability to kill. The tiny assault force included 16 horses and 14 pieces of artillery, but its strength was boosted by Cortés's use of diplomacy, and its success was achieved through the exploitation of the segmented groups under Aztec control. In fact, Cortés's victory was a precedent that repeated itself over and over again for generations in other parts of the Americas. Much is made of the novelty and shock of gunpowder and horses and of the disease epidemics that hit the Aztec armies, but Spanish success was underwritten by the cooptation of many of the subordinated peoples of Montezuma's empire. The final collapse of Aztec power was accompanied by internal revolt. For the amphibious assault on Tenochtitlan, Cortés had his assault vessels built on site with the aid of local natives. His success was achieved at least in part by his machinations, and, although he was, however briefly, a liberator, the "liberation" immediately became a straightforward transfer of power, from a Mexican imperialist to another from across the seas.

Accompanying the conquerors was Bernal Diaz, whose 1568 account of the expedition, published in English as *The True History of the Conquest of New Spain,* reveals some of the Spanish invaders' motives, impressions, and attitudes as they swept through Mexico. His summary of Cortés's campaign rolls off the page in grand heroic celebration as he laments the passing of the generation of *conquistadores* and the dual nature of the Spanish mission in America: "The names of [Cortés's soldiers] ought to be written in gold. [They] died so cruel a death, for the service of God and His Majesty, to give light to those who were in darkness, and to procure wealth which all men desire." Cortés and the *conquistadores* who followed him made Mexico a Spanish and Christian possession. But Spain had only just begun to make its mark on the continent; the rest of America beckoned. In 1533, in the wake of Cortés's Mexican triumph on the violent road to Spanish imperialism in America, Francisco Pizarro's ambitious expedition to the Andes brought down the great Inca Empire.

Pizarro was born in the tough, austere region of Estremadura and so shared a birthplace with Cortés. But Cortés was trained in law and worked as a bureaucrat in the Caribbean while the illegitimate Pizarro spent his youth as a semiliterate swineherd. After he learned of Columbus's feat, he managed to get to the Caribbean in 1502 as a member of a large group of immigrants to Hispaniola in an impressive fleet of 30 ships. He served on an expedition to Colombia in 1510 and thereafter made a career for himself by engaging in any colonial or exploratory enterprise that would employ him. He was part of the 1513 Vasco Núñez de Balboa expedition that crossed the narrow Panama isthmus to the Pacific. He gradually joined in the intrigues of the colonial network taking shape in the Caribbean, Panama, and Colombia. His hard personality and desire for status did not endear him to many of the empire's administrators, soldiers, and entrepreneurs, and he made enemies.

Exploration and settlement in the early sixteenth century Indies required fundraising and connecting with influential backers. In 1528, Pizarro went back to Spain to finance a campaign on the Pacific side of South America to conquer the empire of the Incas, a territory that the *conquistador* described as very rich in gold and silver. (Ten or so years later, Gonzalo Pizarro, the younger half-brother of Francisco, led an expedition east of Quito with Francisco de Orellana in search of the fabled city of El Dorado.) Francisco Pizarro managed to outfit an armed force and left Seville in 1530 for the Indies. He sailed from Panama in 1531, made his way down the Pacific coast and went on to overwhelm the Inca Empire. He accomplished this with luck, force, and deceit in equal measure. His small army trekked into the heart of the empire, befriended and then kidnapped the Inca Prince Atahualpa and held him for a fortune in ransom. When it was paid, Pizarro had the Prince garroted and a native client installed as monarch. By 1535, the Spanish claimed sovereignty over a huge area that became formalized as the Vice Royalty of Peru. Pizarro established Spanish Lima and redesigned the Inca capital of Cuzco. He was rewarded with a title, made a governor, and celebrated at the Spanish Court. But his greed, belligerence, and arrogance continued to antagonize his rivals. His treachery was notorious even by the harsh ethics of the *conquistadores*, and, in 1541, he died at the hands of some of the enemies he had encouraged.

The Spanish Colonial System

The legacies of Cortés and Pizarro and tales of their exploits reverberate to the present. The early Spanish conquests often combined Christian mission with straightforward pillaging. They were often begun by private individuals under the auspices of the state. Eventually, the state took control of the policies, programs, and administration of Spanish America. A system of imperial organization operated in the name of Spain and the church. The key to success for individuals in Spanish America was possession of an *encomienda*, literally, a commission, to an individual or corporation to certain rights over the population of a defined area in Spanish America. It did not grant title to any land, as it did in some cases in Spain, but did specifically assign labor or other service along with tribute (dues) from indigenous peoples or settlers in the area to the *encomiendero*. A New World, new style feudalism was established, with natives as the new serfs. The commissions required that a fifth (*quinto*) went to the Crown of all the profits realized from gold and silver, native tribute, duties, and church tithes and the selling of indulgencies. The Spanish Empire in America took shape as a structured top-down bureaucratic organization somewhat as follows:

- *The Council of the Indies (Consejo de las Indias)* in Spain was a formal control group, not unlike a modern cabinet. It designed and oversaw policy.

- *The Board of Trade (Casa de Contratacion)* administered the policies of the Council of the Indies and collected taxes, shipping charges, and other administrative dues. It issued licenses for a variety of colonial activities including trade and exploration.

- *The viceroyalties* were the largest administrative subdivisions of the Spanish Empire in America and included the viceroyalties of New Spain and Peru in the early period and New Granada in the early eighteenth century.

- *Audiencias* were subdivisions of the viceroyalties, with a major function as law courts.

- *Captaincy generals* were further subdivisions of the *audiencias*.

- *The cabildo* or town council (*ayuntamiento*) defined local civil authority.

Along with the systematic redrawing of community and authority, the Spanish began a program of cathedral building. Universities were built at Mexico City and Lima in 1551.

The Spanish sought treasure in gold but found silver. After 1545, the silver produced at Potosi in present-day Bolivia supported the Spanish treasury. Indeed, by 1600, Potosi was home to the largest concentration of Europeans in the western hemisphere. Otherwise, it was large-scale agricultural land holding, the so called latifundia, that spread the Spanish and *criolo* populations through the Americas, although, of course, these huge slave-operated farms adjusted to regional differences in climate, geography, and agricultural land use potential and land availability. The large estates established in Mexico, Argentina, the Caribbean, and the valleys and coastal plains of the Pacific *audiencias,* as well as the *hacienda* culture they inspired, marked a new permanent European aristocracy in the New World. These social and institutional characteristics were, of course, subject to change over time, keeping in mind the long history of the Spanish American Empire. It lasted for over 400 years. But some basic characteristics of the Spanish Empire were laid down very early.

From the very start of conquest and occupation, the Spanish explored the continent with persistence. Acuncion, in present-day Paraguay, was founded in 1535. As early as 1513, Juan Ponce de León had explored Florida, which was claimed for Spain by the indefatigable Álvar Núñez Cabeza de Vaca in 1528. Cabeza de Vaca (the name translates as "cow head" in English) was among the most widely traveled of the era's peripatetic Spaniards. His travels took him from Texas, possibly to California, and then to Mexico City and eventually thousands of miles south to Paraguay. His chronicles likely inspired the searches for the fabled Cibola, a group of seven wealthy "cities of gold" that were reputed to be in the New World. Another intrepid explorer, Hernando de Soto, for example, found his way to the Mississippi and crossed it by 1541, looking for rumored caches of gold. Another gold seeker, Francisco Coronado saw the Grand Canyon in his epic trek to the west from northern Mexico.

Mythical cities of gold were not the only lure for the Spanish. Reputedly, Ponce de León had explored Florida, as the legend goes, looking for the fabulous "fountain of youth." Dreams, fantasies, rumors, and legend aside, straightforward conquest, exploration, and colonization were what sustained Spain in America, and the Spanish continued to probe by land and sea for over two centuries. As late at the 1790s its sailors were competing with British and American traders and explorers all the way to the northern coastline of present-day British Columbia. Spain's expansion was impressive in its range and pace and in its unremitting suppression of native peoples and traditions. Within a few decades, the western hemisphere had been shaken, and its many cultures distorted by Spain's soldiers, priests, administrators, entrepreneurs, and settlers. In Asia, under the terms of the Treaty of Tordesillas, the Spanish established Manila in 1571 and the Philippines were then subject to a similar process of subjugation. A broad transoceanic Spanish Empire was underway within two generations of Columbus.

The Portuguese World

While Spain was imposing itself on America and the Pacific, the Portuguese Empire took hold in Brazil and in parts of Africa, India, and the Orient. The decision at Tordesillas had suggested a *carte blanche* for Portugal in its half of the globe, and the enterprising Portuguese made the most of it. As noted, they had been moving down the west coast of Africa for decades. After Vasco da Gama's voyage, they established trading and slaving outposts on both the Atlantic and Indian Ocean coasts of Africa. In 1501, in a remarkable twist of fortune, Álvares Cabral, on his way south and then east around the Cape of Good Hope to India, sailed so far into the Atlantic that he made landfall on the most easterly point of South America near present-day Bahia, Brazil. Cabral saw no potential in the place, left, and continued on his original route. Not until 1530 did the Portuguese decide that there might be value there. The area was then organized into 13 *capitanias* along the coastline from the mouth of the Amazon River south to the present-day site of Rio de Janeiro. These resembled the Spanish *audiencias* as administrative units, where a *donatario* held sway over the land and the people. The system was imported from the Azores and Madeira and included sugar culture and slavery. In the Atlantic islands, the use of local natives as slave labor had given way to African slaves who would provide the massive labor force that propelled Brazil's development. By 1600, the founding of landed estates and sugar plantations and the flow of millions of African slaves into Brazil were underway. By 1650, over 300 sugar mills (*engenhos*) were in operation; the number reached 500 by 1700. In the coastal areas, the displacement and destruction of indigenous peoples had begun in earnest by the end of the sixteenth century.

Meanwhile, a succession of gun-wielding Portuguese traders and administrators set up a string of outposts across Africa and Asia: from Angola in West Africa to Mozambique in East Africa and including Goa and Malabar in India (in the wake of Arab and Muslim traders), Malacca on the Malay Peninsula, Colombo in present-day Sri Lanka, and Macao in southeastern China. The reach of the Portuguese was astonishing even if the demand in Asia for their goods was not as great as hoped. The Chinese and Indians regarded much of Europe's merchandise as inferior, but the Portuguese still found ways to extract useful commodities from Asia. From dealings with African and Arab slave traders in Africa to Muslim rulers and traders in the Far East, the Portuguese established themselves as the pioneers of Europe's global reach through diplomacy, war, and economic investment. For America, Brazil's "treasure" turned out to be sugar in the sixteenth and seventeenth centuries. While minerals, especially gold, replaced sugar as Brazil's greatest resource after 1700, sugar remained vital to the Brazilian economy well into the nineteenth century. By 1600, as a result of their global successes, Portugal and Spain were rising in prominence in European affairs and Lisbon and Madrid had become major centers in money matters, politics, and diplomacy. Across the Atlantic the habitable coastline and the immediate hinterlands of Central and South America were under Iberian control. Then, in a rush, the Spanish and Portuguese were joined in America by other European colonizers to the north.

SUGGESTED READINGS

The European background to colonization is briefly summarized in Carlo Cipolla, *Before the Industrial Revolution: European Society and Economy, 1000–1700* (New York: Norton, 1976) and *Guns, Sails and Empire: Technological Innovation and the Early Phases of European Expansion, 1400–1700* (Manhattan, KS: Sunflower University Press, 1985). Cipolla takes a longer, gradual view of European development rather than looking for paradigm events, and his treatment of technology as a way of measuring change and persistence is persuasive. J.R. Hale, *Renaissance Europe, 1480–1520,* 2nd ed. (Oxford: Blackwell, 2000) is a recognized authority on the era that coincided with European expansion. A recommended shorter, topical survey is Jonathan W. Zophy, *A Short History of Renaissance and Reformation Europe,* 2nd ed. (Upper Saddle River, NJ: Prentice Hall, 1999). See also James D. Hardy, Jr., *Prologue to Modernity: Early Modern Europe* (New York: Wiley, 1974) and Peter Rietbergen, *Europe: A Cultural History* (New York: Routledge, 1998). A stimulating and beautifully written example of using art to capture a contemporary worldview is Timothy Brook, *Vermeer's Hat: The Seventeenth Century and the Dawn of the Global World* (New York: Bloomsbury Press, 2008). Keith Thomas, *Religion and the Decline of Magic* (New York: Scribner, 1971) is a stimulating book that sees pre-industrial popular culture through the medium of folk beliefs. One of its themes deals with the impact of Protestantism on folk culture. Peter Laslett, *The World We Have Lost,* 3rd ed. (London: Methuen, 1983) remains valuable as a study of pre-industrial England, even if he does paint a too rosy picture of sixteenth and seventeenth century social conditions. A long respected study of Elizabethan culture, politics, and foreign affairs is A.L. Rowse, *The Expansion of Elizabethan England* (1955; repr., Basingstoke, UK: Palgrave MacMillan, 2003). The reasons for and short-term effects of European expansion are superbly summarized in J.H. Parry, *The Establishment of the European Hegemony, 1415–1715,* 3rd. ed. rev. (New York: Harper & Row, 1966). This brief, lively survey has no peer as an introduction to the subject. J.H. Elliott, *Empires of the Atlantic World: Britain and Spain in America, 1492–1830* (New Haven: Yale University Press, 2007) takes a broader chronological comparative view. European concepts of hegemony and empire have spawned a wealth of studies including Nicholas Canny and Anthony Pagden, eds., *Colonial Identity in the Atlantic World, 1500–1800* (Princeton, NJ: Princeton University Press, 1987); Richard Kagan and Geoffrey Parker, eds., *Spain, Europe and the Atlantic World: Essays in Honor of John H. Elliott* (Cambridge, UK: Cambridge University Press, 1995); Anthony Pagden, *Lords of All the Worlds: Ideologies of Empire in Spain, Britain and France, 1500–1800* (New Haven: Yale University Press, 1995); and an older but valuable comparative view, John J. TePaske, ed.,

Three American Empires (New York: Harper & Row, 1967). David B. Quinn, *Explorers and Colonies: America, 1500–1625* (London: Hambledon Press, 1990) is a collection of previously published essays and is recommended for its author's stimulating reinterpretations of some of the common treatments of European expansion. The massive literature on Christopher Columbus continues to grow, but Samuel E. Morison, *Admiral of the Ocean Sea: A Life of Christopher Columbus* (Boston: Little Brown, 1942) is as good a starting point as any. See also "Book Two" in Hugh Thomas, *Rivers of Gold: The Rise of the Spanish Empire* (London: Weidenfeld and Nicolson, 2003). The rest of this book is also recommended as an introduction to the subject and Thomas uses a great deal of Spanish language scholarship. A richly detailed and well-written text on the early Spanish and Portuguese empires is Lyle N. McAlister, *Spain and Portugal in the New World, 1492–1700* (Minneapolis: University of Minnesota Press, 1984).

Time Line

* * * * * ★ ★ ★ * * * *

CHAPTER 2

The French and Dutch in North America and the Caribbean Melting Pot

The King has two principal objectives with regard to the native Indians. The first is to procure their conversion to the Christian and Catholic faith.... The second objective of His Majesty is eventually to make of these Indians His subjects.... His intention is that... these measures be carried out with goodwill and that these Indians take it up out of their own proper interest.

—King Louis XIV (1663) after he established New France as a royal colony under direct control.

The French in America

BEGINNINGS, 1500–1600

While the English, Dutch, and French would not make permanent colonies in the Americas for a century after the Spanish, the French in particular had shown early interest in the possibilities of settlement. Indeed, French explorers, traders, and fishers were active in the northern reaches of the North Atlantic throughout the sixteenth century, leaving behind failed settlements and temporary trading posts. Even after the French established permanent enclaves in Acadia in 1605 and at Quebec in 1608, it took another half century before Louis XIV officially committed France to an American Empire.

Between the end of the fifteenth century and the 1520s, the Valois dynasty had begun to unify France into something like its modern shape. Like other formative European nations, France had many localities and dialects (*patois*), which remained intact, but the concentration of military and taxing power lodged increasing authority in the monarchy. The political integration achieved under Louis XI in the decades after 1461 paved the way for France's rising importance in Europe and the Atlantic. After the English-sponsored 1497 North Atlantic crossing by John Cabot, numbers of Breton and Basque fishers appeared around Newfoundland and the Grand Banks. Francophile Giovanni da Verrazano (ca.1485–1528) used the term *Nova Gallia* (New France) to describe the northern reaches of North America, and his 1524 voyage inspired French traders and fishers to set up stations as far south as the coast of Brazil.

Jacques Cartier (1491–1557) made his first voyage to the Gulf of St. Lawrence in 1534 with the encouragement of the Valois King Francis I, who had been Verrazano's patron. Francis, like so many others, imagined that there was a northwest passage to the Orient and consequently commissioned Cartier's three voyages of exploration, in 1534, 1535–1536, and 1541–1542. Cartier's first impressions of the barren coasts of Labrador—"I believe that this is the land God gave to Cain"—moderated as he made his way south into the area around Gaspé and present-day Prince Edward Island and New Brunswick. Cartier had entered the mouth of a great river that he named the Saint-Laurent (St. Lawrence), and he appears to be the first European to record the word "Canada" to describe the region. He must be counted as one of the great navigators of the age. In small ships, taking two on the first voyage and five on the last, he sailed along thousands of miles of coastline and deep into the continent, 1,000 navigable miles up the St. Lawrence to the rapids west of Montreal. He entered dozens of harbors, explored the seas around islands large and small and never lost a ship in waters that were often violent and usually frigid. In the course of his three voyages, he set up strategic outposts at Stadacona (Quebec) and Hochelaga (Montreal). These were short lived but suggested the likelihood of settlement. He had good relations with the natives, which indirectly set the tone for future French policy in North America.

Despite the encouraging fact that the French king had funded the expeditions, the attempts to settle failed. On Cartier's last voyage, Jean-

François Roberval installed a party of 200 settlers at Quebec that included convicts and women, but scurvy and cold took a mortal toll on the group. The settlers eventually alienated the local natives. Threatened, depressed, and discouraged, the survivors went back to France. The end of the Cartier era began a long interlude of inactivity before the first permanent settlements were confirmed. Still, although no colony was established during the sixteenth century, the French presence in America was sustained by traders and fishers. The contact was intermittent, but French interests had not entirely abandoned the land that Cartier had claimed for France. Meanwhile, continental France was caught up in the religious and political disruptions of the Reformation.

The response to Protestantism, the aptly named Counter-Reformation, led to greater solidarity among Catholics and caused dangerous divisions within and between nations. As noted in Chapter 1, a peasant revolt in Germany in 1524 triggered a full-scale class war that was fueled by the Lutheran attachments of the lower classes and the attachment to Rome of the ruling classes. A century of religious wars in Europe followed, eased only by the Treaty of Westphalia after the devastation of much of German-speaking Europe in the Thirty Years' War of 1618–1648. That war was an especially vicious one that exhausted the resources of civilian populations who were often the primary targets of military operations. It made a wasteland of parts of northern Europe.

No part of Europe escaped the Reformation. It came to France at the moment Jacques Cartier was exploring in the name of the Catholic king, and, by the 1560s, many French nobles and merchants had embraced Calvinism, referring to themselves as Huguenots (a French derivative of the German *Eidgenossen*, "sworn confederates"). Although Protestantism appeared to threaten the solid Catholic traditions of France, there was some toleration of the Huguenots because the French Monarchy controlled the church's bishops and guaranteed that Catholic hegemony could be maintained, Huguenots tolerated, and Rome kept at arm's length.

Sectarian war nevertheless plagued the country during the latter part of the sixteenth century until the Edict of Nantes (1598) marked an official recognition, that is, toleration, of Protestants. The series of wars also involved a serious challenge to the Valois dynasty from rival factions. The major threat to the regime came from the Bourbon family, which controlled Navarre after 1555 and eventually came to rule France in 1589 in a bewildering atmosphere of assassination, intrigue, interfamily marriage, and sectarian controversy. Such were the convolutions of Europe's dynastic politics. In a way that repeated itself in other conflicts, Elizabeth's Protestant England and Philip's Catholic Spain each supported their religious proxies in France. Meanwhile, French Huguenots had attempted to settle in America. One venture to Rio de Janeiro in 1555–1557 ended in disaster when one of the Huguenot leaders recanted, and the 300 or so French immigrants split into factions. Many went back to France, but most of those who remained in Brazil as Protestants were slaughtered by the Portuguese. The tough-minded Huguenots were not deterred and, in the 1560s, provoked Spanish outrage by trying to settle in Florida. These incursions sparked a more serious Spanish commitment to Florida, and St. Augustine was settled permanently in 1565. At the same time, French pirates had seen the possibilities of setting up posts for easy plundering of the Spanish fleets. They joined briefly with the Huguenots in Florida in 1562–1564 in settlements that were destroyed by the Spanish in 1565.

The North American mainland all the way to the Chesapeake called out for Spanish attention, but native resistance and the logistical and financial difficulties of missionary work or conquest retarded the Spanish and kept them in Florida. The French continued trading and fishing, and, together with the ambitious but failed English settlement at Roanoke off the coast of Carolina (1584–1587), they signaled to the Spanish that they would not be alone in North America. But, until the turn of the seventeenth century, French and English excursions into the Americas were half-baked, poorly sponsored, or freelance experiments, or they resulted in temporary trading and fishing outposts—nothing of consequence. But traffic in the Atlantic was growing. There is no way of knowing how many ships in a given year plied the waters of the northwestern Atlantic between Greenland and New England, but contemporaries estimated them to be in the thousands. All the European maritime nations were represented, and the growing activity in the areas to the south attracted freelance raiders. The opportunistic Francis Drake and the French buccaneer Jean Ribaut profited from piracy. Their informal war on Spanish shipping demonstrated the limits of Spanish control. One of the major factors in the ultimate success of the northwestern Europeans in northeastern North America was the failure of the Spanish to establish firm, defensible settlements north of the Caribbean and Florida and north and east of the lower Mississippi.

NEW FRANCE, ACADIA, AND FURS

There is a grand statue on the ramparts in Quebec City of Samuel de Champlain (1567–1635) standing tall above the St. Lawrence River. It salutes the permanence of Franco America. Along with Spanish St. Augustine, the English Jamestown, and the multinational St. John's in Newfoundland, Quebec City made an early, permanent European imprint on North America.

Champlain was a well-rounded man, the son of a sea captain, intelligent, multitalented, trained in navigation, and experienced in warfare. He led a cavalry unit during France's civil wars. In 1599, he sailed with a Spanish fleet to America and visited the West Indies, Vera Cruz, and Panama before he made his way north in 1603–1604 as a recorder and cartographer under the auspices of the first of the French Bourbons, Henry of Navarre (King Henry IV). He helped establish a small colony in Acadia (Nova Scotia) at Port-Royal in 1605. It got by with some rudimentary farming and fishing. It was destroyed by a group of English intruders in 1613 but was rebuilt by the French and prospered until the British offensives of the War of the Spanish Succession (1702–1713). Acadia's few thousand inhabitants in 1713, when the colony was ceded to the English, had farmed lots under royal grant. But the colony was considered a secondary concern of French imperial policy. The priority was in the St. Lawrence Valley, the heart of New France, and in the vast fur-rich regions beyond.

Where the great St. Lawrence widened on its way to the Atlantic, Champlain established a small settlement in 1608 and named it "Quebec," the Algonquian word for "narrows." Quebec had been the site of the failed Cartier-Roberval settlement of the early 1540s. Now, however, it was chosen for its commanding overview of the St. Lawrence and as a jumping off point for further upstream and interior exploration. The surrounding terrain was certainly forbidding. Endless, dense forests seemed to enclose Quebec along with the long bitter winters that froze the river for months. Yet it became a haven for the small and resourceful population that stayed. Trade with the natives brought in furs with the expectation of greater volume. The beaver became New France's great North American "cash crop" and took traders, ultimately, to the Great Lakes and beyond. If the St. Lawrence region sometimes appeared to the French to be a vacant wilderness, it was home to many thousands of Montagnais, Abenaki, Algonkin (or Algonquin), Huron, and, farther west, Iroquois peoples. The Iroquois Confederacy was formed 150 years before the Europeans colonized North America. The confederacy was perhaps the most powerful political and military native power north of Mexico and was composed, originally, of "Five Nations": the Mohawk (in the east), Oneida, Onondaga, Cayuga, and Seneca.

For security reasons, Champlain aligned himself with the Algonkin and Huron, a policy that had serious consequences for the French when they headed west and collided with the Iroquois. Metal goods, textiles, alcohol, and guns made their way into the native communities as trade and diplomatic exchange mediums. The French, Dutch, and English all engaged in the practice of using muskets (with the requisite powder and shot) as trade items. Natives sought the guns for the advantage they provided over their enemies and the enemies of their European allies. Even the heavy, difficult to use matchlocks (the charge set off with a "match" or taper) were effective against arrows and edged weapons. For Europeans, the downside to this trade was that native alliances sometimes failed and guns stayed in circulation and ended up being used against the colonists. Normally, the Europeans retained an advantage in firepower and controlled the repair of weapons and the source of gunpowder and shot, but the introduction of guns into native politics and warfare was a mixed blessing for the colonizers. The problem was exacerbated after the late seventeenth century and all the way to the late eighteenth century; alliances became more important as Europeans fought each other, with native help, and musket technology improved with the flintlock (no match required) and lighter and more durable manufacture.

After 20 years, there were only 100 people at Quebec. By comparison, after 20 years of settlement, the English to the south in New England had a population that was rising steadily toward the thousands. To encourage specialized immigration to New France, Cardinal Richelieu, the persuasive advisor to Louis XIII, formed the Company of One Hundred Associates in 1627. However, there was no mechanism for open settlement in New France, and the sparse populations throughout its history attest to the restrictive policies of successive authorities. The English charter system, on the other hand, encouraged groups of various predispositions to migrate to America. The French never used that approach. By the 1760s, there was a ratio of some 30 British to 1 French settler in North America.

Richelieu forbade all but Catholics from settling. That tack continued into the eighteenth century and denied the immigration of useful Huguenots who were being expelled from France after the tolerance law of 1598, the Edict of Nantes, was revoked in 1685. About 200,000 Huguenots were scattered throughout the world after the revocation, including a substantial number who ended up in British America. In any case, paltry immigration, the cold, and the overwhelming depth of what was seen as wilderness always deterred large-scale French agrarianism in North America. To be sure, land was assigned to investors who were granted *seigneuries,* in another example of American neo-feudalism. The *seigneurs* brought in indentured servants, *engagés,* who were allowed generous use of land as incentives, but there was no population boom in that method.

Early on, Champlain was made governor of the colony, which, in 1629, was attacked, seized by a rogue English group, and held by the English for three years. It was shut off to the French before it was recovered through diplomatic accords encouraged by Champlain and the French ambassador in London. When Champlain returned to New France in 1632, he helped found a trading post at Trois-Rivières, pushing the French presence farther west and lending his name to the large lake south of Montreal that feeds the Richelieu River, a major north-flowing tributary of the St. Lawrence. The colony's survival was guaranteed by the beaver. The fur trading economy took off in the following decades and pushed French interests deep into North America following Champlain's death in 1635. Unlike the tobacco and sugar commodity cultures to the south, the fur trade did not depend on white servitude or native or African slaves but rather on a network of trade relations with native nations in an area that eventually covered over a million square miles. In the seventeenth century, the European demand for beaver and other furs soared, and pelts joined the other consumables that poured out of the Americas onto the backs and into the mouths of Europe's consumer classes. Following Richelieu's settlement plan, Jesuits and other Christian missionaries such as the Recollets, who were members of the Franciscan order, launched themselves enthusiastically into New France.

By the 1640s, the Jesuits had converted many Huron people to the Christian faith and had appeared in the eastern regions of the Great Lakes. Hochelaga was renamed Ville-Marie and later Montreal. It was settled by Paul de Chomedy de Maisonneuve and a small missionary group. Although its future was tenuous, given the difficulty of communication, the relative trickle of immigrants, the risk of disease, malnutrition, native hostility, and the ever-severe climate, it survived. It was, in fact, another example of the tendency for settlements to defy the odds in New France, where Jesuits managed to pursue their spiritual objectives and fur traders continued to expand their trading range. The *seigneuries* and the *habitants* were strung thinly along the St. Lawrence shores in land divisions that ran from narrow river frontages to long north to south sections called *arpents*. Fish, grains, livestock, and game, as well as an abundance of mineral and wood resources, bolstered the tiny settlements along the great river. Still, after 30 years of settlement and struggle, only three sizable settlements had been established along the St. Lawrence, and the sedentary French population still numbered in the hundreds. By contrast, after 30 years of settlement, there were close to 25,000 English in New England by 1650. Beyond the farms and hamlets along the St. Lawrence, the fur trade and the Jesuit mission were the only marks of permanence in New France.

THE JESUITS

The Jesuits were a force to be reckoned with everywhere in Catholic America. Fearless and deeply committed to missionary work, they were vital to the colonial policies of Spain, Portugal, and France. They often ventured far beyond settlements to contact and negotiate with natives. As they did, they also irritated and even alienated civil authority with their often liberal approach to native rights, especially the rights of converts. Their commitment to papal authority was unimpeachable. The order was but one of many, such as the

Franciscans, whose zeal animated the Catholic Church's mission in America. But Jesuits were especially aggressive and, one might say, the most successful in pushing the boundaries of the Catholic world mission. The Jesuit order, the Society of Jesus, was founded in 1540 and authorized by Pope Paul III. Its leader, the Spaniard Ignatius Loyola (1491–1556) saw the role of the order as being more mobile than monastic. Loyola preached a sacrificial message, as his 1548 "Prayer for Generosity" shows: "To give and not to count the cost; To fight and not to heed the wounds; To toil and not to seek for rest; To labor and not to ask for any reward."

The Society of Jesus began by trying to convert Muslims to Christianity, but, as it grew in numbers and militancy during the Counter-Reformation, it broadened its target. It believed its mandate to derive solely from the Vatican and was often at odds with national and local Catholic officials. The training of Jesuit priests was the most rigorous of any order, and intellectual discipline, toughness of character, and complete commitment was expected from its trainees and clerics. The order instilled in its missionaries and teachers the ability to suffer any privation and to persevere through any hardship. It shaped *individuals* who were self-directed in fulfilling their assignments to redeem the world on behalf of a strict collective. These priests were as doctrinaire as the Calvinists with whom they competed, and they were perhaps more willing to sacrifice their lives to their missions. It took years to become a Jesuit priest. The order went after aristocrats and peasants alike, and, if there was an *army* in the name of Christianity in the early modern era, it was the Jesuit movement. The Chinese missions of the sixteenth and seventeenth centuries, for example, were typical extensions of the Jesuit mandate to go anywhere, into known and remote regions, to spread their message. For generations, in addition to their international mission for converts, the Jesuits were the principal teachers of children in Catholic Europe.

The Jesuits arrived in New France in 1625 to help the more humble Recollets, but soon replaced them. In 1635, they established a school for teaching native boys and, in 1639, built the famous mission at Sainte-Marie in Huronia. In the St. Lawrence Valley, the Jesuits brought in *engagés* on three-year terms to provide agricultural support for their missions. The Ursuline nuns and other orders did the same. The Ursulines, in fact, added what might be seen as a liberal touch to Christian colonization when, in 1639, they arrived and established a school for young females, the first educational institution for women in North America. The order maintains a convent in Quebec City to this day.

NATIVE POLITICS AND THE FUTURE OF NEW FRANCE

The major native cultures in New France were the Algonquian speakers north of the St. Lawrence and the Iroquoian-speaking tribes to the west and south. The term "Algonquian" usually refers to the major linguistic family east of the Appalachians. The Powhatan in the Chesapeake, for example, were Algonquian. Often, the linguistic designation "Algonquian" is distinguished from the term "Algonquin" or "Algonkin," which is used to describe a specific tribe north of the St. Lawrence River. As noted, Champlain had been obliged to ally his outpost to the Algonkin and to the Huron (the "good Iroquois" as he saw them). This left the way open for the wrath of the Iroquois who were renowned for their military prowess and feared for their ritual of slowly and elaborately torturing captives. Trade had begun to influence traditional native politics and diplomacy in the region from the mouth of the St. Lawrence to the Great Lakes. The flow of pelts to French traders rose dramatically from a few thousand in 1614 to hundreds of thousands by the 1640s. Along with the French traders came the Jesuits. Their efforts during the 1630s and 1640s to convert Huron people were heroic in that they were always in danger of capture and torture.

The mission at Sainte-Marie near Georgian Bay, on Lake Huron, promised to be a boon to Christian expansionism. However, reported conversion rates should be qualified by a bit of skepticism. The Huron knew that being Christian helped them to negotiate favorable trade deals. Moreover, the antipathy of natives to Jesuit customs, including the priests' celibacy and outspoken disapproval of Huron social and ethical mores limited the numbers of genuine conversions. Besides, the disease thinning the Huron population from time to time was not unreasonably blamed on the French generally and the Jesuits in particular. The Jesuits may have helped to secure the French presence, but entire Huron villages were emptied by disease epidemics. Meanwhile, the Huron leadership rejected an offer to join the Iroquois, and, after repeated confrontations through the 1640s, a numerically superior and better armed Iroquois force successfully invaded Huronia. The Jesuits burned the Sainte-Marie mission to keep it from the Iroquois, and the remnants of the native community joined the Jesuits as they drifted east back to Quebec. Although the Jesuits continued to chase after converts throughout North America, the sad fact is that more natives died from disease or internecine warfare or conflict with Europeans than were ever converted to Christianity. By mid century, the formerly powerful Huron nation, numbering between 20,000 and 30,000 at one time, was reduced to a few thousand survivors scattered throughout New France. An entire society had been destroyed.

The collapse of Huronia at the end of the 1640s meant the loss of an important source of furs. Entrepreneurial French *coureurs du bois,* "runners of the woods," however, picked up the trade and expanded it to the west. They were succeeded by officially licensed *voyageurs* and a far-reaching network of depots and trading posts. These were the first steps in expanding the geographic range of the French Empire in America. At the same time, more *engagés* were staying on in the St. Lawrence after their terms were up. Small as it was, the agricultural society succeeded in clearing land in the harshest conditions and the shortest of growing seasons. Agricultural work in the pre-mechanical age was difficult in any setting, but, in the St. Lawrence, it required more than usual patience, care, and hard work. The region also lacked the social amenities and cohesiveness of village life because this was still, in the 1640s, a predominantly male society with few families. It would be decades before numbers of female servants, as wives and mothers, were brought in to the colony. Then, a more stable local culture would develop. Before that time, however, the colony's future was a tenuous one. The ambitious Iroquois turned against the French in the 1650s, in bitter wars that reached Montreal and Quebec at one point. As reports of Iroquois pillage and torture made their way through the vulnerable little settlements, the French experiment in the St. Lawrence was transferred from the ill-defined system created by Richelieu to direct royal control.

Louis XIV formalized the status of New France as a royal colony in 1663 and sent out 1,000 regular troops who succeeded in drawing the Iroquois into a peace treaty in 1667. Some 400 of the troops took their discharge in New France. The officers received large tracts of land in the Montreal area, adding hope for the colony's survival. A Catholic presence was confirmed in North America, even if it was only a few days travel away from equally exclusionary English Protestant communities with far greater population densities to the south. Moreover, the Dutch had extended their fur trading interests up the Hudson River Valley. New France seemed hemmed in on three sides by wilderness and to the south by New England and Dutch New Netherland.

The French nevertheless claimed huge tracts of North America. Their trading networks were marvels of administration, logistics, and political dealings with natives. The French energetically explored, mapped, and described much of the continent's interior. By way of contrast, apart from the probing Frobisher and Hudson and some traders, the English and the Dutch were content to settle, albeit in larger numbers, east of the Appalachians and leave tracing the interior to the French. The Spanish had explored the southwestern quadrant of North America, but French adventurers, explorers, fur traders, and missionaries went into the heart of the continent, almost entirely by water transport through the Great Lakes and their river systems. By the end of the seventeenth century, France claimed all of North America north of New Spain and north and west of the English settlements.

THE FRENCH AND THE WEST

As early as the 1630s, Jean Nicollet, a former clerk turned *coureur du bois,* had reached the north shore of Lake Superior, 1,500 miles west of Quebec, revealing the potential of the west for an expanded fur trade. Despite the fall of Huronia, the fur traders pushed farther into the Great Lakes regions, and, by the 1670s, had established a post at Michilimackinac at the junction of Lake Michigan and Lake Huron. Commerce was central to French intentions in the interior, but the desire to claim land for the Crown and preempt the Spanish or English, prompted much of the exploration after the 1650s. In an affair that had major historical consequences, two speculators, Pierre-Esprit Radisson and Médard Chouart des Groseilliers made their way into what is now Minnesota and returned to Montreal in 1660 with an immense cargo of pelts. The load was confiscated because the traders had no license. In a pique, Radisson and Groseilliers went to work for the English, and, in 1668, a group of English merchants funded Groseilliers on a trip to the fur-rich area south of Hudson Bay. Its success led to the granting of a charter in 1670 by Charles II to the Hudson's Bay Company. The territory was named Rupert's Land in honor of the company's patron, Prince Rupert, a cousin of Charles II.

The Hudson's Bay Company eventually controlled the fur and other trade in a vast domain that reached the Pacific in one direction and the Arctic in the other. The opportunism of Radisson and Groseilliers coincided with England's post-1660 imperial designs in America and demonstrated to the French that their claims to territory were only as good as their ability to defend them. The French persisted with their combined policies of exploration, native trading, and Christian mission. A wonderful example of the commercial lengths to which they would go was the construction of a splendid ship, the *Griffon,* near Niagara in 1679. The *Griffon* was intended to transport great quantities of furs from the far west through the Great Lakes to the St. Lawrence ports. The maiden voyage was commanded by René-Robert Cavelier de La Salle (1643–1687), a former Jesuit novice. It sailed all the way to La Baie Verte (today's Green Bay, Wisconsin) on Lake Superior but was lost on the return trip. La Salle, meanwhile, had gone south to explore. Earlier, in 1673, in an extended journey that stretches the imagination, Louis Jolliet and the Jesuit missionary Jacques Marquette had made their way from the Great Lakes south through Illinois to Arkansas. They paved the way for La Salle, who in 1682 reached the Mississippi Delta.

The Spanish explorer Cabeza de Vaca had likely passed through the region 150 years earlier but now La Salle planted a flag and claimed for France all the territory within the river systems that flowed into the Mississippi, one of the largest drainage areas in the world. He named the vast territory Louisiana. This European habit, as old as Columbus, Cortés, and Cartier (who had raised a cross on the Gaspé shore in 1541) was continued into the eighteenth and nineteenth centuries. A symbolic flag or marker or cross and a few words were seen to be enough to claim jurisdiction. Then, in the eyes of the claimants, residence confirmed jurisdiction. On his explorations, La Salle was accompanied by a Franciscan priest, Father Louis Hennepin, whose missionary efforts balanced La Salle's diplomatic agenda. La Salle envisioned a great French empire in the heart of North America. He met an ignominious end, however, and was murdered in 1687 during a mutiny as he led a party of settlers to Louisiana from the Gulf of Mexico in Texas, where his fleet had inadvertently landed.

To appreciate the French presence in North America one should not confine oneself to the Canadian Maritimes and Quebec. Seventeenth century French priests, traders, soldiers, and explorers are remembered in a multitude of place names in the heart of the present United States. In the north, Antoine de la Mothe, Sieur de Cadillac, who was later governor of Louisiana, founded Detroit in 1701, and, between 1730 and the early 1740s, Pierre Gaultier de Varennes et de La Vérendrye, established forts in what is now Manitoba, reached south and west to the Missouri River, and possibly made it as far west as present-day Wyoming. For all that, the French could not hope to settle or set up extensive civil authority in the huge areas they claimed. Rather, they established trade and diplomatic relations with natives wherever they could. By the start of the eighteenth century, France's North American empire consisted of New France, Acadia, Newfoundland, Hudson's Bay, and Louisiana. With the exception of New France (increasingly referred to as Canada) and Acadia, the French colonies were little more than trading posts. In New France, after the royal takeover, the population grew from 3,215 in 1665 to 9,677 in 1681 and then to 13,815 in 1698; it was 24,434 in 1720 and 42,701 in 1739. Overall, some 30,000 people immigrated to New France but only about a third of them stayed. To put the demography into context, on the eve of the Seven Years' War, in 1754, the white, European population of New France was 55,000 while the non-native population of the British colonies in North America was about 1.2 million.

Champlain's legacy was the establishment of a fixed French presence in America. The statues of him in Quebec City, Ottawa, and elsewhere present him as the father of New France, and, insofar as he kept the Canadian colony going, that is a fair assessment. But early French Canadian society was shaped by others such as Richelieu, the *seigneurs* and the *habitant* community, and the Jesuits and fur traders who successfully negotiated with natives even as they frequently alienated them. The chief architect of French American society surely must be Louis XIV and his nationalist and imperial vision for the French in Canada. Louis is also responsible for driving France itself along the road to a dominant place in European and world affairs.

Even in the Age of Absolutism, Louis XIV, the "Sun King," stands out as exceptional. He controlled the church, the nobles, and taxation and was obsessed with the idea of a glorious destiny for France. His transformation of the Château de Versailles and its gardens and grounds into the spectacular Palace of Versailles, his personal seat of power away from Paris, reflects his ego to be sure. Versailles remains one of Europe's most celebrated architectural landmarks. Louis was also the engine that drove France's rise in world affairs. In the late seventeenth century, he set in motion a series of wars with England that lasted for over a century. In the meantime, he gave New France stability, and his intercession in the 1660s was followed by vigorous settlement and trade policies. He encouraged permanence in the agricultural settlements along the St. Lawrence, in part through the importation of marriageable women, the so-called *filles du roi*. Jean Talon, the *intendant* from 1665 to 1672, set up a competent administration and ensured that furs were counted, taxes raised, and the royal "fifth" was given by the *seigneurs*. Royal support for La Salle's and others' expeditions stamped an official French presence on much of the west and the north, in particular with the native populations. Even if the numbers of French remained small in some places and negligible in most, Louis XIV made sure that France mattered in America.

Map 2.1 Early European Permanent Settlements

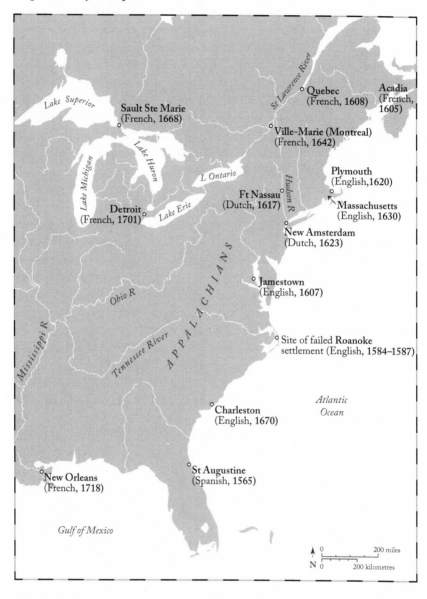

The Dutch

The arrival of 20 "Negars," as the Virginian settler John Rolfe put it, aboard a Dutch ship at Jamestown in late 1619, is worth noting as the start of an

African presence in what was to become the United States. But the arrival of the 20 slaves did not affect the colony's early development nor did it lead in a demonstrable way to institutionalized slavery. The 20 blacks were taken as servants and either died early or slipped into the population after completion of their service. What we should ask is what was a Dutch ship doing in Jamestown with a cargo that included slaves? The answer is simple: in 1619, the Dutch were everywhere else in the world, and their ships carried everything that mattered in the Atlantic economy, including slaves. In the sixteenth and seventeenth centuries, they juggled war, state building, trade, colonization, and religious reform. By the start of the seventeenth century, a thriving map publishing industry had been established in the Netherlands, and, by 1600, the Dutch controlled the largest fleet of ships in the world, some 10,000 by some estimates.

Their reach was global. Dutch merchants, armed escorts, and bureaucrats had even taken away some of the Portuguese privileges in Asia. By the middle of the seventeenth century, they had established colonies in America; had begun to overtake the Portuguese in Java; and, through the Dutch East India Company, had by 1652 started a colony in South Africa at the Cape of Good Hope. The founding of the Dutch East India Company in 1602—shortly after that of the English East India Company in 1600—and of the Dutch West India Company in 1621 set up elaborate trading networks throughout Asia and America respectively. The Dutch East India Company was a striking example of Dutch innovation. It was perhaps the first European joint stock company to offer its stocks to the public, through the Amsterdam stock exchange. It had particular success in the archipelago that would eventually be the Dutch East Indies, today's Indonesia. Holland's people were industrious and efficient and produced high quality metal goods, ships, agricultural products, and fine consumer durables. Dutch merchants and investors were very good at making money. The Dutch produced great pictorial art, and their craftsmen were renowned for the fine design and finish in their work. Antwerp's stock exchange, the *bourse,* was the largest in the world and dominated European investment and capital flow, and the Dutch, per capita, were the richest people in the world in the seventeenth century. Holland was a refuge for religious dissenters and a fit meeting place for Europe's intellectuals, offering a healthy climate for scientific and technological experimentation. It had a booming printing and publishing industry. By any measure, it was more cosmopolitan than its neighbors. It was a major player in all the colonial developments all over the Americas, even if its own settlements were relatively limited. Its legacy is often overlooked or subordinated to the ultimate impact of the Spanish, Portuguese, French, and English in the shaping of the modern American nations, but, in the seventeenth century, the

Dutch mattered a great deal in the intertwined affairs of Europe, America, and Africa.

Holland was favorably located for its role, with access by land to all of northern Europe as well as maritime access to the North Sea and Baltic Sea. For example, when the fish stocks of the Baltic began to decline, the Dutch simply turned to the North Sea. They became the major international carriers of Europe's and then the world's commerce. The *fluyt,* a large, plain, functional cargo ship, helped make Dutch transoceanic trade cost effective. Holland achieved its status in the world in spite of or, just as likely, because of its small population (about 1.5 million in 1600) and its compressed territory, which made logistics, capital networks, and communications easily integrated. It had long been an important player in Europe's economy, but, by the beginning of the seventeenth century, it was a global force to be reckoned with. The southern part of the so-called Low Countries, the Spanish Netherlands, remained part of Spain's European empire; but the northern, liberated areas, Holland and other independent regions or the "United Provinces of the Netherlands," became a formidable national force in the late sixteenth and early seventeenth century.

Independent Holland was forged out of seven provinces in the north while the ten southern provinces remained Catholic and Francophone. The latter became the basis for modern Belgium. The term Holland was applied to the United Provinces and survived along with the older and prosaic Netherlands or Low Countries. The term "Dutch" is a corruption of "Deutsch," a form of the language used in the northern Netherlands. This was a busy society of burghers, multilingual merchants and bankers, scholars, artists, craftsmen, and entrepreneurs, as well as efficient farmers. Land was recovered from tidal waters, and the designs of their extensive retaining dikes were marvels of engineering.

Holland produced the outstanding European military tactician of the age in Maurice of Nassau and, at the same time, was home to one of the great thinkers of the age, Baruch de Spinoza. It also produced the great humanist and political theorist Hugo Grotius, who influenced a generation of scholars and writers on the law. Holland was a crossroads for the reformist religious currents of the age, and although the population was generally Calvinist, there was a substantial Catholic minority. The nation entertained an array of Protestant sects, including the ultraradical Anabaptists, and exuded cultural and economic energy and social equilibrium. This small state was an economic, intellectual, artistic, and naval powerhouse. Its settlement in mainland North America was at first assured by those qualities but was displaced in the middle of the seventeenth century by the rising power of the English.

The Dutch came to America with confidence. As early as the 1590s, hundreds of their ships were trading along the South American coast from Venezuela to Brazil. At the same time, speculators set up forts in the area between the Orinoco and Amazon Rivers, traded with the Spanish, and planned settlements in what would later be Dutch Guiana (today's Suriname). After Hudson's 1609 voyage for the Dutch East India Company, the Dutch seriously considered permanent settlement in the area north of Virginia, and the Dutch West India Company of 1621 was empowered to exploit territory that was in fact described in English charters and ascribed to the holders of those charters. New Amsterdam (later New York) was the result. By the end of the 1620s, the Dutch had joined the other European colonizers in America. The New Netherland Company, chartered in 1614, began trading with natives, mostly for furs, up the Hudson River as far as Albany, pushing close to French interests. The charter lapsed after 1617, but, by then, Dutch vessels had visited Rhode Island and Manhattan. A new map by the explorer Adriaen Block had shown Manhattan and Long Island in detail.

The main force in the development of the colony was the West India Company, which had begun to monopolize Dutch trade and settlements not only in North and South America but also on the west coast of Africa. It was an elaborately designed organization, and, although the state controlled some aspects of general policy, the company operated with considerable autonomy. For the Manhattan area, the company's Amsterdam chapter drew up a settlement plan in 1624. The company intended to run its own farms (*bouweries*), but private investors were given leases and help with livestock, seeds, and tools. Pieter Minuit and Pieter Stuyvesant, directors general of the colony from 1626 to 1635 and from 1647 to 1664, respectively, helped with the colony's stability and promoted its potential for agriculture and for expanded fur trading.

The Dutch had come to stay. As in New France, population growth in New Netherland was slow. In 1630, there were scarcely 300 people in the colony and those were mostly French-speaking Walloons. By the 1650s, however, the population was rising, and its ethnic character changed. In 1664, the population reached 9,000, but, ironically, English, German, Swedish, Finnish, and other nationalities had made the Dutch a minority. In fact, there was an estimated 2,000 English people in the colony in the 1660s. A community of Amsterdam Jews had arrived along with Africans, whose legal status was vague. The colony was Dutch in name and was certainly under Dutch control, even down to its official language, but it was, in fact, an ethnic and cultural mélange.

From the start, the colony reached into native territory, especially to the north among the Mohawk members of the Iroquois Confederacy. Dutch claims now abutted French and English claims in the north, as, after 1620, there was a permanent English colony near Cape Cod at Plymouth. South of the

Dutch was the Virginia Company. New Netherland was effectively bracketed by English colonies. Manhattan Island had been settled as early as 1616 as New Amsterdam, allegedly purchased for 60 Dutch guilders from the local natives. The transaction is legendary for the absurdity of the inflation that has made Manhattan among today's most expensive plots of land on earth. Versions of the Manhattan transaction were repeated thousands of times in North America and should be seen for what they were, a not unusual contrast between the values of America's indigenous peoples and the calculating economic values of European "investors."

By 1630, the Dutch West India Company had issued grants to several *patroons* of huge tracts of land that measured 16 miles of frontage on the navigable rivers lying within the Dutch claim. These grants went away from the rivers to the limits of productive agricultural land. To encourage settlement, a grant was available only if an investor could bring in 50 settlers. These were manorial estates, really, with their own courts and generous tax abatements. Rensselaerswyck, named for the absentee landholder Kiliaen Van Rensselaer, an Amsterdam gem trader, was the only one to survive. But the outline of the plan remained, and the later estates and manors on the Hudson River were among the most impressive residues of the Dutch Empire in America. The West India Company tenaciously protected its claim, and, when the New Sweden Company invested along the Delaware River in 1638, it violated what the Dutch, in a typical contemporary application of the double standard, assumed to be their territory. Sweden was by then prominent in Scandinavian and eastern European affairs, and its American venture was appropriate to its ambitions, but the armed hostility of the Dutch and their superior naval logistics ended the Swedish venture by force in the 1650s.

After a promising start, the colony's future was threatened, first by native resistance and eventually, as we shall see, by the English. In the early 1640s, one of the deadliest native-white confrontations in North American colonial history took place in New Netherland. It shook the population's confidence and caused many settlers to leave, stunting the colony's development. The so-called Kieft's War of 1643–1645 broke out when some Weckquaesgeek natives killed a Dutch settler. At the same time, Director General Willem Kieft's profit strategy, for himself and the company, included demanding taxes from the natives. His logic, in that case, was seriously flawed. He noted that the Puritan English to the north had recently defeated natives in the Pequot War and had wrested "wampum," that is, tribute, from local native groups. Kieft's tax plan exacerbated already tense relations between natives and settlers. Then, in retaliation for the death of that single settler, Dutch militia massacred over 100 natives including women, children, and the elderly. In the war that ensued, several hundred whites and as many as 1,600 natives were killed. Dutch firepower was used to great effect in the conflict that followed. The pattern was reminiscent of the Pequot War of 1636–1637 and anticipated the equally destructive King Philip's War of 1675–1676, both in southern New England. These intense outbreaks everywhere in North America punctuated a near constant atmosphere of murder, reprisal, tension, and intermittent military conflict along the fault line between white settlement and native lands.

Following a half century of settlement and investment and despite the slow pace of immigration and economic development, the nearby presence of imperial rivals, and the traumatic aftermath of Kieft's War, the Dutch colony survived. After 1650, however, England began to adjust its trade policies to counter the Dutch in the West Indies and North America. The policies intensified existing rivalries and led to a series of wars between the two Protestant nations. Such was the priority of national self-interest that an economic contest could triumph over religious compatibility. The English prevailed, and New Netherland was absorbed into English North America in the 1660s.

The Caribbean Crossroads: European Colonizers Collide

The Dutch, at times, seemed more like marauders than colonizers, testing Spanish and Portuguese claims everywhere. Their audacity and abilities helped them capture Pernambuco in northeastern Brazil, and they controlled most of the Angolan coast of West Africa between 1641 and 1648. In the Americas, they made themselves conspicuous in the Caribbean. They encouraged sugar production and slavery and marketed slaves throughout the West Indies, even providing loans where necessary. It is no stretch to suggest that they helped convert the French and English labor systems in the West Indies from using white servant labor to using African slave labor. Holland's seventeenth century role in the economic development of the West Indies challenged the territorial control and trading mechanisms of the bigger colonizing powers. The European colonizers collided with each other all over the Americas but nowhere more frequently than among the Caribbean islands in the seventeenth century.

Map 2.2 The Colonial Caribbean

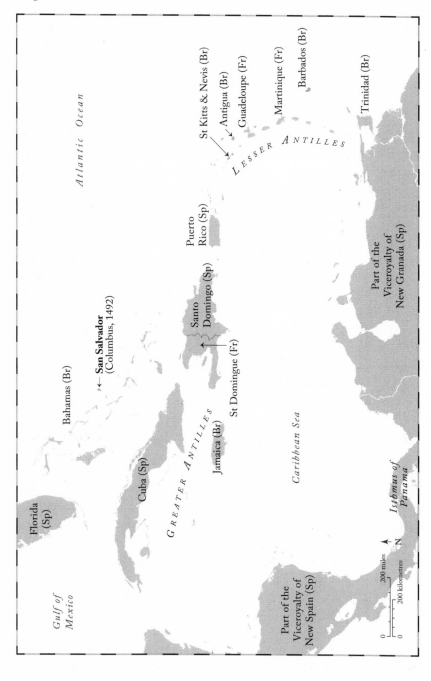

The islands, the Antilles or, more commonly, the West Indies, run on a north-south arc from the southeast coast of Florida at 25 degrees north and 80 degrees west to the island of Trinidad, within view of mainland Venezuela, at about 10 degrees north and 62 degrees west. The islands can be seen as a single large archipelago or as three smaller ones: the Bahamas, where Columbus first made land; the Greater Antilles, including Cuba and Hispaniola; and the Lesser Antilles, including the smaller Windward and Leeward islands. There are some 115 islands by definition in the Caribbean Sea but more than 3,000 rocky islets and cays (small sand or coral islets). The sea itself demands refined navigational skills to negotiate the labyrinthine channels, inlets, and harbors. Cuba is 42,000 square miles and Hispaniola (Haiti and the Dominican Republic), 29,000, while some islands are specks of a few square miles of land. Coming in from the North Atlantic, Columbus found some of the currents in the Caribbean running counterclockwise, even though the islands are in the northern hemisphere.

In important ways, the history of the West Indies during the colonial period paralleled that of the North American mainland: native depopulation accompanied settlement, as did the rampant use of African slave labor on plantations. Slavery transformed the demographics of the sugar-producing islands in the sixteenth and seventeenth centuries. The European competition in the West Indies was chaotic at times. North America experienced similar tension and intrusion, but an English takeover of New Spain, for example, or French control of New England was unlikely. Spanish and Portuguese boundaries in South America were contested from time to time, but national interests were mostly secured by occupation. In the seventeenth century, New Netherland fell under English control, but it was not until the Seven Years' War that French and Spanish claims in eastern North America collapsed. In the West Indies, because of its tighter geography, where the sea gave easy access to all the islands, every European colony was vulnerable to the designs and naval abilities of rivals.

Still, Spain had been left alone in the West Indies for most of the sixteenth century. It established settlements on the major islands and produced sugar, but the chief transportation and distribution center for the Spanish West Indies was at Cartagena on the mainland. It became a target of frequent attacks by English privateers, Sir Francis Drake being the most dangerous. In 1572 and from 1585 to 1587, he terrorized Panama, Cartagena, Portobello, and Florida, exposing Spanish weakness in the Caribbean basin. Drake was not alone. By 1600, privateers had been preying on the Spanish fleets for decades, beginning soon after the northern Europeans moved into the Caribbean, just as they moved into North America. By the middle to late seventeenth century, the non-slave population in the islands was composed of an exotic mix of armed officials, planters, merchants, political and religious refugees, free-loaders, military deserters, runaway slaves and white servants, transported criminals, and escaped convicts. In some places, the ragged tendrils of society created an atmosphere of openness and liberalism and sometimes anarchy.

It was a far cry from the standards of order found in New England, New Netherland, New France, New Spain, or even Virginia, once it had set-tled down. A floating population of misfits, outcasts, and opportunists sup-plied the crews for the privateers and pirate ships that scoured the sea lanes and turned many of the non-Spanish Caribbean ports into wide open, excit-ing, and dangerous places. This international free for all gave way, in time, to formal colonies, mostly French and English, replete with law, order, and government, but, from the moment the outposts began to appear until formal institutional development was established, the Caribbean was the interna-tional free market crossroads of the New World. It was a place where droves of outcasts, exiles, and adventurers crossed paths. As an English observer noted in 1655, Barbados was a human "dunghill." But the Caribbean's potential for development, in sugar production and as a strategic zone for rival national interests, brought the region formally within the orbit of the European impe-rialists by the end of the seventeenth century.

PRIVATEERS AND PIRATES

Two factors put an end to the melting pot: one was the formalization of set-tlement by the northern European imperialists and the second was the explo-sion in the slave population and the gradual shaping of the West Indies into a giant sugar factory, where, by the second half of the eighteenth century, up to 90 per cent of the population was black and most of that was in bond-age. As Virginia and the English mainland colonies moved away from white indentured servitude for their cash-crop labor needs in the late seventeenth century, so too did the English, Dutch, and French in the Caribbean. For the English, official policies for settling the West Indies began in earnest with the Restoration of the Stuarts after 1660. Thereafter the Crown's toleration of English pirates and even privateers vanished. From Drake to Henry Morgan (ca. 1635–1688), privateers had acted as sanctioned adjuncts to the Crown in international affairs. Morgan, for example, wrought havoc among the Spanish and the Dutch while he was making money for himself. He was as ruthless as he was efficient and allegedly committed atrocities against Spanish prison-ers. Like most privateers, he was a talented seaman, politically shrewd, and effective as a commander. Yet his days were numbered, and time ran out for sanctioned freebooters. After the Restoration, the Royal Navy became the single agency of English maritime war making.

As for the legendary pirate culture of the West Indies, it was even further from official approval. The thin line between the privateer and the pirate was still a measurable one. For the most part, privateers were officially condoned to serve the nation's interests, while pirates neither sought nor received official sanction. Some pirates enjoyed the support of settlers in the West Indies and on the mainland coast of North America, trading their expensive loot or paying hard cash for supplies. They were usually immune from prosecution as long as they attacked the commerce of foreigners. However, one of the most famous pirates of the age, the Scot Captain William Kidd (1645–1701), was charged with treason and hanged publicly in London for plundering a British ship. Pirates, nevertheless, continued to stalk the world's rich traffic routes far into the eighteenth century and stirred romantic ideals long after the end of the era. Another legendary figure, Edward Teach, "Blackbeard," affected a fearsome dress and manner and was one of the most notorious pirates of the age. Following days of riotous partying with other pirates, he was eventually trapped and killed in 1718 by the Royal Navy near Pamlico Sound, North Carolina.

Although the image of the pirate as an easy-going antiestablishment rogue who was loyal to his comrades in arms has been the stock and trade of popular films and novels, the reality was, for the most part, different. Some recent scholarship has celebrated seventeenth and early eighteenth century pirate culture as being structured democratically. Egalitarian economics among the crews and a camaraderie drawn from principles of ethnic and racial equality certainly occurred. This view sees pirate society as a counter to the rigid race and class hierarchies that were developing in the British colonies in particular. Whatever the case, the alleged communal solidarity of the multi-ethnic, multiracial pirate cultures, on land or sea, had little hope of surviving the British Empire's designs for the Caribbean or the mainland. For the most part, pirate crews were fickle. They could be indiscriminate in their violence and sometimes feeble in the face of serious opposition. But they identify an era in the history of American development that passed with the arrival of state-chartered settlements in the moneymaking colonies.

Moreover, the pirate "community" was a small one. In one of the most active periods of British piracy, the first three decades of the eighteenth century, there were seldom more than 100 pirate ships at sea in the Atlantic and Indian Oceans and no more the 2,000 pirates employed on them. Yet some 2,500 ships were attacked, and about 10 per cent of those were destroyed by pirates: two factors that hastened the end of the pirate heyday. The rise and fall of privateering and piracy parallel important phases of colonial development. Its rise coincided with an era of indeterminate policies for the Caribbean. Its fall indicated a developing interest among northern imperialists in applying

the kinds of political and economic control in the Caribbean that were forming on the mainland. Sugar, slaves, and commercial profits, even taxable ones,
were what finally decided the future of the West Indies.

THE SLAVERY BOOM IN THE WEST INDIES

African slaves were already present in Hispaniola when the northern Europeans
began claiming islands in the Caribbean. From the time the Portuguese had
set up their first slave-trading posts on the west coast of Africa in the 1440s,
the movement of African slaves, first to the Atlantic islands and then to the
American tropics, had been steady. In 1600, there were likely fewer than 20,000
slaves in Brazil and only a few hundred in the Spanish Caribbean. What happened after 1600 was nothing less than a demographic revolution. Brazil and
the West Indies *each* imported about 500,000 Africans between 1600 and 1700.
The rising value of slave labor was such that elaborate infrastructures, logistics,
intermediaries, and financing were created with great speed in order to transport those one million slaves. The volume of arrivals met what seemed like an
insatiable demand caused by growth and the need to replenish the numbers of
slaves who succumbed to disease, alienation, and overwork in the expanding
sugar plantations. There was a terrible toll on Africans as they made their way
to America, but the death rates in the colonies were appalling too. The tropics
could be deadly for the English, Dutch, and French, but the labor demands and
the infectious diseases that greeted African slaves cut deeply into their numbers
in the Caribbean and in tropical Brazil.

The seventeenth century volume of the slave trade was surpassed in the
eighteenth century when several million Africans made their sad way to the
Americas and the slave trade had grown into an industry of bewildering scale.
By 1750, nearly 60,000 slaves annually were being shipped across the Atlantic.
This was pushed by the rapid expansion of northern European colonizers in
the Caribbean after 1600, the advance of sugar demand and prices in Brazil
and the West Indies, and the relentless need for labor to satisfy those changes.
Sugar and slaves had come to the Caribbean with the Spanish within two
decades of Columbus, but Spain's immigrants to and investments in America
had been drawn early to Central and South America, and the Spanish were
inclined to use the sugar resources of the Caribbean to supply their mainland
settlements rather than engage in heavy volume production for the European
market. For several decades, Europe got most of its sugar from Brazil. In
the middle of the seventeenth century, as the English, French, and Dutch
came into the West Indies to stay, sugar production boomed and so did the
demand for labor. Over time, the decline in available white servants meant

failure to meet labor demand, and the Africanization of the Caribbean began in earnest. It was complete by the middle of the eighteenth century.

The Spanish labor economy in the Caribbean contrasted dramatically with the economies of other West Indian colonies. At the end of the eighteenth century, there were some 80,000 black slaves in the Spanish Caribbean and over 160,000 *free* blacks. Those figures were likely the long-term outcome of high rates of manumission (freeing). In addition, as the historian Herbert Klein notes, the general Spanish encouragement of manumission was made even easier in an economy of small-scale, individual sugar operations. By contrast, blacks completely replaced white servants in the large, export-heavy and labor-extensive French and English plantations during the late seventeenth and eighteenth centuries. In 1775, the British Caribbean had over 450,000 black slaves and only 13,000 free blacks, an arresting 20 to 1 ratio. The French figures are similar: 575,000 slaves and a mere 30,000 free blacks. Those figures reflect both the scale of sugar operations and the long-term trend of absenteeism among French and English planters. The plantations were effectively depersonalized at every level, except perhaps inside the slave communities where distinct black West Indian cultures began to take root. Nevertheless, the small permanent populations of whites, having no way of coping with free blacks, kept blacks permanently in bondage, under strict scrutiny. The absence of any acceptable English or French mechanism for freeing slaves perpetuated their systems and stands in contrast to the Spanish system, which had several ways of providing freedom for slaves, beginning with a consideration of the slave's possession of a Christian soul.

The major English islands were Barbados, settled in 1627; the Bahamas, in 1647; and Antigua, in 1632. Jamaica was wrested from the Spanish in 1655. St. Kitts (St. Christopher) and Nevis were settled in 1624, but the claim was disputed by the French until the Treaty of Utrecht in 1713, when they were confirmed as British. As early as 1620, the English had settled Bermuda, which is north and east of the Caribbean and strictly speaking not in the West Indies. It remains a British dependency to this day. The larger French islands of Martinique and Guadeloupe were settled in 1635. The western end of Hispaniola was neglected, abandoned really, by the Spanish, so the claims of the French, who had settled in the area after 1659, were recognized in 1697. Saint-Domingue (Haiti after 1804) to the west became French, while the remainder stayed with the Spanish as Santo Domingo (the Dominican Republic). By the mid- to late-eighteenth century, a great transformation had occurred, and more than half the West Indian slave population was in French hands. Wherever commercial volumes of sugar were produced, slavery boomed. In the sugar islands of the Caribbean, by the early eighteenth century, blacks outnumbered whites, eventually resulting in a ratio of 1:9, white to black. In some of the British islands, the white population not only fell as a percentage of the whole, to 10 per cent or less, but the actual numbers of whites declined over time. For comparison, note that, in 1775, the ratio of whites to blacks in the lower south of the British mainland colonies, the Carolinas and Georgia, was about 1.3 to 1; in New England, it was 35 to 1. The trend from white servitude to black slavery in the British Caribbean can be seen in the following table.

Table 2.1 Racial Composition of the British Caribbean Population, 1660–1760 (percentages in brackets)

These are aggregate figures. The ratio of whites to blacks was roughly similar in each colony, but there was some variation from island to island.

	WHITE		**BLACK**		**TOTAL**
1660	33,139	(50.3)	32,732	(49.7)	65,871
1710	27,461	(17)	133,800	(83)	161,261
1760	42,686	(12)	313,177[*]	(88)	355,863

[*] That number rose to 450,000 by 1775.

Source: Adapted from Jack P. Greene, *Pursuits of Happiness: The Social Development of Early Modern British Colonies and the Formation of American Culture* (Chapel Hill: University of North Carolina Press, 1988), 178–179 and Orlando Patterson, *Slavery and Social Death: A Comparative Study* (Cambridge, MA: Harvard University Press, 1982), 353–364.

Some areas of Brazil and some coastal counties in the southern colonies of the English mainland eventually became predominantly black. But the most intensively African places in the western hemisphere were in the English and French islands in the Antilles, where the ratio of African slaves to square mile of territory was the highest recorded anywhere during the era of slavery. On the island of Barbados, for example, there were 400 slaves per square mile of land in 1768. The Caribbean became the destination of over one-third of the more than 10 million slaves who were transported to the Americas in the three-plus centuries of the slave trade.

SUGGESTED READINGS

The rise of the Dutch is dealt with in depth in Jan de Vries and Ad van der Woude, *The First Modern Economy: Success, Failure, and Perseverance of the Dutch Economy, 1500–1815* (Cambridge: Cambridge University Press, 1997); Simon Schama, *The Embarrassment of Riches: An Interpretation of Dutch Culture in the Golden Age* (Berkeley: University of California Press, 1987) is another large study of the Dutch phenomenon. See also Oliver Rink, *Holland on the Hudson: An Economic and Social History of Dutch New York* (Ithaca, NY: Cornell University Press, 1986) and Paul Otto, *The Dutch-Munsee Encounter in America: The Struggle for Sovereignty in the Hudson Valley* (New York: Berghahn Books, 2006). An original and eloquent approach to Dutch globalism is Timothy Brook, *Vermeer's Hat,* cited in Chapter 1.

Richard Dunn, *Sugar and Slaves: The Rise of the Planter Class in the English West Indies* (Chapel Hill: University of North Carolina Press, 1972) retains its prominence as an introduction to English Caribbean colonization, and Richard Sheridan, *Sugar and Slavery: An Economic History of the British West Indies* (Baltimore: Johns Hopkins University Press, 1974) is drier but dependable.

An invaluable study of the French in America is W. J. Eccles, *France in America,* rev. ed. (E. Lansing, MI: Michigan State University Press, 1990) and his *The Canadian Frontier, 1534–1760* (New York: Holt, Rinehart and Winston, 1969) is an accessible and intelligent survey. See also Ian Steele, *Warpaths,* cited in the suggested readings for the preface. Steele's sections on Dutch and French relations with natives and the wars that these encounters produced are superb. The book, as a whole, is a lively history of colonial North America and is a model of sound research and judgement. An unconventional and much debated theory of imperial history from the bottom up is argued in Peter Linebaugh and Marcus Rediker, *The Many-Headed Hydra: Sailors, Slaves, Commoners, and the Hidden History of the Revolutionary Atlantic* (Boston: Beacon Press, 2000). See also Marcus Rediker, *Villains of all Nations: Atlantic Pirates in the Golden Age* (London: Verso, 2004).

Time Line

1497	John Cabot's voyage.
1534	Henry VIII of England rejects Rome and establishes the national Church of England.
1558	The accession of Elizabeth I.
1584–1587	The Roanoke failure.
1588	The defeat of the Spanish Armada.
1603	The death of Elizabeth and the accession of the Stuarts.
1607	The founding of Jamestown.
1620	The Plymouth settlement.
1622	The beginning of Powhatan's War.
1624	The collapse of the Virginia Company.
1630	The Puritan founding of Massachusetts.
1634	The founding of Maryland.
1636–1637	Pequot War.

CHAPTER 3

* * * * * * ★ ★ * * * * *

The English Colonies in Mainland North America Before 1650

Carpenters, Joyners, Glaziers, Painters follow their trades only; Gun-smiths, Lock-smiths, Black-smiths, Naylers, Cutlers, have left the husbandman to follow the Plow and Cart, and they their trades, Weavers, Brewers, Bakers, Costermongers, Feltmakers, Braziers, Pewterers, and Tinkers, Ropemakers, Masons, Lime, Brick, and Tilemakers, Cardmakers... Turners, Pumpmakers and Wheelers, Glovers, Fellmungers, and Furriers, are orderly turn'd to their trades, besides divers sorts of Shopkeepers, and some who have a mystery beyond others, as have the Vintners. Thus hath the Lord been pleased to turn one of the most hideous, boundless, and unknown Wildernesses in the world in an instant... to a well-ordered Commonwealth... to serve his Churches.

—Edward Johnson, commenting on the economy of Boston and other towns in 1647 (the total Massachusetts population was then about 13,000), from Johnson, *Wonder-Working Providence of Sions Saviour in New England* (1654), Chapter 6. Johnson exaggerated the economy's ability to support many of those trades on a fulltime basis, or to support more than a few practitioners. Most artisans and tradesmen were also farmers.

From the moment the northern Europeans followed the Iberians to America, Africa, and Asia, they began to eclipse the Spanish in global importance. Changes came quickly. By the early seventeenth century, they had established permanent colonies in the Americas and intruded upon Spanish trade and Portuguese claims in Africa and Asia. By 1700, the English and French had established settlements and trade relations in India, and the Dutch had wrested control away from the Portuguese in what is now Indonesia. As noted, the Dutch even intruded temporarily into the northern coastal area of Portuguese Brazil. Spain ended up competing in the Caribbean rather than controlling it. In Central and South America, the Iberians consolidated their empires, even acting together when the Portuguese and Spanish merged under the Habsburgs from 1580 to 1640. But the northern Europeans now defined the territorial limits of Spain in America and the world, thus making the mandate of the Treaty of Tordesillas of 1494 a dead letter.

The delay in English, French, and Dutch colonization was caused not simply by the absence of a Henry the Navigator or a Ferdinand and Isabella but rather by a combination of domestic preoccupations and a general lack of interest in American settlement. Even knowing of the "Indies" was not enough to inspire the French or English to colonize it in any formal or official way. When John Cabot had explored the area from Newfoundland to Long Island in 1497 under contract to England's first Tudor monarch, Henry VII, he did not recommend colonization, and the early Tudors could see no practical reason for funding or organizing an American settlement. The French monarchy funded Cartier's voyages between 1534 and 1541 but then backed away when the tentative settlement at Quebec failed. However, several decades later, the French set up permanent settlements in Acadia in 1605 and at Quebec (New France) in 1608. The English settled permanently in Virginia in 1607. The Dutch emerged as a national entity by shaking off Spanish Habsburg rule and developing an international outlook, which included colonies in America. A new era in American colonization was begun in a relative flash of time. What changed for the new imperialists during the sixteenth century were prospects for profits and the means, opportunity, and methods to acquire them.

Like the Dutch and French, the English found ways to encourage settlement without straining the state's coffers, and publicly supported but privately funded settlements characterized the new colonies in North America. As noted, the French Crown was slow to fund and then govern its colonies. In the 1660s, the haphazard early experiments along the St. Lawrence and in Acadia finally gave way to a policy of permanent royal administration. The Dutch approach to colonization was marked by private enterprise sanctioned by official policy and support. The early English model derived from the Crown's nominal authority to grant licenses to groups of colonizers who would fund their own settlements. The charter system was born. In a way that parallels the French experience, the English Crown did not have a firm policy for the North American colonies until the 1660s, when a clearer system of trade and planning emerged. All the European empires in America evolved from experiment and ill-defined authority. The English were no different in that sense. But in important ways, their early settlements were fundamentally different, not only from those of their rivals but also from each other.

The Background to English Colonization in America

English adventurers led the way, and then commercial and religious groups set the tone for development. Sir Walter Raleigh (ca.1552–1618), for example, poet, raconteur, schemer, dreamer, and politician, steeped in Elizabethan Renaissance culture and with an eye to profit, paved the way for the Virginia experiment. On the other hand, the English Reformation inspired the sober-minded Christian objectives of the Plymouth and Massachusetts Bay colonies. The model for the early charters can be seen in the monopoly franchises granted to trading organizations such as the Muscovy Company (1555) and the East India Company (1600). Another way of understanding the character of early English colonization is to note that the English, and the French and Dutch for that matter, knew where they were going and what they were doing. The ocean charts and usable land maps that were available in the early seventeenth century were so much more refined than the materials Columbus, Cabot, and Cartier used. Men could sit in London, Paris, or Amsterdam and point to a spot on a map of North America and indicate a claim for it. Also, Spanish success in Mexico, the Caribbean, and the Andes, as well as the profits the Portuguese took from Brazilian sugar, had made such claims attractive.

In the first few decades, the northern Europeans did not touch directly on each other's claims. Their settlements were pods separated by borderlands still controlled by indigenous nations. Those native communities would be squeezed and shrunk as the volume of English immigration and colonial development increased during the seventeenth century. The borderlands filled in, more by English settlement than by either the French or the Dutch. In the end, the English became the dominant colonizers in North America by conquering the Dutch in the middle of the seventeenth century and the French a century later. But throughout, the rates of immigration, slave importation, and healthy birthrates pushed English colonial populations far beyond those of their neighbors, the French, whose policies and locations kept the Franco-American population sparse.

The Tudor consolidation of English politics paved the way for England's foray to America. Henry VII (Henry Tudor) returned from a French exile, ascended the throne of England in 1485, and began to edge England toward a national politics. The thirty-year Wars of the Roses had exhausted the Houses of York and Lancaster in their violent struggle for dynastic supremacy, and Henry Tudor moved aggressively into the aftermath. Henry VII also saw the need to make England secure from the rising continental powers. He understood the need for a national navy, controlled by the Crown, and authorized the building of Europe's first permanent dry dock for the construction and maintenance of ocean-going ships. He arranged the marriage of his daughter to the Scottish royal family, the Stuarts. That union and its succession yielded a monarchical alliance with the Scots a century later. His son, Henry VIII, made an even greater mark on English history by creating a national Protestant Church in the 1530s.

While he is often depicted in popular caricature as a gluttonous hedonist, an egoist so obsessed with having a son and heir that he removed a succession of wives in the process, the legacy of Henry VIII is more substantial. In 1533, he made himself head of what would be the Church of England, known in America as the Anglican Church. By doing so, he effectively rejected the Catholic Church and Rome's nominal spiritual and administrative authority. By 1536, the new state church began to seize the Catholic monasteries in England. Henry also saw to it that Sir Thomas More, the former chancellor of England, Renaissance scholar, and friend of Erasmus, was executed for refusing to recognize the rights of the Protestant succession in England. Henry's radical actions were in part an angry attempt to control his own marital status, to annul or divorce as he saw fit, but there was a clear national interest. An independent church meant that England's diplomatic policies could now be formed without concern for papal scrutiny.

Henry's Reformation left some of the ritual and protocols of Catholicism in place, as well as some of the administrative structure of archbishops, bishops, priests, and parishes, but the result was a dramatic act of independence from Rome. That break not only gradually separated English politics from those of France and Spain but also added an ecclesiastical difference to the national rivalries that followed. In England, the ecclesiastical pyramid now stopped at the Monarchy and not at Rome. As the century wore on, "Englishness" came to identify a culture and language linked to a state religion. By the time the English decided to settle in America, their laws, political organization, arts and letters, and a new church were on display.

Between 1536 and 1543, Henry VIII consolidated the unification of Wales and England, after 300 years of quasi-military English control of the region. The subjugation of Ireland was another and somewhat different outlet for Tudor energy. English intrusions into Ireland dated back to the Norman era but rose under the Tudors. Symbolism mattered, and, although the English controlled only a small area around Dublin, the so-called Pale, Henry proclaimed himself King of Ireland in 1541. In Elizabeth's reign, after the 1560s, the English moved deeper into Ireland, creating a colonial culture as they went, with lands and titles being distributed to a new category of Anglo-Irish aristocrats.

Beyond Ireland, the western Atlantic now beckoned. Martin Frobisher, searching for the Northwest Passage to China, made it as far north as the Arctic Circle and Baffin Island in 1576. Another Englishman, Henry Hudson, who also had worked for the Dutch, gave his name to a river and the great bay he reached in 1610, where he died following a mutiny. Henry VIII had died in 1547 and was succeeded by his son, the 10-year-old Edward VI, who died in 1553 following years of intrigue and plots; he was succeeded by his half-sister Mary. There was then a brief revival of Catholic fortunes under Queen Mary, "Bloody Mary" as she was called because of her persecution of Protestant opponents. But, in 1558, the accession of Elizabeth, another half-sister of poor Edward, restored Protestantism. Elizabeth's impact and reputation, as a vigorous internationalist and national inspiration, has left us with an epoch identified simply as the "Elizabethan age."

THE ELIZABETHAN OUTLOOK

When Elizabeth assumed the throne, the so-called Marian attacks on the Reformation Church halted. Elizabeth restored the unilateral authority of the Protestant Church of England, brought stability to politics, and spurred English self-awareness and Anglo-centrism. "God's Englishman" was a Protestant and an Elizabethan. The "virgin queen" was also and more importantly "good Queen Bess." Her influence on the public and on the rising class of patriots and entrepreneurs was unprecedented. She captivated the English imagination and today is celebrated as the patron of a generation of heroes whose names resonate through the English historical imagination: Drake, Hawkins, Grenville, and Raleigh.

More than any other, Sir Francis Drake (ca.1540–1596), who died at sea, came to personify the English virtues of intelligence, loyalty, and bravery. Drake raided Spanish outposts in the Caribbean and Panama in the 1560s and 1570s. Elizabeth I granted him a privateering license to wage independent war, for profit, on Spanish shipping. He was also the first Englishman to sail around the world (1577–1580). He plundered Spanish settlements on the west coast of South America during that voyage and then audaciously claimed California for Elizabeth as "New Albion." He was knighted for his exploits and then mounted a great raid on a Spanish fleet at Cadiz in 1587, burning and sinking 30 ships and, as he put it, "singeing the [Don's] beard." He was front and center in the defeat of the Spanish Armada in 1588, an event that secured his place in the pantheon of larger-than-life English heroes.

Drake was not alone. As the century wore on, English explorers and privateers continued to harass Spanish shipping. The break with Rome had released England to form its own foreign policy, and Catholic Spain became, in turn, a religious and political rival. The redoubtable Sir John Hawkins (1532–1595), Drake's relative, was a major force in England's international trade. He was likely the first Englishman to deal in African slaves, as early as the 1560s. He was aware of the need for England to confront the Spanish with naval parity, and his positions, first as the Royal Navy's treasurer and later as an admiral, were crucial in England's rise to globalism. His son Richard continued the family's maritime exploits, and the name Hawkins (or Hawkyns) became synonymous with English courage and ambition. Sir Richard Grenville, Raleigh's cousin, was another naval enterpriser who took part in Raleigh's Roanoke colonization experiment in 1585. His fearless aggression perfectly fit the image of England's martial spirit. He died heroically after taking on a superior Spanish fleet near the Azores in 1591.

Another optimistic expansionist, Sir Humphrey Gilbert, received formal permission from Elizabeth in 1578 to establish a colony in North America, and the way it was designed anticipated the early seventeenth century chartered colonies. The Queen's "patent," a charter or exclusive license, allowed for the private settlement of new lands while serving the national interest. Fixed settlements in North America would retard Spanish expansion and create a base for continued interruption of Spanish commerce in the Atlantic. Spain and England had been antagonizing each other before Elizabeth's grant to Gilbert, and the growing English presence in the Atlantic augured more tension. Gilbert finally got his venture going in 1583, but his small fleet went no farther than Newfoundland before the voyage was aborted. He and his ship were lost on the return to England. Nevertheless, Englishmen were now seriously looking for a permanent place in the western Atlantic. In 1584, Raleigh's proposed colony in North America was the logical outcome to a period of probing, but the colony at Roanoke, just off the North American coast, failed, and England's settling of North America was delayed for a generation.

THE ROANOKE DISASTER, THE ARMADA,
AND THE HAKLUYT IMPERATIVE

Two important criteria for English colonization had been established. The first was a method, rather than a policy, of royal support and authorization for private exploration, settlement, and profit. This system in the first phase of English colonization in America obliged the charter recipient to serve the interests of the nation and maintain English religious and legal standards while enjoying free rein in local governance and development. A second and necessary component was a class or culture of either individuals or groups ready and eager to use the charter system. Grenville, Gilbert, Raleigh, and others of their ilk drove the colonization engine. Raleigh had picked up Gilbert's patent, to try to succeed where the former had failed.

His reconnaissance mission to mainland North America reported on a suitable spot south of Chesapeake Bay, near Albemarle Sound on an island just off the coast of what is now North Carolina. Raleigh named the entire area "Virginia" to honor the Queen and advertise her reputed chastity. The name endured but the colony at Roanoke Island did not. The settlement established in 1585 was abandoned a year later. Francis Drake actually stopped by during one of his raiding expeditions to the south. He removed the settlers and returned them to England. Grenville went back to Roanoke and left a small group of men to care for the site, but, when a final expedition reached the island in 1587, they had disappeared. The leader of the 1587 expedition, John White, had scouted the Chesapeake Bay region in 1585, recording his impressions in writing and in watercolors of landscapes, fauna, and the Algonquian people. He also drew maps of the area. The drawings are impressive and among the first European visual images we have of North American places and peoples. He went back to England for supplies, but war with Spain delayed his return, and White did not get back to Roanoke until 1590. He found the settlement abandoned and no trace of any English settlers.

To this day the Roanoke "mystery" teases the imagination. Scholarship and popular literature have puzzled over the eerie outcome. Did the settlers leave under their own initiative and end up on an adjacent island or the mainland? Were they assimilated by local natives? Were they killed and their remains scattered? Symbolically, the Roanoke misadventure produced what is purported to be the first English child born in the present United States. She was named in celebration of Elizabeth's America, *Virginia* Dare. But it would be 20 years before another formal English attempt was made to settle in America, on the mainland at Jamestown in 1607. At Roanoke, the colonists were clearly unprepared and ill equipped for survival, and they eventually antagonized the natives who originally helped them. The expectation of riches evaporated shortly after arrival, and the settlers seemed unmotivated to try to feed themselves by cultivating crops and breeding livestock. Disease, despair, and malnutrition, along with conflict with the natives, doomed the experiment. For all their confidence and verve, the English were far from infallible. Twenty years later and shortly after it was founded, the Jamestown colony, that is, Virginia, barely survived some of the same problems.

The eventual colonization of Virginia owed much to propaganda. The melancholy fate of the Roanoke settlement might have given potential investors pause, but it did not deter Richard Hakluyt (1552–1616) from promoting the need for England to claim a stake in America. His *Principall Navigations, Voiages, and Discoveries of the English Nation* (1589) was expanded in 1598–1600 and has been called the "prose epic of the English nation." As the literature of Edmund Spenser and Shakespeare are to Elizabethan poetry and drama, Hakluyt's prose work comes to us in another register of the English spirit. As historian, geographer, and booster, Richard Hakluyt, not to be confused with his father and a cousin of the same name, added scientific logic to patriotic enthusiasm. Regrettably, his writings are mostly neglected today, but they offer a clear *entrée* into England's late Renaissance scholarly, political, and nationalistic mood. In his 1584 treatise, *A Discourse Concerning Western Planting*, published at the start of the Roanoke venture, Hakluyt argues strongly for English settlement in America as a way to preempt other Europeans, specifically the Spanish, from monopolizing trade. Why, asks Hakluyt, should England negotiate with European powers for materials that were available in America? In a decisive summary, Hakluyt says:

> This enterprise [English settlement] may staye the Spanish Kinge from flowinge over all the face of that waste firme [land] of America, yf wee seate and plante [settle] there in time, in tyme I say…[for] there is no comparison between the portes of the coastes that the Kinge of Spaine dothe nowe possesse…and the portes of the coastes that our nation is to possesse by plantinge at Norumbega [present-day New England].
>
> *A Discourse Concerning Western Planting* (1584; repr., Cambridge: Press of J. Wilson and Son, 1877), 154.

Norumbega was supposed to have been the site of a Norse settlement and had appeared on Giovanni da Verrazano's 1529 map of America. It identified a stretch along the coast in the region of what would become New England. Hakluyt predicted the development of a great shipbuilding industry there, where timber was plentiful. Locally built and English ships could then disrupt Spanish shipping in the western Atlantic more efficiently. He was also downright belligerent in his desire to take on the power of Philip II. Once the English were established in North America they could, he said,

> spoile Phillipps Indian [American] navye, and...deprive him of yerely passage of his treasure into Europe and...abate the pride of Spaine and of the supporter of the greate Antechriste of Rome and to pull him down in equalitie to his neighbour princes, and...cutt of the common mischefes that come to all Europe by the peculiar aboundaunce of his Indian [American] treasure, and thiss withoute difficultie.

A Discourse Concerning Western Planting, 155.

Hakluyt was suggesting a rationale for Elizabethan policy in America, and, as the English began a serious consideration of American colonization, relations with Spain deteriorated, leading to one of the great military events of the Renaissance, the attempted invasion of England by the Spanish Armada in 1588. The term "armada" simply means "large fleet," but it has come to describe an event considered among the most important in English history. Habsburg Spain under Philip II, who ruled from 1556 to 1598, had become increasingly stretched by the Dutch independence movement and by English affiliations with other Protestants in Holland, Scotland, and Germany, as well as with French Huguenots. Philip was a militant imperialist and passionately anti-Protestant. While he oversaw Spain's "golden age," he also overestimated its resources and perhaps underestimated the rising powers to the north. He was aroused in 1588 to launch an invasion of England to suppress rising English power and Dutch insurrection in the Spanish Netherlands and to squash Reformation heresies. A year earlier, the English Parliament had executed Mary Queen of Scots, a Catholic Stuart with a Tudor grandmother who laid claim to the English throne. Europe's Catholic princes, including the Spanish Crown, saw this as an affront, but it was really Elizabeth's rising glory, influence, and prestige that most worried Spain. Philip's great flotilla was the largest ever assembled in Europe to that date. It consisted of 130 ships, some 30,000 men, and over 2,000 pieces of artillery. It was a frightening juggernaut and headed to Holland to meet up with the army of the Prince of Parma and thence to a landing in England.

From its conception to its operation, the Armada was a gamble. The fleet itself was made up of vessels that were either too ponderous for maneuverable combat or too light for the storms of the Bay of Biscay, the English Channel, and the North Sea. Its command was incompetent, and its crews and army comprised a medley of nationalities and languages, including Catalans, Portuguese, Irish, and English Catholics. The story of the English attack on the fleet has a great heroic ring to it. It celebrates Drake's great poise as vice admiral and records the pluck of the English crews in their lighter, faster, and better armed vessels as they isolated the Spanish warships one by one and shattered the behemoths. During the encounter, the Spanish formation was split into confused parts. It was then driven from the refuge it had taken at Calais after the English sent burning ships into the harbor. The great fleet was ultimately destroyed by what some have called the "Protestant wind," a great storm that drove the Armada into the North Sea and around the north of Scotland to the west coast of Ireland and the North Atlantic. Storms and a lack of navigation charts resulted in many wayward Spanish ships and countless bodies being dumped on rocky coasts around the British Isles before a bedraggled 80 or so vessels returned to Spain. England had survived a great threat and now was a bona fide rival of Spain. England's European star rose at the moment of its first American failure at Roanoke.

THE STUARTS

Elizabeth died in 1603 without an heir, and, because a Tudor had earlier married a Scottish Stuart, the crowns of Scotland and England were combined under the Stuarts. It began with James VI of Scotland, who became James I under the new joint monarchy. James Stuart and his successors lacked Elizabeth's style, common sense, and popular appeal, and they led Britain into one of the most tumultuous periods in its history. For the next century, Britain's history was punctuated by religious turmoil, constitutional conflict between the Monarch and Parliament, civil war and insurrection, the execution of one Stuart king, and the expulsion of another. Economic depression, ideological extremism, the great plague of 1665, and the great fire of London in 1666 added to the anxieties of the era. But the ultimate resolution of the century's convulsions shaped modern Britain and led to the creation and particular form of Britain's American Empire, which, by the start of the eighteenth century, was firmly established. The mainland American and Caribbean colonies boomed, British trade and political influence in the Atlantic and Indian Oceans expanded steadily, and a global rivalry with France intensified. Moreover, in the wake of the Stuarts, Britain reached a level of political stability, and the great strains between the Crown and Parliament had been mostly resolved by the time the Stuart reign ended. In 1707, the parliaments of Scotland and England were united and Great Britain was born.

Before all that, in the first half of the seventeenth century, the Stuarts struggled to adjust to the changing moods and values in English political life.

James's reign (1603–1625) was a mix of good sense in economics, stubbornness in politics, questionable personal behavior (his penchant for having young handsome male friends as companions), and failed foreign policies. While insisting on protecting the Church of England's status, he managed to alienate both England's Catholic minority and the more radical elements of English Protestantism. The so-called Guy Fawkes plot to blow up Parliament in 1605 led to a purge of Catholics. There was more trouble for the Stuarts stemming from Protestant reformers. Protestant separatists attacked the Church of England, and the more radical of those ended up in Holland. Within the Church itself, the seeds of reform created a movement, later known as "Puritanism," that is, a movement to "purify" the Church of England and go even further with the Reformation. The movement had formed in the later years of Elizabeth's reign but became more aggressive because of what the reformers saw as Stuart ambivalence. As noted, James himself was a controversial figure and aroused much comment by contemporaries regarding his many talents as well as his foibles. Henri IV of France is alleged to have called James the "wisest fool in Christendom," a not inaccurate epithet.

By all accounts, he was a mixed blessing for the English, but he had both an immediate and a long-lasting effect on the course of modern history. He and his son Charles issued the charters for the first permanent American colonies in Virginia, Massachusetts, and Maryland and acknowledged the unchartered Plymouth settlement. James also commissioned a new Bible in English. The so-called King James Version was put together by a team of scholars and churchmen and is surely one of the great literary achievements of the English language. It was based, ironically, on the English translation of William Tyndale (ca.1494–1536), a tenacious reformer who was executed as a heretic in Belgium.

In the early years of the seventeenth century, English interests committed themselves to "planting" the area that is now New England. The efforts of English sailors such as Bartholomew Gosnold in 1602 and George Waymouth (or Weymouth) in 1605 to establish settlements attest to the growing determination of English entrepreneurs. The natives all along the coast from Florida to Cape Breton were routinely trading with anyone who touched land. For the English, the time seemed ripe to preempt the French and, as Hakluyt had put it, "staye the Spanish kinge." In 1606, James, as head of state, granted patents for two claims on the North American coast to groups of London and Plymouth merchants. The London Company received a patent for South Virginia, between 34 degrees and 41 degrees north, and the Plymouth Company for the zone between 38 degrees and 45 degrees north. The claims overlapped, but a clause stipulated a 100-mile buffer between them with no settlement allowed. The designated territories reached inland for 100 miles.

The London Company settled its claim in 1607 at Jamestown in Chesapeake Bay, and the colony adopted "Virginia" as its designation. The first permanent English presence in the Americas followed. Using refined cartography, the London Company knew where it was going. Roanoke sailors had visited the Chesapeake during the brief life of that colony. The company chose the appealing and bountiful Chesapeake Bay for settlement, and then, with disastrous consequences, colonists set up their homes in a low-lying malarial swamp.

The Troubled Origins of Virginia 1607–1624

Hakluyt had pointed the way for English expansion, but neither he nor any other imperialist had devised an easy strategy for permanent settlement. Spain and Portugal did not offer an appropriate example for the English or for the French or Dutch for that matter. The Roanoke disaster should have served as a caution to the next set of optimists, the London Company's shareholders and servants. It apparently did not. The lessons of Roanoke seemed to have been lost on the ill-prepared private chartered group that blundered into confusion and destitution in the Chesapeake. In the longer run, Virginia survived where Roanoke failed, but, from the moment it was founded in 1607 to the stabilization offered by a royal charter of 1624, the London Company's Virginia gambit flirted with the fate of Roanoke. For the thousands of servants and settlers who perished in the swamps and woods around Jamestown in its early decades, Virginia was a hell. The mortality rate among immigrants in its first two decades was an appalling 80 per cent. As much as the image of Elizabethan or Jacobean glory persists, the early American picture has ragged, starving servants dying in droves in Virginia. And far from the chivalrous Raleigh or the flamboyant John Smith, the "first gentlemen of Virginia" were the hardened survivors whose tobacco wealth came from the exploitation of white labor and the later enslavement of Africans. Tobacco and its profits saved Virginia.

Virginia's early history is a story of human incompetence, inhumanity, and avarice. It was, however, England's first fixed foothold in America. That it would produce the likes of Washington, Jefferson, and Madison hardly seemed likely from the condition of the beleaguered sufferers in the Jamestown mire. But the founding of Jamestown has come to represent a threshold moment in history, and 1607 has a place alongside 1776 as a paradigm for American nationalism. As a puff from a 1907 Virginia guidebook put it, to celebrate the tercentenary of Jamestown, "America's only shrines are her altars of patriotism—the first and most potent being Jamestown, the sire of Virginia, and Virginia the mother of this great Republic." That claim for an American genesis has been challenged by Massachusetts's "city upon the hill" and Pennsylvania's "best poor man's country." If the Virginia colony can be used as a metaphorical shrine to the origins of the United States, we do well to remember that, in the seventeenth and eighteenth centuries, it was the place where the native Algonquian people, the Powhatan, were decimated. It also saw the cruel destination of tens of thousands of white indentured servants and of enslaved Africans. It was a crude graveyard for many of the first generation of white immigrants.

The three ships of the London Company that sailed into the Chesapeake in 1607 carried 105 people. By the company's own definitions, about a third of the settlers were "gentlemen" and the rest were tradesmen, laborers, and "boyes." What did those "gentlemen" expect to do? Relax while their male servants gathered wealth? Be favored as princes by the natives? A governing council was set up that included John Smith, the worldly adventurer, and Bartholomew Gosnold, the sailor-explorer. On paper, the group was not functionally suited to what lay ahead. In practice, it suffered the consequences of sloppy thinking and the rough realities of the Chesapeake. Disease, starvation, depression, and confusion decimated the settlers' numbers. Within a year, only two-thirds of the original party remained at the site, which survived only because the company sent supplies and additional settlers.

By the fall of 1608, it was still struggling to rationalize the experiment, and the number of gentlemen still outnumbered laborers. A census of 1608, for example, includes a "Mistresse Forrest, and Anne Burras her maide" (a John Burras was listed as a tradesman). Among the servants were several "Dutch men and Poles, with some others." Once again, torpor, incompetence, and ignorance ate at the population. There is something terribly forlorn about a venture that simply plunked down an assemblage of ill-suited hopefuls in a harsh environment without any particular strategy for survival, let alone profit. The experiences of the first groups of hapless settlers would be repeated, with interesting modifications, for nearly two decades before political stability, sustained economic means, and optimism prevailed. There was no gold or silver, nor any other useful commodity. The Virginia Company Council in London had no plan for sensible settlement. In what was believed to be a land of plenty, tired settlers starved to death.

John Smith was one of the era's great boosters. His *Generall Historie of Virginia, New-England and the Summer Isles* (1624) and *True Travels, Adventures, and Observations* (1630) are concoctions of ego and exaggeration. Smith cuts a heroic figure as he details his various adventures, including the uncorroborated, albeit plausible story of his capture by the Powhatan tribe while he was foraging and negotiating for food for his starving fellow settlers. The "Princess" Pocahontas's intercession to save his life has joined the stock of legend. The romantic flavor of the event, alleged by Smith in his 1608 book, *A True Relation... of Virginia,* still appeals to twenty-first century audiences. Although we might question Smith's accounts and criticize his hyperbole and self-serving fictions, he was an important figure in the early colonization period. He ran afoul of enemies at Jamestown and was almost hanged by factional rivals before Captain Christopher Newport, returning from England, interceded on his behalf.

Smith took a prominent role in the London Company's operation in 1608–1609 and recorded in his *Generall Historie,* "This was that time...we called the starving time; it were too vile to say, and scarce to be believed what we endured...for want of providence, industry and government and not from the...defect of the country." The self-promoting Smith, traveler and chronicler extraordinaire, helped to advertise Virginia's potential but was quick to see its present condition as a flawed, mismanaged travesty. He encouraged the settlers to plant corn and commit their depleted energies to farming and trading with the natives rather than follow the company's orders to find gold. He left in 1609, but returned to America in 1614, sponsored by some London merchants. From that trip, he brought fish and furs back to England from the coastal area north of the Chesapeake and used them to entice settlers to what he called "New England." Although the popular image of Smith derives from his own descriptions of his adventures in Europe and America, he should be remembered for his efforts to show the value of coexistence with natives, his descriptions of landscape and climate, his maps, and his analysis of colonial enterprise.

Smith criticized the company's strategies and so lent a sobering tone to grandiose expectations. He was later joined in his cautionary admonitions by the English philosopher Francis Bacon who, in 1625, wrote an essay "Of Plantations" that used the unhappy lessons of early Virginia to urge future colonists to be more modest in their outlook and more careful in how they populate, where they settle (he is specific in using the malarial Jamestown site as a caveat), and how they use the land. His advice on white-native relations strikes a commonsensical, if patronizing, note:

> If you plant where savages are, do not only entertain them with trifles and gingles, but use them justly and graciously, with sufficient guard nevertheless; and do not win their favour by helping them to invade their enemies, but for their defence it is not amiss; and send oft of them over to the country that plants [for example, England], that they may see a better condition than their own, and commend it when they return.
>
> *The Works of Francis Bacon, Lord Chancellor of England,* modernized and ed. Basil Montagu (Philadelphia: A. Hart, 1852), 41.

In some later cases, Francis Bacon's suggested diplomatic tactics were employed, but impatience, greed, and hubris accompanied white settlement in the Chesapeake. The colonies founded after Virginia and before 1660 avoided many of that colony's problems, either from the lessons it presented or, more likely, from their own inherently careful, longer term, and communal objectives. Meanwhile, Virginia would flounder for a while until it became stabilized by commercial tobacco crops.

Despite the horrendous death rates of the "starving time," the London Company persisted in sending people to the colony. Despite or because it lacked a clear plan of development, it received a second and revised charter in 1609 that lodged control in a company-appointed council and expanded the company's territorial claims north and south and most significantly from "sea to sea." The magnitude of the territorial claim mocks the reality of the tiny clusters of hungry, confused settlers and the mortality rates among them. Several thousand immigrants landed in the colony in its first decade, but, in 1619, there were only about 700 people left. One set of figures shows that between 1619 and 1622 some 3,750 migrants set off for Virginia. Yet, in 1622, the population remained at about 700. What happened to over 3,000 of the 1619–1622 immigrants? Most died shortly after getting to Virginia. Some died at sea, others in the native uprising of 1622, and it is likely that many made off into the forests or up the rivers. English migrants kept the flow going, but Jamestown's woeful conditions kept killing them off. In the starving time, for example, the settlers simply could not cope with the near tropical heat and humidity in summer, the contaminated water, and the outbreaks of typhus, dysentery, and malaria. During the cold snaps of winter, because they did not prepare properly, they had to burn their furnishings and even parts of their crude dwellings for heat and trade their metal tools with the natives for bits of food.

Provisions from England were often delayed, and, because no food had been stored, the settlers often ate the livestock as it arrived and then turned to mice and rats and eventually their own dead. There is at least one recorded case of cannibalism, of a man eating his deceased wife during the winter of 1609–1610. When a group of previously shipwrecked settlers arrived from Bermuda in 1610, they were shocked by what they found—a tiny group of emaciated survivors. The absence of any social or economic cooperation, the misplaced "gentlemen" who could not and would not labor, and the laborers who lacked direction created a desperate atmosphere. There was dissension at the top, no consistent leadership, and depression throughout.

Still, the London Company attracted titled men to run the colony. Smith was succeeded by Lord De La Warr, but both men were forced back to England, by injury and sickness, respectively. In 1611, Sir Thomas Dale, De La Warr's deputy, took over. He published *Lawes Divine, Morall and Martiall* and with an armed force began to apply order to the settlement. The "martiall" laws were the key to his reforms. Settlers were obliged, under threat of severe penalty, to plant vegetables and corn and then to care for them. In other words, Dale's laws were designed to compel people to stay alive by taking care of their own nutritional needs under the threat of punishment. There were usually enough healthy survivors or newcomers to enhance the settlement's chances for survival, and Dale enlisted enough able hands to erect a fort at Henrico, 50 miles up the James River from Jamestown. By the time Dale was succeeded by Sir Thomas Gates in 1612, the London Company received its third, revised charter. Bermuda, far out into the Atlantic, was added to its jurisdiction. Also, in 1612, John Rolfe cultivated a crop of "tall tobacco," likely from Spanish Caribbean seeds. After he shipped his first load to England in 1614, he put Virginia on the road to survival.

TOBACCO, LAND, AND LABOR

A weed, dried and smoked by natives for centuries for ceremonial and social purposes, was refined, probably hybridized, and then cultivated in the Caribbean and Central and South America by Europeans for their own ceremonial and social habits. The Spanish and Portuguese had taken American tobacco back to Europe in the early sixteenth century and had produced commercial volumes by 1600. Rolfe himself was a pipe smoker when he arrived in Virginia, and, in 1608, one of the listed immigrants, Robert Cotton, was identified as "A Tobacco-pipe-maker." While there is no evidence that he practiced his trade in Virginia, he had clearly done so in England. After a short time the so-called sot weed gave Virginia a future. Land was subdivided into lots and distributed under company auspices to be cleared and farmed by tenants. The availability of land to tenants or owners and the suitability of the soil and climate for tobacco helped turn Virginians into survivors.

Meanwhile, Rolfe married the legendary Pocahontas in 1614. It has been suggested that this was a diplomatic decision (Rolfe needed both the English governor's permission and that of Powhatan), but it was most likely spurred by genuine affection. English authorities did not easily condone interracial marriage, and Rolfe's decision ran against English mores. Before her marriage, Pocahontas had been captured, converted to Christianity, and, technically, held hostage while Thomas Dale's soldiers had hammered Powhatan's people. The peace that followed was essentially a forced one that Powhatan silently adhered to for several years. Rolfe took Pocahontas to England in 1616 where she met with the king and queen. Because of her lineage, she was feted as royalty. This example of European recognition of native royalty was not unusual, even if most aspects of native culture were disdained.

Pocahontas died in 1617, in England, as she prepared to return to America. The cause of her death was vaguely ascribed to an "infection" and might have been pneumonia or consumption. Some historians have inferred smallpox from her condition and history. She was barely 23 years old.

After the death of Pocahontas, Rolfe returned to Virginia to promote the tobacco economy. A group led by the Earl of Southampton and Sir Edwin Sandys took over the running of the Virginia Company of London. With George Yeardley as governor, the company repealed the severe civil codes and in a momentous decision allowed for a legislative assembly for the colony. The Virginia General Assembly, the House of Burgesses, is correctly seen as the first elected, representative legislature anywhere in European America. Initially, its 22 members were chosen by taxable planters in eleven sparsely populated "towns" or districts, referred to as "hundreds." The company appointed the governor and council, but legislation originated from the representatives, the landowners. We must not see this as a sudden burst of egalitarian politics, however. It was hardly democratic, but it formalized a local legislative authority that would have a major impact on the way Virginia developed. It was a mechanism that allowed landowners to serve landowners' needs, and it helped turn the corner on Virginia's viability. By 1619, the three pillars of Virginia's future were in place. The first two, tobacco cultivation and a forum for local representative government, the House of Burgesses, were reinforced by a third, the *headright* system of 1618.

The headright system was similar to Dutch practice. In Virginia, the policy called for the outright grant of two 50-acre plots to any person in the colony at the time who was not bound to service, that is so-called "freemen." It allowed 50-acre grants to any immigrants paying their own way to the colony and each family member—man, woman, or child. More important was the provision for grants to those who paid the way of immigrants, a further incentive to population growth. The Virginia Company of London endorsed the scheme, and, after 1619, the burgesses administered it. As tobacco exports rose, the legal control of land distribution was in their hands, and a local formula for creating and maintaining wealth was confirmed. Soon, successful planters armed with deeds to land and seeds for tobacco fanned out and up the river systems of the western Chesapeake shore, even as disease-related mortality rates remained high. The company had finally introduced strategies for management and growth, but its days were numbered. It was tottering on the brink of bankruptcy by 1620, and, in 1624, it failed. But it left behind an infrastructure under the control of private landowners with local political authority.

The paradox of Virginia is that out of the ashes of the early catastrophes rose one of the most powerful societies in colonial America, the

Virginia "plantocracy," that is, a ruling class of planters. The headright policy was intended to save the Virginia Company and encourage self-sufficiency and growth. It failed in the first instance and succeeded in the second. The earlier land distribution system of "patents" to groups such as the "Society of Smith's Hundred" continued up to the company's collapse in 1624. But the future was already being shaped by individual ownership. The James, the York, the Rappahannock, and the Potomac Rivers were navigable for many miles upstream so that tobacco could be grown inland, processed, packed, and shipped downstream to and across the Atlantic.

By the early 1620s, the planters of Virginia were confronted with a dilemma: land was available for tobacco cultivation, but it was worthless without labor, and lots of it. The cliché that, in England, land was scarce but people were plentiful was inverted in Virginia where land was plentiful and labor scarce. Virginia's planters would have to devise ways of getting and keeping a steady supply of labor. In 1618, about 20,000 pounds of tobacco were shipped out of the colony, and, by 1627, 500,000 pounds were sent to market. By mid-century, the colonies of Virginia and Maryland, which began growing tobacco after its founding in 1634, were producing millions of pounds of the crop annually, and, by the 1680s, the Chesapeake planters sent over 20 million pounds of tobacco yearly to England. Rising volumes drove down prices, but profits could still be made by increased production. Tobacco cultivation and processing was labor intensive. Seeding it, weeding it, picking it, curing it, and packing it involved a set of backbreaking routines. It was a year-round enterprise. Smallholders were obliged to make do with their own or their family's labor and sometimes with a single servant. The newly emerging Virginia gentry, the plantocracy, began controlling larger numbers of servants, and a powerful minority emerged that based its wealth as much on its ability to control labor as to acquire land. Before that, however, the last days of the Virginia Company of London were accompanied by a complete breakdown in relations with the Powhatan.

CONSOLIDATION

From the beginning, dealings between the immigrants and the local Powhatan natives had ranged from generosity and respect to suspicion, fear, mischief, and outright hostility. Chief Powhatan died in 1618 and was succeeded by his half brother Opechancanough. The tenuous peace of 1617 ended, and, in 1622, relations had become so poisoned that Opechancanough launched full-scale attacks on the English in and around Jamestown in what was, for the Powhatan, total war. He killed about 350 colonists. The English response was predictable. They were now capable of reprisal and conducted vicious counterattacks using pikes and matchlock muskets against the Powhatan, destroying native lodgings and food stocks as they killed Powhatan warriors. Although Jamestown survived and marketable tobacco began to appear in quantity, disease and malnutrition continued to take their toll. The Virginia Company in London had already begun to break up over personal rivalries and the lack of profits. It surrendered its charter, and Virginia became a "royal province," that is to say that the Crown held the charter and the king appointed the governor. A new era in Virginia's history began. The Crown, if necessary, could subsidize the colony with supplies and military help, and, even if it assumed some legal authority in its right to appoint governors, it did not and logistically could not administer the colony directly. The burgesses were in control of day-to-day operations, making and supervising their own laws. A model for all the royal colonies in English America had appeared. In 1639, Charles I granted Virginians the right to call the Virginia General Assembly together annually and, by doing so, technically conceded a form of self-rule to the colony.

A census of 1625 confirms the meager Virginia population after two decades of struggle. It also provides a snapshot of the colony's social and gender composition. A total of 1,227 people were identified, including 873 adult males of whom 441 were "servants" and 222 females of whom 46 were servants. There were 107 children listed, two "indians" and 23 "negroes." The overwhelming ratio of white servants to "negroes" would continue as the tobacco economy flourished, before its reversal in the late seventeenth century. Natives living outside the white settlements were not included, and, in any case, their numbers were in precipitous decline. The male to female ratio had moved closer since the early days of the settlement but would not balance for several decades until immigration and natural increase closed the gap.

By the 1640s, Virginia's non-native population had reached 10,000, a quadrupling over 10 years. By 1660, it was 27,000, including nearly 1,000 Africans. The mortality rates in the colony dropped, and, with the influx of thousands of servants and some natural increase, population rose quickly. In addition, mills, workshops, roads, and rudimentary towns appeared. In 1644, Opechancanough launched another war against the English, and, although several hundred English lives were lost, the campaign crippled the Powhatan's abilities to resist further. Opechancanough was killed, apparently by a shot in the back at Jamestown. In 1651, English America's first "Indian" reservation was set up near Richmond to accommodate the remnants of the Powhatan population, the residue of a vibrant society that had welcomed the English a few decades earlier. The physical environment was also being remade. Planters early on had experimented with wine grapes, silkworms and mulberry trees, indigo, various fruits, nuts and spices, and even some West Indian cotton, but none took hold commercially. Tobacco did, and its production came to define Virginia's politics and culture. Some large planters and hundreds of small farmers also raised livestock and grew "indian corn," wheat ("English corn"), and other edible grains along with flax and hemp for "homespun" clothing fibers.

LABOR

The English who crossed the Atlantic to mainland North America in the 1630s and 1640s were drawn either to the religious sanctuaries of New England or to the tobacco fields of the Chesapeake. Virginia attracted huge numbers. The immigrants came to purchase the land, if they had the means, or to work for others if they did not. For the well off, Virginia was an investment in status, but the poor were more often pushed by having no prospects at home. Conditions in England provided a pool of needy English families and individuals. Poor harvests and a rising landless population put pressure on limited resources. The continuing enclosure movement threw large numbers of families off the land and into poverty as landlords converted their small, rented, or leased holdings into pasture for livestock in response to a rising demand for sheep's wool.

New World cash-crop economies required investment capital, land, suitable climate and soils, and, most important, dependable sources of abundant labor, as well as legal control of it. In Virginia, the demand for labor was met with a system of term servitude, by way of "indentures," whereby a servant and a planter or his agent signed a mutually binding contract for a period of four to seven years. These contracts were ostensibly beneficial to both parties. The planter had control of the servant's labor and was obligated to clothe, feed, house, and protect the servant for the duration of the indenture.

In practice, the relationship favored the planter, and the lowly status of the servant, a dependent, was automatically translated into statutory deference. In the seventeenth century, anyone who worked for anyone else was technically a servant, whether the terms were for a day, a year, or longer. Under the common Virginia indentures, servants agreed to strict obedience and could be punished for running away, striking the master or offending a mistress, refusing to work, drinking, fornicating, or swearing. In some cases, branding or mutilation by the master under the auspices of the local courts was acceptable punishment. If a runaway were caught and returned, he or she could be penalized by a doubling of the time left on the indenture, turning five years, for example, into ten. The master's obligation was simply to care for the servant and, at the completion of the contract, supply the servant with a parcel of land, seed, tools, and perhaps some cured tobacco, which served as currency in the early days of the colony.

Those throngs of servants fueled the economy. In an age when manual labor was the lot of most servants, tobacco work was more than usually onerous. The heat of a Chesapeake summer was difficult enough to endure for any English person, but to be bent over tobacco plants, hoeing and weeding and under the supervision of often-impatient masters, exacerbated what was, for many, already a harsh life. Attrition was high, through illness and death; servants sometimes gave up and ran off into the forests. Yet the supply of servants was assured in the early decades, and planters were free to exploit them. The conditions were not bad everywhere, of course, but, when we see estimates of only 20 to 25 per cent of indentured servants redeeming their contracts, the picture is a depressing one.

This system of open, sanctioned abuse continued into the early eighteenth century, until white indentured servitude was replaced by the more dreadful system of race-based bonded slavery. With the exception of the slave labor system, which appeared after 1660 and took hold in law and practice before the end of the century, Virginia's basic social, economic, and political features were taking root by the 1660s. The survivors of the Virginia Company disaster were melding into a class with special political powers. There were churches and some royal officials to be found, but they offered little in the way of restraint on the emerging power of the plantocracy. If Virginia was "the mother of this great Republic," as the twentieth-century celebrations attested, then it was a mother that favored some at the expense of others. Virginia was a class-based society, reflecting English practices in most regards but shaping its own particular brand of preference and privilege early on.

Maryland

Virginia's Chesapeake neighbor, Maryland, shared most of its economic and social conditions but was founded in a different way—as a proprietorship and a potential religious outpost for English Catholics. In 1634, it became the second chartered colony in the Chesapeake and, after Massachusetts to the north, the third formally chartered English colony on the North American mainland. It began with an interesting twist on the charter system. George Calvert, who served as secretary of state to James I after 1619, resigned in 1624 and converted to Catholicism but was, nevertheless, knighted as Lord Baltimore by a sympathetic James. The enterprising Baltimore had been a member of both the Virginia Company and the Council of New England. His effort to establish a community on what he named the Avalon Peninsula in Newfoundland failed in large part because of settlers' inability to cope with the hard and unpredictable climate. He then visited the Chesapeake in the late 1620s and saw the prospects for growth, although he died before his request for a chartered tract on the northern edge of Virginia was approved by Charles I in 1632. His son, Cecil Calvert, the second Lord Baltimore, like his father, never visited the proposed colony, but he inherited a unique license. The terms of the charter made him sole *proprietor* and silently permitted Catholic settlement by not excluding it.

The first group of 200 settlers arrived in 1634. Regardless of the charter's open mandate and the fact that Catholics, including two Jesuits, were among the first arrivals, Catholics were never a majority in Maryland. As proprietor, Baltimore had the authority to assign governors and councils so long as the colony respected the rights of "freemen" and did not violate English law. The colony was named for the wife of Charles I and took shape north of the Potomac River and on the eastern shore of Chesapeake Bay. It imitated the economic model of the Virginia tobacco plantations, and, for several years, there were formal disputes and even armed conflict between the two colonies, mostly over boundaries. In the end, the Crown acknowledged Maryland's territorial claims. The colony's leadership settled into good relations with local natives and distributed land in a modified manorial system, allowing for large tobacco estates and introducing a labor system similar to Virginia's. Yet, after several years of clearing land and producing tobacco, only a few hundred people had come to the colony, so, in the mid-1640s, Maryland continued to be at the mercy of its more powerful neighbor. In fact, armed Virginians calling for the Maryland charter to be revoked attacked the colony and, likely, only the intercession of Sir William Berkeley (1606–1677), the new royal governor of Virginia, assured Maryland's survival. Berkeley was committed to peace in the English settlements and, in that spirit, supported the Maryland proprietor.

Maryland had survived, but only by the skin of its teeth. Then, its population climbed to 4,500 in 1650 and to nearly 8,500 in 1660. Even when it affirmed its charter boundaries, Maryland was still hemmed in by Virginia and was further restricted in space later by Pennsylvania to the north and Delaware to the east. But it boomed, especially after 1700. By the time of the Declaration of Independence, Maryland's population, white and black, reached 45 per cent of Virginia's and 31 per cent of the total Chesapeake population. The combined population of Virginia and Maryland, white and black, in the mid-1770s was approximately 650,000, figures that were unforeseeable in the desperate days of the early seventeenth century. The Chesapeake colonies survived by discovering sustainable economic methods not in the original prospects of the founders. Tobacco cultivation, servant and then slave labor, and the creation of an economic, social, and political class structure to control workers set the Chesapeake on a unique path in mainland North America.

The history of the early Chesapeake is instructive in understanding the precarious, erratic, and muddled histories of the early English chartered settlements. Factions thrived and permanence was attained only after the original intentions of the charter holders or the first generations of settlers were modified. Virginia is a perfect example of that. Maryland's problems were unique to Maryland, but every one of the early chartered colonies encountered teething problems. The Atlantic was a highway, but it was a slow one. The American colonies were many weeks away from English ports, and communications were consequently delayed. That meant that the civilian authorities on site, courtesy of the charter system, could operate, sometimes out of necessity, in ways that precluded direct interference from the company, the Crown, or the proprietor. The foundations for the future development of all colonial societies were laid down by very small numbers of people.

New England

THE PILGRIMS

The northern component of the original Virginia grant of 1606, the Virginia Company of Plymouth (also called the Plymouth Company), used a variety of subcontracts to establish itself. None of them created a viable, permanent hold on the territory until it was settled as a religious refuge by the so-called Pilgrims of 1620. Before then Sir Ferdinando Gorges (ca.1566–1647), a flamboyant English entrepreneur, established a colony at Sagadahoc, Maine in 1607 and built a fort there at about the time the Chesapeake colony was started at Jamestown. The venture failed the following year because, not unlike at Jamestown, the colonists squabbled with each other and seemed indifferent to the need for collective agriculture. The area was then used by fishers and traders, and Spanish, Dutch, and French ships joined the English in establishing semipermanent outposts along the northern New England coast. Gorges, however, was not deterred by the 1608 failure. In 1614, the ever-busy John Smith, after an exploratory voyage, convinced Gorges of the potential for fishing profits. One of Gorges's agents spent a winter at the mouth of the Saco River and reported on Smith's findings. Gorges resumed his plans for a colony, and the old Plymouth Company charter was replaced by an organization known as the Council for New England in 1620. The term "Virginia" was now confined to the old London Company claim in the Chesapeake, and the northern portion became known as New England. It identified an area between 40 degrees and 48 degrees north, from the northern edges of Virginia to the Gulf of St. Lawrence and "from sea to sea."

Those who made the first continuous English settlement in New England have come down to us as the "Pilgrims" after the posthumous printing of William Bradford's *History of Plymouth Plantation, 1606–1646*, in which he notes that the immigrants "knew they were pilgrims." (Bradford's manuscript remained unpublished until 1841, but colonial historians such as Nathaniel Morton made free use of it much earlier.) Bradford (1590–1657) was the driving force of the experiment and the colony's governor for all but a few years between 1621 and 1657. The Pilgrims had not taken part in the Plymouth Company's plans or in Gorges's schemes. They were a small tightly knit group of families from Nottinghamshire who had separated from the Church of England and moved to Holland in 1608. They worried about the end of the 12-year peace between Holland and Spain because the religious freedom they enjoyed in Holland was fragile, and, if there were any resumption of Spanish control or influence, they would certainly lose their Dutch sanctuary. Alternatively, they feared that their children might be absorbed into Dutch society and lose their English identity. The Pilgrims lacked a charter of their own but the group's leaders, including William Brewster, helped by Sir Edwin Sandys of Virginia, secured permission to settle in the old Plymouth grant. They sailed from Holland to Plymouth, England and joined with a larger group of migrants who had either bought or were granted shares from stay-at-home investors. When it sailed, the 180-ton merchant ship the *Mayflower* carried just over 100 passengers in addition to its 25-man crew. The self-absorbed Pilgrims referred to the other passengers as "strangers." In late 1620, after several weeks at sea, the *Mayflower* reached Cape Cod, and the Pilgrims decided to part ways with the rest of the travelers and set up their own "Godly" community while the "strangers" dispersed.

On November 11, 1620, the so-called Mayflower Compact was signed by 41 male adults at Plymouth, New England. They agreed among themselves to establish a "covenant" to order and secure their intended community:

> In the Name of God...We...the Loyal Subjects of our dread Sovereign Lord King James...Having undertaken for the Glory of God, and Advancement of the Christian Faith, and the Honour of our King and Country...to plant the first Colony in the northern Parts of Virginia; Do by these Presents, solemnly and mutually, in the Presence of God and one another, covenant and combine ourselves together into a civil Body Politick, for our better Ordering and Preservation, and Furtherance of the Ends

aforesaid... [to] enact, constitute, and frame, such just and equal Laws, Ordinances, Constitutions, and Officers... for the general Good of the Colony.

Reproduced in *Classics of American Political and Constitutional Thought*, ed. Scott Hammond, Kevin Hardwick, and Howard Lubert (Indianapolis: Hackett, 2007), 7.

Three things are worth noting: first, the signers vowed to do "our dread Sovereign" James's work in America even though they had conspicuously separated from the Church of England. Second, the agreement had a specific civil purpose. Third, the method of assuming "rights" to mutually agreed authority, without a patent or charter, served as a precedent for later spontaneous communities in Providence (Rhode Island) and New Haven (Connecticut). Also, although half the settlers died during the first winter, the remaining Pilgrims did not leave with the departing *Mayflower* but persevered with a fatalism that drew deeply from the community's spiritual integrity.

As soon as the Pilgrims had distanced themselves from the other migrants, they quickly tied their ecclesiastical ends to their civil and economic needs. The use of "first comers," to distinguish the original group, was a sign of the symbolic importance of "founders." Still, the experiment rested on the principle of voluntary uniformity. The otherwise plain manner of worship and the participatory roles in congregational organization were upheld by fasting days, obligatory social behavior, mandatory attendance at prayers and services, and a strict regimen of charity and morality. The Plymouth colony was a commune. Although it acknowledged a spiritual and church leadership and the notion of "visible saints," there was a plan to operate the colony as an economic collective. That plan was modified early. Lots were assigned to individual families, and farms were started. Land was deeded, that is, fixed to personal ownership with the individual's right to its disposal. Gender roles favored males, as in England, in legal and political matters.

English common law and practice and its American version determined that a married woman was legally *feme covert* (Norman French), that is, a woman "covered" by her husband. In formal law, the term "coverture" defined the woman's status. The principle, assumed to be correct on the basis of gender, determined, in effect, that a husband and wife were one person, that a wife was defined by the husband's status and subsumed within the husband's sovereignty. A single woman or widow fell under a different set of legal principles as a *feme sole* (Norman French), a woman alone, and had rights to own property and make contracts under her own name. Single women seldom could exercise any political rights. If we wonder why a woman would surrender a measure of autonomy for marriage, we do well to note that single women had few economic or social opportunities to function independently. In all English jurisdictions, property descended to males. The term "spinster" conjures up the image of spinning wheels, but it slips into the language as an "unmarried" woman, a rare and suspicious status. Except in the circumstance of a serious gender imbalance, there was a prejudice against unmarried men too. The family, in particular the nuclear family, had become the norm by the seventeenth century.

The family unit was at the heart of the community's ethos. Women and children were central to the economic survival of the colony. Their labor was as vital as any man's, and no small farm could function without the coordinated labor of the family. Some tasks were gender or age specific, but the family acted as a single unit in the sowing and harvesting of crops and tending to livestock. As noted in Chapter 7, the household economy in the preindustrial New England farm required a sophisticated distribution of tasks that were coordinated in a common purpose. Some of the colony's leaders did have servants, but, for the most part, the settlement was sustained by the family farm and cooperative exchanges of goods, labor, and services. Houses, barns, and meeting houses were erected *by* the community acting in concert.

A future New England pattern was first seen in Plymouth, where a covenanted group, a genuine community, also allowed for individual property ownership. Its social and economic model rested on the principle of family farms for basic needs and as a means of engendering personal and social responsibility. The church was also the meeting house for civil issues. Taxes were voted on, land was distributed, and roads built by tax assessment, all done in open public forums. The needs of the corporate whole merged with personal responsibility and spiritual conformity. Because of its separatist ethic, it was a somewhat closed, insular society, and the somewhat arbitrary territorial boundaries of the "little commonwealth" were narrowly and poorly defined. The Pilgrims were dreamers and optimists seeking a harmonious sanctuary in America, but they were also practical in how they went about fulfilling those dreams.

Throughout the 1620s, other, mostly ephemeral groups attempted to set up fishing and trading posts in the vicinity. The inhabitants of one of these settlements, at nearby Mount Wollaston ("Merrymount"), provoked the Pilgrims, who in an odd moral juxtaposition complained of their wanton living *and* their successful trading with the area's natives. But Englishmen were setting up all along the New England coast. The ever-resourceful Ferdinando Gorges founded a colony in Maine in 1622–1623, and John Mason another to the south in what became New Hampshire, with trading rights that reached to the borders of New France. Meanwhile, the Plymouth community legalized and defined its territory by buying up the shares of the original Plymouth Company stock.

Pictured in tall hats and dark capes, the Pilgrims have been carica-
tured in American folklore as costumed characters who invented the thanks-
giving and turkey tradition. They are so much more important in ways that
mark off the diversity of the early English colonizers and their settlements.
They stand in contrast, for a start, to the avaricious but befuddled early
Virginians, by having a sensible mode of organization and a clear communal
order. The "Godly enterprise" they started in America included the American
Congregational Church that appeared throughout New England with the
Puritan migration of the 1630s.

As they settled in, the Pilgrims encountered area natives, including
the talented and bilingual Squanto (Tisquantum) who was a member of the
Pawtuxet tribe, a part of the larger Narragansett nation. His story is a dramatic
one, unique in some ways but not unlike that of other native intermediaries.
For decades, Europeans had forced or lured natives to Europe to be trained in
European languages as translators in order to return as spokesmen for traders,
settlers, or Christian missionaries. As early as 1605, George Waymouth had
kidnapped five natives and taken them to England. Squanto was one of them.
He returned to New England as a translator with the John Smith expedition of
1613–1614 but was kidnapped a second time by an English trader. He was taken
back to Europe and sold into slavery. Again he made it back to New England,
via Newfoundland, as a guide and translator on one of the era's many exploratory expeditions. Again he escaped and made his way home only to find that
his tribe had been decimated by disease. Squanto then became a close advisor
to the Pilgrims, and, as an intermediary, he helped secure a peace treaty with
local sachem (chief) Massasoit. He also showed the English the best places to
build weirs for fishing the streams and how to plant, tend, and harvest corn.
But as he tried to navigate between two cultures, he ran afoul of Massasoit
when he sided with the English in an alleged native plot. Before he died in 1622,
Squanto reconciled his differences with Massasoit, but his troubled experiences
linger as evidence of the way native translators and diplomatic intermediaries
often ended up with no clear place in either world.

Meanwhile, the fate of Squanto's people was repeated countless times
before and during the contact era. Governor Bradford's *On Plymouth* contains
a description of the impact these epidemics had on local native towns. On a
trip to pay tribute to the local sachem Massasoit, Bradford notes:

> They [an expedition of Pilgrims] found…the people not many,
> being dead and abundantly wasted in the late great mortality
> which fell in *all* these parts about three years before the com-
> ing of the English, wherein thousands of them died. They not
> being able to bury one another, their skulls and bones were found

in many places lying still above ground where their houses and dwellings had been, a very sad spectacle to behold.

The Mayflower Papers (New York: Penguin Books, 2007), 19 (emphasis added).

After 1630, Plymouth was overshadowed by its neighbor, Massachusetts. The 400 or so Pilgrims of 1630 were immediately outnumbered by the first few shiploads of Massachusetts Bay immigrants, and, by 1640, the latter's population, including Maine, was nearing 10,000, compared to Plymouth's 1,000 people. Massachusetts hemmed in Plymouth as it came to dominate New England by the second half of the seventeenth century. When Plymouth was finally absorbed into Massachusetts in 1691, the latter's population was seven times greater than Plymouth's. Unlike Plymouth, the Massachusetts Bay colony was intended to be more than a refuge. Its "errand into the wilderness" was more ambitious than what the more parochial Pilgrims had in mind, and, when the Puritans arrived in New England in 1630, John Winthrop's idealized "city upon the hill" announced the arrival of a special Christian mission to New England.

PURITANS

The term "puritan" with an upper or lower case "p" was used in the sixteenth century as an epithet for the "precisionists" who sought to expunge the residual Catholic customs from the Church of England. Unlike the Pilgrim Separatists, the Puritans were committed to change from within. Also, in England, the movement was not isolationist in the way the Separatists tended to be but increasingly attached itself to Parliament and its growing conflict with the Stuarts. Indeed, Parliament's triumph in the English Civil War in the 1640s was achieved with the support of an intensely religious rank and file that had been around for decades. English Calvinism had also become a highly politicized revolutionary ideology that went beyond a program of church reform. Ironically, the most extreme English Puritans did not make their way to America but stayed and appeared as "Levellers" in the war-torn England of the 1640s. These radical egalitarians sought the dismantling of hereditary privilege based on property, the end of the nobility and monarchy, and universal manhood suffrage. Before that, however, after Charles I became king in 1625, some groups of dissenters chose voluntary exile to Massachusetts.

In 1629, Charles I granted the Massachusetts Bay Company a charter. This disaffected Church of England group, a persistent nuisance to the church hierarchy, decided to move to America, to the open stretches of the older

Plymouth Company grant. The Stuart King was happy to see them go. Unlike the Virginia Company of London, the Massachusetts Bay Company did not retain an English headquarters and the charter, in effect the legal authority of the company, went to America with the first group of migrants under the terms of their organizational purpose, the Cambridge Agreement of 1629.

With that group was John Winthrop (1588–1649) the company's governor or deputy for most of its formative years. The son of a middle-class family, Winthrop was educated at Cambridge and trained for the law at Gray's Inn. He was a "commoner" in the sense that he did not possess a title, but his father was a successful landholder, and Winthrop himself was a lawyer and member of a growing professional English "gentry" class. He was a writer of great clarity and his journals, edited and published under a variety of titles over the years, stand with William Bradford's and John Smith's histories as the most important personal accounts of the first settlements of English America. Winthrop's ruminations allow us inside the mind of a committed Puritan ideologue during the founding period of the Massachusetts experiment and combine diary, history, and policy, all set in deeply Christian themes.

In 1630, two fleets, one of four vessels and one of seven, carried 700 Puritans, mostly in family units, to New England. They brought with them a settlement model that blended community with ecclesiastical discipline. Covenants marked the company's social design so that communities would be held together by collective agreement. There would be no repeat of the Jamestown fiasco at either Plymouth or Massachusetts. The Massachusetts Bay Company established a string of settlements along the coast from Plymouth to Salem and then proceeded to settle inland. The civil authority consisted of a governor and assistants in a legislative body, the General Court. Representation was restricted to church members, so-called freemen, until participation was expanded in 1664 to include "polls," that is, taxable men. The early restriction technically violated the charter but was applied in any case because the magistrates had the charter in their possession and controlled its implementation. Towns were established once a church was authorized. These towns were ordered to send representatives to the General Court initially to receive instruction and advice, but, over time, brought local issues to bear on the General Court. Still, the General Court maintained considerable taxing authority over the towns.

The New England town was a combination of congregation, family farms, and a local political unit functioning in the "town meeting." Major tracts of land were distributed to groups rather than individuals. A congregation, quite simply a covenanting group, was granted a large section of land for a church and residential settlement. The larger grant was then subdivided into lots that varied in size according to the status of the recipient. The stated religious objective of the Massachusetts Bay Company was maintained in a model that combined spiritual conformity with civic order, to ensure harmony and permanence. There was no cash crop and no precious minerals. Settlers were granted enough land, in fee simple title (effective ownership) to optimize their material needs, with enough land in reserve for the next generation. Treaties with natives were originally designed to separate large parcels from traditional native use. Over time, the steady pressure of English settlement pushed native groups into narrower and tighter spaces. At the start, settlers made a conscious effort to replicate the *idealized* English village setting: a commons and small home lots clustered around the meeting house, with larger acreages farther out but within the surveyed bounds of the town.

All this was anticipated in Winthrop's famous sermon *A Modell of Christian Charity* given on the flagship *Arbella* as it approached the New England shore. The essay is rightly noted for its stress on the spiritual "mission" ("we are entered into a covenant with Him") but it is just as sociological. First, Winthrop reminded his fellow voyagers that "God almighty in His most holy and wise providence, hath so disposed of the condition of mankind, as in all times some must be rich, some poor, some high and eminent in power and dignity, others mean and in submission." (See the modernized version in *Classics of American Political and Constitutional Thought*, 13–18.) Winthrop was no egalitarian. Indeed, he brought several servants with him to Massachusetts, as did others. A third of the Pilgrims had come with servants. Winthrop's point was that the obvious social conditions of the age were the result of God's will. But then Winthrop enjoins his audience to understand that "every man might have need of others, and from hence might be all knit more nearly together in the bonds of brotherly affection." Here, Winthrop appeals to the need for the stabilizing social effects of neighborliness. He warns of the dangers that await the fragile community in New England and leans heavily on the need for togetherness with phrases such as "make others' conditions our own" and "delight in each other" and "mourn together, labor and suffer together, always having before our eyes our commission and community as members of the same body." God would then "delight to dwell among us." The great flourish near the end of the sermon sets the mission in grandiose terms:

> We shall find that the God of Israel is among us when ten of us shall be able to resist a thousand of our enemies; when He shall make us a praise and glory that men shall say of succeeding plantations [settlements], "may the Lord make it like that of New England." For we must consider that we shall be as a city upon a hill... So that if we deal falsely with our God in this work

we have undertaken, and so cause Him to withdraw His present help...we shall be made a story and by-word through the
world.... We shall shame the faces of many of God's worthy
servants.

One of the great American aphorisms, "the city on the hill," drawn from
the Gospel of St. Matthew's Sermon on the Mount is lodged in that sermon.
So too is a grand vision, a subjective importance, and, perhaps, a great deal
of optimism. The model blended communal need with self-interest; it asked
for altruism and put the onus on individuals to adhere to it. The harmony that
Winthrop pleaded for would hold in Massachusetts even as time and circumstance modified the experiment.

By 1633, two important ministers had come to stay in Massachusetts:
John Cotton (1584–1652) and Thomas Hooker (1586–1647). These activists
helped establish theological conventions based on the tenets of a century-old
Calvinism. The key to the doctrine was the notion of fundamental human
depravity, the "fall" from grace, and "predestination," the fact that God had
determined those to be saved, even before the creation of the earth. Christ
had died *only* for the elect, and, because only God could regenerate the sinner,
good works were irrelevant. In Calvinist thought, a saint, that is, one of the
elect for whom salvation was predestined, was always a saint. Once grace was
recognized it could not be taken or given away. The community of dissenters,
fleeing from Church of England imperatives and intolerance, was early on
administering its own hard doctrines. Massachusetts spread territorially as
its population grew. This growth affected the doctrinal ambitions of the magistrates (the leaders and churchmen), and, over time, the theological rigidity
of the leadership was modified. The town, as a social and political unit, was
a fixture. The initial design held, and the town defined Massachusetts society
throughout the colonial period.

GROWTH, DISSENT, AND WINTHROP'S LEGACY

Within a decade of their arrival, Puritans in Massachusetts had established
35 congregations in some 30 mostly agrarian towns of varying sizes. The communities on the immediate shoreline combined farming with maritime trade
and fishing. Some of the town grants were as large as a few hundred square
miles and others, a mere thirty or so square miles. Most were about 100 square
miles, and, over time, larger grants were subdivided into two or more towns
as populations increased and new congregations formed out of older, larger
ones. As noted, the plan was to have so-called home lots for housing clustered
together near the church and meeting house and a main farm lot farther

out. The congregations quickly cleared land, erected simple dwellings, and acquired plows, rakes, hoes, and rudimentary furnishings. Within a generation, families were living in improved housing away from the "commons" on their larger lots. This dispersal allowed individual families some day-to-day privacy for the family unit but did not weaken the town meeting's vitality, and regular church attendance ensured social as well as instructional consistency.

The "Great Migration," which included and followed the Winthrop settlers, spurred the number of new town grants. In England, bad harvests, rising landlessness, religious and political disorder, civil war, and the Cromwell Protectorate of the 1650s resulted in the migration of some 220,000 people (about 4 per cent of the English population) between 1630 and 1660, a substantial number of which left in the 1630s. Large numbers were drawn to the Caribbean and Chesapeake as servants, and many Puritan-leaning families of various economic means were naturally drawn to New England and by the Massachusetts Bay Company. By 1640, the population of Massachusetts Bay and Maine was 10,000.

The decade of the 1630s was also marked by disputes over church and theological matters. The General Court established a college in New Town (Cambridge) in 1636 to train ministers. It was named for a benefactor, John Harvard, shortly after his death in 1638. Over time, the school became an important institution of classical learning, but, in the short term, it served to parallel the colony's own Christian mandate. It also responded to the Puritan priority of having a literate community. Although Winthrop and the magistrates sought to control the colony's development, there was never any chance of a full-blown theocracy, in large part because of the charter's political specifications. Moreover, the practical necessity of establishing a sustainable economy engaged the population in ways that moderated the magistrates' oversight of everyday matters. Nevertheless, the colony's leaders did push their versions of church orthodoxy and their presumed supervisory role in the spiritual lives of the people. But there were flaws in the façade of orthodoxy. Roger Williams (1603–1683) arrived in the colony as John Cotton's friend. The men soon parted ways. As minister in the Salem church, Williams immediately questioned the civil authorities' attempts to control the forms and content of worship and, in 1635, was summarily banished from the colony. Williams's view of Congregationalism was open and liberal. To Winthrop and others, that approach constituted political defiance. As John Cotton became more committed to a fusion of political and church authority, his eyes were closed to any form of spiritual pluralism. Williams's views went in the other direction. When he left Massachusetts he took his theories with him, purchased land from natives, and founded a settlement at

Providence in what would become Rhode Island. A faction had broken away within a few years of settlement. Ironically, after dissenting from the Church of England's orthodoxies, the New England Puritan leadership had discovered its own problems with dissent and the need to suppress it.

Another important challenge to Massachusetts's authority came from the remarkable Anne Hutchinson (1591–1643) who went even further than Roger Williams in offending the magistrates. She was a self-directed, confident female with an outstanding intellect who challenged the orthodox theology promoted by male clerics in a male-dominated world. Her case exposed the potential strains inside the holy utopia. She arrived in Massachusetts with her husband in 1634, already in her early 40s. She had 15 children, was a busy and popular midwife, and shortly became well known in what was still a close-knit community. She was audacious in her rejection of the way predestination was explained in Massachusetts and criticized the colony's leadership for stressing artificial "good works" over simple faith. She argued for a more personalized relation with God in which each practicing Christian could reach God and seek salvation through a faith-based "covenant of grace." Her denial of the Calvinist imperative was bad enough, but her promotion of an alternative approach was akin to heresy. She had crossed a line by not conforming to *official* Puritanism. That meant she was guilty of "antinomianism," meaning that she rejected a moral law as defined by the Massachusetts magistrates. She had presumed to teach a radical theology in meetings in her home that had been attended by men as well as women. Antinomianism became a controversial issue in New England, always suggesting dissent of the magistrates' theological dictates.

Hutchinson was charged with sedition, having gone so far as to accuse the Massachusetts clergy with engaging in a "covenant of works." She charged the clergy with pushing the rule of obedience as a moral imperative with political ends. Her emphasis on a "covenant of grace," which allowed the individual to find a personal relationship with God through Jesus was anathema to the Massachusetts leadership. Hutchinson's logical, emotional, and spiritual integrity actually threatened Winthrop's model of orthodoxy. The arcane detail in these disputed matters was supremely important to that generation of Christian thinkers and especially to Puritan perfectionists. The interpretations came from places deeply embedded in scriptural reference. At first, John Cotton and others had indicated support for Hutchinson, but, in a lamentable act of retraction, Cotton moved with Winthrop and the others to condemn her.

On the face of it, Hutchinson was not persecuted specifically for being an outspoken woman. Indeed, women, although technically subordinate in legal as well as church status, were understood to be capable of having grace. Yet, in a revealing way, Hutchinson's gender did play a part in her fate. At her trial, the prosecution's case focused on her "heresy" and her encouraging of "lewdness" by having men and women together at her Sunday meetings. It also attacked her for stepping outside her role as a wife and mother. Her response was neither docile nor contrite. During Winthrop's interrogations and accusations, Hutchinson's testimony was firm, intelligent, and defiant. In the end, she was found guilty of breaking the law and violating the edict of St. Paul that stipulated that women should not preach. This was no doubt a show trial and a grim bit of theater, and Winthrop had his way. But by any standard of English jurisprudence, the trial was as much an ideological, clerical persecution as a formal litigation.

The guilty sentence of the "court" was inevitable, but the authorities did not rest there. Hutchinson had attended the birth of the badly deformed, stillborn child of her friend and fellow radical Mary Dyer, who would later convert to Quakerism and, as we shall see, run afoul of Massachusetts authorities two decades later. The stillborn child's appearance was used to suggest an association with the devil with an obvious inference of witchcraft. In 1638, Hutchinson was banished and moved with her family to Rhode Island. She later moved to Long Island and then to the present environs of New York City, where she was murdered by natives in 1643. What her experience and the Williams episode reveal is that, although the basic lines of religious and civil order remained in Massachusetts, they were challenged. The New England frontier allowed for an escape hatch for dissenters and Puritan liberals. In Massachusetts, towns continued to spread outward from the Boston hub, but settlements were now being founded outside Massachusetts's jurisdiction, especially in Connecticut and Rhode Island.

By the mid-1630s, three colonies had been chartered, Virginia, Maryland, and Massachusetts, and, by 1650, the English were everywhere on the eastern seaboard of North America. In New England alone, along with the Plymouth colony, there were permanent communities in Connecticut, New Hampshire, Rhode Island, and Maine. Elsewhere, trade and fishing outposts dotted the coastlines from Newfoundland to the Caribbean. The English were in North America to stay. But so were the French to the north and the Spanish to the south and west. In the 1620s, the Dutch and others also set up formal colonies and carved out claims in eastern North America and the Caribbean. Native peoples were drawn deeper into European ambitions and confrontations.

Like all Christian settlers in all the Americas, the Puritans assumed spiritual and cultural superiority and a right to the land they occupied. In 1636–1637, New Englanders found that their assumptions were not shared. The natives of southern New England, depleted in numbers and, in some cases, still confused over the purposes of permanent English communities, began to question the intrusions. They protested and then resisted the spread of English farms. In 1636, armed English militia attacked a Pequot group to avenge the murder of a white trader. The Pequot retaliated with attacks on white settlements that led, in the summer of 1637, to militia from Massachusetts, Plymouth, and Connecticut destroying the main Pequot village near New Haven and slaughtering most of the survivors. The Pequot War was ostensibly a case of a violent quid pro quo, but its roots were deeper and more complex. Natives were conscious of the erosion of their traditional hold on the land and of the cultural bullying that went with white expansion. An issue as simple as an English pig running through a native corn patch became a clash of cultures. The Pequot affair rang a warning bell about the potential insecurity of the English settlements in the region. It also reinforced English notions of native savagery, even as it evinced and encouraged English savagery.

In addition to the problems with natives, New Englanders in the late 1630s and early 1640s were very much aware of the Dutch presence immediately to the south and west of them. From Long Island to the upper Hudson, Dutch settlements appeared to be a greater impediment to expansion than were the French farther north. With the shock of the Pequot "uprising" still resounding through the settlements, and conscious of their imperial neighbors, Massachusetts, Plymouth, Connecticut, and New Haven created a union in 1643. It was known variously as the United Colonies of New England or the New England Confederation and lasted until 1684. Its effectiveness was limited by the retention by each member of its own ultimate authority. By agreeing only to a limited union, a conditional defense compact, each New England settlement jealously protected its political autonomy.

The founding and settling of Plymouth and Massachusetts were models of order and competence in comparison to the mess at Jamestown. But each of the early colonies and non-chartered settlements experienced a sharp lesson in the realities of colonization. Whatever was intended or expected by the early groups was subject to internal strain, environmental correction, and unanticipated violence. The futures of these colonies was planned in England but ultimately determined in America. After two generations, there appeared in mainland North America several quite distinct English communities, all coping with their necessary adaptations to the realities of colonial enterprise.

Table 3.1   The Thirteen Mainland Colonies—Settlement and Charter Dates of the English Colonies in North America

ORIGINAL 13 COLONIES	DATE AND TYPE OF CHARTER
Virginia	1606–Company Renewed 1609; 1612
Massachusetts	1629–Company
Maryland	1632–Proprietary
Connecticut	1662–Self-Governing (Royal approval)
Rhode Island	1663–Self-Governing (Royal approval)
North Carolina	1663–As part of Carolina Proprietary Charter
South Carolina	1663–As part of Carolina Proprietary Charter
New York	1664–Proprietary
New Jersey	None
Delaware	1682–Proprietary (part of Pennsylvania) Separate assembly in 1701
New Hampshire	1679
Pennsylvania	1681–Proprietary
Georgia	1733–Trustees

Source: Adapted from Jeffrey Morris and Richard B. Morris, eds., *Encyclopedia of American History*, 7th ed. (New York: Harper Collins, 1996) and Thomas L. Purvis, *Almanacs of American Life: Colonial America to 1763* (New York: Facts on File, 1999).

PERMANENT EUROPEAN SETTLEMENT OF AREA	DATE OF ROYAL CHARTER	STATUS IN 1776
1607	1624	Royal
1630 *	1691 *	Royal
1634	-	Proprietary
1635 **	-	As in 1662
1636 ***	-	As in 1663
1653	1729	Royal
1670	1729	Royal
1614 (Dutch)	1685	Royal
1624 (Dutch)	1702	Royal
1631 (Dutch)	-	Proprietary
1623	1679	Royal
1681	-	Proprietary
1732	1752	Royal

*   Plymouth—Founded without a charter and settled in 1620; absorbed by Massachusetts in 1691.

     Maine—Much of the territory was also claimed by France; settled without a charter in 1623; chartered to private interests in 1639; purchased by Massachusetts in 1677.

**   New Haven—Settled in 1638; absorbed by Connecticut in 1665.

*** Rhode Island—Originally a cluster of settlements that combined in 1644 under a charter granted to Roger Williams; formal charter was issued in 1663.

SUGGESTED READINGS

K.R. Andrews, N.P. Canny, P.E.H. Hair, eds., *The Westward Enterprise: English Activities in Ireland, the Atlantic, and America, 1480–1650* (Liverpool: Liverpool University Press, 1978); J.H. Elliott, *Empires of the Atlantic World: Britain and Spain in America, 1492–1830,* cited previously, and James Axtell, *Beyond 1492: Encounters in Colonial America* (New York: Oxford University Press, 1992) deal with the era of early English colonization experiences. Garrett Mattingly, *The Armada* (Boston: Houghton Mifflin, 1959) is not only a compelling account of the event but sees the Anglo-Spanish conflict as a spur to English Atlantic policy. The best source for the Hakluyt papers is E.G.R. Taylor, ed., *The Original Writings and Correspondence of the Two Richard Hakluyts* (London: The Hakluyt Society, 1935). The background to Hakluyt's Elizabethan environment is found in Peter C. Mancall, *Hakluyt's Promise: An Elizabethan's Obsession for an English America* (New Haven: Yale University Press, 2007). Karen Kupperman, *Roanoke, The Abandoned Colony* (Totowa, NJ: Rowan & Allenheld, 1984) remains the best short introduction to Roanoke. Interpretations of the early English colonization experiences abound. Among those recommended are Francis J. Bremer *John Winthrop: America's Forgotten Founding Father* (New York: Oxford University Press, 2003) for its emphasis on Winthrop's influence in defining English America and James Horn, *A Land as God Made It: Jamestown and the Birth of America* (New York: Basic Books, 2006) which revises some earlier treatments of Virginia's origins as does Karen Kupperman, *The Jamestown Project* (Cambridge, MA: Belknap, 2007). A welcome comprehensive anthology of contemporary writings is James Horn, ed., *Captain John Smith: Writings with Other Narratives of Roanoke, Jamestown and the First English Settlement in America* (New York: Library of America, 2007). Horn has included excellent reproductions of John White's paintings. Another stimulating view of the Chesapeake settlements is David B. Quinn, ed., *Early Maryland in a Wider World* (Detroit: Wayne State University Press, 1982). Sumner Chilton Powell, *Puritan Village: The Formation of a New England Town* (Garden City, NY: Doubleday, 1965) postulated the thesis that the British sought to replicate their social and economic agrarianism in New England. This book led to an explosion of local studies in colonial American social history with a strong emphasis on the New England town. See the reference to the monographs by Cook, Greven, Lockridge, and Zuckerman in the suggested readings at the end of Chapter 7. John Demos, *A Little Commonwealth: Family Life in Plymouth Colony* (New York: Oxford University Press, 1970) is a sharply observed study of the communal nature of New England's first permanent settlement. Migratory patterns are treated in a variety of ways and the following is recommended: Alison Games, *Migration and the Origins of the English Atlantic World* (Cambridge, MA: Harvard University Press, 1999). This is a detailed description of the mostly Puritan migrants who went to New England and the West Indies after 1630. The demand for labor throughout the colonial period is dealt with in David W. Galenson, *White Servitude in Colonial America* (Cambridge: Cambridge University Press, 1981) and the older but still useful Marcus Jernegan, *Laboring and Dependent Classes in Colonial America, 1607–1783* (New York: Ungar, 1931). A vivid and engaging picture of life in seventeenth century Chesapeake is recreated in John Barth's picaresque novel *The Sot-Weed Factor* (Garden City, NY: Doubleday, 1960) written in the literary style of the seventeenth century.

Time Line

CHAPTER 4

* * * * * * ★ * ★ * * * * *

The Growth of New England and the Chesapeake

1650–1700

Whereas the most wise & holy God for severall yeares past hath...chastized us...to be effectually humbled for our sinns to repent of them and amend our wayes; hence it is the righteous God hath heightened our calamity...and given commission to the barbarous heathen to rise up against us.

—Preamble of an act of the Massachusetts General Court, November 1675, explaining the reason for the outbreak of King Philip's War.

Bee itt Enacted...That all Negroes and other slaues [slaves] already within the Province...and hereafter imported...And all Children born of any Negro...shall be Slaues as their ffathers were for the terme of their liues [lives].

—Maryland General Assembly, *An Act Concerning Negroes & Other Slaues*, 1664.

Massachusetts: Adaptation and Growth

The Massachusetts Bay enterprise was the most self-conscious of the early chartered communities. It wasted no time in defining itself, and the clearest example of the Puritans' rush to record the mission is Winthrop's journal of 1630–1649, including his *History of New England*. Sermons were published with an eye to posterity, and descriptive letters flowed across the Atlantic to England, describing the new Zion. There was promotional literature too, and William Wood's *New England's Prospect* of 1634 is a lively celebration of New England's condition and potential. One of the most important of the era's chronicles is Edward Johnson's *Wonder-Working Providence of Sions Saviour in New England* (1654), an often polemical account of the founding and growth of the colony and of its special place in God's design. On a more prosaic level, ordinary settlers began to project their own self-conscious meaning into Massachusetts's future, for example, in the way they named their children. Most children were given scriptural or other popular names, but there was also a pattern of symbolic naming. One finds in the records female names such as Patience, Prudence, Thankful, Expedience, Charity, Waitstill, Mercy, Submit, Deliverance, Experience, Amity, Mindwell, Silence, and Remember. Male christenings included Preserved, Consider, Hopestill, Recompence, and Increase. These have a particular New England quality.

Children's names notwithstanding, the projections of the first two generations created a rather closed civil society sustained by both the town polity and the moral and spiritual imperative of the Congregational Church. Population grew quickly from the start, however, doubling every generation and leading to the creation of more congregations, more towns, and more cultivated land. All of eastern and southern New England was transformed as forests were thinned and planted with English crops; older native pastures were occupied by English sheep, swine, and cattle; coves, natural harbors, and riverbanks were converted into permanent fishing communities. The simple huts and lean-tos of the first settlers gave way to more substantial houses that suited the climate. Brick public buildings appeared. Decent roads appeared, linking the towns, some of which, on the coast and inland, exceeded 1,000 inhabitants. By the end of the seventeenth century, Boston emerged as a vital Atlantic port with a healthy, locally owned shipbuilding industry and a significant merchant class whose affairs took them into the Atlantic and the New England hinterland. Breweries, distilleries, sugar refineries, and other manufactories flourished in a very compact urban space. By the end of the century, Massachusetts was home to 60 per cent of New England's 100,000 people.

Map 4. 1 Population Distribution in Colonial British North America:
1650, 1720, and 1750

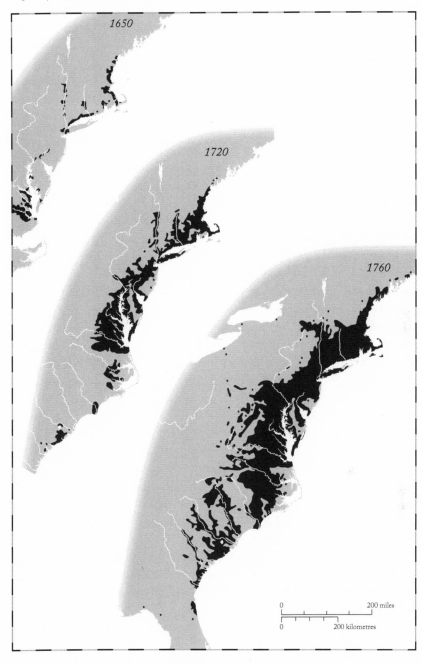

Growth and time affected the original Puritan mission in Massachusetts, for the most part by simply scattering the population farther away from the control of the Boston magistrates. The local, everyday preoccupations of the towns and local congregations moderated the doctrinal ideals of the "holy commonwealth." Historians have used the term "declension" to describe the gradual easing of the founders' social and spiritual control over the population, especially after 1650. Certainly, there was an outpouring of "jeremiad" sermons and editorial literature from the colony's leadership lamenting the apparent decline of the missionary zeal of the founders. The jeremiad sermon survived as a literary form well into the eighteenth century. A poor harvest, a native uprising, a war with France, an epidemic of influenza or smallpox, a questioning of authority (as in the Hutchinson case) could be taken as a sign, as Winthrop had threatened, of God's abandonment of the mission. The necessary easing of the conditions for church membership to accommodate a far-flung and growing population was also interpreted as decline by a theologically reactionary minority.

In most respects, however, over the course of the seventeenth century, Massachusetts retained a great deal of its Calvinist mandate. Change indicated adjustment rather than failure. A social, religious, and economic conservatism prevailed in the colony and in most of New England. The Congregational Church remained monolithic down to the 1690s and dominant to and beyond the Revolution. Strict Calvinist predestination theory relaxed as the church and its doctrines adapted to natural increase and immigration. The core group of 1630 had controlled the small original community, but social and religious cohesion would have to be maintained in a different way as the century wore on. The inevitable reforms of the 1660s, instigated by the "halfway covenant," led to salvation becoming universally attainable. We do well to remember that Puritanism never represented a completely static theological instrument or intellectual doctrine. It was a reformist way of dealing with the intersections of politics and ecclesiastical and social norms. Those who came to Plymouth and Massachusetts were in the process of defining their purposes and their methods of practicing Christianity. Even though dissidents were unwelcome and the maintenance of order was a priority in early Massachusetts, logic insists that change was integral to the tradition of Protestantism and that Massachusetts adapted to necessity and opportunity, adjusted to growth and complexity, and modified Winthrop's Zionist vision to suit reality.

From the beginning, for all the high purpose and aggressive optimism of its founders, Massachusetts was very much an experiment in voluntary conformity. The first chink in its façade appeared when the leadership sought to *enforce* conformity. The voluntary departure of Roger Williams and the forced exile of Anne Hutchinson in the 1630s attest to that. If the Puritan collective could be threatened from within, it certainly wanted to avoid external taint. Sectarian discrimination lasted to the end of the seventeenth century. In 1651, three Baptists were hounded out of the colony, and a handful of Quakers were imprisoned and expelled in 1656. The General Court went so far as to impose the death penalty on any Quaker who reentered the colony after being expelled. As a result, two Quakers were hanged in 1659.

Then, the friend and former disciple of Anne Hutchinson, Mary Dyer, was hanged on Boston Common in 1660. Dyer had earlier defied the authorities by converting to Quakerism and reappearing in Boston to challenge the magistrates and Massachusetts law. She was expelled but fearlessly returned to provoke the authorities. The hard-nosed magistrates hanged Dyer as a warning to others. She went to her death serene and unrepentant as a Quaker martyr in America's Puritan community. But Dyer and Hutchinson had already been demonized with vivid if concocted evidence of satanic links. After the Hutchinson trial in 1638, Winthrop had ordered the public exhumation of Dyer's "monstrous birth," the stillborn fetus. It was described as having "a face, but no head...no forehead, but over the eyes four horns, hard and sharp...the nose hooked upward;...between the shoulders, it had two mouths...it had on each foot three claws" (*History of New England*, 314). Winthrop circulated those descriptions, and his use of satanic imagery is a telling example of how a tangible devil could still be a frightening presence in the minds of Puritan leaders.

After the Dyer hanging in 1660, the newly restored Stuarts stepped in and ordered the Massachusetts Bay Company to release any Quakers in custody. But the magistrates continued to exclude Quakers and others from residency and reapplied a corporal punishment law against nonconformists. As early as 1641, the company had yielded to criticism of its policies with its "Body of Liberties," legislation that appeared to soften its penal codes and limit the sometimes arbitrary power of the magistrates. But, in 1646, John Winthrop and the colony's leadership defied criticism of these exclusionary policies and announced that "allegiance binds us not to the laws of England any longer [if we do not] live in England." This was not so much a denunciation of citizenship or a declaration of independence as it was an affirmation of the prerogatives of local authorities far away from English settings. Puritans sought to replicate the English village or, in Boston, the English market town and seaport, but those social and economic models were inevitably modified, by the system of land distribution and the particular functions of the Congregational Church. Moreover, Massachusetts early on claimed a measure of political autonomy under the terms of its charter.

As for the Congregational Church, an agreement, the Cambridge Platform of 1648, was endorsed by the Connecticut settlements and by the Massachusetts General Court. It announced the supremacy of the Congregational model. It emphasized the local authority of each congregation and rejected the hierarchical models of the Church of England and the synod model of the Presbyterians. But, in its own way, it advocated a centralized format for the many individual congregations adhering to Puritan principles. The result was an odd mix of a formal *established* church, with colony-wide authority, alongside local congregations with certain administrative rights. Quakers, Baptists, and others were still excluded, however, and the Cambridge settlement suggested a standardized, mandatory, colony-wide ecclesiology while allowing local control over the choosing, housing, and paying of ministers.

Devolution also extended to civil matters. In 1644, the General Court created a bicameral legislature where the magistrates sat as one body and the deputies, the representatives from the towns, constituted another. Until 1664, the only voters were "freemen," church members as distinct from churchgoers. Church attendance was expected and often enforced, and, as the numbers of churchgoers who were not freemen increased, so did their civil influence in the towns of Massachusetts and elsewhere in New England. Town meetings were attended by taxpayers, whether they were church members or not. In 1647, all towns of more than 50 families were obliged by law to establish schools for the rudimentary education of children, a policy that was intended to ensure scripture readers for the future. A growing population and the spread of new towns demanded some adjustment, however, in the company's regulations and in the church's doctrinal rules.

Perhaps the most controversial and meaningful adjustment made by the Puritan leadership in the seventeenth century was the so-called halfway covenant. It was designed, debated, and adopted between 1657 and 1662 and issued by the General Court in 1664. It attempted to modify the apparent sophistry of strict predestination with an equally sophistic road to salvation. The halfway covenant was well named. What it said was that the children of baptized parents who were not among the elect could be admitted to the church through the baptism process. This apparently reasonable concession by the colony's leadership was in fact brought on by the expansion of the settlements and new congregations. Thus, the system that allowed for common civil rights while insisting on the protocols of a minority was challenged by demographics and geography. The older magistrates, whose number was shrinking relative to the non-elect but observant Puritan majority, were faced with making accommodations in order to maintain their authority.

The decision incurred the wrath of many of the old guard who saw it as a clear sign of the softening of the Calvinist imperative.

THE TOWN

As noted, the town was perhaps Winthrop's and the magistrates' greatest legacy. It was and, in some respects, remains New England's most dynamic institution. The term is an awkward one for today's generations. It was not a series of streets, bungalows, lawns, and subdivisions with a downtown business district, malls, hospitals, and schools. The seventeenth century towns of New England might be all of that today, but most conform to the boundaries of the colonial era, and most retain the civic political institutions of that time. The preindustrial, rural New England town was a defined, legally sanctioned civil community within surveyed boundaries containing a few dozen to two or three hundred families on farm plots of a few dozen to several hundred acres. Town grants had been larger, for the most part, in the early decades of the colony but, over time, approached a fairly common size of about 30 to 40 square miles or 20,000 to 30,000 acres.

Often, a new town was simply hived off from a larger existing one, or the result of social conflict, inadequate church space, or simply the desire to move west, south, or north. Individual family lots were distributed according to status or influence, but they were usually adequate to a family's ability to feed itself and provide some other basic needs, such as fuel, hides, wool, or other fibers. There was common land for grazing. Lots were scattered in a rough pattern to the boundaries of the grant, and, although most towns ended up with a tavern or store, the most common central feature was the church/meeting house, a building where the taxpayers met for civic matters and where the majority attended services and lectures. There were inevitable variations in town size, population, and economy. Topography, soil types, woodlot potential, and the adequacy of river or stream water also varied. There were fishing towns and frontier settlements and port towns such as Boston and Salem. There was usually a mixture of social and economic groups; some families and individuals persisted as political or church leaders, and some were economically better off than the majority.

What all towns had in common, from New Hampshire to Long Island Sound, was integrated political, social, and economic conditions. Most towns gave the *appearance* of egalitarian homogeneity, and, although that was never fully the case, the civil covenant sustained the towns' corporate integrity. Militia training and shared religious, agrarian, and educational habits made for a shared New England culture. It was at the town level that the Puritans' emphasis on individual moral and economic responsibility blended with the communal politics of the covenanted town. Individualism thrived inside a communal setting. That apparent paradox led to a distinctive politics: the individual family was tied to a larger corporation, the town, which in turn was bound to the larger aggregate community. As noted, towns were represented in the General Court. The election of individuals to represent the towns was conducted in the towns. As we shall see in Chapter 7, by the second half of the eighteenth century, there were hundreds of mature versions of those towns in New England.

Greater New England and the Restoration

Until the 1660s, Massachusetts was the only chartered colony in New England, and it remained the dominant jurisdiction throughout the colonial period and beyond. When Roger Williams and Anne Hutchinson fled Massachusetts for Rhode Island, they paved the way for other settlements, some of which refused to join the New England Confederation of 1643, naturally fearing Massachusetts's power. By 1656, the towns of Providence, Newport, Warwick, and Portsmouth had formed a government that allowed for freedom of religious expression, liberty of conscience, and explicit separation of church and state. The future colony of Rhode Island was in the making. Town government and political representation resembled those in Massachusetts, and, although the Congregational Church was dominant, it was not the force it was in Massachusetts.

The area defined by Connecticut was settled by English opportunists along with Massachusetts people seeking to preempt the Dutch. Its first formal governor was Winthrop's son, John the Younger. The liberal-minded Reverend Thomas Hooker influenced the settlements' "Fundamental Orders" of 1639, which formalized a group of semiautonomous towns into a functioning colony with political institutions that resembled those of Massachusetts. Some 15 towns were established in Connecticut before 1660 in the vicinity of the unchartered New Haven colony of 1638. New Haven was especially rigid and limited the franchise to church members. After the royal charter of 1662 created a unified Connecticut, the colony absorbed New Haven in 1665.

Even before the Connecticut General Court successfully petitioned King Charles II to accept a unified Connecticut as "a little branch of your mighty Empire," the intersection of religious and royal authority in England affected New England's development. In the two decades before his execution by Parliament in 1649, Charles I threw English politics into a series of shocks that began with his attempt to control judicial and taxing procedures and ended with the collapse of his regime in the English Civil War.

That was followed by Oliver Cromwell's Protestant republic, which failed and led to restoration of the Stuart monarchy under Charles II in 1660. What followed was a coordinated, focused agenda for English overseas development. New Englanders had openly supported Cromwell's English Commonwealth, and the Restoration gave them pause. Indeed, two of the judges who had sentenced Charles I to death ended up in exile in New Haven when the Stuarts were restored. But most New Englanders recognized the reality of Charles II's legitimacy, and, in rapid, succession the authorities in Rhode Island, Connecticut, New Haven, and Massachusetts all "proclaimed" him "their" monarch between October 1660 and August 1661. This contrition was calculated to appease the new royal regime. Government and legal authority in the various Connecticut, Rhode Island, and New Haven settlements had been *assumed* by settlers but not officially sanctioned by the Crown. But then New Haven was absorbed into Connecticut's 1662 charter, and Rhode Island was chartered in 1663. The Rhode Island charter reflected its society's character and included a guarantee of sectarian "differences...in matters of religion." The General Assembly of Rhode Island was, in effect, a centralized alternative to the previous "federation" of smaller units in the independent towns. Plymouth's status was maintained. In 1677 the old Gorges claim was bought out by Massachusetts and the whole of Maine was formally absorbed into the Province of Massachusetts Bay under the royal charter of 1691. New Hampshire was an informal adjunct to Massachusetts but was separated from the latter to be administered directly by the Crown in 1679–1680.

Between 1664 and 1666 four royal "commissioners" roamed through New England to settle boundaries and record individual oaths of allegiance to the new king. All antimonarchical (that is anti-Stuart) language was withdrawn from official documents, and religious toleration was urged. Rhode Island, Connecticut, and Plymouth complied, but Massachusetts balked and evaded the strict letter of the demands, even when the removal of its charter was threatened. The commissioners instructed all assemblies that political rights and "freeman" status were to be extended to all men with "competent" means in land or other economic activities, an example of the English Crown ordering American colonists to be more liberal. At the same time, the colonies were instructed to comply with the new trade rules being introduced in the Navigation Acts.

The Navigation Acts were at the center of Restoration trade and general colonial policy for America, and the codes included mechanisms for their enforcement. Cromwell had begun the process with the Navigation Ordinance of 1651. After 1660, it became the model for trade regulations under the restored Stuarts. An organized, regulated English Empire was in the making.

Table 4.1 The Navigation Acts and Trade Regulations

NAVIGATION ORDINANCE OF 1651	This was inspired in part by Dutch competition. Under this regulation *most* goods were to be shipped on English or colonial vessels with crews to be composed of a majority of English sailors.
NAVIGATION ACT OF 1660	Here *all* colonial trade was to be carried in English ships and at least three-quarters of the crew were to be English, including the ship's captain. The list of "enumerated" (classified) articles that had to be landed in English or colonial ports included tobacco and sugar.
STAPLE ACT OF 1663	Materials shipped from continental Europe, Asia, and Africa had to go through English ports and then to the colonies.
PLANTATION DUTY ACT OF 1673	This was essentially an anti-smuggling regulation. It imposed a bond on captains of colonial ships to ensure that they would pay duties.
NAVIGATION ACT OF 1696	This established vice-admiralty courts in colonial ports to enforce the regulations. It tightened the earlier acts. If there was a single navigation act that confirmed the British Empire's economic objectives, it was this one. It followed the Glorious Revolution of 1688–1689 as the first important post-Stuart imperial regulation.
WOOLEN ACT OF 1699*	Banned the export of colonial woolen cloth.
HAT ACT OF 1732*	Banned the export of colonial-made hats.
MOLASSES ACT OF 1733	Applied a prohibitive tax on foreign molasses imported into the colonies to protect British West Indian producers.

*The Woolen and Hat Acts were designed explicitly to protect industries in the British Isles.

Source: Adapted from John J. McCusker and Russell R. Menard, *The Economy of British America* (Chapel Hill: University of North Carolina Press, 1985), *passim*.

King Philip's War

Even as the Navigation Acts were raising the British Empire's economic prospects, the marginalizing of native peoples continued apace in New England and elsewhere in the colonies. The 1629 charter had enjoined the Massachusetts Bay Company to undertake missionary work to convert the many small tribes in New England to Christianity. The most persistent missionary was the tireless Reverend John Eliot, who had come to the colony in 1631 and, after 1646, worked among the natives, learning many local dialects and eventually creating an alphabet and publishing a Bible in the Algonquian language in 1661–1663. His approach was an interesting combination of arrogance and enlightenment. He understood the need for most indigenous peoples to live separately and worked to establish about a dozen towns for about 1,000 Christian natives ("praying Indians" and "praying towns"). But the great native uprising of 1675–1676, King Philip's War, shattered Eliot's model and ended any viable native communities in coastal southern New England. John Eliot's "praying towns" had been a success of sorts but mainly from the English perspective. Tensions between a dwindling, desperate native population and the ever-expanding English settlements had grown in intensity. By the 1670s, the number of natives remaining in southern New England was less than 20 per cent of the precontact population. Then, in 1675, one of the most vicious wars in American history broke out in southern New England, shattering the limited native hold on traditional lands.

King Philip's War, so named by the English for the Wampanoag sachem (chief) Metacom, also called Philip, was a disaster waiting to happen. The Wampanoag, Narragansett, Mohegan, Podunk, and Nipmuck nations had been pushed away from their original lands by the steady spread of New England towns. English settlement now ran in an ever-expanding arc from Boston and Plymouth on the coast to the Connecticut River in the west, reaching the Connecticut and Rhode Island shorelines along Long Island Sound. While some land had been formally obtained by treaty from tribal leaders, many traditional hunting, farming, and fishing sites had been simply expropriated by whites. Although the Pequot War of 1637 might be seen as a precedent, the dimensions and severity of King Philip's War went far beyond the scale and shock of the Pequot War.

If there was a single immediate trigger for the war it was the unfortunate experience of John Sassamon, a bilingual native intermediary who was found murdered in the spring of 1675. Sassamon had been involved in a negotiated native disarmament and may have been mistrusted by whites and natives alike. He brings to mind the awkward status of Squanto in 1621 Plymouth. In any case, three natives were tried and hanged by the English for Sassamon's murder, sparking a response from Philip's Wampanoags, who began attacking English towns with a fury that shocked New Englanders. Well-armed Boston and Plymouth militias then attacked Wampanoag towns. Revenge, reprisal, and atrocity were the main features of the conflict, which heralded a yearlong suspension of Puritan social order and the ultimate collapse of native resistance and social viability in southern New England. The war's strategic patterns were established early, when New England militias and native warriors engaged each other in a series of fronts that moved across the New England landscape from south to north and to the west. The conflict was driven into more and more bitterness by reciprocal acts of cruelty against civilians on both sides, brutal acts that stretch credulity. In one particularly bloody episode, an estimated 300 Narragansett women, children, and elderly males were massacred in Rhode Island by a combined militia army of the New England Confederation. Natives also routinely tortured women and children and destroyed whole towns, killed livestock, burned crops and farm houses, and took prisoners. New England militia, sometimes intimidated by native warrior bands, often focused violence specifically on native women and children. The war was also more lethal than earlier colonial encounters because of the extensive use on both sides of newer flintlock muskets. Even though most jurisdictions forbade selling guns to natives throughout the colonies, there were ways of acquiring firearms through illicit trade.

The war produced the great saga of a captured Englishwoman recounted in one of the most important books in New England history, *The Soveraignty & Goodness of God, Together with the Faithfulness of His Promises Displayed; Being a Narrative of the Captivity and Restoration of Mrs. Mary Rowlandson.* She was taken hostage with others from Lancaster, Massachusetts in February 1676 and ransomed in May of that year. Her account of the three months she spent as a captive, on the move, hungry, fatigued, and under constant threat of physical and psychological abuse or death, is a compelling story. Rowlandson's narrative also revealed the desperate plight of the natives who held her and who themselves starved, fell ill, and were under constant threat from angry and vengeful English forces. More to the point, she introduced a literature in the making, the captive narrative as drama and spectacle and proof of Puritan integrity and English resolve. Although there is evidence of many English captives being absorbed into native society and taking up with their captors, the Rowlandson name became a byword for the inherent power of New England's Christian civilization in a war that tested Puritan moral fortitude. Her strengths were ascribed to her background, which, it was assumed, had given her the resilience to endure. The book was promoted anonymously by Increase Mather (1639–1723), a Massachusetts-born Puritan leader, as an example of Christianity's power in adversity. It remains a compelling dramatic account as well as a window into the seventeenth century Puritan mentality.

In the war of attrition during 1676, native warrior groups and their communities were scattered to the west and north and killed off in increasing numbers. Every native success was punished by ruthless militia response. In the end, the native effort exhausted itself, manpower was seriously depleted, and the coalition fragmented. It likely had no chance of success to begin with, given the resources of the New England colonies and the fact that a sizable minority of the native population remained loyal to the English. Native motivation came from a widely felt sense of desperation, of fatalism. The war ended in the Assowamset swamp in Rhode Island with an appalling massacre of natives and the death there of King Philip. His wife and son were sold into slavery in the West Indies, along with a great many other captives. In a symbolic act, the Puritans allowed native allies to behead and quarter Philip's corpse, and the head was displayed on a pike at Plymouth to broadcast his alleged treason.

Mary Rowlandson's story may have been uplifting, but the aftermath of King Philip's War left a scar on the Puritan conscience. A flood of books followed and reminded New Englanders that the savage and primitive behavior usually ascribed to natives had been spectacularly evident in the actions of English people. If Mary Rowlandson's ordeal had shown tough New England fiber, the vengeful brutality of the militia raised questions about the character of Christian New Englanders. The war killed 600 English and 3,000 natives, and the ratio of fatalities to total population makes King Philip's War the bloodiest in colonial history. Some 1,200 houses were destroyed by fire. Over half the towns of New England suffered damage, and 12 were completely destroyed. The monetary costs likely exceeded the gross domestic product of the New England Confederation.

This was a total war that involved the complete human and material resources of each side. The very survival of each was threatened, and the usual restraints of war against noncombatants were ignored. The long-term consequences of the Puritan victory were catastrophic for the demoralized native survivors, whose chance of retaining any semblance of independence was gone. Their presence in New England was diminished. The English communities recovered, were rebuilt, and the expansion of New England continued, although doubts had been raised about the moral superiority of the Puritan mandate.

The Dominion of New England

In the aftermath of the war, Massachusetts's resistance to the Stuart Restoration of 1660 finally caught up with it. Stuart commissioners had been pressing for the end of the original Massachusetts Bay Company charter for years for a variety of what they considered were less than strict interpretations of its mandate. The recalcitrant magistrates finally but reluctantly accepted the resumption of Stuart authority. However, in 1684, they paid for their early defiance with the loss of the 1629 charter. The protests of the Massachusetts General Court went for naught. The annulment of the charter coincided with the death of Charles II in 1685, the accession of James II, and the creation that same year of a revised administrative structure for all of New England. The Dominion of New England was formalized in 1686 and initially lumped together Massachusetts and New Hampshire and then included Rhode Island and Connecticut—followed by a sweeping expansion to include the newer colonies of Pennsylvania, New Jersey, and New York. Of course Plymouth and settlements in Maine also came under its authority. This was a radical departure from the earlier practice of allowing each colony the right to its own administration. The ostensible reason for the dominion was to provide for a more effective military presence in a possible French war and to streamline the enforcement of the Navigation Acts.

To colonists affected by the decision, it was more like a power grab and an attempt to undercut local charter rights. The royal governor of the newly created dominion was the former governor of New York, Sir Edmund Andros, who walked into a storm of anger, resistance, and, ultimately, rebellion. His heavy-handed approach in his new role echoed the arbitrary policies of the Catholic-leaning, anti-Parliament James II. Once again, a Stuart was in the thick of constitutional and religious controversy. Confident of his authority, Andros began reappraising everything within his purview, including the legality of land titles. He wanted to apply "quitrents," that is, payments to the Crown of fixed charges for the use of assigned farm acreages. He went so far as to try to use Boston's Old South Meeting House for Church of England services, and, heaping outrage upon outrage, he also proposed limiting town meetings to one a year and placing local militias under his control. To colonists, these were affronts to their English rights and usurped long-held local prerogatives.

Andros's future in America depended on the ability of his patron, James II, to maintain power in England. But James's ego and his blatant Catholic leanings had sparked a national uprising that deposed him within four years of his accession. The single-minded James allowed the admission of Catholics to high office and formally tolerated Catholics and nonconformists in his "declarations of indulgence." Then, to top it off, in 1688 he fathered a son, a potential Catholic heir to the throne. By the time James's supporters had prosecuted several Church of England bishops for refusing his declarations of indulgence, a major confrontation was clearly in the offing. In late 1688, a group of seven influential political figures, including the Bishop of London, invited William of Orange to lead an army to depose James. William landed with an impressive Dutch army of some 15,000 troops. James was deserted by his senior people and took refuge in France. He returned in 1689 and raised an army in Ireland, but he was defeated by William's forces at the Boyne, near Londonderry, and sent into permanent exile. The so-called Glorious Revolution was secured when William and his wife Mary, a Stuart, agreed to assume the English throne. Mary legitimized the succession, and William became William III. However, in a very important way, a revolution had taken place, as a coda to the events of the Civil War of the 1640s, and Parliament had secured an unshakable role in the constitution. In 1701, it passed a new Act of Succession, which ensured a Protestant monarchy and allowed Parliament a say in the succession.

Andros was deposed as the events in old England reverberated through New England. An enthusiastic armed mob chased Andros into hiding in the Boston fort, charging him with leaning toward a French alliance and a "popish plot." He gave himself up. But even with his reputation damaged, he resurfaced in 1692 as governor of Virginia, under the aegis of his new commander, William III, the man who had displaced his former patron. The much maligned but opportunistic Sir Edmund Andros, despite his humiliation in Boston, emerged as a shrewd bureaucratic survivor in the ashes of the Stuart dynasty.

Salem, Witches, and the New Massachusetts Charter, 1691–1692

The expulsion of Andros did not end late-century convulsions in Massachusetts. These began with debates over the halfway covenant in 1662–1664 and continued with the miseries of King Philip's War, the loss of the original charter, disappointments in the war with France that started in 1689, and uncertainty over the new royal charter of 1691. The Puritan world seemed to be turned upside down, and the century ended with the calamity of the witch hunts and trials at Salem and in other towns. The recorded trial testimonies, in particular, have left a rich record, but a satisfactory explanation for its fearsome intensity evades researchers. This persecution remains one of the most tantalizing episodes in New England's history. On the surface, the story is straightforward: in early 1692, some adolescent girls began accusing some mostly menopausal women of being witches. The numbers of accused grew, and magistrates from the General Court prosecuted dozens of women, in addition to some men, executing 20 for diabolical associations. At least four others died in prison. The devil was assumed to be loose and abetting in the alleged malefactions.

Between 1647 and 1691, episodes of witchcraft in New England resulted in at least 57 trials with several ending in executions. Notably, Increase Mather, then New England's foremost intellectual, published *An Essay for the Recording of Illustrious Providences* in 1684, a compendium of recorded cases of witchcraft in New England. It is written in lurid language describing as satanic behavior conditions that today would be diagnosed as psychotic, deranged, violent, or simply offensive. Increase Mather wrote for a literate, intelligent audience, but we can be sure that the unlettered and illiterate in the population received the same message. In that way, the Salem event is instructive and tells us that witches and witchcraft survived in the folk-beliefs of Calvinist Congregationalists.

There was nothing like this in contemporaneous Christian Virginia. Indeed, although there were scattered witch trials elsewhere in the colonies in the second half of the seventeenth century, only in Massachusetts, and to a lesser extent in Connecticut, did prosecutions persist. The Salem episode is a sorry blip in the sorry history of a species of persecution that murdered thousands of people, mostly women, in Europe during the Reformation. But it is a blip that teases the imagination and cries out for an explanation. How could it have happened in a presumably civilized and rational society? It was not a pogrom against religious dissidents but derived from a belief that Massachusetts had been targeted by the devil. In the end, the victims were put through a harrowing process of interrogation and terror. The chief prosecutors were members of the residual but still powerful class of old-style magistrates, including Increase Mather's son, Cotton Mather (1663–1728). Only when the public and some of the prosecutors recoiled from the proceedings did the trials, convictions, and executions cease. Many of the accusers, prosecutors, and jurors recanted after witnessing the sobering spectacle of hangings and prison deaths, and the magistrates began to question the value of spectral evidence (from disembodied spirits or ghosts).

Of the 24 who died, 6 were men. Nineteen of the accused were hanged, and 80-year-old Giles Gorey (or Cory) was crushed to death for refusing to enter a plea. As noted, at least 4 died in prison, and, in the bizarre atmosphere of fear and uncertainty, 2 dogs were executed. The numbers of accused or "named" beggars belief as the witch hunt went beyond Salem. In a total of 24 towns, some 156 people were accused, and another 250 were under suspicion. Historians have suggested a range of explanations that run the gamut from lead poisoning to socioeconomic divisions in a Salem that was commercial on one side and agricultural on the other. There are theories about the unwelcome appointment of a minister, a simple neighborly dispute that got out of hand, and other sociological, psychological, and political possibilities. Another theory is that the authorities used the accusations as a means to reassert themselves in an era when the older verities were under siege. Why not see the upheavals of war, declension, and the loss of the charter as devil's work? The very abundance of possibilities suggests that no single explanation will do. In 1711, the Massachusetts government reversed the Salem convictions in a belated act of contrition. People found suspected witches or "sorcerers" throughout the northern colonies during the eighteenth century, and, as late as 1787 in Philadelphia, for example, a mob stoned an elderly woman as a suspected witch. The last witch to be convicted, formally, in the British Empire, was tried in Great Britain in 1712.

Salem's painful experience was but one of a series of issues that preoccupied New Englanders. A war with the French was already underway, and trade, civic politics, and the day-to-day economic concerns of farmers and fishers always consumed attention. The status of the Puritan mission was still a topic of concern, and intellectual and theological debates continued even as the Salem episode receded in importance. The errand into the wilderness was not over. The Congregational Church and town model were intact. But New England was no longer the petri dish for experimental Calvinism, and the city on the hill was increasingly more a political and cultural symbol than it was a demonstration of Christian perfection.

The Massachusetts Charter of 1691 came with a royal governor, but the basic political structure remained, with town representation in the Massachusetts Assembly (the General Court) and the governor's council drawn from the assembly. But an important milestone was reached when property qualifications superseded church membership in local politics. The Congregational Church retained its superior position as the established church and was supported by taxes (tithes) drawn from the whole population, regardless of church membership. Still, the way was cleared for sectarian diversity because of the new charter issued by the new English monarch. Massachusetts's claim to Maine was upheld and the inevitable absorption of Plymouth was confirmed. The Dominion of New England was moribund, and the 1660s charters of Massachusetts's southern New England neighbors were reaffirmed. After independence was achieved post 1776, those charters survived by removing the references to England and the Crown. They formed the basis of the republican state constitutions, up to 1818 in the case of Connecticut and to 1842 in Rhode Island.

Virginia after the Restoration

The 1625 "Proclamation Settling the Affairs of Virginia" rationalized Virginia's political status as a royal colony, and tobacco had already promised profit and permanence. The survivors of the London Company debacle were tough, usually English-born gentlemen who saw their futures in land and tobacco. They were joined by ambitious newcomers encouraged by the headright system that offered land to those with means. By the 1670s, in fact, the fertile tidewater land had been taken up, and family dynasties were taking shape. A Virginia version of a ruling class of "landed gentry" was being established, replete with control of the House of Burgesses and with institutional consistency in the form of an established church, the Church of England, and a royal administration favoring planter interests. Junior members extended the reach of the planter class by moving on to land stretching over several parishes and even counties.

At the top of Virginia's wealth pyramid were families such as the Carters. Robert Carter (1663–1732) was born in the tidewater and became known as "King Carter." He was likely the wealthiest man in Virginia when he died. His progeny continued the family's prominence in Virginia affairs. By the time of the Revolution, seven members of the Carter family controlled some 170,000 acres of land in several counties and together owned over 2,000 slaves on several plantations. Throughout the second half of the seventeenth century, the accumulation of increasing parcels of land by family interests had begun to outline Virginia's future. Even when voter eligibility among small landowners passed the 50 per cent mark, the reins of power lay with a minority of wealthy and often interrelated families. Marriages tended to be made within a web of linked family ties. Names like Byrd, Fitzhugh, Lee, Washington, Randolph, and others dominated local politics in separate parishes and counties and especially in the House of Burgesses.

From 1630 to 1660, from a small base, the annual volume of tobacco exports from the Chesapeake had risen by a factor of ten. It then doubled by the end of the century. By 1700, the Chesapeake was shipping 30 million pounds of cured tobacco per annum into the British economy, that is, about 340 pounds for *every* man, woman, and child, free and slave, in Virginia and Maryland. It bears repeating that huge land holdings were useless without the labor to make them productive. The tobacco yields from large acreages demanded year-round gang labor. In January, the seeding of the year's plants began with stooped labor preparing and seeding beds by hand. With wet spring weather, the seedlings were delicately transplanted. Thereafter, as the plants matured, daily hoeing was needed to keep the soil loose. The backbreaking weeding and topping of excessive growth and the vigilance required to remove worms and other parasites wore down all but the hardiest workers.

Harvest time in the fall of the year was even more demanding; each plant stalk needed to be cut, and, when limp, the leaves were gathered up and taken into enclosed curing sheds to be carefully hung before being packed into huge barrels. Those "hogsheads" held 400 to 500 pounds of compacted tobacco leaf. Many were equipped with an axle and could be rolled to the nearest river or bay dock for shipping. In the summer and fall, field hands worked the proverbial sunup to sundown day in exhausting and repetitive chores. Small-scale independent and tenant farmers cultivated small crops of tobacco along with mixed livestock and grain farming. In many cases, these small operators worked alongside one or two servants or slaves. In 1624–1625 a Crown census had identified 40 per cent of the white population as servants. That ratio persisted into the second half of the century. As demand for labor increased, landowners ran into a supply problem. The number of available immigrant white servants fell. Then, the trend to adopt a legalized, codified system of African slave labor began in earnest. By the 1660s, the House of Burgesses had begun to put into law what was already happening in practice. Planters were simply holding on to black "servants" at will.

THE LEGALIZATION OF SLAVERY IN THE CHESAPEAKE

Slavery was defined in a 1661 statute that legalized permanent bondage for blacks, making their status distinct from term-restricted white servitude. Any child of a black mother was automatically considered black, regardless of the father's race, while an interracial child of a white mother occupied an ambiguous status until the beginning of the eighteenth century, when mixed-race children inherited the status of either black parent. Eventually, grandparents and great-grandparents could determine the racial and thus the legal status of a child. Hence the notorious "single drop" principle was in effect by the end of the seventeenth century and affixed permanently to American race relations. Race-specific categories were emphasized in a 1664 Maryland statute, "An Act Concerning Negroes & other Slaves," that read in part

> That all Negroes or other slaves…within the Province, and…[those] hereafter imported…shall serve Durante Vita [for life]. And all Children born of any Negro or other slave shall be Slaves as their ffathers were for the terme of their lives. And forasmuch as divers freeborne English women…to the disgrace of our Nation doe intermarry [that is, have coital relations or have cohabited] with Negro Slaves…the Issue [child] of such

women...shall serve the Masters of their Parents [shall be the property of the master].

Root of Bitterness: Documents of the Social History of American Women, ed. Nancy Cott, 2nd ed. (Boston: Northeastern University Press, 1996), 29–30.

The statute goes on to note that any white woman who "marries" a slave will henceforth become the property of the slave's master. Of note is the term "other slaves," likely referring to natives who, while never a significant percentage of the slave population, could nevertheless be found within the system. Evidence suggests that, although many enslaved natives were prisoners of war, or the offspring of captives, there was likely a frontier trade in kidnapped native slaves. Also, the reference to white women "marrying" slaves was a direct prohibition of interracial sexual relations. Premarital or extramarital sex, usually noted as "fornication," was forbidden in law everywhere in the colonies. In seventeenth century New England, for example, giving birth to a "bastard" could result in hanging. At the very least, the "fornication" of a black male and white female brought shame and ostracism to the woman and the community.

White males, especially masters, were less likely to be harassed, scorned, or punished for copulating with female slaves. Although miscegenation was subject to legal penalties, it occurred on a scale that belied the laws against it or the public reporting of it. In any case, there were precious few women, white, black, or native, in the Chesapeake in the 1660s. Some rough estimates indicate a 75 to 25 per cent ratio of white males to white females in the 1660s, a difference that closed to 55 to 45 per cent by the early eighteenth century.

The early codes led inexorably to an unequivocal definition of legal slavery as race based and to the slave as taxable and disposable property. In a relatively short time, Africans in English America were stripped of their moral, legal, and social identities. Slave *equaled* black, and black *equaled* slave. By the turn of the eighteenth century, slavery was codified everywhere in the American colonies. In 1705, Robert Beverley (ca.1673–1722) an English-born Virginia planter and administrator wrote *The History and Present State of Virginia* in which he summarized the codes:

[In Virginia] Servants they distinguish by the Names of Slaves for Life, and Servants for a time. Slaves are the Negroes, and their Posterity, following the Condition of the Mother, according to the Maxim, *partus sequitur ventrem*. They are call'd Slaves, in Respect of the Time of their Servitude, because it is for Life.

Servants, are those which serve only for a few Years, according to…their Indenture, or the Custom of the Country.…The Male-Servants, and Slaves of both Sexes, are imployed together…in sowing and planting Tobacco, Corn, &c.…Female-Servants [are]…rarely or never put to work in the Ground, if she be good for any thing else.…Whereas on the other hand, it is a common thing to work a Woman Slave out of Doors.

Beverley identifies several characteristics of the origins of the racial divide in the colonial period and later in the independent republic. The term *partus sequitur ventrem* can be understood simply to mean that a child inherits the status of the mother. This matrilineal provision would blend everywhere with Maryland's patrilineal standard to make any child with any African genes a subject of property. Beverley also succinctly notes some useful terminology: "servant" meant a white person on limited term service. "Slave" meant a black person in permanent bondage, as chattel. As Beverley notes, "Slaves are the Negroes, and their Posterity." A few decades earlier the word "servant" may very well have been used equally to describe a black or white person. In fact, by 1655, Anthony Johnson, a black man and possibly a survivor of the 1619 inaugural arrival of Africans in Virginia had been granted 200 acres of headright land because he somehow imported five "servants" who were black. Several other black families joined his small community. He later moved to Maryland, but, when he died in 1669, the Maryland government appropriated his estate and he was retroactively defined as an "alien." Johnson's identity, after his death, had run into the new slave codes. The systematic and legal designation of the black servant as a slave and as property was accompanied by legislated bans on intermarriage.

The practice of race-based slavery did not accompany the English to the Americas; they eased into it over time. The transition from servant to slave for black people took place over several decades. It coincided with the rhythms of supply and demand. Another factor that contributed to the demand for black labor was the difficulty in attracting new white servants into the Chesapeake for fieldwork. By the end of the seventeenth century, the cost of acquiring white indentured servants, either by arrangement with a local master or directly from England, was becoming more expensive than buying black slaves outright, with the slaves and their progeny kept for their lifetimes. What had been a noticeable trend in the 1650s and 1660s became a runaway restructuring of Chesapeake society by the early eighteenth century. The small planter was squeezed to the margins by wealthier landholders who could acquire land, increase their slaveholding, and enlarge their planted acreages. When it became necessary, they moved away from depleted soil to raw and more fertile land on the moving frontier that shifted inland from the tidewater.

In 1650, out of an estimated 18,731 population in Virginia, there were 405 blacks, most of them in an informal, sometimes ill-defined state of permanent servitude. In 1670, there were 2,000 slaves in a population of 35,000. In 1700, of the 58,560 people in the colony, 16,390 were slaves. Over two-thirds of the increase to Virginia's population of 23,000 between 1670 and 1700 was due to slavery. In one especially telling 20-year stretch, 1680–1700, Virginia's total white population declined slightly while the black population rose by over 500 per cent. Virginia's black population, which was 6 per cent of the whole in 1670, rose to an astonishing 28 per cent in 1700. It rose to 33 per cent in 1740 and 41 per cent in 1760. In Maryland, the numbers and ratios of blacks to whites were lower but no less significant. By the early eighteenth century, the Chesapeake was socially, economically, and culturally *defined* by slavery; it was, by definition, a slave society. By the middle to late eighteenth century, the trend was duplicated in the tidewater regions of the Carolinas and Georgia. For example, on the eve of the Revolution, South Carolina had a black majority, and, in some tidewater communities, ratios of blacks to whites approached those of the West Indies. All the English colonies adopted racially defined slave codes, but not all were "slave societies." North of the Chesapeake, slaveholding was legalized, but even in places where slaves accounted for over 10 per cent of the population, such as in New York, slavery did not define the society.

The growth of slavery and the reasons for its legalization in English America are among the most active topics in American history. What accounts for the "invention" of slavery in the Chesapeake and elsewhere in the English Atlantic? Did some specifically English form of racism precede the institution? One thing is certain, white planters seemed to prefer white indentured servants, at least up to the time when supply fell behind demand. The so-called origins debate struggles to find explanations for the shift to black slave labor. Historians have taken a longer perspective and noted that, even before the writing of codes, *black* had been used routinely as an identifier. Englishmen had certainly taken part in the Iberian slave trade by the middle of the sixteenth century. Clearly, the English accepted racialism, that is, the assumption of certain biological characteristics based on color. It is hard not to see the English as "racist," in the way the term is used socially and culturally today; but how did perceived racial differences and seeing the differences as black inferiority lead to slavery?

One of the obvious explanations for the origins of English slavery distills into legal opportunism; Africans simply were not protected by church law and without contracts could not be considered subject to common or civil law. In Virginia and elsewhere in the colonies, there was no concerted church opposition to the slave codes, and no legal barriers. In an important extension of legal loopholes, the absence of Christian resistance eased the planters' assumptions of *ownership*, without term, of the black servant. The slave codes, after all, were written to accommodate what was being practiced, black servitude without term. Another explanation notes that, although English settlers were racist, legalized chattel bondage would have been delayed or even avoided without perceived need and a ready supply of slaves. As historian Winthrop Jordan puts it,

> Negro slavery there [in Virginia and Maryland] was neither borrowed from foreigners, nor extracted from books, nor invented out of whole cloth, nor extrapolated from servitude, nor generated from English reaction to Negroes as such, nor necessitated by the exigencies of the New World. Not any one of these made the Negro a slave, but all.

White Over Black: American Attitudes toward the Negro (Chapel Hill: University of North Carolina Press, 1968), 72.

A 1705 Virginia statute decisively stated that "All Negro, mulatto and Indian slaves within this dominion... shall be held as real estate."

As noted, slavery was also codified north of the Chesapeake. During the Pequot War and King Philip's War, Massachusetts authorities had sold native captives into slavery in Bermuda and the West Indies. Indeed, an early legal reference was a Massachusetts law of 1641, which exempted all persons from slavery *except* in the centuries-old tradition of "Captives taken in just warres" and those "strangers [who]... are sold to us." White servants could be "bought" and "sold," but only for the term of service remaining. Even where slavery was banned, in Rhode Island in 1670, for example, the law was ignored. In Massachusetts and other jurisdictions, race-based slavery may have been understood in oblique ways rather than in firm statute law, but it was accepted.

In the cash-crop economies of the Chesapeake and the lower south, the laws were specific and authorities viewed slavery as beneficial. By 1865, when the Thirteenth Amendment outlawed slavery after the Civil War, many in the southern states, after 200 years, still saw it as a "positive good." Logically, institutionalized slavery and the race-based caste system it created in America led, over time, to deeply held white assumptions of black inferiority and degradation. If the biological explanation was not sufficient, then apologists used sociology to make the point. The American tragedy of race, slavery, segregation, and the cultural divide that went with it began with what Winthrop

Jordan called an "unthinking decision," the gradual designation of blacks as slaves and slaves as black. Few slaveholders in the eighteenth century or, for that matter, all the way to the Civil War cared enough to guess at the long-term consequences of institutionalized slavery, and the few who did often saw the institution as too firmly entrenched to be removed.

BACON'S REBELLION

After the first Navigation Acts and the disruptions of the three Anglo-Dutch wars (1652–1654; 1665–1667; 1672–1674), the prices for Chesapeake tobacco collapsed to about a fifth or sixth of their pre-1660 values. They recovered but not before many small planters and tenants abandoned tobacco growing for other crops. Overproduction and competition hit the industry hard. Then, in the early 1670s, disease ravaged cattle herds and a series of servant protests made for more trouble for Virginia's planters and farmers. A common means of raising monies for local and colonial government expenses was the poll tax. This traditional levy was applied to land values, incomes, and assets. In Virginia, it had been suspended during the tobacco boom because excise revenues had been high, but, in the 1670s, the colony needed money for public projects and the House of Burgesses reintroduced the tax. Although some of the voting members of the House felt it in their own pockets, the burden fell heaviest on smallholders. Also, Charles II, in an extraordinary decision, granted proprietary rights of several million acres between the Rappahannock and Potomac Rivers to a court favorite. He followed that with what appeared to be a 30-year grant of *all* of Virginia to two other court favorites. This somewhat ridiculous action was eventually withdrawn. The favorites, however, were given rights to quitrents, a form of tax that could be applied to any colonial land and was payable to the proprietor—a company or the Crown, whoever had distribution rights under the charter. In this case the quitrents were reinstated to the Crown's use in 1684. Before that time, however, confused land deals, shaky economic conditions, and misguided use of royal prerogative in the 1670s aggravated the sour mood of most of the Virginia population, rich and poor. In a further blunder, Governor Berkeley refused to schedule any elections to the House of Burgesses.

Those distempers took a back seat to some frightening events on the frontier, which, in 1675 was still only 30 to 50 miles from Jamestown. Intertribal native wars to the north sent large numbers of Susquehannocks across the Potomac and into Virginia where they attacked white settlements. Efforts by the Virginia and Maryland militias to respond failed, sending shock waves through the region and turning many frontier families into refugees. On one particularly violent day in early 1676, over 30 settlers were killed.

Berkeley was criticized by friend and foe alike for refusing to retaliate. It was suggested, plausibly, that he was afraid to jeopardize his personal stake in the fur trade.

Nathaniel Bacon (ca.1647–1676), a relative of the philosopher and scientist Sir Francis Bacon, was an ambitious, well-connected planter and a member of the advisory Virginia Council. In the wake of Berkeley's prevarications and without formal permission, he raised a small army of disaffected frontier settlers and defeated a Susquehannock army. What followed was the stuff of high drama. Berkeley declared Bacon a traitor and had him arrested for defying the council and fomenting an insurrection. Bacon at first appeared to repent, and Berkeley pardoned him, but in June 1676, Bacon reversed his field and raised another army estimated at 500 men, mostly tenants, former indentured servants, and small landowners. They marched into Jamestown and forced Berkeley to sanction a major campaign against frontier natives. In the midst of the turmoil, land and tax reforms were pushed through the House of Burgesses in an attempt to appease some of the dissenters. Berkeley then denounced Bacon in the name of the King and, for the second time, declared him a rebel and traitor.

By August of 1676, Berkeley was without the means to subdue Bacon, who now had the support of some large planters and launched another expedition against the frontier natives. In September, Berkeley managed to organize a force of armed supporters and verbally reclaimed his authority at Jamestown. The seesaw continued. Bacon's army returned from its frontier campaign and drove Berkeley out of Jamestown yet again and, in a dramatic flourish, burned the town. In October, a full-fledged coup was underway, and, although the longer-term objectives of the rebels remained vague, the affair was threatening to bring the Crown in force to Virginia to prevent what was potentially a collapse of civil order. But then Bacon died suddenly of complications of malaria. His army broke up, and the rebellion fell apart. Berkeley's rejuvenated forces eventually hunted down most of the rebels, and many surrendered on a promise of amnesty. A royal commission from England was sent to investigate the affair and to restore political order. The rebels were pardoned, but Berkeley cavalierly defied the commission's order and had 23 of Bacon's supporters executed. His position was now untenable, and he retired immediately to England where he died the following year.

The Bacon and Berkeley episode allows us to see inside the intense politics of Virginia. It is also a threshold moment in Virginia's evolution from a failed commercial enterprise to the tough planter culture that followed and thence to its confirmation in the wake of Bacon's failure. The chief antagonists in the rebellion were men of good breeding, "well-born" Englishmen. They had the talents and drive suited to Virginia's political environment.

Berkeley had taken up his Stuart appointment in 1642, lost his position in 1652 after the Stuarts had been deposed, but came back at the Restoration in 1660 to finish off his career. He was the governor of Virginia for 27 of his 35 years of colonial service. That in itself is a remarkable record of longevity in the fluid world of early colonial politics. He was privileged, haughty, and arbitrary, and he alienated many of the small farmer "freemen."

In the short term, Bacon's stunning uprising led to a better representation of regional and class interests in the House of Burgesses. But the main characteristics of Berkeley's long tenure remained, however, and, when the smoke cleared, a firmly established ruling class still controlled Virginia's politics. The rebellion revealed the class discords in the society. Bacon attempted to overturn the ruling coterie and its land and frontier policies; he sought to open up Virginia to a more pluralistic politics and a different land distribution policy. Ironically, in the wake of his failure, Virginia adopted the slave-based labor economy that cemented the elite's control of Virginia's future. Although there were a few reforms in its wake, it should be remembered that Bacon's coup failed, and Virginia continued on its route to the hierarchical society it became. Bacon's Rebellion is an important milestone in the shaping of one of the founding cultures of the United States. At a crucial time in the colony's development, there was a serious attempt to change the course of its history. Bacon's failure guaranteed that Virginia would flourish as a highly structured, top-down society, with a secure ruling class.

SUGGESTED READINGS

For a recent study of Jamestown and Virginia's settlement see James Horn, *A Land as God Made It*, cited in Chapter 3. Among the best of an extensive literature on seventeenth century Virginia are Edmund Morgan, *American Slavery, American Freedom: The Ordeal of Colonial Virginia* (New York: Norton, 1975) a superb and original thesis on the origins, history, and effects of Virginia's racial divide and Darrett Rutman and Anita Rutman, *A Place in Time: Middlesex County, Virginia*, 1650–1750 (New York: Norton, 1984) a case study and fine example of social history methodology. A welcome addition to the "origins" debate is Edward Countryman, ed., *How Did American Slavery Begin?* (Boston: Bedford, 1999), a well-designed compilation of the various theories of slavery's American origins. The early chapters in Winthrop Jordan, *White Over Black: American Attitudes toward the Negro, 1550–1812* Chapel Hill: University of North Carolina Press, 1968) after 40 years remain potent in their analyses of racial attitudes in the sixteenth and seventeenth centuries. Wilcomb Washburn, *The Governor and the Rebel: A History of Bacon's Rebellion in Virginia* (Chapel Hill: University of North Carolina Press, 1957) is recommended for its narrative approach. For a provocative analysis of the longer-term consequences of Bacon's failure, see Stephen S. Webb, *1676: The End of American Independence* (1984; repr., Syracuse, NY: Syracuse University Press, 1995). Two anthologies of Puritan New England worth consulting are David D. Hall, ed., *Puritanism in Seventeenth Century Massachusetts* (New York: Holt Rinehart, 1968) a collection of seventeenth century documents and his *Puritans in the New World: A Critical Anthology* (Princeton: Princeton University Press, 2004). The work of the late Perry Miller has influenced two generations of scholarship on American Puritanism, and his theses on Puritan orthodoxy and declension continue to generate controversy. His *The New England Mind: The Seventeenth Century* (Boston: Beacon Press, 1961) and *The New England Mind: From Colony to Province* (Cambridge, MA: Harvard University Press, 1953) are representative of his scholarship and interpretations. An older, short comparative overview of the Puritan phenomenon is Alan Simpson, *Puritanism in Old and New England* (Chicago: University of Chicago Press, 1955). The most recent study of Anne Hutchinson is Michael Winship, *The Times and Trials of Anne Hutchinson* (Lawrence, KS: University Press of Kansas, 2005). Daniel Vickers, *Farmers and Fisherman: Two Centuries of Work in Essex County, Massachusetts, 1630–1830* (Chapel Hill: University of North Carolina Press, 1994) shows the way seventeenth century settlements became engines of persistence and how occupations and the nature of work and economic relations shaped New England society. Of the great many town studies that dominated New England social history for a generation Kenneth

Lockridge, *A New England Town: The First Hundred Years* (New York: Norton, 1970) serves as a general example. William Cronon, *Changes in the Land: Indians, Colonists, and the Ecology of New England* (New York: Hill and Wang, 1983) describes the way the New England landscape was affected by colonization. There is an extensive literature of the Salem episode including some useful recent interpretations, but Paul Boyer and Stephen Nissenbaum, *Salem Possessed: The Social Origins of Witchcraft* (Cambridge, MA: Harvard University Press, 1974) is a fine introduction to the complex and tantalizing phenomenon. A recent treatment of the Salem phenomenon is Mary Beth Norton, *In the Devil's Snare: The Salem Witchcraft Crisis of 1692* (New York: Knopf, 2002). Jill Lepore, *The Name of War: King Philip's War and the Origins of American Identity* (New York: Knopf, 1998) is an interesting analysis of King Philip's War and serves as a good example of the scholarly interest in "history as memory." The book is another illustration of the scholarly habit of seeing "origins" of some aspect of American civilization in every important event. The best single treatment of the impact of the later Stuarts and the Glorious Revolution on New England is Richard Johnson, *Adjustment to Empire: The New England Colonies, 1675–1715* (New Brunswick, NJ: Rutgers University Press, 1981).

Time Line

1625	Death of James I.
1642–1649	English Civil War (first and second armed conflicts).
1649	Execution of Charles I.
1649–1651	English Civil War (third conflict between supporters of Charles II and Parliament).
1649–1660	Interregnum (The Protectorate, 1653–1659).
1660	Restoration of the Stuarts (Charles II).
1652–1674	Dutch Wars (the first through the third).
1664–1681	Creation of colonies in New York, New Jersey, Pennsylvania, Delaware, New Hampshire, and the Carolinas.

CHAPTER 5

* * * * * ★ * ★ * ★ * * * *

The English Civil War, the Restoration, and the First British Empire in America

The great question which, in all ages, has disturbed mankind... and disordered the peace of the world, has been, not whether there be power in the world, nor whence it came, but who should have it.

—John Locke, *Two Treatises of Government* (1690).

The Stuarts, Parliament, and the Temper of English Politics

The creation of permanent English societies in scattered parts of the Caribbean and North America marked a turning point in the history of the British Isles and led the way to a *bona fide* empire in the western Atlantic. But, while the outlines of colonial British America were being traced, an explosive series of political issues shook the British homeland. Early Stuart ideas and policies provoked a string of political crises that culminated in the English Civil War and the trial and execution of Charles I in 1649. Then, in the brief interlude between 1649 and 1660, before the resumption of Stuart rule, Oliver Cromwell's interregnum government fought the Dutch, revised English trade policies, and pulled Scotland and Northern Ireland deeper into the English orbit. After the Stuarts were restored to power in 1660, under Charles II, England embarked on a more aggressive imperialism, especially in America. By the end of the seventeenth century, the Stuarts were gone, again, in the aftermath of the overthrow of James II in 1689. The outlines of the eighteenth century British Empire had appeared. As the number of American colonies increased and the older ones matured, new trade policies were introduced.

When James I died in 1625, he left behind in England a cloud of doubt about his religious ambiguities and his presumption of a "divine right" to rule, shape legislation, and impose taxes if he wished. He had offended Parliament. In foreign affairs, he had allied England to Protestant Holland after the start of the Thirty Years' War in 1618. However, his peace with Catholic Spain as early as 1604 was considered foolish, and his son Charles, by marrying a Catholic Bourbon princess, had linked England's royal family to France. In a variety of ways, James had assumed powers for the throne that were not possible in the England of the seventeenth century. The absolute monarchy of France and Spain was simply not possible in the more open atmosphere of English politics. As the Tudors had shown, the monarchy was a powerful institution with strong constitutional rights, but its authority was tempered by Parliament. Even though political representation was confined to a tiny percentage of the total population, Parliament had achieved a constitutional role that stood as a barrier against autocracy.

The monarchy was certainly capable of engaging popular support for its actions and policies. Elizabeth had offered a model for it, but the Stuarts lacked her flexibility in domestic affairs, her certainty in foreign affairs, and her innate "Englishness." James left his son Charles I, with at least two expectations that were redundant: one, that he could curb Parliament's rising assertiveness and two, that he could stem the growing radicalism of some reform-minded religious groups. By supporting the Church of England's attacks on separatists and reformers, who were mostly Puritans, he ran afoul of many House of Commons members. Charles had substantial support at the highest levels as head of the Church of England, the nation's most powerful institution outside Parliament. Because the bishops who sat in the House of Lords had the ear of the king, as did most of the privileged landed classes, support for Charles's version of the royal prerogative was acceptable to an important stratum of English society. But, in Parliament, a serious division had developed in English politics that made Puritan reform of the church, for example, a form of political opposition.

The rift that had been evident during James's reign opened wider within a few years of his death. In 1629, Charles refused to call a sitting of Parliament. He had a constitutional right to do so, but it had seldom been used. His action aroused open parliamentary dissent, and he responded by refusing to call a sitting of Parliament for over a decade, the so-called eleven years' tyranny. Charles ran government under his executive authority. He enlisted the support of Thomas Wentworth, the first Earl of Strafford (1593–1641), and William Laud (1573–1645), who became bishop of London in 1628 and archbishop of Canterbury after 1633. Strafford was a powerful member of the king's privy council, the administrative precursor of the modern cabinet, in effect the executive body of the realm. In the absence of Parliament, the Charles, Strafford, Laud triumvirate was known appropriately as "thorough" government and pushed a royal agenda while marginalizing the petulant opposition of now idle parliamentarians. Together, Charles and his executive sought to "Anglicize" Ireland and enforce the Church of England's singular authority throughout the British Isles. Laud's relentless enforcement of the church's authority and protocols drove many Puritans to emigrate and pushed those who remained to intensify their opposition.

Parliament's constitutional authority to tax was circumvented in 1634 when Charles applied what was actually a legitimate means of raising money for naval expenses: a levy on ports. He then expanded the range of the levy, the "ship money," to include inland towns. The furor this caused bedeviled him for the remainder of his reign even though, in a test case, the courts ruled in favor of his method. It did little to assuage the sour taste his actions left among parliamentarians. In 1639, flawed attempts to impose Laud's church model on the Scots led to two Scottish wars (the "Bishops' Wars"), which succeeded only in emptying the royal treasury. Still, until then, Charles had done reasonably well financially without Parliament. By 1640, however, his administration needed money and recalled Parliament so that it could raise funds through its taxing authority. It met for a few weeks, but the king dissolved it when his requests for funds were made conditional. Parliament wanted redress of its complaints and a contrite Charles. Those were fanciful demands, and, given his abiding hauteur, he was bound to demur. But he was insolvent and was forced to recall Parliament later that year, with fateful results.

To his opposition there was clearly more desperation than equanimity in Charles's decision. In 1640, the personal attacks on him had become loud and constant, and, in 1641, Parliament presented him with its Grand Remonstrance, a list of 204 grievances and demands for reforms to government that would restore Parliament's role and diminish the influence of the church in political matters. Charles rejected the entire list of proposals, which were, in effect, a manifesto of Parliament's rights. The Grand Remonstrance itself and Charles's open contempt for it then became the central points of reference for opponents to the Stuarts. The chief architect of the Grand Remonstrance was the Puritan, John Pym (1584–1643), perhaps the leading parliamentarian of the age, and, now that it was finally in session, Parliament vented the frustrations of a decade. In a controversial demonstration of political revenge, it had impeached Laud and Strafford in 1640 for treason for violating Parliament's constitutional authority. John Pym was the main prosecutor. When the charges of treason were not proven, Parliament used a "bill of attainder," in this case, an order or writ by Parliament, to override the court's decisions, and Strafford was executed in 1641 as was Laud in 1645. In the chaos that followed Stafford's death, Charles attempted to have five members of Parliament, including Pym, indicted for treason, under his version of constitutional protocols. With each part of the government charging members of the other part with treason, a dangerous impasse was reached. The system then collapsed. Government failed.

Charles was not without support. As the majority in Parliament flexed its presumptive rights, the king went off to raise an army to put down what he and many others saw as insurrection. Indeed, what is now referred to as the English Civil War (the first phase, 1642–1646; the second phase, 1647–1649) was known to contemporaries as "the rebellion." It was, in any case, an historic contest between two parts of the national government vying to assert a superior place in what had been a shared sovereignty. Charles's support was largely regional and centered in the north and west. There was some obvious sympathy for the Stuarts among the Scots, but Pym negotiated the support of the radical Presbyterian Covenanters. Later, their "Covenant" was rejected by Parliament's army, which led in a contradictory way to Covenanter support for the Crown in Scotland during the second phase of the war in 1648. Oliver Cromwell waged a relentless campaign against them after 1650, and not until the Glorious Revolution was there a full restoration of the Presbyterian Church and a place for it throughout the British Isles.

Pym also organized loans and designed taxes that boosted Parliament's ability to fund its war against Charles. Pitched battles, sieges, and a gradual wearing down of the royal cause led to a triumph for Parliament. And, although this was a political war with religious undertones and at times quite vicious, it was nothing like the horrors experienced by the civilian populations in the Thirty Years' War on the European continent. The parliamentary cause was bolstered by the crusading zeal and leadership of Oliver Cromwell (1599–1658), whose military skills were as impressive as any in British history, and by Sir Thomas Fairfax. The latter commanded the 20,000-strong New Model Army of 1645, which succeeded the piecemeal militias of the early years of the war.

The New Model Army was large, disciplined, and skilled and became the decisive variable in the war. It outnumbered by two to one a 7,500-strong royalist army at the Battle of Naseby in 1645 and defeated it decisively, ending the first phase of the English Civil War. The New Model Army was also highly politicized, and, at the Putney debates in the fall of 1647, factions within it argued with each other on the revolutionary purposes of the war. For many in the ranks, the war offered the opportunity to reform English society into an egalitarian one rather than simply to assert Parliament's sovereignty. The aptly named "Levellers" in the New Model Army wanted to open up Parliament to wider representation. Other revolutionary groups went even further. The "Diggers," for example, pressed Parliament for the most extreme reform, the redistribution of all land, a truly dangerous proposal to the landed classes who controlled Parliament. But the civil war was not fought to raise the masses to political equality; it was the outcome of a political confrontation that centered on institutional reform and not revolution from the bottom up. In that sense, the objective of the victors was more socially conservative, even if it sought radical institutional reform.

The most sensational event of the war was the trial and beheading of Charles I by a triumphant Parliament. He was caught, he escaped, and was caught again in the latter part of the war. He refused to acknowledge the charges against him, supposing that he would legitimate them if he did, and went to his death unrepentant and with dignity on January 30, 1649. While in prison, Charles wrote, or had written for him, a theoretical justification for his position, *Eikon Basilike,* which has merit as an explanation of his version of royal executive privilege, that the Monarch was ordained by God to rule the nation peacefully for its sake. But events made Charles a loser and his theories of kingship obsolete. His essay was rebuffed by the pro-republican *Eikonoklastes* of John Milton (1608–1674), the great poet and essayist who became a secretary to Oliver Cromwell until, in 1652, blindness overtook him. His aggressive republicanism and connection to Cromwell made his life difficult under the Stuart Restoration, but he managed to compose what is perhaps the most impressive poem in English literature, *Paradise Lost* (1667).

Milton's defense of republicanism, his earlier attack on censorship in *Areopagetica* (1644), in which he excluded Catholics from freedom of speech rights, along with the emergence of Levellers, Diggers, and the ultraradical, theocratic Fifth Monarchy men were all part of a buoyant political culture that had waged a war against a legitimately placed king. The short-term impact of the ideas and upheavals was less revolutionary than it might have been. The war and the Commonwealth of England did not lead to a remaking of English social or electoral standards. Parliament had asserted itself, appeared more potent than ever, and would apply its power again to depose another Stuart in 1688–1689. The death of Charles I marked the first stage of a reform of the mechanisms in English political life. Parliament demonstrated its central role in the constitutional arrangement but then discovered that it could not govern unilaterally. Eventually, the republican experiment failed, and the Stuarts were restored to their executive position in 1660, but a significant shift in the locus of power in England had begun.

Cromwell's Commonwealth and the Protectorate (1653–1660) curbed the extremism of visionaries like Gerrard Winstanley, the Digger and Quaker whose radical egalitarianism frightened Puritans and Royalists alike. The Fifth Monarchy men and their proposed model theocracy went in the other direction, and opposition to it revealed an interesting civil strain in English Protestantism. The Fifth Monarchists had earlier supported Cromwell as "God's instrument," but, after he established the centralized Protectorate with himself as dictatorial Lord Protector, they dropped their support and were hounded to irrelevancy over the next decade. The eleven years from the death of Charles I to the accession of Charles II, part of the "Long Parliament" (1640–1660) inspired thoughtful treatises on civil authority, such as James Harrington's fascinating *Commonwealth of Oceana* (1656). Harrington's utopian political designs on land reform and political separation of powers influenced William Penn and, a century later, the leadership in the American Revolution. The English Civil War inspired other theories, such as Thomas Hobbes's *Leviathan* (1651). Here was a call for a social and political contract that would be impervious to interest or faction. The war had terrified him and others in that it exposed England's need for a restraining agency to prevent power struggles. What he suggested was something like a disinterested king, perhaps, with the means to ensure liberty and security while restraining the "natural" potential for "war of every man against every man."

The humorless Cromwell stifled public entertainments and denounced the popular vestiges of English Jacobean arts and letters. He and his Puritan support in Parliament introduced dress codes and standards of behavior that amounted to moral censorship, as they suppressed the radical left of the Puritan movement. He died, a dour and unfulfilled Christian republican, in 1658, and his son Richard succeeded him, and when Richard died, popular taste for *their* model of executive authority was gone. By then, interest groups inside and outside Parliament sought a return of the monarchy, under suitable terms. The republican experiment seemed out of place and contradicted itself with its top-down authoritarianism. Indeed, the "republic" was one in name only, describing a system without a hereditary monarch. It was not a republic in the full sense of accommodating the pluralistic interests of the population.

But England had been set on a somewhat different future by the events of 1640–1660. An elected assembly that included a large number of commoners had charged a king with treason against the realm, tried him, found him guilty, and had executed him. Clearly, this was a profoundly decisive act and declared Parliament's capacity for exercising its strengths. The Stuarts were restored under Charles II in 1660 to bring efficiency, balance, and familiarity back to government. The term "Restoration" is used routinely to acknowledge the return of the Stuart executive. But Parliament was also restored to its place in the constitution with enhanced confidence and a demonstrated will to act in its own interest.

It might be said that Cromwell squandered a chance to make fundamental changes in England's social structure. But the nation was wary of the radicalism thrown up in the conflict, and those doubts were confirmed by Cromwell's failures in the 1650s. Ironically, Parliament had attacked the Stuarts for their tendency to arbitrary rule, but the Stuarts were restored to curb Parliament's tendencies in the same direction. In international affairs, however, Cromwell's brief rule was a busy one. In 1651, to arrest Dutch expansionism, Parliament passed the first of the Navigation Acts (the Navigation Ordinance), which signaled a major shift in English imperial design. It attempted to exclude the Dutch from exploiting the English economy in America. The act sought to control trade between the colonies and England. England went to war with Holland in 1652–1654, and again under Charles II in 1665–1667 and 1672–1674. The wars cost the Dutch their North American colony, and England found a permanent place in the middle regions of the North American mainland.

Cromwell left another imperial legacy. In the 1650s, he began to move Scottish settlers en masse into the north of Ireland as part of his strategy to convert the Irish to Protestantism and to displace as many Catholics as possible with an influx of mostly Presbyterian Scottish settlers. This has affected Ireland to the present, and the six counties of Ulster retain deep sectarian divisions. The northern Irish impact on America began in the early eighteenth century as thousands of the successors of those settlers, the so-called Scotch Irish, made their way to the American frontier, in particular, to Pennsylvania, Virginia, and the Carolinas.

The Anglo-Dutch Wars

There had been a festering commercial rivalry between England and Holland for some time, and the implementation of the 1651 Navigation Ordinance raised the stakes. Scuffles in the English Channel and the Baltic Sea and disputes over herring fisheries precipitated a full-scale maritime war in 1652 that lasted for two years. Economic fatigue forced a truce, but the English had made a dent in Dutch influence in the Atlantic economy. The second Anglo-Dutch War of 1664–1667 spread to West Africa, the Far East, and America and resulted in the loss of the New Netherland and Dutch claims in the

Delaware area. The English took control of Dutch North America but left Suriname (Dutch Guiana) alone. The first two wars were fought for the most part on the high seas, and, although the Dutch were often more than a match for the English in ship design, seamanship, and leadership, they were eventually worn down by England's superior resources. Yet England, at one point, was forced for a time to cut back on naval spending because of two great national disasters, the great bubonic plague of 1665 and the Great Fire of London, 1666. In addition to those crises, the Dutch, in a display of panache, forced their way up the Thames, causing panic along the way before the invasion was turned back. One of the more important consequences of the Dutch wars was the way they encouraged England to make greater investments in ships and infrastructure and, in general, to reform its military organization.

The first two wars had blunted Dutch maritime power, and the third war (1672–1674) struck hard at the Dutch on land. The English cynically supported a French landward invasion of Holland, which failed but served notice of French power in northwestern Europe. Meanwhile, Holland held off a planned English amphibian invasion and managed to break an Anglo-French blockade. Ironically, the future William III of England, William of Orange, held the Dutch together, while the man he replaced as King of England in 1689, James II, the Duke of York, acquitted himself well as an admiral in his brother Charles's Royal Navy.

Because Charles had openly tolerated James's declared Catholicism, Parliament in 1673 passed the "Test Act," which required all public officeholders to be members of the Church of England and to take communion in the church. As for the Dutch, the wars slowed their remarkable global ascent. Protestant Holland survived, and, although it was removed from North America, it continued to maintain the highest standard of living, per capita, in Europe and remained important in European and world affairs. The third war also revealed an improvisational approach to military and diplomatic alliances. In their diplomatic or military alliances, nations often applied the principle of opportunity rather than holding to formality, precedent, cultural or religious compatibility, or loyalty. On the face of it, there was no dynastic or cultural logic in an Anglo-French alliance against Protestant Holland, although Charles II favored toleration of Catholics and had pro-French leanings. The Catholic Habsburgs of Spain sided with Holland in that war after having spent nearly a century waging war against the Dutch. Across the Atlantic, the Dutch losses confirmed the realpolitik of imperial relations with the English takeover of Holland's North American settlement.

After the fall of New Netherland, English North American claims formed a belt running along the Atlantic coast from the Spanish borderlands of what is now northern Florida and Georgia to the intersection of New

England with New France and Acadia. Even before the end of the Dutch wars, these claims led Charles II and Parliament into a surge of colony making. Charters were issued to the settlements in Connecticut in 1662 and Rhode Island in 1663. The Carolinas were chartered in 1663, New Jersey and New York in 1664, New Hampshire in 1679, and Pennsylvania in 1681. Delaware was first governed through the Pennsylvania charter but formed its own assembly in 1704 after receiving a royal charter in 1702. Georgia was chartered in 1733. Massachusetts absorbed Maine in 1677 and Plymouth in 1691. New Haven became part of the Connecticut Colony in 1665. Nova Scotia (Acadia minus Cape Breton Island) was under British control after 1713 and was granted an assembly in 1758. If these new colonies had anything in common, it was their chartered legality and the political institutions that went with those charters. Otherwise, they represented a kaleidoscope of religious, social, and economic interests. As the British Empire in North America took shape, it resembled a patchwork of little sovereignties.

The New Restoration Colonies and the New Empire

In 1660, there were only a few hundred people living in the area that became Delaware, Pennsylvania, and New Jersey. But, in New Netherland (New York), there were several thousand settlers and as many as 600 African slaves. The Dutch had established in New Amsterdam (New York City) a merchant *entrepôt*, a hub, around the natural harbors of Manhattan. They had pushed north to Albany for the fur trade while enclosing the Swedes and blocking others from the region. The English, in this case, took over an established community and set about revising it. A charter was granted to the king's brother James, the Duke of York, hence the simple replacement of "Netherland" with "York," and the colony was defined geographically in roughly the shape it has since maintained. It included Long Island and the ocean access at the outflow of the Hudson and then a long widening mass of land to the north bordering on western New England and running along the Hudson River to the French claims and west to the Appalachians. The Dutch collapse in New Netherlands was accompanied by a flurry of English chartering in direct commercial formats. The "Company of Royal Adventurers of England Trading into Africa" was reorganized and renamed as the Royal African Company in 1672; it intended to break the Dutch hold on the slave trade. Two years earlier, Charles II had chartered the Hudson's Bay Company, as a territorial claim and a fur trading enterprise to compete with the French in the distant northwest. Meanwhile, the English were careful to recognize existing Dutch legal and cultural rights in New York. When Peter Stuyvesant surrendered to an English fleet in New York harbor, he did so in exchange for some liberal concessions. In 1665, civil and criminal laws, referred to as "Duke's Laws," were announced, derived in part from the models at work in New England. Town deputies, including the Dutch, were acknowledged as representatives in the provincial assembly, which was later extended to include the Delaware settlements.

The civic government of the renamed New York City was reorganized with a mayor appointed by the governor, as were aldermen and a sheriff. The second Anglo-Dutch War (1664–1667) threatened ethnic harmony, and English officials seized Dutch property from the Dutch West India Company and from individuals who would not swear allegiance to England. Then during the third Anglo-Dutch War, New York City fell to a combined Dutch naval and land assault and was briefly renamed New Orange, after the Dutch royal family. Dutch rule was temporarily resumed. The fur-trading *entrepôt* to the north, on the Hudson, had long been known as Fort Orange (present-day Albany). The city reverted to English control after the peace treaty of 1674. The Duke of York had the charter restored to him, and he appointed Sir Edmund Andros (1637–1714), the later head of the Dominion of New England, as governor.

The English were in the region to stay with a system superimposed on a non-English population. In time, the Dutch majority was overwhelmed, but the language functioned for several decades, and churches, villages, and some Dutch customs remained. New York's Dutch heritage was a harbinger of the later ethnic diversity of the middle colonies and the backcountry, as Scotch-Irish, German, Scottish, Irish, and other non-English immigration poured in during the early eighteenth century. By the time of the American Revolution, 40 per cent of the thirteen colonies' white population was not English, and in the middle colonies of New York, New Jersey, and Pennsylvania, the English were a minority.

In the shorter term, New York entered into disputes with Connecticut over territorial jurisdiction, a common issue everywhere in the colonies. Although these overlapping claims were usually resolved between the disputants themselves, sometimes, the Crown had to adjudicate. Charters usually made clear concessions, but not always, and, at one time or another, New York claimed Nantucket, Martha's Vineyard, and parts of Maine. Cultural and territorial adjustments aside, New York politics were complicated by the Duke of York's provocations. It was one thing for him, as proprietor, to control land distribution, but he had sidelined demands for a popularly elected assembly since 1670.

In 1685, the Duke of York became King James II and lasted a mere four years before his Catholicism, errors of judgement, and pathological arrogance brought him down. As noted earlier, in America, he fashioned his vision for empire with the Dominion of New England, a forced union of all the colonies and settlements from Maine to Pennsylvania under the supreme management of Edmund Andros. New York was brought into the dominion in 1688. The union failed when James failed. Even as the Duke of York, the future King of England had no qualms about flaunting his religious preferences in the exclusively Protestant northern colonies. As early as 1683, as proprietor, he had given the governorship of New York to an Irish Catholic, Thomas Dongan. James's persistent rejection of appeals to open New York politics to more popular representation and his heavy handed and very unpopular extension of the Dominion of New England when he became king, meant that opposition to him in England would be echoed in North America.

Leisler's Rebellion

Jacob Leisler (1640–1691) was a German soldier who came to America in 1660 as an employee of the Dutch West India Company in New York. He married well, made a fortune in trade, stayed after the English conquest, and was well known in the community. He was a devoted Protestant who had earlier opposed the appointment of the Catholic Thomas Dongan as governor. He also incurred the wrath of Andros for his openly antiestablishment views. In the explosive atmosphere of 1688 and 1689, when news of Andros's expulsion from Boston and James's exile to France reached New York, Leisler proclaimed William III as king. He and his followers ("a rabble" according to one report) seized Fort James in Manhattan. At the same time, war broke out between France and England, a war that would last intermittently until 1697. Leisler assumed control of the New York Assembly and expanded his presumptive part in the Glorious Revolution by leading an ambitious but ultimately failed campaign to French Canada as part of the imperial war effort. He then defied an order to stand down and recognize the appointment of the new royal governor in 1691. For a time, he had the support of most of the people in most of the towns of New York, but the flamboyant Leisler had overstepped himself, and his earlier pledge to King William did not bring forgiveness. He was overpowered by a regiment of royal troops sent to restore order, tried for treason, and hanged along with his chief lieutenant. A spectacular moment in New York politics ended with his death.

Leisler's illegal power grab has left his reputation a bit fuzzy despite his popular opposition to and overthrow of the Andros and the Jacobite New York establishment. But he simply prolonged his coup d'état when there was no need for it, and he might have lived had he recognized the new post-Stuart regime in New York after 1690. His participation in what he saw as a patriotic attack on the Stuarts demonstrated the close relationship between the politics of England and local colonial affairs. But he can be seen in another light, as a rebel who seized power in a royal colony with an agenda that, after the expulsion of James, had little to with the empire. In that way, his coup resembles Bacon's Rebellion of 1676, revealing internal conflict in two separate colonial societies with quite different cultures. Each attempted to redefine their societies: Bacon by challenging Virginia's ruling classes and reforming land distribution and Leisler by removing the Crown's executive authority in New York. As is the case after many failed rebellions, the status quo was resumed stronger than before.

The Middle Colonies Take Shape

In 1664, the Duke of York transferred to loyal Royalists Lord John Berkeley (who was not related to the Virginia Berkeley) and Sir George Carteret the settlement rights to an area between the Hudson and Delaware Rivers that marked off the future chartered colony of New Jersey (1702). They designed a set of guidelines or "Concessions and Agreements" that allowed for freedom of conscience, settlement through a system of quitrents (with the rents to be gathered by the proprietors), and a representative assembly.

Without a formal charter, New Jersey's non-native population rose from a few hundred to nearly 4,000 in 1680 and to nearly 15,000 in 1700. Nominal proprietors came and went, and, for a time, the area was divided into two jurisdictions, East and West Jersey. In 1688, it became part of Andros's Dominion of New England, which by then was on its last legs. West Jersey had earlier attracted Quaker interests and introduced William Penn to the possibilities of American settlement. But the Jerseys were always subject to New York's influence, politically, economically, and constitutionally. The end result of the rotating proprietorships was the revocation of all the proprietors' political authority and the issuing of a royal charter in 1702. Even then, New Jersey continued to be under the executive banner of the "Governor of New York." Still, in the almost two decades between the final fall of the Dutch in America (1674) and the fall of James II (1689), New Jersey took shape as a viable and distinct community marked by ethnic and religious pluralism.

The creation of Pennsylvania in 1681 is a striking example of how North American "vacant" space could be arbitrarily dispensed by a distant king. Charles II's granting of a proprietary charter to William Penn (1644–1718) of a territory that, on paper, spread over 29 million acres, or about the size of England, has extravagance written all over it. It was an unusual act on a number of levels. On the surface, the size of the grant and the fact that the charter was given to an individual, a dissenter, a Quaker, is puzzling. The Crown noted that the area to be settled was the last major piece of territory open to an English claim, and the grant to the Quaker Penn was, on the face of it, a bit incongruous. But Charles had a quite rational motivation. It would retire a debt of 16,000 pounds sterling that the king owed to Penn's late father, and a successful Quaker enclave in America might siphon off numbers of troublesome English Quakers. That suited Penn. From his perspective, the charter would allow for a self-governing Quaker community in America that might also turn a profit.

Penn's own story is a fascinating one. His father William (ca.1621–1670), Charles's creditor, was a wealthy and committed Church of England adherent. William junior was more than normally pious growing up and was destined to follow his father's Anglican path until he fell in with Puritans and was expelled from his Church of England–dominated college at Oxford. He saw naval service in the Anglo-Dutch Wars and managed some of his father's Irish properties before he was drawn to Quakerism. He served time in jail for his beliefs, which are clearly revealed in his pamphlets. He advocated simple living and attacked luxury but, without any sense of contradiction, thought of himself as an economic liberal. His chief ideological virtue, as he saw it, was his belief in freedom of thought and religion as well as in the concept that all "free Englishmen" should have equal political rights. In 1671, he took the Quaker message to Holland and Germany, and, thereafter, he traveled throughout England, provoking many of the opponents of Quaker religious radicalism, military pacifism, and social egalitarianism. He became a trustee of the small Quaker community in West Jersey in the 1670s and then requested repayment of the Stuart debt to his father. After the grant, it was Charles II who named the colony Pennsylvania, "Penn's Woods," in honor of William Penn senior. In 1682, the ever-active Duke of York retired his Delaware claim to Penn as an act of friendship that presents us with another conundrum of sorts. Perhaps the future James II saw his family's friendship with Penn as more important than the deep religious differences between them.

Penn lived in his massive estate, Pennsylvania, for two brief periods in 1682–1684 and 1699–1701, but his influence on the colony's future went far beyond that. He authorized a "Frame of Government" in 1682 that allowed for an elected assembly and encouraged treaties that favored natives. Criminal law was less stringent than in most English jurisdictions: for example, only murder and treason were punishable by death, unlike the scores of capital offences on the books in England and the relatively large numbers on the books in New England. During his first sojourn in the colony, he built a mansion, laid out the distinctive grid plan for Philadelphia, visited other colonies to encourage good relations, and wrote a lively essay on the colony's geographical virtues and potential for settlement. His friendship with the Stuarts made it possible to have about 1,300 Quakers released from jails in England. Even when James II was overthrown in 1689, the claim was reconfirmed under William and Mary, and a busy Penn helped settle a boundary dispute with Maryland, proposed a model, mostly ignored, for a united colonial congress for trade purposes, and set up a public grammar school. His *pièce de résistance* was the Charter of Privileges of 1701, which confirmed and expanded the 1682 "Frame" and opened the way for broad voting rights and a unicameral legislature with significant authority. Penn remained active in the colony's political affairs, which were open and somewhat factious. His contact with his creation declined after 1712 when he was incapacitated with seizures.

Massachusetts and Pennsylvania were each established as Christian "commonwealths." But they were established several decades and several degrees of purpose apart. By 1700, Winthrop's model colony had undergone some charter and ideological modification but remained Congregationalist and ethnically English. What Penn left behind was a political system that reflected the colony's pluralistic religious and ethnic population. By the middle of the eighteenth century, Pennsylvania was home to the most socially and ethnically diverse community in the western world, with Quakers by then in the minority. German and Scotch-Irish immigrants outnumbered the English. Philadelphia became one of the most important ports in the empire, and the rural population of Pennsylvania was perhaps the most prosperous per capita in America. In contrast to the homogeneous populations of the New England colonies or the functionally elitist slave societies of the Chesapeake, the middle colonies after the Restoration introduced lively, polyglot variants to the North American settlements, which were by then expanding south of the Chesapeake.

South of the Chesapeake: The Carolinas

For a long time in the sixteenth and seventeenth centuries, the Spanish had resisted French attempts, including those of the Huguenots, to set up in Florida. Ponce de León had claimed the area as early as 1513, but Spain was unable to maintain any sizable settlement until it founded St. Augustine with 1,500 settlers in 1565. Francis Drake, ever the nemesis of the Spanish, destroyed the fort there in 1586, and Spain's efforts to push north were stalled by fierce native resistance. Still, over time, tenacious Spanish priests founded missions all the way to the northeast corner of the Gulf of Mexico, today's Florida "panhandle." The Franciscans established some 38 missions and converted or influenced over 25,000 natives in northern Florida and adjacent territory. As early as 1629, English speculators had shown interest in the area that is now Georgia and South Carolina or, as the Latin for Charles had it, "Carolana." There was no significant English occupation until after the capitulation of Spanish Jamaica to Cromwell's ships in 1655.

By the middle of the seventeenth century, however, the time appeared ripe for the English to reach out from their Caribbean bases to the Spanish borderlands on the southeastern mainland. There was also movement south from the Chesapeake. In 1653, some Virginians settled near Roanoke in what would become North Carolina. In 1660, a group of New Englanders sponsored by London merchants, set up a short-lived colony at Cape Fear to the south of those Virginia settlers. Then, in 1663, a royal charter was issued to eight prestigious "proprietors." Charles's chief minister, Lord Clarendon, was among them, as was Sir William Berkeley, the long-term governor of Virginia. The venture sparked interest among Barbados's expanding planter class. On paper, the Carolina charter had a pedigree, but it lacked finances and immigrants and not until the 1670s did small permanent settlements appear. Meanwhile, the English claim to the region was given diplomatic legitimacy in 1670, when, in the Treaty of Madrid, England and Spain agreed in principle to their respective occupation rights in America. Although the principle was often ignored, the treaty admitted limits to Spanish claims north of Florida.

Meanwhile, the original plan of government for Carolina was replaced in 1669 by a more elaborate system embedded in a set of "Fundamental Constitutions," reputedly composed by John Locke (1632–1704) and Anthony Ashley Cooper (1621–1683), the future Lord Shaftsbury. The former would later write two of the most influential books in English political history, *An Essay Concerning Human Understanding* (composed from 1671–1687) and *Two Treatises of Government* (published 1689). The liberal themes of the latter were allegedly penned to justify the outcome of the Glorious Revolution, but they might have been written earlier. Locke's themes of social and political contract would strike a chord with eighteenth century political theorists everywhere in the English-speaking world, including in America amongst the revolutionary generation. Shaftsbury was one of the most controversial public figures of the age, serving on Cromwell's council during the Commonwealth and then as chancellor of the exchequer and lord chancellor under Charles II. He was a schemer and agitator, and his involvement in the Carolina project is an example of the way important Englishmen saw the prospects for profit in the Restoration empire. His memory is maintained in South Carolina in the names of two rivers that run through Charleston, the Ashley and the Cooper.

The plan for Carolina was a complicated mix of open political and religious freedoms that included a superstructure, which hoped to replicate the titled and landed hierarchies of England. The proprietors would each have a "seigniory" of 12,000 acres in each of the counties as they were formed. Below this ruling group would be "landgraves" with grants of up to 48,000 acres in total. Then there was a descending strata of landholders that included *caciques*, a term borrowed from the Spanish word for native chief, and below that manor lords and descending categories of landholding down to "freeholders" with 50 acres and voting rights. Although sectarian Christian worship was tolerated, the Church of England was "established" as the official tax-supported church. There was something dreamlike in the assumptions of those proprietors. America was not the place to replicate the English aristocracy.

The proprietors remained in England where they set up what they called the "Palatine Court." It appointed the governor, heard appeals, and generally sought to supervise law in the colony. The proprietors envisioned a future American hereditary aristocracy. It was thought that this could be achieved by making huge land grants with property rights subject to the inheritance provisions in the English custom of primogeniture and entail. In that system, land could not be subdivided but had to be passed to the first son, who was legally bound to hold the land in one piece. The successor then assumed the political status that went with the land. However, by 1693, what emerged in the Carolinas was not an American version of the English hereditary political system but a representative bicameral assembly as planters took control of the government. Absenteeism failed to work in the Carolinas and neither did the proposed hierarchy of New World, land-rich, and leisured hereditary lords. The native threat and attacks by French and Spanish raiders during Queen Anne's War after 1702 prompted the Crown to act, and the proprietors gradually lost their grants and Carolina became a royal colony in 1706 for security reasons. By that time, it had been reconstructed as a mecca for moneyed and ambitious planters. By 1700, the population was about 16,000 of which over 10,500 were in the northern part of the colony directly south of Virginia. The slower population growth in what would be South Carolina masked its eventual appeal to planter investment in cash crops, slave labor, and profit. The emergence of the Carolinas as viable commercial colonies, open to planter entrepreneurs, coincided with the transition to slavery in the Chesapeake labor force. The Carolinas reflected trends in both Chesapeake and Caribbean slave cultures. By 1700, over 40 per cent of South Carolina's people were slaves. Charleston (formally Charles Town before 1783) was founded in 1670, and, by the middle of the decade, its immediate environs were home to several hundred planter-settlers from England and the West Indies.

The South Carolina cash crop economy included rice, the dye plant indigo, and silk. The latter had been part of the lure of settlement, but there turned out to be no profit in it. The weak proprietary hold meant that factions and political conflict marked Carolina's early development. As early as 1677, Culpeper's "rebellion" had demonstrated the folly of absentee proprietorship. The proprietors' agents antagonized the small planter class and an anti-proprietary party set up an alternative government. John Culpeper defended the rebels and their political agenda but was arrested and charged with treason by the appointed resident governor. He was acquitted, with help from the absentee holders of the charter, and he managed to get concessions from the authorities that allowed for more planter participation in government. But stable government eluded the colony, even as its economy improved and population reached several thousand by the 1680s. In the ten years following 1685, six appointed governors came and went in what was an unmanageable political system. There was even a bit of intercolonial strife, for example, when Virginia's assembly prohibited Carolinian tobacco from its territory. This forced the growers to contract New England ships to take their tobacco first to New England and then to Europe, in violation of the Navigation Acts. Still, an important part of Restoration policy had been achieved. Carolina was permanent and completed an extraordinary burst of colony making to go with the Navigation Acts, the possession of Jamaica, the taking of New York, and the creation of Pennsylvania. Slaves began pouring into the Carolinas in increasingly larger numbers, and the stage was set for a new, formidable planter culture in British America.

By the turn of the eighteenth century Carolina consisted of two distinct sections. The northern community was settled around Albemarle Sound on the Virginia boundary and separated from the far southern settlements around Charleston by over 300 miles of territory, parts of which had been traversed by only a few whites. Throughout the Carolinas, trade with natives brought in thousands of deer hides as barter but also created tensions between natives, Spaniards, and Englishmen. However, as they moved in and through the Carolina tidewater, up the rivers, and gradually into the entire habitable region, tenacious English traders displaced and threatened many native people.

The Tuscarora War of 1711–1712 began with a devastating native retaliation against the actions of those fur traders. About 200 white settlers were massacred, and the tit for tat continued until white militiamen killed or enslaved about 20 per cent of the southern Tuscaroras, ending their viability as an independent tribe. They were forced north to join the northern Tuscarora in the Iroquois confederacy. The Yamassee War of 1715–1717 was another bitter and deadly affair. It fit the pattern of reprisal and retaliation that accompanied all native-white conflicts, and, in this case, it pitted one native group against another, when Cherokees aligned themselves with colonial militias against the Yamassee-Creek consortium. Before it ended, the war drove English settlers back to the outskirts of Charleston, but the eventual defeat of the Yamassee ensured easier access to the west for future white settlement. Meanwhile, the original proprietors had hung on to their licensed claims even after the arrival of royal government. They eventually surrendered their patents with the exception of Lord Carteret, who managed, with skill and persistence, to hold on to a part of his grant until after the Revolution. The term *North* Carolina came to denote the Albemarle area after 1691, and in 1712, a separate royal governor was assigned to it. In 1729, a separate charter was issued, and North and South Carolina were confirmed as unique colonial entities.

Three years later, the extreme southern portion of the old Carolina grant was assigned to a group of London philanthropists as a refuge for English paupers. The colony, Georgia, was the last of the thirteen mainland colonies to be chartered. The colony came long after the Restoration surge, but its purpose, to be a haven for the poor, demonstrates that, as late as 1732, colonies were created with mandates that had no exact precedent. Lying adjacent to Spanish territory, Georgia was seen by the Crown as a military and diplomatic buffer. It was the brainchild of British Member of Parliament James Oglethorpe, who, with a group of well-off "trustees," secured a patent to settle and govern the area, Georgia, for a 21-year period. The scheme, in part, was aimed at relieving London of some of the problems of pauperism, crime, and homelessness by sending the poor and debtors and other felons to America to engage them in useful agriculture. Although the plan had strategic and trade objectives, it was also a sincere philanthropic venture. Alas, it was too optimistic. The hope of the trustees was that the availability of land, honest toil, and sobriety (slaves and rum were forbidden) would rehabilitate the destitute throngs who would settle. Reality trumped ideals, and, within a few years, legislation encouraged speculative investment in land. Over time, the utopian vision faded. Rum was allowed in 1742, slavery in 1749, and, by 1752, Parliament had grown tired of subsidizing the colony and the charter passed to royal control. By then, speculators had transformed tidewater Georgia into an extension of tidewater South Carolina's slave society.

SUGGESTED READINGS

Two recommended surveys of seventeenth century England are David Underdown, *A Freeborn People: Politics and the Nation in Seventeenth Century England* (New York: Clarendon Press, 1996) and Barry Coward, *The Stuart Age: England, 1603–1714* (New York: Longman, 1994). Conrad Russell, *The Crisis of Parliaments: English History, 1509–1660* (London: Oxford University Press, 1971) reaches back to the early sixteenth century to convey the era's political and constitutional turmoil and the transformation of the English state. A popular brief overview of the era is Christopher Hill, *The Century of Revolution, 1603–1714* (New York: Norton, 1980). The prolific Hill's Marxist perspective emphasizes the radicalism and ideological underpinnings of the English Civil War. His narrative and judgements are clear and thoughtful. Another prolific historian, H.R. Trevor-Roper, in *From Counter-Reformation to Glorious Revolution* (London: Pimlico, 1993) offers a selection of his essays and lectures on key aspects of seventeenth century English and European history. His brief essay "The Glorious Revolution of 1688" is an interesting analysis of the social and political context of the event. See also J. Plumb, *The Growth of Political Stability in England, 1675–1725* (London: Macmillan, 1967). This slim volume is remarkably comprehensive in its treatment of the intricacies of party politics and patronage from the Restoration to the age of Walpole. A reliable survey is Frank O'Gorman, *The Long Eighteenth Century: British Political and Social History, 1688–1832* (New York: Arnold, 1997). For the rise of British nationalism in the eighteenth century see Linda Colley, *Britons: Forging the Nation, 1707–1837* (New Haven: Yale University Press, 1992). Colley's thesis links Britain's rise to international prominence to militarism and the growth of patriotism, and although it deals with the period following the union of the parliaments, it has useful things to say about the outcome of the Glorious Revolution. The intellectual and theoretical currents of the seventeenth century and later are dealt with in stimulating fashion in C.B. Macpherson, *The Political Theory of Possessive Individualism, Hobbes to Locke* (Oxford: Clarendon Press, 1962). The relevant chapters in Jeremy Black, *The British Seaborne Empire* (New Haven: Yale University Press, 2004) offer a recent and comprehensive review of the way maritime trade accelerated Britain's growth and influence in the Atlantic economy in the late seventeenth and early eighteenth centuries. For useful studies of the early decades of Pennsylvania history see the early chapters in James Lemon, *The Best Poor Man's Country: A Geographical Study of Early Southeastern Pennsylvania* (Baltimore: Johns Hopkins University Press, 1972) and Mary M. Schweitzer, *Custom and Contract: Household, Government, and the Economy in Colonial Pennsylvania* (New York: Columbia University Press, 1987).

Time Line

1688–1697	The War of the League of Augsburg (in America, King William's War, 1689–1697) and the Treaty of Ryswick.
1701–1714	The War of the Spanish Succession (in America, Queen Anne's War, 1702–1713 ended by the Treaty of Utrecht, 1713).
1707	Union of the English and Scottish parliaments.
1715–1716; 1745–1746	Jacobite (Stuart) uprisings in Scotland.
1721–1742	The Robert Walpole era in Parliament.
1740–1748	War of the Austrian Succession (in America, King George's War, 1744–1748) and the Treaty of Aix-la-Chapelle.

CHAPTER 6

✦✦✦✦✦★✦✦✦✦✦

Transition: Imperial Wars and British Politics

1689–1748

Trade is the Wealth of the World; Trade makes the Difference as to Rich and Poor, between one Nation and another; Trade nourishes Industry, Industry begets Trade; Trade dispenses the natural Wealth of the World, and Trade raises new Species of Wealth, which Nature knew nothing of; Trade has two Daughters, whose fruitful Progeny in Arts may be said to employ Mankind: namely MANUFACTURE and NAVIGATION.

—Daniel Defoe, 1728, quoted in J.H. Plumb, *England in the Eighteenth Century* (1950; repr., Harmondsworth, England: Penguin, 1963), 20.

It was an exhaustion of reserves of money and manpower that brought eighteenth century wars to an end rather than decision by clash of arms.

—John Keegan, *A History of Warfare* (New York: Knopf, 1993), 345.

King William's War (The War of the League of Augsburg)

War or the threat of it colored much of the history of colonial North America. The Spanish fought with natives in Florida, as did the French in the St. Lawrence and Great Lakes region, as did the English along the entire Atlantic littoral from the Maine frontier to Florida and west into the Appalachians. These could be as irregular as chance encounters between traders and native hunting parties or involve thousands in awful, organized wars such as the destruction of Huronia, the Powhatan wars, or King Philip's War. The Tuscarora and Yamassee wars in the early eighteenth century followed the expansion of white settlement into the southern backcountry. By the late seventeenth century, natives were being drawn as clients or proxies or allies into the American extensions of European wars as the imperialists fought each other.

Table 6.1 Selected European–Native Wars in the Thirteen Colonies

SECOND POWHATAN WAR (VIRGINIA) MARCH 1622 TO APRIL 1623	This was the result of tension and distrust between the former benefactors of the Virginia Company, the Powhatan, and the company itself. The Powhatan killed 347 settlers, but a rejuvenated and vengeful English population destroyed native villages and food supplies. The event put another nail in the beleaguered Virginia Company's coffin, but it destroyed any long-term viability of the Powhatan. It led eventually to a third war in 1644, which furthered the demise of the Powhatan nation. Steady white encroachment on native land was a factor in both these conflicts.
PEQUOT WAR (SOUTHERN NEW ENGLAND) AUGUST 1636 TO FALL 1637	This bloody affair took place within a few years of the Puritan settlement and resulted in part from native resistance to white expansion and spreading agricultural settlement. The ostensible cause of the war was a native response to an English attack to avenge the murder of a trader. The English struck alliances with other regional natives and waged an angry war of reprisals that nearly exterminated the Pequot.

KIEFT'S WAR (NEW NETHERLAND) FEBRUARY 1643 TO AUGUST 1645	Again, the war was a retaliatory affair. Natives raised havoc in outlying Dutch settlements, but a Dutch offensive in 1644 killed as many as 600 natives. The total toll might have reached 1,500. The war strained Dutch resources, however, and left a residue of fear in the settlements, even as it blunted native opposition to white expansion.
THIRD POWHATAN WAR (VIRGINIA) MARCH 1644 TO OCTOBER 1646	The Powhatan people, in a desperate attempt to retard English encroachment, killed hundreds of whites. The Virginians took to destroying the natives' winter food stocks to starve the population. This was the last serious effort by the Powhatan to retard English domination of the Chesapeake.
KING PHILIP'S WAR (NEW ENGLAND) JUNE 1675 TO FALL 1676 (SPORADIC AFTERSHOCKS INTO 1677)	A great native alliance in southern New England attacked 52 towns, destroyed 12, and killed 600 English settlers. Colonists killed several thousand natives in the war. This war was especially brutal and was waged specifically in some cases against non-combatants. In a way that echoes the third Powhatan War in Virginia, this decisive war ended native resistance to English expansion in New England.
BACON'S REBELLION (VIRGINIA) 1676	While Bacon's uprising against Berkeley's government was grounded in politics, it had begun when Bacon and his supporters, hoping to open up new land for settlement, waged a vicious war against both hostile and friendly natives on the Virginia frontier. Bacon resented Governor Berkeley's more cooperative, trade-related native policies.

KING WILLIAM'S WAR (NORTHERN NEW ENGLAND) MAY 1689 TO SEPTEMBER 1697	In the American theater of the wider War of the League of Augsburg, native allies of the French destroyed Schenectady, New York; Salmon Falls, New Hampshire; and Casco, York, and Wells in Maine. Pro-English Iroquois raided Canada but paid for their actions by the retaliation of France's native allies. A pattern of white-native military alliances began to take shape in this war.
QUEEN ANNE'S WAR (THROUGHOUT THE COLONIES) MAY 1702 TO APRIL 1713	The policy of forming native alliances was confirmed in this war. South Carolina militias waged war against the Spanish in the south, burned St. Augustine, and destroyed missions and enslaved hundreds of natives who had converted to Catholicism. The raid on Deerfield, Massachusetts by French-funded natives remains one of the most notorious events of the war in New England and added to an already deep distrust of and antipathy toward natives.
TUSCARORA WAR (NORTH CAROLINA) SEPTEMBER 1711 TO JUNE 1713	Tuscarora natives destroyed the town of New Bern in North Carolina in a campaign of revenge against white traders. Militia and pro-English natives responded with devastating results for the Tuscarora. The remnants of the tribe went north to join the Five Nations.
YAMASEE WAR (SOUTH CAROLINA) APRIL 1715 TO NOVEMBER 1717	Again, the war was a native reaction to abuse by frontier traders. Yamasee and Creek warriors drove to within 12 miles of Charleston before they were driven back by South Carolina militia with help from other colonial militias and their native allies. The powerful Cherokee were kept out of the war, and the way was opened for settlement south and west and later into Georgia.

DUMMER'S WAR (MAINE, PART OF MASSACHUSETTS) 1721 TO 1725	This small war, named for Governor William Dummer of Massachusetts is unusual. It was less a corollary of imperial war than it was a local conflict between English and French settlers. It stemmed from a Massachusetts–New France dispute over the northern Maine boundary as New England's population moved north in increasing numbers. In 1722, skirmishes between settlers gave way to a declared war against the Abenaki, long-time allies of the French. The Massachusetts militia cleared large parts of central Maine for English settlement. Bounties were offered for native scalps, which encouraged the killing of natives by freelance English scalp hunters.
KING GEORGE'S WAR MARCH 1744 TO OCTOBER 1748	This was an example of the way native groups were drawn into imperial affairs. French-allied natives raided New England and New York, wreaking havoc on frontier settlements while British-supported Iroquois raided Canadian settlements.
SEVEN YEARS' WAR (1756–1763) PART OF THE FRENCH AND INDIAN WAR MAY 1754 TO FEBRUARY 1763	The involvement of native forces increased in this, the fourth of the imperial wars in America. The French met English regular army advances into the Ohio Valley with French-led Indian ambushes. French allies raided New England, New York, Pennsylvania, Maryland, and Virginia. In western Pennsylvania colonial British militias destroyed the Delaware town of Kittaning. They also destroyed the Abenaki town of St. François in New France.

CHEROKEE WAR (THE CAROLINAS) FALL 1759 TO DECEMBER 1761	Cherokee warriors attacked South Carolina frontier settlements to avenge the murder of several of their people. British regulars and colonial militia struck back but the Cherokee persisted and overran Fort Loudoun. After more attacks on civilian settlements, the Cherokee were beaten back by a British expedition that burned many Cherokee towns. The war was distinguished by the fact that both the Cherokee and the British were acting independently, outside any scheme of alliances. This conflict can be seen as a deliberate war of British expansionism at the tail end of the Seven Years' War.

Source: Adapted from Ian Steele, *Warpaths: Invasions of North America* (New York: Oxford University Press, 1994) and from Thomas L. Purvis, *Almanacs of American Life: Colonial America to 1763* (New York: Facts on File, 1999), 29–33.

What the English referred to as King William's War was known in its European phase as the War of the League of Augsburg or the War of the Grand Alliance or even the Nine Years' War. The terms "league" and "alliance" indicate the way Europe's dynastic struggles worked. The League of Augsburg was a mostly token alliance of several states formed in 1686 to oppose Louis XIV and French expansionism in Europe. France had designs on the Rhineland Palatinate and invaded it in 1688. It was resisted by a coalition of the Holy Roman Empire, Savoy, Spain, and, after William's accession, the English and Dutch. In western Europe, at least into the eighteenth century, rivalries often carried religious connotations, but the causes of enmity were neither predictable nor logical. Protestant Holland and England fought each other in the seventeenth century, and Catholic Spain and the Holy Roman Empire allied with Protestant Holland and England to oppose Catholic France in the 1688–1697 war. Scottish Jacobites (from the Latin for James, *Jacobus*) supported the deposed James II and sided with France in the war and, later in the eighteenth century, twice invaded Britain to reclaim Stuart rights.

The 1688–1697 war was a direct struggle between the emergent big powers, England and France, with assorted allies on either side. It was the first of the four North American wars that ended with the capitulation of New France in 1763. The Anglo-French conflict then continued to the end of Napoleon Bonaparte's regime in the early nineteenth century. The 1688 war also underscored a remarkable trend in world history, namely that, since the beginning of European expansion in the fifteenth and sixteenth centuries, Europeans had taken their affairs and conflicts overseas, to Asia, Africa, and America.

In America, King William's War began when New York's ambitious Governor Dongan aroused the Iroquois to attack the French in their forts and on their trade routes all the way from the St. Lawrence River and the eastern Great Lakes to the Mississippi country. The resulting sporadic, small-scale raids and counterraids along the borders set the tone of the war in the American theater. It was generally fought between small groups of regular forces, militias, and native contingents. There were exceptions, one of which was the relatively easy English capture of Port-Royal on the Bay of Fundy in Acadia in the spring of 1690. Governor Sir William Phips (1651–1695) of Massachusetts led a force of several hundred New England militiamen in an amphibious assault on an undermanned Port-Royal, which fell without much trouble. An emboldened Phips then launched another, more costly, amphibious campaign up the St. Lawrence River in the fall of 1690 in an ambitious attempt to seize Quebec. The heavily fortified city was defended by a force that was probably larger than Phips's. The siege foundered. Of an estimated 2,300 troops in the invasion force, as many as 1,000 perished. Smallpox and exposure killed hundreds during the aborted siege, and, on the way home, rough seas and bitter weather added to the death toll. The sorry result of that disaster was compounded when Port-Royal was recovered by the French in 1691.

These events shook New England's pride and drained the Massachusetts treasury, and the sour mood they caused was exacerbated a year later in the heat of the Salem witch trials. On the other hand, Governor Phips managed to survive the setback in Canada and the Salem uproar. His story has a fabulous rags-to-riches shine. He was born on the Maine frontier, apprenticed as a ship's carpenter in Boston, worked his way into command of an expedition to find sunken treasure in the Caribbean, found a fortune, and was knighted for it. Following his return from the Canadian failure, he was appointed the first royal governor of Massachusetts under the new charter of 1691, just in time for the witchcraft hysteria at Salem. He supported the trials at first but then ordered them halted when, in the general hysteria, his wife was charged. His career was brief but colorful and important, given his status as an American-born royal governor. He died in London in 1695.

In any event, the war cautioned New Englanders against assuming an easy removal of the French near their borders. New France survived. French military skills and strategies were enough to stretch New England's superior manpower resources. Under orders from the restored governor general of New France, the Comte de Frontenac, regular troops and militias and their native allies attacked English settlements across northern New York and

New Hampshire and in Maine and western Massachusetts. Elsewhere, the audacious, freewheeling Pierre Le Moyne d'Iberville (1661–1706), in a splendid display of tactical virtuosity, won victories over the English in the distant Hudson Bay region in 1690. Then, in 1696–1697, he laid waste to English settlements in Newfoundland, and burned St. John's. Following those successes, he led an expedition to the mouth of the Mississippi in 1698 to claim New Orleans for France. Meanwhile, French forces and native allies held the formidable Iroquois in check. A French resident population of 12,000 seemed capable of intimidating New England and New York's combined 100,000 population and superior resources. By the time the war was over, a deeper Francophobia had taken root in the northern English colonies to go with a fierce antipathy toward native clients of the French.

Queen Anne's War (The War of the Spanish Succession)

The Treaty of Ryswick of 1697 confirmed the Anglo-French imperial rivalry in North America. English claims to Newfoundland and Hudson Bay were recognized, despite French successes in each region. Acadia had been recovered by France, and the treaty confirmed it as a French possession. For the belligerents, the war had been mostly desultory, an expensive draw, and, in America, some old enmities persisted and some new ones emerged. The Five Nations Iroquois Confederacy (soon to be joined by the southern Tuscaroras to be the Six Nations) continued its decades-long war against the French in the upper St. Lawrence and eastern Great Lakes. The Abenaki and the Massachusetts government engaged in vicious small-scale attacks on each other. Natives often acted independently, but the alliances that were struck during King William's War now appeared set and were revived within a few years of the Ryswyck treaty. In Europe war was resumed between France and England after 1701 in the first round of the so-called War of the Spanish Succession. American colonists prosaically named the conflict Queen Anne's War.

The war began as yet another European power struggle. In 1700, Charles II of Spain died without heirs. His throne was claimed in the name of the grandson of Louis XIV, and France invaded the Spanish Netherlands to help secure it. This sparked a rejuvenated anti-French "Grand Alliance" of England, the Dutch Republic, the Holy Roman Empire, and some German states. The war produced two military legends, Prince Eugene of Saxony and John Churchill, the first Duke of Marlborough (1650–1722). The latter had married well, fought with distinction in the third Anglo-Dutch War, and played a key role in the success of William III in 1688–1689. His talents were many, but his tactical flair and military daring made him a national hero. His name is linked to a series of battles that are among the best known in British history: Blenheim (in Bavaria) in 1704 and Ramillies, Oudenarde, and Malplaquet (in the Low Countries) between 1706 and 1709. Those battles were expensive affairs involving huge armies and much bloodshed. At Oudenarde, for example, the French host, including allies, numbered about 100,000 and Marlborough commanded 80,000. Blenheim was a spectacular success because it saved Vienna from the French and demonstrated Marlborough's élan. In the formal engagements that marked this and other eighteenth century European wars, with ranks of infantry pouring musket volumes into each other, the battlefields became slaughterhouses. As much as half of the French army of 60,000 was killed, wounded, or captured at Blenheim. Improved firearms technology, including field artillery, and massed troop formations contributed to the carnage. The European set pieces contrasted with the tactics and much smaller scale of the battles fought in the woods and meadows of North America by mixed contingents of regulars, militia, and native warriors.

Marlborough was rewarded for his triumphs with an estate that still bears the Blenheim name, and he has been canonized along with Britain's other military heroes, such as Drake, Wolfe, Nelson, and Wellington. In his time, however, he was a controversial figure: he was even charged with embezzlement, fell out of favor with Queen Anne, and was removed from command in 1711. But he survived the scandal and lived to bathe in his own celebrity, eventually personifying British power and influence. His accomplishments and reputation added cachet to the word "British" as it began to appear in the colonies. In 1707, as we shall see, the parliaments of Scotland and England were combined in the Act of Union. The use of the term "Great Britain" was important both as a formal state designation and as a patriotic or nationalist catchall. It found its way to the colonies as a more inclusive term than "English," although the "*rights* of freeborn Englishmen" would be invoked by colonial Britons all the way to the American Revolution. Marlborough's martial exploits embodied an identifiable British ethos, the rising glory of a militant Britannia. But the 1702–1713 war cost the British Treasury about 150 million pounds sterling, an enormous sum considering that normal annual operating expenses ran to about 2 million pounds sterling. The running costs of the war had been met with loans, taxes, and, eventually, state-funded debt, a formula that continued throughout the eighteenth century as war, diplomacy, and trade elevated Britain's place in European affairs.

If the scale of the European war makes the North American phase seem slight by comparison, the consequences of the American campaigns of 1702–1713 nevertheless had serious ramifications. After the Treaty of Ryswick in 1697, the French embarked on an aggressive expansionist program in the Mississippi Valley and Louisiana. They established missions at Cahokia and

Kaskaskia in Illinois country and strengthened or built forts in the north-west, one at Michilimackinac at the junction of Lakes Huron and Michigan (rebuilt 1712–1715) and another at Detroit (1701). They also started a colony near the Gulf of Mexico on the Mobile River. French strategy was intended in part to keep the English out of the fur trade. A glut had depressed prices, and some western trading posts had been closed to limit the supply and force prices to rise.

When the War of the Spanish Succession began, the Abenaki at first attacked nearby Maine settlements but then, in 1704, destroyed Deerfield, Massachusetts. This attack, just west of Boston in New England's heartland, sent shivers through the entire New England population. As with the 1697 attack on Haverhill, only 30 miles north of Boston, the Deerfield raid reminded New Englanders that they were not far from a rough, dangerous frontier and even the settled core of Massachusetts was vulnerable. The Deerfield raid was as fearsome as any of the rampages of King Philip's War. Fifty townspeople were slaughtered, and nearly half of the 250 survivors were carried off and marched north under terrible privation. It took years to ransom and recover most of the hostages. The episode produced an important New England book, John Williams's *The Redeemed Captive Returning to Zion*. But in a way that perplexed contemporaries, some of the hostages chose to stay with their native captors in New France. Deerfield became a byword for native depravity and, because they encouraged the raid, for French immorality.

In response to public demands for revenge, New England militias waged war on Acadia to block supplies to the Abenaki and, after two failed attempts, managed to capture Port-Royal in 1710. There would be no French recovery of Acadia this time, and the colony was ceded permanently to Great Britain in the 1713 Treaty of Utrecht that ended the war. The French had success in Newfoundland in the area around Bonavista and St. John's but surrendered those gains to Britain at the end of the war. As a harbinger of future imperial conflict in North America, the war saw the Spanish siding with the French. A Carolina militia army retaliated by pillaging St. Augustine without managing to level the fort there. Another southern army of mixed white militias and natives destroyed 14 Catholic missions to the west of the Carolinas before French-supported Choctaw warriors stopped them.

British success in Europe and the difficulties facing France in its over-extended American empire gave Britain a strong hand in the peace negotiations at Utrecht. Newfoundland, Acadia, and Hudson Bay were ceded to Britain, while the French held on to Cape Breton (Île Royale, the northern extension of Acadia), the islands in the Gulf of St. Lawrence, and fishing rights in northern waters. The French Empire remained intact in the St. Lawrence, the Great Lakes, and the Mississippi Valley but was as stretched as ever in a vast area dotted with missions and forts and held together with a threaded network of native alliances west of the Appalachians and north of the northern New England and New York frontiers. One of the most important outcomes of the war was the acquisition of the Spanish *asiento*. This was a monopoly granted to an ambitious British company, the South Sea Company of 1711. It called for the transport of 4,800 Africans a year for 30 years into the Spanish American colonies. In 1720, the confident South Sea Company, relishing its potential for profit, was ready to take over part of the British national debt. But it released too many shares, and these rose so rapidly in value that they ran ahead of the company's worth and created a great "bubble," which burst with a ruinous effect on stockholders and with frightening consequences for the British economy. The calamity allowed Chancellor of the Exchequer Robert Walpole to reorganize state finances. Parliament passed the so-called Bubble Act to regulate joint stock companies. Great Britain entered the eighteenth century as a newly designed state, having achieved tangible success in a long, hard war, and with a new hero in the Duke of Marlborough. It had made small but important North American acquisitions, and, even as the South Sea Bubble burst, it was learning valuable lessons in national finance.

Scotland, Britain, and the New Nation State

Parliament passed the first Mutiny Act in 1689. It was in response to the wholesale desertions from the army to James's side during the 1688–1689 conflict, but, when the Crown ceased to pay for the upkeep of the army, its annual review by Parliament became a routine. It was intended to toughen the personnel in the British Army now that the force represented a central place in national policy. It made desertion, mutiny, and conspiracy punishable by death. In the 1760s and 1770s, Parliament attached "quartering" provisions to the act, to have colonists pay for the British Army in America. Parliament also produced legislation in 1689 that addressed the new tone of the nation's politics. The so-called Bill of Rights ("An Act Declaring the Rights and Liberties of the Subject and Settling the Succession of the Crown") is a milestone in British history. The 1689 act was a reaction to the disaster of James II. It rescinded some of the legislation passed during his brief reign and rejected his heirs' claims to the throne. His voluntary exile was proof enough of Stuart irresponsibility and unsuitability. The Bill of Rights banned Catholics from royal succession and demanded oaths of commitment to the Church of England from the Monarchy. The "rights" in the act included legal rights; freedom from arbitrary, that is, royal, taxation; no "standing army" other than one authorized by Parliament; the right to fair and open trials; the right to petition the Crown; and the right to freedom of speech. The act required the Monarch to call a regular sitting of Parliament, a major step that was formalized by the Triennial Act of 1694. The 1689 and 1694 acts naturally favored Parliament and its legislative and legal authority but it in no way rejected or disrespected the Monarch's role in defending the unwritten constitution and administering the affairs of the nation. The overall effect was to correct the most obvious constitutional usurpations of the Stuart era. The temper of the acts had an immediate and long-lasting impact on the colonists' interpretation of *their* citizenship and rights as "English" subjects.

The union with the Scots produced a single Parliament but not without teething pains and not without short-term resistance from the exiled Stuarts. Twice, in 1715 and 1745, Scottish Jacobites rose in rebellion against the Hanoverian succession and Parliament's place in it. For many Scots, the Act of Union of 1707 was a great leap in the dark. Like most of Europe, including England, Scotland was regionally diverse, and highland culture and language, for example, were somewhat alien to lowland Scots. After the Reformation, hardcore Calvinism had jostled with Catholicism and, after the union of the English and Scottish monarchies in 1603, with the probing fingers of the Church of England. Scotland was among the poorest of European nations, and its belated and failed experiment in independent colonization was a sharp reminder of its economic limitations. The Darien scheme of 1698–1700, to establish a trading settlement on the Panama isthmus, drained money from Scotland's small community of merchant and landed classes. Opposition by English and Spanish interests compounded the scheme's difficulties, and its failure wounded Scottish pride. The Scots had fought the English for centuries and had been drawn to France by their mutual antipathy to England. The triumph of Scottish Protestants in the 1560s had ended the "auld alliance" with France, and the accession of the Scottish Stuarts to the English throne together with the upheavals of the seventeenth century had made formal relations with France impossible. Thus Scotland was isolated diplomatically. Its soldiers fought in the Thirty Years' War but did so as hired hands, and Scottish armies of competing attachments were involved both for and against the Stuarts in the English Civil War and Glorious Revolution.

The proposed Act of Union of 1707 was, in part, prompted because Stuart interests in the Scottish Parliament initially refused to accept the pending Hanoverian succession to the throne under the Settlement Act of 1701. This act was one of the most crucial of Parliament's actions during this period. It reiterated much of the succession conditions of the 1689 Bill of Rights but also declared that, in the event that William III and his successor, his sister-in-law Anne, should die without heirs, the succession would fall to the House of Hanover. Thus, on the death of Anne in 1714, George I, a German, was installed as Britain's king. A trace of continuity was assured because George's mother was the granddaughter of James I. Under the 1701 act, the sovereign was required to be a member of the Church of England and reside permanently in the British Isles. Moreover, the Monarchy was forbidden under the act to wage war without Parliament's approval. The act also barred foreigners from sitting in Parliament or holding political office. Those and other conditions were clearly intended to preclude any repeat of the troubles with the Stuarts who had been in part responsible for the breakdown of national security and internal order. Parliament and king could now function in lockstep in public and international affairs. There was also a clearer role for the Monarch in the maturing empire in America.

The Scottish debate on the proposed union of the parliaments was held in the aftermath of the Settlement Act. For some, the act threatened Scottish cultural identity and legislative independence while, for others, the Stuarts remained the legitimate heirs so that the Hanoverian succession technically violated the original Scottish succession. After all, James II had left a son and heir. The issue was heated and divisive, yet, with the support of an aggressive minority, the union was pushed through and the Scottish Parliament dissolved itself. A lingering resentment to the union has fluctuated in intensity to this day. In the beginning, the Scots were granted 45 seats in the House of Commons and 16 in the House of Lords, a one to ten Scottish to English ratio when the population ratio was closer to one to six. Still, by bringing Scotland directly into the empire, the union was a boon to many, even if numerous leading Scots saw it as a surrender of nationhood.

Over the longer term, the highland culture of ancient Scotland disappeared or was badly damaged. Lowland Scots were obliged to "anglicize" themselves if they were to benefit from the British Empire. Yet the union benefited landowners and merchants, brought Scotland fully into the American tobacco economy, and spread Scottish traders, administrators, and military leadership to North America, the West Indies, Africa, India, and wherever British naval power along with engineers and managers reached. By the end of the eighteenth century, Scottish philosophers, scientists, writers, architects, and artists had put Scotland in the forefront of the European Enlightenment. Whether or not the Act of Union of 1707 was responsible for the achievements of Adam Smith, David Hume, David Ramsay, or James Watt is a moot question. In any case, Scotland retained much of its native character, and, if the universal themes of Hume and Smith showed Scotland's cosmopolitanism, then Robert Burns at the end of the eighteenth century reminded Scots of their parochial uniqueness.

References to "settlement" and "union" could not hide the fact that British politics were not quite settled or unified at the beginning of the eighteenth century. If Scotland loomed large in the nation's affairs because of the Stuart issue, there was also residual English support for the Jacobites, which went all the way to Parliament. The Stuarts were not completely finished as a force. Louis XIV had provided refuge for the exiled Stuarts and, for what it was worth, recognized their claims to the British throne, but he died in 1715, leaving doubts about French support for the Stuarts. James II had died in France in 1701, and the Scottish Jacobites proclaimed his son James Edward Stuart James III of England and VIII of Scotland in absentia. In reality, he was, as contemporaries sarcastically named him, the "Pretender" to the throne. His attempt to invade Scotland in 1708 was aborted when the British Navy drove back the French invasion fleet. Then, in 1715, he landed in Scotland, and his supporters won a shallow victory before being thoroughly defeated. The "Old Pretender" fled to the continent, and, because of the death of his French patron Louis XIV, he ended up in Italy, where he died and was buried in St. Peter's Basilica in 1766.

If there was an air of farce in the failed Stuart coup, the Jacobites retained enough support to actually threaten the state after 1715. The Old Pretender's son Charles Edward Stuart, "Bonnie Prince Charlie," launched another campaign in Britain in 1745 as the "Young Pretender." He raised a great highland army, occupied Edinburgh Castle, and alarmed lowland Scotland and much of northern England's population too by reaching Derby in the English midlands before running out of energy and hope. His army retreated, eventually, to the north of Scotland, where a regular army led by the Duke of Cumberland crushed the remnants of Charles's bedraggled warriors at Culloden in April 1746. The battle ended with the execution of many of the wounded Highlanders who were left on the battlefield. Bonnie Prince Charlie remains one of the most revered Scottish icons, Culloden a shrine to the tragedy, and Cumberland a symbol of English ruthlessness. Scottish nationalism and perhaps some revisionism have made the "forty-five" central to the debate over the fate of the Scottish nation. However, even though the event still stirs Anglophobia in Scotland, only a minority of Scots supported the Stuart revival in 1745. The British nation had moved on. But the impact of the uprisings on Scotland was significant. After Culloden, the so-called Highland clearances began in earnest, and the crofter, village, and clan structure of the north was shattered, in many cases by military force. Thousands of families were evicted or chose to leave, and the flight to America continued well after the American Revolution. They went to the aptly named Nova Scotia, part of the former Acadia, and, after the British occupation of Cape Breton Island in 1758, an American version of the Scottish north took hold there. Throughout the eighteenth century, displaced Scots joined displaced Irish, Scotch-Irish, Germans, and other European *émigrés* to populate the colonial American backcountry in Pennsylvania, Virginia, and the Carolinas.

In the seventeenth century, the Bishops' wars, the English Civil War, the Anglo-Dutch wars, and the Glorious Revolution had guided Britain's national and international development. In the eighteenth century, Britain and France fought four wars between 1689 and 1763 and faced off again during the American Revolution. All of those wars involved Spain and various other nations. After 1793, another 20 years of war took Great Britain to the end of the Napoleonic era. Britain fought the United States in the War of 1812. In addition, Britons fought each other in the two abortive Stuart invasions and then once more across the Atlantic in the American War for Independence, when the Crown took on rebelling British subjects. The 1745–1746 Jacobite uprising is noted as the last war fought on British soil, but one might point to a series of Irish uprisings and civil strife to underline the persistence of war on British soil into the late twentieth century. The conquest of Ireland over several generations, the Act of Union with the Scots, and the suppression of the Jacobites provided evidence to many Irish and Scots that the British Isles was in fact a product of *English* imperialism and militarism.

The Stuart collapse on the bloody moor at Culloden in 1746 was a vivid demonstration of state power. But the wars with France were the main cause of the steady militarization of Britain's foreign policy. While the American campaigns in King William's War and Queen Anne's War were not side-shows by any means, a major thrust of British militarism was to fix a key role for itself in European affairs. Wars are costly. As noted, by the end of Anne's reign in 1714, two wars with France had drained the government's coffers despite the rise in colonial and international trade. But war, naval superiority, and diplomacy did advance Great Britain's global reach. On the other hand, a post-1689 reform of domestic politics was underway with important conse-quences for both Britain and the British Empire.

Politics and People in Britain, 1689–1740

British political institutions have never been static. The evolution of the British form of representative government has been long and choppy. Today's Parliament consists of the House of Lords and the House of Commons, as it has for centuries. But their respective functions have changed consider-ably over time. The former had long been the advisory body to which a suc-cession of monarchs had turned for advice and consent. In fact, before the fifteenth century, the Monarch had attended its deliberations. As the name implies, the House of Lords accommodated England's and later Scotland's and Ireland's hereditary peers. In Ireland's case, although it was still technically a colony of Britain in the eighteenth century, it was split between an increasingly Protestant north and a Catholic south. But its aristocracy sat in the House of Lords, where birthright meant an automatic place. This chamber represented the interests of Britain's landed aristocracy and their progeny, which, as a class, presumed to control the political destiny of the nation. By the early eighteenth century, it had a little over 200 members.

The House of Commons was the elected house and represented the counties, towns, and districts. Taxes were applied to all classes who had assets in real estate or trade and investment. The Commons was much larger than the Lords, with over 600 sitting members in the early eighteenth century. Although it presumed to represent the population at large, its members were often elected by acclamation or simply assumed a place, representing a district with few or even no people in it, the so-called rotten boroughs. The size of the electorate after the Glorious Revolution had grown because inflation had expanded the numbers of people with a forty shillings freehold, the threshold for voting rights. Still, the voting population of Britain was tiny, comprising less than 5 per cent of households. The Commons wielded power because, over time, it had assumed the taxing prerogative. Together, the Lords and Commons made the law, but money for the Monarch's executive functions, for any national purpose, was largely at the discretion of the Commons because of their taxing rights. This practice, imitated in the colonial American assemblies, was understood to be at the root of rights embedded in colonial American charters. When the slogan "no taxation without representation" rumbled through the colonies in the 1760s, it was echoing a principle long established by the House of Commons in Britain.

Cromwell had dissolved the Lords in 1649 with the view of abolishing it. It was restored in 1660. Following the Restoration and despite Parliament's victory over the royalist excesses of Charles II, both houses were divided over policy, interest, and influence. The divisions were sometimes ideological but usually came down to contests over the distribution of patronage, of government contracts, and of "places" (offices). As the structure of government afforded the Monarch the authority to administer the law, parliamentary maneuverings rotated around the king and his successors after the Restoration. The divisions settled into two main groups, known by the originally derisive "Tories" and "Whigs." The former term derived from an Irish word for bandit, and "Whig" from an English Civil War reference to Presbyterian rebels in Scotland. The "parties" had begun to appear before the Glorious Revolution, originally as "Court" (Tory) and "Country" (Whig). The Court party presumed to represent landed interests in the royal orbit of power and preference, while the Country party opposed Stuart policies and was strongly anti-Catholic. The terms were applied in interesting ways to the patriot and loyalist factions and their objectives during the American Revolution, with patriots ("rebels") being referred to as "Whigs" and the loyalists as "Tories."

Between 1679 and 1681, the Whigs had introduced "exclusion bills" to prevent James II (then the Duke of York) from gaining the throne. As early as 1673, Parliament, in a generally nonpartisan mood, had pushed through a Test Act to exclude non-Anglicans by "testing" the faith and affiliations of potential officeholders. In the end, those Whigs were ultimately responsible for the accession of William and Mary and then Anne and then the Hanoverian Georges. By the beginning of the eighteenth century, the Tories, as an opposition party, attacked government corruption and national debt and fought with the Whigs over foreign and domestic issues. A measure of the instability in Parliament is best illustrated by noting that, between 1689 and 1715, twelve parliamentary elections were held in England (Britain after 1707) or roughly one every two years. These were expensive and rancorous and illustrate confused and shifting alliances and groupings inside and outside Parliament. The number of elections in that 26-year period contrasts with the thirteen elections that were held in the *remainder* of the eighteenth century. To put that in perspective, the number of general elections in the 1689 to 1715 period is greater than in any other comparable time period in British history.

The heady atmosphere of politics, war, trade, and constitutional excitement was seasoned with vibrant cultural, literary, and intellectual innovation. In a conscious comparison to the era of the Roman emperor Caesar Augustus, Britons celebrated their own "Augustan Age." For decades, beginning in the late seventeenth century, fresh dramas, the poetry of Dryden and Pope, the writings of Swift and Defoe, the political theories of Locke, and the political manifestoes of Trenchard and Gordon in *Cato's Letters* cast a glow over British national self-consciousness. The intellectual energy of Augustan England can be seen in the satires of Pope and Swift and in the illustrations of William Hogarth. In some respects, the moral and deeply Christian universe of seventeenth century giants such as Milton or John Donne gave way to more sociological and rationalist views. Journalism and essay writing flourished. The stirrings of liberal economic thought can be seen in the Dutch-born Bernard Mandeville's 1714 essay the *Fable of the Bees* (arguing "that Private Vices by the dextrous Management of a skilful Politician may be turned into Publick Benefits") and earlier in Sir William Petty's statistical and analytical economic essays. As the Glorious Revolution had drawn colonial Americans into a participation in the politics of the British Empire, the English literature of the age found its way into the libraries of colonial America's political classes. The lively political and social essays of Richard Steele and Joseph Addison were very popular in America. In fact, colonial society was as ready to embrace the new "Augustan" age as were the British, and, like the British, colonists studied, imitated, and revered the new classicism.

Much of preindustrial Britain's rural culture was still intact in the early eighteenth century, but market forces were intruding. Although the landscape was still dominated by villages, farms, and some market towns, London had become an urban monolith and the political and commercial nerve center of the empire. Bristol, Norwich, Edinburgh, Newcastle, and other cities grew in size and importance, and fledgling cities such as Belfast, Glasgow, Liverpool, and Manchester appeared as export, entry, and processing centers. In particular, Liverpool and Glasgow grew rapidly because of the tobacco and slave trade. By the middle of the eighteenth century, nearly 20 per cent of the British population could be considered urban, living in towns and cities of 10,000 or more people. In the half century after 1700, England's population rose by 1 million people to a total of 6 million. By 1750, there were about 10 million people in the British Isles. But this growth rate was slower than in the colonies, where the population doubled every 25 years, reaching 1.2 million in 1750 and over 2 million by 1770. In Britain, however, the greatest change in society was not population growth but the changing activities of that population.

A rising class of commercial and manufacturing capitalists, profiting from the trade policies codified in the Navigation Acts, were now feeding raw materials from the Caribbean and North America into the British Isles and providing colonial markets for English manufactured goods. These goods were mostly the products of hundreds of small factories and specialized wood, metal, and textile workshops, as well as reexported or refined materials from various parts of the empire. During the first half of the eighteenth century, their overland transportation was inefficient. For example, Northumberland coal was easier to ship by sea from Newcastle to the south of England than it was by land. That changed in the second half of the eighteenth century. In the age before steam, the scale of any enterprise was limited by the availability of water or animal power. But investment funds could be had. The Bank of England had been established by an act of Parliament in 1694, and the bank attracted investment "subscribers" whose funds provided the government with low interest loans. Debt was still a problem for the government, but it was a controlled and ultimately manageable debt. The Bank of England stabilized currency and influenced interest rates, and, eventually, it emerged as Britain's central bank. Money and a compliant licensing system led to the building of turnpikes and canals.

By the 1770s, overland transportation was transformed by a dense network of toll roads. Travel times between major centers were reduced by 75 per cent in many cases. Markets in Europe and the colonies kept Britain's economy on the move. Labor, as servitude or for piecework or wages, was available for any investor. The "putting out" system, whereby families contracted for textile work, helped a great many rural villages survive the continuing enclosure movement. This conversion of small acreages into pasture for livestock had already disfigured the English countryside as landowners moved short-term tenants and renters off the land by terminating their agreements. The landed classes, the hereditary aristocracy for the most part, became richer throughout the seventeenth and eighteenth centuries, and they and the rising commercial classes dominated Parliament and the economy.

The Glorious Revolution had removed a wayward Stuart, elevated Parliament's role in the constitutional settlement, and issued rights and standards to manage the royal prerogative. But the Monarchy and its executive function had been preserved as a vital mechanism in government. While merchants and lesser gentry were crowding into the House of Commons, place, privilege, and influence guaranteed that the important members of the aristocracy directed the nation's affairs. Cromwell's republic had failed and so had his social engineering; the Restoration had seen to that. As for the Glorious Revolution, it seemed as much a housecleaning or reform as it was a revolution in any fundamental sense. Political stability came to Britain not by the overthrow of the traditional order but by the refinement of its political institutions and practices. In Parliament itself, ministers and leading parliamentarians were surrounded by assorted toadies and favorites, as before, and they continued to be pursued by sycophantic office seekers. Politics in Britain was a highly personalized business.

Sir Robert Walpole and the Nation 1721–1742

Robert Walpole, the first earl of Orford (1676–1745), looms large in British history. He was the most important individual in the nation's public affairs for over twenty years. Although he is referred to as Britain's original "prime minister," he is more properly understood as the most favored of the king's ministers and the most skilled, effective, and durable parliamentarian of the period. One explanation for Walpole's emergence as "prime minister" is that he substituted for the king in regular meetings and discussions with senior ministers because George I ("German Geordie" to the Scots) spoke no English. The modern cabinet system evolved from those ministerial sessions. The office and separate functions of the prime minister were not constitutionally affirmed until the early twentieth century, but, in practice, the role of a first minister, with the support of a majority of the House of Commons and the collaboration of the Monarch, can be said to have begun with Walpole.

He was a Whig of the older variety who actively opposed royal and Tory prerogatives, yet he owed his position to the direct support of the Monarch. His control over the administration of finances and of "patronage" or the means to dispense offices, along with his enormous influence in Parliament, brought a measure of stability to Britain's politics during the first part of the eighteenth century. The clear presence of parties as brokers of interests and the superior skills of Walpole to dispense favors, even to potential opponents, put an end to the plotting and conspiratorial politics that had thrived during the later Stuart regime.

Walpole had run into trouble with Tory parliamentarians during Anne's reign, but, with the accession of George I in 1714, he managed to control partisan opposition. He was, in effect, the secular head of British politics from 1721 to 1742. Meanwhile, British influence rose in continental affairs during those two decades, due in large part to effective military campaigns in Europe and America and the gradual quieting of domestic dissent. The installation of the Hanoverian line and the rise of Walpole precluded the threat of a conservative Tory, Stuart, High Church of England revival. National interest replaced party or ecclesiastical interest as the glue that both stabilized the nation's business and expanded her international horizons. A permanent national debt was created under Walpole's leadership, and he initiated some questionable foreign policy gambits and he perhaps overstayed his relevance. However, his legacy is assured; he oversaw the consolidation of the state apparatus that accompanied Britain's continued rise to prominence.

While Walpole might have been simply the right man in the right place at the right time, there can be no doubting his skills in pulling together the agencies of power and authority. For example, unlike other titled first ministers, he remained in the Commons and close to the rising interests that controlled the national purse. When he resigned in 1742, Britain was again at war with the French. By the 1760s, however, Britain was on the threshold of an industrial revolution, and the French had been cleared out of India and North America after the Seven Years' War of 1756–1763. The Stuarts' claims were a dead issue, and the harmonious marriage of Parliament and royal executive seemed to work well. Partisan politics colored the nation's business as before, and Tory and Whig factions came and went. They were often cloaked in similar policy and purposes and sometimes appeared to simply exchange roles as government and opposition, as "ins" and "outs." Importantly, however, the constitutional settlement that had been achieved between 1689 and the Hanoverian accession in 1714 remained. British society was politically, culturally, and economically flexible enough to appear to other Europeans as an open, fair, and creative community.

Absolutism prevailed in France, Spain, Prussia, Austria, and Russia, but it had failed to take root with the Stuarts in Britain. Britain was different. The Church of England was the state church, to be sure, and test and conformity acts continued to exclude all but conformists from important civil positions. However, Methodism, a minor but lively movement, offered alternatives, especially to the lower classes. Presbyterianism was a brake on Anglican hegemony in Scotland and Northern Ireland and, in Scotland, enjoyed the status of a national church. Ireland was nominally part of the British state but is best seen as a colony where English and Protestant landholders ruled over a persistent and aggrieved Catholic majority.

In England, the steady rise in population and economic growth were accompanied not only by middle-class materialism but also by landlessness, poverty and crime, and the continued political exclusion of the vast majority of the population. The number of offences designated as capital crimes rose in the eighteenth century. This uneven pattern of development leaves us with the paradox of hungry youths being hanged for stealing silk handkerchiefs while the elevated strains of Handel's music were playing a mile away. Societies for the promotion of arts and letters appeared, and the creation of the Royal Academy of Arts in 1768 stands as a milestone in the nation's self-image. Social order and civil order were maintained by a systematic collaboration between capitalists, by the church, and by a punitive judicial ethic. The intellectual vitality of British letters echoed the nation's social and cultural vigor and fed into the empire's larger meaning: British civilization. The darker side of eighteenth century progress in Britain was the gap between rich and poor and between a class enjoying direct participation in politics and other classes without those opportunities. In America, as they celebrated British ideas and culture and defined their place in the British Empire, colonists may have presumed to emulate British constitutional practices, but their access to political participation was easier and more broadly defined.

THE AMERICAN EMPIRE IN THE AGE OF WALPOLE

While Walpole was guiding British domestic politics, the slave societies of the British West Indies boomed. On the mainland, the major developments were mostly expansions of what had taken form in the late seventeenth and early eighteenth centuries and showed in population growth, territorial expansion, and the maturing of institutions and societies in each of the colonies. For example, Virginia and Massachusetts were several generations old, and, by the middle of the eighteenth century, the thirteen mainland colonies had hived themselves into distinctive regional clusters. New England's farm and town-based society bore little relation to the planter-slave societies of the Chesapeake and tidewater lower south. The religious and ethnic polyglot communities of the middle colonies were quite unlike the homogeneous ethnic, religious, and social structure of New England or the nominally Anglican vestry system of the Chesapeake. Newer communities were forming beyond the older settled coastal areas, and a fourth region, the backcountry, began to take shape. The West Indies clearly represented a fifth region.

Thus, during the first half of the eighteenth century, the colonies had taken permanent shape on the contiguous coastline of North America and in the islands of the Caribbean. These various entities were cohering into the regional social and cultural patterns that defined English-speaking America. The regions were clearly distinct from each other and included the four New England colonies; the middle colonies, dominated by New York and Pennsylvania; the Chesapeake and the lower south, characterized by the Virginia and South Carolina planters; and a frontier zone that comprised parts of most of the colonies from north to south and that reached west into the Appalachians by the 1740s and north to Maine. The West Indian colonies were heading in a different direction. Shrinking white populations meant that the English presence in the Caribbean was mostly politically transient and that the region was now defined socially by the slave majority. Acadia and Newfoundland were nominally under British jurisdiction after 1713 but were sparsely populated and lay outside the burgeoning thirteen colonies to their south. It was not simply geography or climate that marked the mainland colonies off from the dozen other British colonies in the western Atlantic. Each mainland colony was governed from within by local representative assemblies and administered by a royal-, company-, or proprietary-appointed governor and his council.

As Walpole's prominence eased Britain's constitutional perplexities, the colonies slipped into a more casual relationship with the Crown, and a period of "benign" neglect, in terms of imperial intrusion, began. In 1775, as those colonies were rebelling over changes to imperial governance and revenue matters, Edmund Burke attempted to convince Parliament that colonial grievances were legitimate. He coined the phrase "salutary neglect" to describe the Crown's loose administration of the American colonies in trade and administrative matters during the second quarter of the eighteenth century. Burke noted that, after about 1720 until the 1750s or later, the colonies had been left alone to conduct their local political and economic affairs and their internal development. In short, during the Walpole era the American mainland colonies grew and matured while the Crown was mostly absent. The British Empire settled into a fluid, integrated, and growing Atlantic community. An interesting paradox was developing in the first half of the eighteenth century. As colonists became more attached to their own unique circumstances and local identities, they also became increasingly committed in spirit and culture to a benign, protective, expanding, and permissive British Empire. Those attachments were taking hold as a third imperial war broke out.

The Third Imperial War in America, 1740–1748

The War of the Austrian Succession, or King George's War in the colonies, raised the stakes in the rivalry between France and Britain. In a telling prelude, war broke out between Spain and Britain in 1739 over increasing British incursions into Spanish America. The conflict was immediately given the colorful title of the "War of Jenkins' Ear" referring to a 1731 incident when Spanish seamen allegedly cut off the ear of a captured British privateer, Captain Jenkins. As proof of his humiliation, Jenkins had appeared in London with his shriveled, pickled ear. Although the story may have been a folkloric fable, it outraged the British public to the extent that, when war with Spain did break out, for entirely different causes, "Jenkins' ear" was used as an example of Spanish crudity. Verbal symbolism was in the air in other ways. For example, James Thomson's and David Mallett's stirring 1740 lines, "Rule, Britannia, rule the waves: / Britons never shall be slaves," coincided with rising British passion. British pride was also matched to music in the public rendering of the melody and lyric of "God Save the King," during the heady atmosphere of the Jacobite Rebellion of 1745.

The term "Britannia" and the visual image of her were familiar. But now the symbol was raised as a synonym for national and imperial identity. Meanwhile, the war with Spain in the Caribbean and adjacent Spanish territory became part of a wider war in Europe, the War of the Austrian Succession. As Maria Theresa of Austria assumed the Habsburg throne, Frederick II of Prussia invaded the contested Polish borderlands of German-speaking Silesia. The Prussian military had been raised to an intimidating standard by Frederick I. The war had the hallmarks of another dynastic struggle among Europe's absolutist monarchs. Louis XV of France and Spain's Philip V both opposed Maria Theresa. Louis wanted to break up the Habsburg Empire and Philip opposed Austrian claims to large parts of Italy. The British were already at war with Spain but decided to broker any alliance it could against France. It funded Prussia's land war against the French and fought the French at sea in the Atlantic, Caribbean, and Mediterranean, as well as on land in India and America. In the latter case, the war fit earlier patterns of mostly small-scale engagements with militias and native proxies doing much of the fighting. Still, there were major campaigns in America. In Acadia, the French launched a failed attempt to recover Port-Royal, which had been renamed Annapolis Royal. At the tip of Cape Breton Island, strategically overlooking the Gulf of St. Lawrence, the apparently impregnable fort at Louisbourg fell to a colonial militia army acting in concert with the Royal Navy. But, after the war, British negotiators needed to get the conflict settled quickly and made what concessions they could, including the return of Louisbourg to the French. This gesture offended the New Englanders who had captured it. The Treaty of Aix-la-Chapelle of 1748 was settled by mutual exigency brought on by sheer military exhaustion and unsustainable expense. In Europe, the war's greatest legacy was the emergence of Prussia as a serious power. In America, New Englanders had committed enthusiastically to the war but would harbor an annoyance with the Crown over the return of Louisbourg. James Oglethorpe of Georgia, with various native allies including Cherokees, had taken the war to the Spanish all the way to St. Augustine. In the end, all parties understood that the outcome of the war was inconclusive. The way was cleared for yet another showdown between Britain and France a decade later. That war would be for bigger global stakes and, among other things, would redefine British North America. Meanwhile, the colonies continued to celebrate their local virtues while settling comfortably under Britannia's protective mantle.

SUGGESTED READINGS

The best overview of colonial American warfare is Ian Steele, *Warpaths: Invasions of North America* (New York: Oxford University Press, 1994). See also the same author's *The English Atlantic, 1675–1740: An Exploration of Communication and Community* (New York: Oxford University Press, 1986). On the politics and imperial economics of the era, see Plumb's *The Growth of Political Stability in England, 1675–1725*, cited in Chapter 5, and D.C. Coleman, *The Economy of England, 1450–1750* (London: Oxford University Press, 1977). James Henretta, *"Salutary Neglect": Colonial Administration under the Duke of Newcastle* (Princeton, NJ: Princeton University Press, 1972) continues to influence the study of Parliament's policies and relations with the colonies. As for the practices, development, and significance of government in the colonies, Bernard Bailyn, *The Origins of American Politics* (New York: Knopf, 1968) is indispensable as a broad overview. See also Jack Sosin, *English America and the Revolution of 1688: Royal Administration and the Structure of Provincial Government* (Lincoln, NE: University of Nebraska Press, 1982).

CHAPTER 7

The Regions of Colonial America: Northern Society and Politics in the Eighteenth Century

I do not find a model in the world, that time, place, and some singular emergences have not necessarily altered; nor is it easy to frame a civil government, that shall serve all places alike.

—William Penn, *Frame of Government with Laws Agreed upon in England* (1682), quoted in Jon Wakelyn, ed., *America's Founding Charters: Primary Documents of Colonial and Revolutionary Era Governance* (Westport, CT: Greenwood Press, 2006), 257.

The Regional Character of Colonial America

The *white* population of the thirteen mainland colonies reached 1 million in 1750. It then doubled and, by 1790, doubled again. Britain's economy began its transition to manufacturing, capital accumulation, urbanism, and technological innovation as Anglo-America, with some minor exceptions, remained steadfastly agricultural into the Revolutionary era. In 1750, England had begun a steady march toward urbanization. While the term "urban" has no absolute parameters, estimates suggest that, if one uses a base measurement of 10,000 for a town or city, 16 per cent of the English population was "urban" in 1750, rising to 21 per cent by the end of the century. The urban figures for Scotland and Ireland were lower, at 9 per cent and 5 per cent, respectively. Scotland's urban population grew rapidly after 1750, reaching 17 per cent by 1800. Using similar criteria, only about 3 per cent of the mainland colonial population was urban in 1750. Only Boston, Philadelphia, and New York had more than 10,000 inhabitants. Indeed, according to the 1790 federal census, with a population of nearly 4 million, the newly created United States contained only six cities of over 8,000 people. An expanding supply of agricultural space allowed the rural population to spread. In the rural British Isles, the trend was away from agrarian replication. Rural and village society, particularly in England, was being transformed into a mix of agriculture, mining, woolen textile manufacturing, and iron foundries. The development of an urban culture was clearly showing, but what drove change in the British economy and culture was the seeping into rural Britain of the commercial, capitalist, and industrial trends of the modern era.

In the mainland colonies, progress and growth were measured by a moving frontier and more of the same: more farms or plantations. The sugar plantations of the West Indies and the tobacco and rice plantations and some commercial farms of the mainland were part of a capitalist world, and tobacco curing and sugar refining suggested some low-level industrial activity, but, for the most part, the commercial economies of the British American colonies were emphatically agricultural. Where there were small concentrations of people, they occurred on plantations or in a few regional towns or ports. Immigration rose in the backcountry in the middle third of the eighteenth century in an arc that ran from Pennsylvania to Georgia and tended to add another stratum of white family farm culture. In Virginia, coastal North Carolina, South Carolina, and Georgia, slave populations boomed but remained largely confined to the tidewater regions and the immediate piedmont areas. To the west, after 1720, growth came from large trans-colonial and transatlantic migration. North Carolina was the fastest growing colony in British America in the few decades before the Revolution, as white families flocked to its backcountry. In fact, by the 1740s, white Virginians and Pennsylvanians had begun to look across the Appalachians to the French-claimed Ohio Valley. Farther north, in a process that had begun with the original settlements, New Yorkers and New Englanders pressed north and west to take up arable land.

Map 7. 1 Regional British America, ca.1750

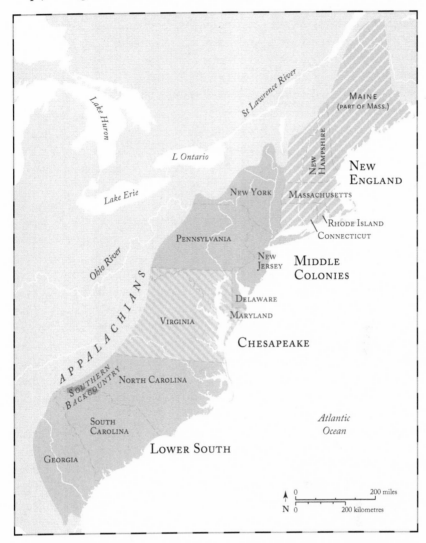

By the middle of the eighteenth century, the migratory trends in all the colonies meant that English colonists had begun to press against French- and Spanish-controlled territories and against western native communities. The internal migrants were, for the most part, subsistence farm families and land speculators. By 1750, British America from Georgia to Maine was a much-expanded version of what it had been in the late seventeenth century. Over half of colonial Americans were engaged in what historians have referred to as "subsistence" farming, an awkward term that presumes that small-scale farming produced enough, or nearly enough, for nuclear families to subsist on.

Another 20 per cent of family units ran profitable farm operations, either as full-time slave-holding planters, all of them in the Chesapeake and south, or full-time commercial grain and livestock farmers, predominantly in the middle colonies. Another 5 per cent or so of families functioned as rural merchants or full-time artisans. The rest of the family economies were engaged in fishing, milling, or in the few urban economies. The identification of occupations has to be qualified. In all regions and in most enterprises, individuals and families had to be flexible. The woman who spun fibers or tended a vegetable garden also took part in every other household, farm, or plantation activity. Certainly there was a gender division of labor, but, like all work, it was not defined by specialty. Children as young as eight or nine labored at appropriate chores as part of the labor resource of the nuclear family unit.

Iron foundries and sawmills and gristmills dotted the rural landscape, but these were invariably small-scale operations serving the needs of local communities. The rural blacksmith made horseshoes, farm implements, and other small metal appliances, often while farming a small family plot. With some exceptions, forges were usually one-man operations. Their clientele was usually from the immediate neighborhood, and income was, in part, the result of barter; a plowshare might bring several bushels of wheat or some shoes from a local cobbler. Farmers wove fibers and developed fabrics from flax or wool of their own or of neighbors. Weavers, tailors, carpenters, and masons exchanged services or goods with each other, as most were also farmers. The 90 to 95 per cent of colonial people who lived in farming environments looked after their basic household clothing, metallurgical needs, and sustenance without any manufacturing of scale.

The urban face of colonial America was in the seaports, in particular in Boston, New York, Philadelphia, and Newport, and in Baltimore and Charleston on a lesser scale. By the first few decades of the eighteenth century, these cities had become regional political and commercial centers. The larger seaports thrived in the expanding Atlantic economy. Docks, wharves, and warehouses employed many hundreds of laborers, and thousands of part- and full-time seamen called them home. The larger centers provided legal and financial services and were the centers of provincial politics and major distribution hubs for the goods that came into the colonies. The lower south, however, lacked even a rudimentary urban culture. Charleston in South Carolina was perhaps the only southern town with any claim to urbanism, although its population did not reach 10,000 until 1770. It was the main port of entry for the slaves who flooded into the southern colonies after the turn of the eighteenth century. Although Williamsburg, New Bern, and Savannah were the seats of the colonial governments in Virginia, North Carolina, and Georgia, respectively, they were as rural as the farming clusters and plantations they served.

Some production of scale did occur in places like Boston, for example, which had thriving shipbuilding industries that encouraged ancil-
lary manufacturing in rope and sail making and ships' repairs and supplies.
Sugar refining and distilling gave Boston a unique feel and function in contrast to the rural hinterland. In any urban, that is, nonagricultural setting,
there were bakers and tailors, tanners and shoemakers who employed male
and female servants and paid wages and trained apprentices but never on a
scale that resembled British practice. The social structures and economies of
Philadelphia and New York were similar to Boston's. They were marked by
warehousing, import and export facilities, and fixed populations of craftsmen,
seamen, dockworkers, and laborers. The largest concentration of African
slaves to be found north of the Chesapeake was in New York City.

Beyond the seaports, the commercial market for basic household
commodities was limited, given the capacity of the local rural economies to
produce and distribute household and farming basics. Increased demand for
imported cloth, expensive household goods, tea, crafted metal products, and
so on did not break down the local economies. Even regional attempts to break
into the rural economies failed. For example, in Boston and Philadelphia in
the mid-eighteenth century, investors' efforts to mass-produce linen textiles
using the labor of the poor and widowed populations failed because these
products could not displace or compete with rural homespun. Rural colonial
British America in the first half of the eighteenth century comprised a multitude of localized rural economies, some of which were exclusively regional:
for example, the whaling community of Nantucket, the cod fisheries of New
England, or the deerskin traders of the southwest. Even though slavery was
a legalized, institutionalized labor system everywhere, we need to differen-
tiate the slaves in tidewater South Carolina and Georgia, who were mostly
African born and worked as gang laborers, from the smaller labor units of
Virginia and Maryland, where a majority of the slave population was either
American born or assimilated by the middle of the eighteenth century.

There was no single colonial economy but rather a separate Pennsylvania
economy, New Hampshire economy, South Carolina economy, and so on—
and perhaps regional extensions of these economies. The climate, geography, and linked histories of New England's colonies constituted a colonial
region, and the demographic, economic, social, and cultural characteristics of New Hampshire resembled those of its neighbors: Massachusetts,
Connecticut, and Rhode Island. Three levels of association best describe the
maturing thirteen colonies: 1) the chartered colony itself connected to its
sub-localities of towns, counties, or parishes; 2) a regional linkage with common intercolonial features such as slavery in the Chesapeake and lower south,
town life in New England, and pluralism in the middle colonies; and 3) the

bond to the British Empire itself. As to the latter, there was an assumption in Britain that constitutional and actual authority descended from the Crown to the colony and then to the local community. However, from the colonial perspective, the nominal order was reversed so that the primary level of authority lay at the narrower local level. Each colony was jealous of its constitutional and legislative identity, and each understood that it possessed a measure of political autonomy. This autonomy was perhaps the single most common characteristic shared by the mainland colonies. As noted, colonists were British in their cultural and "national" identities and took their common political ideas and institutions as their evidence of being British. At another level, each colony, with an ever-rising population, was locked into the British imperial economy even as its locally circulating economies continued.

Table 7.1 Selected Population Figures for the Mainland North American Colonies, 1630–1780

NEW ENGLAND

		NEW HAMPSHIRE	MASSACHU-SETTS	RHODE ISLAND	CONNECTI-CUT
1630	W	500	506	—	—
	B	—	—	—	—
1660	W	1,505	19,660	1,474	7,995
	B	50	422	65	25
1680	W	1,972	39,582	2,902	17,211
	B	75	170	115	35
1700	W	4,828	55,151	5,594	25,520
	B	130	800	300	450
1720	W	9,205	88,858	11,137	57,737
	B	170	2,150	543	1,093
1750	W	26,955	183,925	29,897	108,270
	B	550	3,035	3,347	3,010
1770	W	61,742	*261,336	54,435	178,183
	B	654	*5,229	3,761	5,698
1780	W	87,261	*317,760	**50,275	200,816
	B	541	*5,280	**2,671	5,885

W = White B = Black

*   Includes the Maine counties of Massachusetts, which were listed separately after 1750. The Massachusetts figures for 1770 included 30,783 whites and 475 blacks in the Maine counties; for 1780 the figures were 48,675 and 458, respectively.

**   Rhode Island's population declined as the British wartime occupation of Newport drove many inhabitants into neighboring provinces.

Total New England Population in 1780:
White: 656,112
Black: 14,377 (a drop of 975 persons from the 1770 figures)

MIDDLE COLONIES

		NEW YORK	NEW JERSEY	PENN-SYLVANIA	DELAWARE
1630	W	350	—	—	—
	B	10	—	—	—
1660	W	4,336	—	—	510
	B	600	—	—	30
1680	W	8,630	3,200	665	950
	B	1,200	200	25	55
1700	W	16,851	13,170	17,520	2,335
	B	2,256	840	430	135
1720	W	31,179	27,433	28,962	4,685
	B	5,740	2,385	2,000	700
1750	W	65,682	66,039	116,794	27,208
	B	11,014	5,354	2,872	1,496
1770	W	143,808	109,211	234,296	33,660
	B	19,112	8,220	5,761	1,836
1780	W	189,487	128,987	319,450	42,389
	B	21,054	10,460	7,855	2,996

W = White B = Black

Total Middle Colonies Population in 1780:
White: 680,313
Black: 42,365

SOUTHERN COLONIES

		MARY-LAND	VIRGINIA	NORTH CAROLINA	SOUTH CAROLINA	GEORGIA
1630	W	—	2,450	—	—	—
	B	—	50	—	—	—
1660	W	7,668	26,070	980	—	—
	B	758	950	20	—	—
1680	W	16,293	43,296	5,220	1,000	—
	B	1,611	3,000	210	200	—
1700	W	26,377	42,170	10,305	3,260	—
	B	3,227	16,390	415	2,444	—
1720	W	53,634	61,158	18,270	5,048	—
	B	12,499	26,599	3,000	12,000	—
1750	W	97,623	129,581	53,184	25,000	4,200
	B	43,450	101,452	19,800	39,000	1,000
1770	W	138,781	259,411	127,600	49,066	12,750
	B	63,818	187,605	69,600	75,178	10,625
1780	W	164,959	317,422	179,133	83,000	35,240
	B	80,515	220,582	91,000	97,000	20,831

W = White B = Black

Total Southern Colonies Population in 1780:
White: 779,754
Black: 509,928

ALL COLONIES

	*** TOTALS FOR 1770	*** TOTALS FOR 1780
White	1,688,254	2,204,949
Black	459,822	575,420
Total	2,148,076	2,780,369

*** The aggregate totals include some 23,975 whites and 2,725 blacks (1770) and 88,770 whites and 8,750 blacks (1780) in Kentucky, Tennessee, and Vermont. The figures for those territories and settlements are not listed among the state populations in the foregoing charts.

Source: *Historical Statistics of the United States, Colonial Times to 1970* (Washington, DC: Bureau of the Census, 1975), Part 2, Section Z, pp. 1168ff.

REGIONS: NEW ENGLAND

Many symbols, stereotypes, and popular images of eighteenth century New England exist today. Among the most durable is the theme of transition, of the way collectivism gave way to individualism and acquisitiveness. As the historian Richard Bushman put it, New Englanders moved from being "Puritans" to being "Yankees." To be sure, hard work was seen as a virtue, but it was also necessary in an environment that did not yield its resources easily. Eighteenth century sermons often served as lectures attacking idleness while holding to Winthrop's enjoinder to help the "worthy" poor and needy. Another popular image of colonial New Englanders presents them as taciturn and private. Yet another sees a lingering Calvinism, a severity in moral values and behavior and a persistent respect for authority. The typography of colonial New Englanders is replete with symbolic adjectives such as "hardy" Nantucket whalers and Gloucester fishers and "self-directed" subsistence farmers who cleared and worked the "thin" rocky soil to make a living in a "harsh" climate that fostered toughness and social solidarity. These clichés are more accurate than mythical or fanciful. New Englanders did make what they saw as a tough physical environment into a productive one in a way that reflected strength of character. The archetypal Boston merchant was canny and hardworking, and there was hardly anything like a leisured class in

New England. The original social organization of the town and the family farm persisted and maintained common attachments to locality.

The New England practice of partible inheritance allowed for residential and social continuity. The system meant that, when a father died, the family land was divided among the surviving adult sons. In other words, if there were three male survivors, there would normally be a tripartite division of the land. Although widows and single daughters were provided for, the title to the land went to the male survivors. The extension of political rights that went with land meant that, in the eighteenth century, New Englanders added to the electorate when they bequeathed their land, so long as their heirs paid taxes. The assumed rights of successors helped create the highly politicized, cantankerous, and collectivist New Englanders. They challenged the British during the Stamp Act crisis in 1765. Boston merchants and artisans set the course for dramatic revolutionary activism with the "Tea Party" of 1773. Meanwhile, by resisting British martial law, farmers, en masse, as the symbolic "minutemen," prepared the way for the War for Independence at Lexington-Concord and Bunker Hill.

At the start of the eighteenth century, New England's intellectual life was dominated by Boston's Cotton Mather, the prodigious writer and theologian who, with his father Increase, maintained a link to the high ideals of Winthrop's grand design for a Christian New England. In the first paragraph of the "general" introduction to his seven-volume magnum opus, *Magnalia Christi Americana* of 1702, Mather announces the purposes and outcome of the Puritan mission in what he called "The Ecclesiastical History of New-England":

> [F]lying from the deprivations of Europe, to the American Strand; and, assisted by the Holy Author [of the Christian religion]... I do...report the wonderful displays of His infinite Power, Wisdom, Goodness, and Faithfulness, *wherewith His Divine Providence hath irradiated an Indian Wilderness.* (Emphasis added)

The brilliant Cotton Mather was aggressively conservative on the one hand but fair minded and open to change on the other. He encouraged the prosecution of the Salem witches but could not accept the evidence that was used to prosecute and sought lighter sentences for the convicted. He was also an experimenter in rational medicine and promoted smallpox inoculation. His passion for the Massachusetts ethos drove him to attack the Andros regime in the turmoil of 1689. In 1713, he was the first American to be admitted to the prestigious Royal Society of London for his scientific contributions. In some ways, Mather deserves his reputation as a stern "puritanical" busybody and pedant. He had enemies in Boston, which was changing with the age.

But Cotton Mather also lived at the start of a new age in New England. He published an astonishing 450 books that included sociological, philosophical, and historical works, and he wrote political and moral pamphlets to go with his many theological treatises. His importance lies in his prominence in New England politics and intellectual life and in the fact that his cosmopolitanism and intellect were used to promote New England's exceptional place in the Christian world. Some of his writings influenced later eighteenth century intellectuals. For example, Benjamin Franklin found much sound practical and moral use for Mather's *Bonifacius* or *Essays to do Good* (1710).

If Cotton Mather stands as a pivotal figure in a transitional period in New England history, by the time of the Revolution, merchants such as John Hancock and lawyers such as John Adams had come to dominate public affairs in Massachusetts using language that was increasingly secular. Symbolic references to the "city on the hill" no longer had Saint Matthew in mind, but they did presume to identify a special place in America and the world for New England and, in particular, for Massachusetts. However, the fact remains that each region, indeed, each colony produced its own symbols, ideals, images, and stereotypes of American "originals" and American "exceptionalism." Even Jamestown's wretched beginnings and eventual survival serve to identify America's originality, and Virginia eventually produced George Washington, Thomas Jefferson, and a host of "founders." William Penn's experiment gave rise to American religious and political pluralism, and Pennsylvania cultivated the ultimate American everyman, the Boston-born but Philadelphia-based Benjamin Franklin. So there was no single genesis but rather a set of threads that came together politically, over time, but retained their parochialism well beyond the Revolution.

The most enduring legacy of colonial New England perhaps is the *town*. In its design, role, and legacy, there were no comparable examples elsewhere in colonial America. Today, there are over 1,500 towns in the six New England states (Maine and Vermont are postcolonial creations), each of which owes its local political prerogatives to standards that were designed in the seventeenth century and refined in the eighteenth. In 1750, half the region's 360,000 people lived in Massachusetts. In 1770, there were nearly 350 towns and 580,000 people in the four colonies. Nearly 50 per cent of them lived in Massachusetts.

As noted in Chapter 3, the town, as a subdivision of the larger colony's grant, was assigned to a congregation. It was both ecclesiastical and civil. The town grant was then subdivided into family lots. In Massachusetts, for example, depending on social or ecclesiastical status and economic means, landholders received more or fewer acres, but, in legal terms, each landholder was nominally equal to the next. The initial distribution of land usually ran from lots of 100 acres to 400 acres. Although they were creations of the seventeenth century legislatures, which set the rules for municipal government, towns controlled their own specific affairs in the town meeting. Here, all tax-paying male residents met to discuss bylaws and elect civic officials, usually in the combined meeting house–church. These town meetings petitioned senior governments regarding tax assessments or infrastructure funding or to settle boundary and other conflicts with neighboring towns. A distinct form of municipal government emerged from this model. The town meeting annually elected or appointed selectmen, the equivalent of aldermen or councilors or reeves to serve for a year. The same town meeting appointed constables, tax assessors, weights and measures inspectors, surveyors, and others to manage the town's affairs. Each town, from time to time in peacetime and regularly in wartime, mustered a compulsory militia made up of all able-bodied adult males. Toward the end of the colonial period, some larger towns employed jailers and appointed overseers of the poor.

There was a conscious attempt early on to follow established English patterns of land use, which saw private homesteads supplemented by commons. Local authority and governance borrowed heavily from older Tudor English statutes regarding the poor, the criminal, and the transient. The practice of "warning out" impoverished transients or unsavory, unsponsored, or unknown migrants reflected English vagrancy laws and reinforced the towns' somewhat insular purposes. The most distinctive role of the towns was to serve as the representative units in the New England colonial assemblies. The elected members of the legislative assemblies of Connecticut, Massachusetts (including Maine), New Hampshire, and Rhode Island represented the towns that sent them. Towns, as communal entities rather than as groups of individuals, parties, or ethnic or religious delegates were the agents of representative government. New England's politics evolved into a unique system that contrasted both with traditional, preferential British parliamentary representation and with the economic, ethnic, or proprietary priorities of West Indian and some other British North American jurisdictions. Counties were created in New England but had no political purpose apart from the administration of civil and criminal courts. In all of preindustrial America, the face of authority first presented itself at the local level, and, in New England, *local* meant *town*.

Over time, the town as the fount of New England's culture has been both idealized and scorned. In 1871, for example, the reformer Wendell Phillips looked back and announced breezily that his "ideal of a civilization…is a New-England town of some two thousand inhabitants, with no rich man and no poor man in it, all mingling in the same society…no poorhouse, no beggar, opportunities equal.…That's New England as it was" (*The Labor Question* [Boston: Lee and Shepard, 1884], 19). Professional historians have since revealed cracks in that image. Not all towns in the mid- to late-eighteenth century were harmonious municipal islands of self-sufficient farmers. Population densities or "crowding" in southeastern New England, especially in eastern Massachusetts, began to shrink the stock of available arable land. After a century or more of the subdivision of many of the original land grants, farmers had fewer and fewer acres to leave to the next generation. New towns were created all over New England well into the nineteenth century. However, the towns were smaller, and, even before the Revolution, most new towns were being hived off from the older town grants.

For Massachusetts, the New Hampshire and Maine frontier absorbed some of the constantly expanding population, and there was an outflow of population to the west and north. On the eve of the Revolution, however, as much as 50 per cent of Massachusetts's population lived within 25 miles of Boston. There was a rise in landlessness as too many sons chased too few acres in the older, settled parts of the colonies. Population density in Massachusetts, excluding Maine, rose from 7 to 26 persons per square mile between 1700 and 1760. Population concentrations were very high in maritime and fishing communities along the coast and in the agrarian arc around Boston, where density reached 44 persons per square mile compared to about 12 per square mile in the rest of the province. This long-term trend also occurred in the environs of New York City and Philadelphia. In western Massachusetts, Springfield grew to dominance as an important regional center but, for the most part, the agricultural towns remained relatively small. In all of New England, over half the rural towns contained only a few hundred families and had populations of between one and two thousand people. In Connecticut, there were population pods around New Haven and Hartford and along Long Island Sound and in Rhode Island, the town of Newport dominated the small agricultural hinterland of that colony.

Rivers determined settlement patterns everywhere in the mainland colonies. The Hudson in New York; the Delaware in Pennsylvania; the Potomac, Rappahannock, and James in Virginia; and the Savannah farther south had all served as highways and settlement strips. In New England, the Connecticut River Valley had, by the middle of the eighteenth century, become a major strip of settlement as the river flowed through New Hampshire, Massachusetts, and Connecticut into Long Island Sound. Along the Merrimack River, a ribbon of settlements ran back from eastern Massachusetts into New Hampshire. In Maine, population concentrated itself along the Penobscot River. For over a century, timber and fur influenced Maine's growth and access to the Atlantic kept a population of farmers, fishers, traders, and shippers active. Although Maine remained a part of Massachusetts until 1820, its counties had become a semiautonomous subdivision of the Massachusetts General Court by the middle of the eighteenth century. It continued to be the fastest growing part of New England into the nineteenth century as its settlements pushed north and west. The governance of Maine towns closely resembled those in the southern parts of the region.

The Town and the Farm

Historians of New England have categorized towns by size, location, function, and wealth. Thus, depending on a variety of factors such as soil types, region, and average land holdings, there might be an emphasis in a particular town or area on grains or cattle or sheep rearing. Some statistics show *average* farm acreages of about 100 acres in southern New England, but the figures have to be viewed with caution because the size of working farms ranged from as few as 20 acres in the older settled regions to several hundred acres in the west and north. Moreover, 100 acres dominated by exhausted soil, woodlots, uneven terrain, marshes, and rock was less useful to a family than 10 to 20 acres of good soil and pasture. On some larger holdings, with the help of one or two servants, landholders produced agricultural surpluses for market. But the majority of New England's farmers worked as few as 10 or 15 acres based on the extent of their property and the size of the family labor unit, and they filled out their material needs with labor and other forms of exchange. Out of necessity, this rural economy produced a versatile labor and skills population in which crafts or trades identities usually accompanied a major occupation as "farmer" or "husbandman." There was no clear division of labor or assignment of specialty in those environments. In fact, only a few rural towns could support a full-time carpenter, blacksmith, weaver, tailor, shoemaker, or tanner. With the necessary tools for spinning, weaving, or tanning, a farmer or neighbor could custom make clothing from wool, linen (flax), or leather at home. These micro economies produced considerable social intimacy and political and economic interdependency, but their agricultural inefficiencies were obvious. As late as the 1790s, Timothy Dwight observed that "the husbandry of New England is far inferior to that of Great Britain." He noted "a deficiency in the quantity of labour" and "insufficient manuring; the want of a good rotation of crops; and slovenliness in cleaning the ground. The soil is not sufficiently pulverized [broken]; nor sufficiently manured. [Farmers]...are generally ignorant of what crop will best succeed another; and...fields are covered with a rank growth of weeds" (*Travels in New-England and New-York* [New Haven: S. Converse, 1821], 109). As the twentieth century economist Percy Bidwell noted, New Englanders knew of the improvements in agricultural science, those "of Tull, Bakewell, Townsend, Coke, and Arthur Young" but appear to have ignored them because, in New England, "implements were rough and clumsy, livestock was neglected [and the quality of] the land exhausted" (*History of Agriculture in the Northern United States, 1620–1860* [1925; repr., New York: P. Smith, 1941], 84).

Why then was there no great innovation or advance in New England's agricultural methods or technology? The improvements in British agriculture and, to some extent, on larger and commercially productive farms in America were not possible on New England's multitude of small farms. Even if it occupied more than 10 acres, a family could barely cultivate or work that much land. A husband and wife and perhaps two grown children might be able to grow two or three acres of grain crops; raise a few cattle, sheep, or pigs; and tend to a vegetable garden and orchard. Family members might even manage the labor to make cider and soap and many households spun fibers from their own flax or wool. During the winter break from intensive agriculture, the family might even find a market to exchange some other skills such as weaving, shoemaking, or carpentry. But the limits to subsistence farming did not mean that New England farmers were economically primitive. The cost of maintaining the family farm as the family's vital socio-economic agency limited the farmers' ability to improve the farm. The smallholder could not hire labor to properly maintain the land or expand crops or improve livestock management. The subsistence farmer could not amass enough capital or credit to afford improved farm implements such as a superior harrow or plow or the oxen to pull them. Families on those small farms were self-employed units that managed their own accounts. Even servitude was bartered, as parents, from time to time, sent their children to neighbors to learn specific skills or to work off debts or obligations and, in many ways, to integrate the children into their wider community. Account books were kept, and, even if little money circulated, debts and credits, labor costs and materials were always assessed as monetary value.

As in virtually all of rural North America, wage labor was rare. For the vast majority of rural New Englanders, there was no nearby alternative to the family farm, so it persisted as a cultural and economic imperative into the nineteenth century. In an important way, that very persistence also precluded the sale and aggregation of smaller parcels into larger commercial holdings that might have encouraged innovation for profit. The subsistence economy began at the very edge of the maritime and commercial urban societies. For example, the town of Roxbury, immediately adjacent to Boston, was still agricultural in the middle of the eighteenth century; the majority of its families held deed to some land, even though some of the holdings were as small as a few acres. In southern New England, fewer than 10 per cent of farmers produced annual surpluses for market on a full-time basis. Perhaps another 10 per cent of rural adult males were not farmers but full-time merchants or mill owners or retired elders. Another 10 per cent were occupied full time in a craft such as masonry, carpentry, or blacksmithing. Even those families might raise some livestock on a few acres or tend to an orchard or woodlot.

Farmer-laborer, farmer-shoemaker, farmer-blacksmith, or farmer-carpenter (and so on) was the common status of males in the eighteenth century farm towns. Many of the hundreds of surviving account books indicate the intricate dealings of rural families with their neighbors in this system of flexible economic exchange. A good example of the exchange and interdependency habits of the rural community can be seen in the following summary of some of the accounts of John Reed, a farmer-shoemaker in Weymouth, Massachusetts, 12 miles from Boston. Reed's farm contained 20 acres of combined tillage, cultivated grass, pasture, and orchard. His account book and many others of similar content are today housed in the Baker Library at Harvard. The sample here deals with the variety of goods Reed received for shoe manufacture and repair involving some 30 separate customers for the 12 months following February 1743. All entries have attached monetary values, but none is given here; little money changed hands and the purpose here is to denote the varieties of exchange and not "income."

Among the items Reed received as credit for making or repairing shoes were hides, milk, rye, calf-skins, a pound of fat, cash, turnips, flax, honey, meat, earthenware, an almanac, dry fish, two pigs, wool, salt, hay, molasses, oil, plums, biscuits, cider, casks, and fish. Reed built (or had built) a house in 1742–1743, and he received the following construction materials in barter: posts, clay, rails, one thousand shingles, one thousand bricks, pavements, lime, clapboards, and planks. For his shop, Reed received in barter from local suppliers four-dozen heels, a side of cured leather, and tacks. Reed received the following farm and related labor: from a client's slave, Sambo, splitting rails, plowing, driving plow for two acres, and sliding six loads of wood; from a client's white servant carting hides to Braintree, a day's work planting, one day thatching a barn, a day's work hoeing, and mortising eight posts; and from customers themselves, Reed received carting dung and hay, helping in carrying hay, carting corn, carting stones, gathering corn and picking apples, hoeing, mowing, and butchering. For the construction of his dwelling, Reed credited a mason with chimney work, laying paths, plastering, making mortar, underpinning, and "you and Nathaniel's work." From a blacksmith, he received axe sharpening, a hoe, and a spindle. From a tailor, he obtained a frock, doublet, jacket and britches, and also "driving my plow" and "your wife for work." He also had a deed written and "borrowed horses." Each commodity and work assignment had a monetary value given to it, though less than 10 per cent of all dealings concluded with a money settlement.

In most of southern New England, interspersed among the thousands of farms and hundreds of meeting houses, were brick kilns, forges, woodlots, and ore diggings. On streams and rivers, dozens of sawmills and gristmills served local communities. Roads and trails crisscrossed the region, and, in some towns, taverns and retail shops were located at crossroads. Some larger farms did use servants by the day or week or longer, but most small farms exchanged their labor or hired a neighbor's son or daughter on a reciprocal basis. In any case, New England did not produce or maintain a permanent class of servants. In the coastal and mercantile economies of Newport, Salem, and Boston, merchants and shipowners did contract with household servants and, in some cases, slaves. However, labor options on the coast were broader than those available in towns inland, where the nature of the agrarian world meant that travel beyond walking distances required a horse, and few rural New Englanders possessed one. Tillage, too, was limited by a family's capacity to work a few acres of soil, as, in most areas, only a few oxen were available, and humans often pulled plows. As the family operated as a productive unit, its functions during the seeding, growing, and harvesting seasons were concentrated on harmonized labor.

As the John Reed sample above indicates, there was little or no time for rest. When winter curtailed most outdoor work and darkness drew families even closer to the homestead, hard work was still required from all to make ends meet. Wool carding, leather tanning, and flax to linen processing followed the harvest season. Spinning, weaving, dyeing, and tailoring were also done locally. Although not all farms produced all the fibers they needed, most produced some part of their clothing and food needs. The refining of flax, from plant to seed removal to the pummeling of the stalks, was among the dirtiest and tiring of winter farm tasks, but flax-based linen was the most economical and accessible fabric available to farmers. Leather, from cattle, game, or swine, and spun sheep's wool went into the more durable and winter clothing. Animals provided the fats and tallow for making candles and soap (lye was tediously leached from wood ashes); these chores required heavy and skilled labor and were among the many tasks that devolved to wives and daughters. Charcoal pits produced potash, which, along with dung, provided fertilizer. The pre-mechanical rural world was quieter than ours but perhaps smellier. The odors of cooking, boiling clothes, and burning wood mingled with those of humans to produce pungent indoor air. Bathing was rare and absent in winter. Outdoor work was subject to the amount of natural light available and to favorable weather. Winter kept people indoors or close to home for days on end.

Even the most modest farm produced apples, turnips, flax, and oats or English corn (wheat) or "Indian" corn. Most owned one or more animals for fibers and meat. Colonists had to salt meat, preserve vegetables and fruits, and make cider or beer. Heavy manual labor demanded high calorie diets. Records show that the rations allotted to campaigning soldiers usually contained over

4,000 calories a day, for each man. In campaigns against the French in the middle of the eighteenth century, New England militias consumed huge amounts of starchy and protein-rich foods. The sheer physical output of a day's march in the forests and the setting up and tearing down of camps placed enormous demands on strength and stamina. Farm labor, at times, was no less demanding, and diets were rich in carbohydrates and proteins. Beef, mutton, or pork (salted, cured, or fresh) was complemented with milk, bread, and root vegetables. Sugar came with some of the carbohydrates, but, in most towns, it was also available in cake form produced in the refineries of Boston or Newport. Beer was used as nourishment as well as an intoxicant.

In broad terms, in the first half of the eighteenth century, life expectancy for both males and females in New England was approximately 42 years. This average was determined by fairly high rates of infant mortality. Primitive standards of sanitation and rudimentary medical procedures merged with postnatal infections, congenital defects, and delivery complications to cause high levels of infant mortality. White women throughout the northern colonies averaged eight or more births during their fertile years; some four or five children usually survived. However, surviving infancy meant that an individual's life expectancy rose dramatically. The majority of rural New Englanders and middle colony farmers who reached the age of 20 could expect to live to 70. Beyond the infant death figures, the general mortality rate, that is, the number of deaths per capita, was very low in New England and not much higher than in the general population of today's United States. The rural environment, from Maine to Pennsylvania and even in parts of the white south, was healthier than Europe's. Diets in the colonies were generally superior in quantity and variety, and lower population densities meant that the effects of the inevitable epidemics of infectious diseases were less devastating than they were in Europe. Nevertheless, in the late 1730s and early 1740s, repeated outbreaks of diphtheria north of the Chesapeake killed thousands of rural inhabitants. Higher population densities meant that, in Boston, Newport, New York City, Philadelphia, and Charleston, mortality rates were three or four times higher than in the countryside. Smallpox, the scourge of the native populations, struck hard at whites too, often with terrifying results. In 1721, in Boston, for example, over half the population was infected and nearly 900 died. Over 700 deaths resulted from a 1760 outbreak in Charleston, South Carolina. Although smallpox hit rural communities, its greatest impact was in the periodic outbursts that ravaged the seaports. Without the increasing application of inoculation through the eighteenth century, the death tolls from smallpox would have been even more alarming.

By the 1760s, coastal New England had developed in different ways from the world of the farm. A string of towns ran from Castine, Maine, a small trading outpost in Penobscot Bay, all the way south to Long Island Sound. These were a mix of fishing, whaling, and shipping ports. Immediately north of Boston, Gloucester and Marblehead were home to fleets of commercial fishing vessels that swept the north Atlantic for cod from the Grand Banks to Newfoundland. In the late 1760s, cod accounted for a third of the value of New England's exports. Because of the 1692 witchcraft crisis, Salem survives in lore as a dramatic symbol of parochial New England. It was even used to parallel the paranoia of mid-twentieth century cold war America in Arthur Miller's *The Crucible*. But, in the middle of the eighteenth century, Salem was becoming a major regional port of entry. As its docks and warehouses expanded, it rose in status to become the second largest port in Massachusetts by the time of the Revolution. To the south, Newport and, indeed, Rhode Island itself were the most heterogeneous of New England's communities. There was more religious and ethnic variety in Rhode Island than elsewhere in the region, and Newport's sophisticated merchant community rivaled Boston's in wealth, influence, and international enterprise. Newport was home to America's largest Jewish community, and its homes, shops, and wharves employed the largest slave community north of New York City, as much as 14 per cent of the total population. Still, throughout the entire colonial period, Boston was the region's major economic *entrepôt* and the heart of New England politics and culture.

Boston

From the top of Beacon Hill in Boston, looking south or west, an observer in 1760 saw fields, farmsteads, some wooded patches, pastures, and open space that began at the very edge of the town. Looking the other way, that is, to the north or east from Beacon Hill, the viewer would first see a jumble of tenements and wharves and a web of narrow and crooked streets and lanes; then the mouth of the Charles River, Boston's extensive harbor, and a cluster of small islands; and finally the Atlantic horizon. What would most likely strike the observer was the concentration of habitation. In the 1760s, the population density of Massachusetts, excluding Maine, was about 26 persons per square mile. In Boston, the population per square mile was a stunning 12,000, as people had settled onto a small peninsula, separated dramatically from its rural environs by a narrow strand of land, the "neck." Beacon Hill and the Commons took up a major part of the town's area, leaving 15,000 people crammed into less than one and a half square miles on the peninsula. Boston was a walking city. No person was farther than a half hour or so by foot from the most distant friend, relative, or commercial associates.

In 1713, the town was subdivided into eight wards, which grew to twelve in 1735. These precincts served as administrative neighborhoods where fire wardens, overseers of the poor, and other corporate functionaries were established. Boston's economy was unlike any other in the region. Its merchants had their own ships built, equipped, and manned locally before sending them whaling or trading. Sails, ropes, and barrels were manufactured locally to supply the shipbuilding industry and to service the large numbers of domestic and imperial ships that used the port of Boston. Coopers, for example, thrived in Boston and other seaports because foods and liquids had to be transported or preserved in barrels. Barrels came in a variety of sizes and forms, "pipes," "hogsheads," "firkins," and so on, and staves and rims were required in huge quantities everywhere in the Atlantic world. Other merchants imported consumer goods that were increasingly in demand throughout the region. Miles of docks were run by wharfingers, who owned or managed the wharves as shippers and receivers. Hundreds of dockhands, carters, and sailors worked the wharves and lived in the nearby tenements and alleys.

There was an internal, town-based retail sector of bakeries, breweries, butchers, and tailors on a scale and in an economy that simply could not exist in rural New England. Widows, including "grass widows," that is, wives whose husbands had run off to sea or were long absent, were favored in the licensing of taverns or were, in a few instances, employed in large numbers in private or public supported schemes to spin or process cloth for sale. Boston was no larger than a moderate-sized English market town, but it exercised a form of domestic imperialism *vis-à-vis* the region. It also printed the newspapers, books, pamphlets, and sermons that circulated in Massachusetts and beyond. It housed specialized craftsmen and retailers— from silversmiths to wigmakers to tobacco merchants. Apprentices, servants, and laborers hustled around the docks and shops, and wives and daughters kept the small household economies going. Working- or middle-class youth were groomed for trades or crafts at an early age while the male children of the "better sorts" studied the classics and accounting for a future in business or law. The daughters of the well to do studied manners and decorum and prepared for a suitable marriage. The daughters of the majority learned useful household skills while they too prepared for a suitable marriage. There were no "careers" open to women of any class, only the prospect of a central role in the household economy. Rural adolescent males learned a useful skill to go with their future in farming, and, in Boston or Newport or in the fishing towns, youth were likely to be more focused, that is, more specialized, in crafts or in fishing or seamanship.

When Bostonians of all classes gathered in huge numbers to protest the British Parliament's new legislation in the 1760s and 1770s, they were reflecting a long history of collective civic activism. From time to time, laborers and artisans gathered to protest food and commodity prices. The population would turn out for the annual "Pope's Day" parade, a Boston version of "Guy Fawkes Day," named after the failed 1605 Catholic plot to blow up James I and England's Houses of Parliament. Town officials paraded through the wards of the town in annual displays of civic collectivism. By the 1740s, Boston had peaked in its growth and reached its optimum prerevolutionary size, but its importance to Massachusetts and regional New England continued. Ultimately, after 1763, it became the most active center of protest in the colonies.

New England's Regional Culture and Society

The hum of Boston commerce, the rural New England town as social organ, the legislative process, the agrarian nuclear family, and a common history defined a regional culture. The ethnic face of New England remained predominantly English, but what had been modified was the Congregational Church's hegemony. The orthodox Calvinism of the first half of the seventeenth century had been softened. After the first generation of ministers and theologians, there was much lamenting of the weakening of the holy mission of the founders, the so-called declension thesis that focused on the decline of spiritual integrity. The "jeremiad" and the cautionary sermons of failure and defeat gave way in the eighteenth century to sermons that concentrated on self-help and personal responsibility. Preachers railed against idleness and social disorder as much as they attempted to retain, revive, or redesign Calvinist doctrine. Socially, even in the midst of visible demographic change, New Englanders were busy expanding north or west in search of fertile and accessible land. New towns continued to be created on the fringes of settlement and by subdividing existing towns. But there was also significant multigenerational residential persistence. Although the New England colonies attracted fewer immigrants than the rest of mainland British America, the high levels of natural increase, a healthy population, and longevity kept the population growing at an impressive rate. As noted, there were periodic outbreaks of diphtheria, influenza, and the apparently contagious "throat distemper" along with the dreaded smallpox, but, by any contemporary measure, anywhere in the world, New England was a healthy place.

Despite New Englanders having to face the constant threat of war with natives or with the French and their native allies, New England society was not particularly violent internally. Compared to Britain and to Europe in general, crime rates were low. New England appears tranquil when one considers the numbers of capital crimes in Britain in the eighteenth century, the frequency of hangings and deportations, and the size of prison populations.

Certainly, most of the social and economic causes of theft, assault, and murder that existed in Britain were absent in New England, and colonists were less likely in 1760 to find witches or adulterers to hang than they had been wont to do a century earlier. Although the material standard of living improved in statistical terms, there were increasing numbers of poor people in eastern and southern New England. Most of the larger towns engaged public officials to regulate poor relief. Boston had a separate almshouse for the "deserving poor," a workhouse for the "able" poor, and a prison. Poverty in England and Scotland was systemic, and the poor laws reflected a persistently high level of people without the means or opportunity for subsistence. In New England, poverty and dependency were seldom life-long conditions for all but a small minority.

The late seventeenth century English census of Gregory King lumped together "servants" with "paupers" and "cottagers" to suggest that the majority of families in England were dependent on landlords, employers, charity, or servitude. That was not the case in New England, where "dependency" was usually a phase rather than a lifetime status. But there were destitute and transient people in the population: orphans, abandoned or widowed wives, incompetent or infirm dependents. Many made their way into Boston, for example, where they joined with the urban needy to put pressure on the tax base and, at times, strain the patience of the authorities. There were large numbers of young rural New England men who were without an inheritance or whose inheritance had been delayed. They worked as laborers or applied what talents they had to other occupations to earn enough money or credit to lease or buy a home, or to eventually outfit an inherited farm. And misfortune could strike by way of a failed crop, the death of a father, or the lack of suitable land to pass on to a son. The urban economies of Boston and Newport and other commercial towns fluctuated as trade volume ebbed and flowed and shifted to other commodities and locations. Indeed, Boston's economy collapsed following the boom created by King George's War. The incidence of full-blown unemployment (a lack of available employment) was low, but many urban, maritime, and day laborers everywhere did encounter periods of underemployment during their lifetimes.

Still, living standards improved for the majority. Deeds, inventories, and account books are common sources for gauging material standards, and they indicate a broad general improvement across the northern colonies. A concept that appeared in this period in the northern colonies was "competency." What it meant was the idea that the rural family applied its energies, skills, and human resources to achieving a level of sufficiency, a measure of economic independence—a competency. A useful place to look at the effects of time and permanence is in the changing quality of housing standards.

Homes were more substantial and refined by the second half of the eighteenth century. Wall hangings, glass windows, plank flooring, brick exterior walls, lath and plaster interior walls, stone foundations, manufactured furniture, dishes, cutlery, kitchen appliances, and other accoutrements had made their way into rural New England. Interiors were less likely to be single shared spaces, and a trend to privacy became part of the functional separation of space within homes. Homespun dominated, but there was a measurable trend to imported luxury goods. The crude lean-tos, dugouts, and ramshackle temporary houses of the initial settlements had long since given way to permanence. Public structures such as meeting houses, courthouses, churches, granaries and gunpowder houses, and legislative buildings were more substantial. Commercial buildings such as markets, warehouses, and workshops were larger. Today, a wide variety of mid-eighteenth century architecture can still be seen in cities such as, for example, Boston, Newport, and Salem.

There were differences in social status everywhere. Deference toward the well off, the clergy, and the educated business and legal classes created a social ramp of "better sorts," "middling sorts," and "lesser sorts." But New England's common civil institutions, similar religious outlooks, and a persistent ethnic homogeneity gave the region an internal coherence that also marked it off from other parts of Britain's North American Empire. The majority of New Englanders were now native born. Older sumptuary codes were disappearing, ending the rules for dressing according to status. Permanence meant paved roads, taverns, coach travel, and rural stores. Artisans, physicians, and lawyers joined ministers as well-educated members of rural middling sorts. There were pockets of squalor, drunkenness, and even destitution in Boston, for example, but they did not disfigure the society. There was refinement among the Harvard and Yale cognoscenti and their libraries, clubs, and associations. Rich merchants spent hours in their counting houses and more hours studying languages and reading the classics and the latest political and philosophical treatises from Europe. By the middle of the eighteenth century, New England society was self-defined even as it retained an attachment to the empire and to the major features of British culture, politics, and law.

REGIONS: THE MIDDLE COLONIES

What made the colonies of Delaware, New Jersey, New York, and Pennsylvania a region? The use of "middle" to define the group is at first a geographical convenience, but the term also helps distinguish the four colonies from the ethnic and sectarian homogeneity of New England and the slave dependent colonies of their southern neighbors. Still, each colony in the region was distinct from the others in some important ways. New York's origins, development, and economic character stemmed in part from the Dutch to English transition of the late seventeenth century. Pennsylvania began as an immense proprietary grant with Quaker and neo-feudal purpose but became the most accessible colony for the masses of white, land-seeking, multiethnic, multi-sectarian immigrants. Delaware shared some of the characteristics of its Chesapeake neighbors and, at the same time, reflected some of New Jersey's and Pennsylvania's social features. Parts of New York on Long Island and along portions of the Hudson River were settled by New Englanders and resembled New England's corporate society.

It is not enough, however, to define the middle colonies simply as *not* New England and *not* the Chesapeake and south; we should view the region as a distinctive component of the North American Empire. For the most part, land was granted to individuals who formed communities of counties, townships, and villages. Climate differences with the Chesapeake meant that landholders in the middle colonies farmed in conventional family-based ways and produced grains, livestock, and consumables for their own use as well as for local and overseas markets. The mixed farm was dominant. Slaves were found in places like Philadelphia and New York City and on some of the larger estates. But only in New York and the adjoining parts of New Jersey and, particularly, in New York City were they present in conspicuous numbers. In 1770, slaves and free blacks made up nearly 12 per cent of New York's total population and 7 per cent of New Jersey's. Delaware's slave population was slightly more than 5 per cent of the whole. The rapid growth of the white population in the region in the eighteenth century was due to high levels of white immigration and healthy natural increase. On the other hand, the colonies of the Chesapeake and the south owed much of their population growth to the growth of slave labor. As noted, the slave population of Virginia grew at nearly twice the rate of the colony's white population.

An estimated 585,000 people came to the British mainland colonies between 1700 and 1775, with over four-fifths of them arriving after 1730. The numbers included 278,000 African slaves who were being landed at a rate of seven or eight thousand annually in the 1760s. The middle colonies attracted much of the white European immigration because of generous land distribution practices, especially in Pennsylvania, and because of "push" factors in places like Northern Ireland and Germany. Only 17 per cent of the 300,000 white immigrants were English while some 33 per cent were Germans. Over half of the white total came from British societies other than England. The southern Irish, the Scotch-Irish, and the Scots and Welsh were identified by the English as ethnic groups and considered themselves as culturally and linguistically distinct. Being "British" did not translate into cultural homogeneity. There were some Gaelic speakers among the British immigrants, but the majority spoke English. They did so, however, in many dialects and accents. Even among the native English, there were patterns of speech and dialects that came from the colloquial diversity of England itself.

One of the outcomes of the British colonial experience in America was the slow blending of that wide range of accents, dialects, and vocabularies—and even the Dutch and German languages—into a narrower set of sounds. All of them were essentially *new* English accents that corresponded to the regional subdivisions of mainland North America. In the lower south, the accents and hybridized linguistics of African and African American slaves found their way into white speech mannerisms. From the start, some native terms for the physical world had entered the colonial idiom. Occasionally, a French or Spanish term entered the lexicon. The sound and style of today's American English began to take shape in the mingling of peoples in the colonial period.

Most of the Scots who went to America before the Revolution were Lowlanders. The Highlanders exodus came later. As the immigrants dispersed, many of them integrated directly into existing populations. But there was considerable voluntary and convenient segregation, as Scotch-Irish families and groups made their way to the western fringes of Pennsylvania, for example, or Germans established unilingual townships or sectarian enclaves. An early group of German immigrants in 1710 tried to settle in New York's Hudson Valley, but restrictive land policies there drove them to the frontier. Thereafter, Germans tended to go to Pennsylvania. In 1719 an estimated 7,000 southwestern and Palatine Germans along with Swiss migrants landed in Pennsylvania. The flow continued at roughly 2,000 a year until the Revolution. In the first United States census of 1790, one-third of Pennsylvania's population was German or of German descent, and, although the majority of the remaining two-thirds was British, only one-third claimed English ancestry.

A new British America was taking shape. The people who came in the eighteenth century, for the most part, flowed into established communities or settled near them. Much had changed. For most of the seventeenth century, the majority of newcomers were white servants. They might have arrived for short- or long-term service, arriving alone or with families, or perhaps they were indentured to Chesapeake planters. They were mostly young and male. White servants constituted 55 per cent of all arrivals, including slaves, in the seventeenth century. In the eighteenth century, the proportion of white servants to the whole immigrant population fell to 18 per cent. The proportion of exiled British convicts, who were sent into service in America, rose from 2 per cent of the whole to 9 per cent on the eve of the Revolution. Meanwhile, the most striking change was in the surging importation of African or West

Indian slaves, from 7 per cent of the whole to 45 per cent of all immigrants. British America became increasingly more racially, culturally, and ethnically complex in the decades before the Revolution. New England remained mostly white and mostly English.

The royal charters of the late seventeenth century in New England had opened up settlement to all English immigrants, and the 1707 union with Scotland had given Scots equal rights to settle. Although there was considerable tolerance in northern New England to Scottish, Scotch-Irish, and Irish settlement, Massachusetts passed a law in 1720 to discourage Irish settlement. Scottish and Scotch-Irish Presbyterians who did manage to get into Massachusetts were ostracized and, in some cases, verbally and physically abused by Congregationalists. The combination of sectarian hostility and limited space kept immigration to southern New England to a minimum, and the Massachusetts population remained overwhelmingly English by descent, over 82 per cent, into the revolutionary era.

Immigration statistics give us numbers and other pertinent data such as immigrant origin, destination, and, sometimes, economic status. Beyond the hard data, however, the recorded experiences of ordinary humans as they traversed the Atlantic and then struggled to set up in North America reveal the drama of immigration. The passage itself was an ordeal for most and only slightly less horrendous for the minority of passengers with means to afford a bit of shipboard comfort. In the first place, the crossing from Europe or the British Isles to the mainland ports of North America took from one to four months depending on weather, stopovers, and seamanship. For the groups of Germans making their way down the Rhine to Rotterdam or elsewhere, another two months could be added to the trip. In the Atlantic, the possibility of storms, damage, and pirates and, during war, the threat of enemy ships added uncertainty to any voyager's prospects. The ships carrying the immigrants were usually too small or at best poorly designed to accommodate the numbers who packed into them. Although paying travelers were afforded more comfortable and spacious quarters than the throngs of servants and redemptioners crammed into the lower decks, they too were exposed to indiscriminate infectious diseases. Food and water were always vulnerable to taint and waste. Seasickness affected everyone on unstable ships in the cold, often stormy, and seasonally violent North Atlantic.

Yet the thousands of passenger, cargo, military, and slave ships that annually crossed the Atlantic during the centuries of sail were remarkably reliable even if passengers and crews had quite awful shipboard experiences. Hunger, thirst, fear, and detachment troubled emigrants, and illnesses were sometimes fatal. Typhus ("ship's fever"), scurvy, an array of gastrointestinal afflictions, and dysentery (the "bloody flux") were common. An outbreak of any infectious disease could decimate a ship's crew and passenger list. Among the accounts that survive, one of the most famous is that of Gottlieb Mittelberger, a minor church functionary who claimed to have been associated with the delivery of an organ from his base in Baden-Württemberg to a German congregation in Pennsylvania. He spent six months getting to his destination, arriving in Philadelphia in October 1750 in the company of about 400 German and Swiss-German redemptioners. Although Mittelberger's hostility to the agents in Europe who had recruited and misled the boatload of servants motivated him to write and publish his journal, the conditions he witnessed and recorded were not altogether unusual.

Mittelberger emphasized the physical and emotional misery of the passengers. In a much-cited passage, he noted that 500 passengers were jammed into a ship, "packed densely, like herrings." The adults had a "bedstead" in a space of about two feet by six feet with only a few inches between each body. Mittelberger recorded "smells, fumes, horrors, vomiting...sea sickness, fever, dysentery, headaches, heat, constipation, boils, scurvy, cancer, mouth-rot.... [the] highly-salted state of the...meat...and filthy water...very black, thick with dirt, and full of worms...[and] toward the end of the voyage, ...the ship's biscuit, which had already been spoiled for a long time...full of red worms and spiders' nests" (*Journey to Pennsylvania* [Cambridge: Belknap Press of Harvard University, 1960], 12–15.) He reported that 32 children had died and been thrown into the sea, noting that these crossings were especially hard on children who "from 1 to 7 years rarely survive the voyage."

The hardships of getting to a port of departure, boarding and then spending days waiting for clearance, followed by a lengthy, arduous voyage were bad enough. Then there was uncertainty for many once they reached America, which would temper any idea of unalloyed enthusiasm for arrival. Yet the attraction of America and the ultimate rewards it promised kept the throngs coming. Mittelberger was relentless in reporting death and despondency, and if his fellow passengers were in fact as demoralized as he saw them, there was also fatalism in their decisions. Few, if any, would make the return voyage. Upon arrival at any of the ports, immigrant servants were divided into categories: those who came with contracts or others who were available to be "bought" or hired to redeem their fares. Some suffered for days waiting to be employed. There were family members who were met by their donors and others who had arranged for their own passage.

This elaborate dispersal method depended on some system of communication. Ships' regular departure and arrival schedules were often published, but there were also unscheduled sailings. The need to improvise because of bad weather, diversions, stopovers, or other impediments meant that ships might sit for a time in a harbor until the news of their presence could be broadcast in and beyond the port by written notice or word of mouth. In any case, the immigration of so many tens of thousands of Europeans, especially into the middle colonies, reshaped American society in the two generations before the Revolution, just as increased volumes of slave imports affected the Carolinas. Natural increase accounted for most of the growth in the colonial population, but immigration played a major role in the *way* the colonies grew. Although the basic institutional structures of politics and economics seemed set, the cultural and social face of most of the colonies south of New England were influenced by the medley of people, with their distinctive tongues, sects, and aptitudes, who arrived in the eighteenth century. Certainly many immigrants were absorbed and assimilated into English ways, but many found their way into ethnic enclaves, especially in Pennsylvania, New Jersey, and the northern Chesapeake. Still others, arriving in groups, congregations, or even shiploads established themselves in new communities, especially on the frontier.

The Chesapeake absorbed a portion of the influx, but the majority went to the middle colonies. In 1700, New York and Pennsylvania each had slightly less than 20,000 inhabitants, but, by 1760, Pennsylvania's population was 183,000 while New York's was about 117,000. That trend was reversed after 1800 when New York's commercial and industrial sectors dominated the region's economy. Prerevolutionary Pennsylvania's growth was one of the most significant demographic factors in the history of the colonies north of the Chesapeake. As for New York, much of the settlement of the fertile land on Long Island resembled New England, and many towns had in fact been established by Puritans in the seventeenth century. Otherwise, the huge landed estates north along the Hudson were in the hands of a few important families. Their "manors" engrossed much of the area's arable land and kept it from potential immigrants who otherwise had the means to purchase it. Thus, in the Hudson Valley, tenancy was more common than in most parts of the colonies, and, although some of the terms offered to tenants were generous by European standards, immigrants preferred the system of land distribution in Pennsylvania. There, a land bank was established to help with mortgages and loans, and land was distributed to settlers in return for quitrents, a system whereby the leaseholder paid an annual fee to the government or the private deed holder.

Land was the lure everywhere, of course, but, in Pennsylvania, it was available to immigrant servants with industry, patience, and ambition. Immigrants known as redemptioners were important in Pennsylvania's expansion. Strictly speaking, the term redemptioner refers to any immigrant who came to America and redeemed the cost of the passage by committing to a term of service. In that sense, the Chesapeake's indentured servants of the seventeenth century were redemptioners but with a significant difference from the eighteenth century servant immigrants. The latter were obliged, in most cases, to repay their transportation costs with service. Therefore, the term redemptioner is a useful one in thinking of the way the poor made their way to the British colonies in the eighteenth century. A man, woman, or a family *redeemed* the cost of transportation by contracting with a sponsor to perform a term of servitude. In some cases, ships' captains and agents brought immigrants to America without contracts and had them assigned in the ports of the Delaware River and the Chesapeake. The overworked white indentured servants of seventeenth century Virginia and Maryland redeemed the cost of their passages with prior contracts, the indenture, but the comparison ends there, in nomenclature.

The eighteenth century's redemptioners were not subject to the same levels of exploitation. White families made up a larger proportion of the immigrants to the middle colonies and the Chesapeake in the eighteenth century than had been the case earlier, when single men predominated. Thus the middle colonies in the eighteenth century were attractive to a more self-conscious class of immigrants. Nevertheless, there was still a flow of coerced or needy servants into the colonies. Most of the several thousand English convicts who were transported in the 1750s as servants ended up in the Chesapeake and lower south. Many of the servants, individual families, and convicts came without any sense of organized community, but many groups, like Mittelberger's Germans, did. There was not only ethnic cohesion in the throngs of Scotch-Irish, Scottish, Irish, and German arrivals but also, often, religious collectivism. The German Mennonite, Amish, and Lutherans and the British Presbyterians and even Catholics shaped the middle colonies into a religious mosaic in the decades before the Revolution.

The proprietary grants that established New York and Pennsylvania in 1664 and 1681 respectively were huge. As noted, Pennsylvania was as large in area as England. Although common boundaries were vigorously contested, especially between Pennsylvania and its neighbors, the charter authority claimed by New York and Pennsylvania each extended far into the interior. New Jersey's and Delaware's territorial boundaries, like Maryland's and Rhode Island's, were restricted in the west. The Pennsylvania grant went directly west to beyond the Allegheny Mountains. Its backcountry was massive in scale and topographically varied. Beginning in the 1720s, that area began to attract large numbers of settlers. Pennsylvania's western development differed from New England's. Once past the Connecticut River Valley, the western New England frontier became difficult because it ran into New York's claims. In Pennsylvania, the land suited farm settlement into the eastern slopes of the Allegheny-Appalachian chain. Pennsylvanians and Virginians coveted the fertile land beyond the mountains, the French-claimed, rich soil of the Ohio country. New York's frontier headed north before it turned west along the

Mohawk Valley to the Great Lakes. Yet on the western side of the Hudson River there was little defined agricultural settlement. To the east of it lay the great estates, the "patents" descended from the original Dutch grants to patroons. These enormous tracts of land ran east from the Hudson to the often-disputed boundaries with Massachusetts and Connecticut and had been shaped into manorial estates by the middle of the eighteenth century. That is, the holders of the patents kept title to the land but subdivided it into leaseholds, tenancies, and rentals, ranging in terms of three or more "life-leases" held in one name for three or more lifetimes to annual arrangements that could be terminated at will. This distribution of the land resembled older English, feudal-like arrangements that called for rents and lease payments to be made regularly. The land was used as a revenue generator for the patent holders and their heirs. In a series of contiguous estates running north from Manhattan to an area just north of Albany, the system was defined by the names of the holders of the great patents: Phillipse, Cortlandt, Beekman, Livingston, Rensselaerswyck, and others.

Although the emphasis was on attracting and exploiting white tenant farming, many of the rich families in the patents employed African and African American slaves in numbers not seen elsewhere in the countryside north of the Chesapeake. Still, the available acreages were relatively large, and, with industry and good management, a tenant family could produce enough grains and livestock to create surpluses. On the other hand, as the yields on tenant holdings were not always satisfactory, the rents and charges acted as a disincentive to families with means who could arrange for deeded land elsewhere. Squatters on unoccupied lands were a problem for the New York manor-tenant system, and law enforcement was spotty. In its land-use practices, ethnic and religious diversity, and political factionalism, New York was far removed from its next-door neighbors in New England. Its politics in the early eighteenth century were marked by competing interests seeking to influence or secure the support of the royal government in the colony.

The New York frontier from the 1740s to the early 1770s was controlled for the Crown by Sir William Johnson (1715–1774). The Irish-born and indefatigable Johnson, whose baronetcy was granted by the Crown during the French and Indian War, came to America as an immigrant with means. He administered a tract in the Mohawk Valley owned by his uncle and later acquired a large swath of his own. He rose in status and influence by developing strong trade and diplomatic relations with the Iroquois Six Nations and acting as a merchant to the small white settlements at the edge of British-controlled territory. He amassed a fortune, was appointed Crown commissioner for Indian affairs, and, after 1755, secured the alliance of the Six Nations against the French in the war that followed. His son succeeded him and, during the War for Independence, remained loyal to the Crown. The New York frontier differed from Pennsylvania's and New England's in that it was effectively Johnson's personal fiefdom.

In Pennsylvania, the frontier moved west into the Allegheny foothills as settlers pressed against the native populations. As in the case of Virginia and the Carolinas, the frontier was exploited by the Scotch Irish, whose clannish belligerence thrived in the loosely organized settlements of the west. It is not too much to suggest that the spread of a largely Celtic population into the farthest reaches of arable land was useful as a quasi-military barrier against the native populations who still held fast in the Appalachians. By the middle of the eighteenth century, frontier settlement had developed its own unique character. The often-remote settlements in the frontier regions were often no more than clusters of small farms in forest clearances. The farms were often inefficient and the standard of living marginal. The images of crude cabins, whisky stills, and hogs rooting among the corn patches on the eastern slopes of the Appalachians persist as stereotypes of populations that were carving out a world that was unlike those of the older communities to the east. The cultural values in those frontier environments were shaped by religious, communal, familial, and, ultimately, political loyalties that were among the most parochial in all of the colonial regions. For the Celtic settlers whose leases had expired or whose tenuous hold on a scrap of land in Ulster had been forcefully ended, the American frontier, for all its hardships, afforded its settlers with a way to break generations of restraint in the old countries. The frontier's basic, highly personalized politics invited individuals and groups to shape their own futures.

The American promise, the land of opportunity for the masses, appeared to be the frontier that ran from western Pennsylvania south to Georgia. There was no comparable settlement in New York's western and northern reaches. In New England, by contrast, the Maine and New Hampshire frontiers grew, but they did so by replicating, for the most part, the institutional and cultural models of older, denser, settled southern New England. From the middle of the eighteenth century, the great surge of population into the backcountry created a rare social and political environment on the frontier.

THE URBAN ENVIRONMENTS: NEW YORK CITY AND PHILADELPHIA

New York City and Philadelphia shared many of the urban characteristics of 1760s Boston. Each was a major seaport and the gravitational political, intellectual, and economic core for their regions. They were even more crowded than Boston and, like the latter, populated by tradesmen, artisans, laborers, sailors, and merchants. New York City contained a higher proportion of slaves than did the others, and the majority of its white population was Anglican. Philadelphia had a greater mix of sects including Quakers, while Boston, for all its adaptations, was still dominated by Congregationalists. Still, by the standards of the day, all three cities were urban and served as doorways into and out of America. Yet New York City and Philadelphia each differed from Boston in some basic ways. For a start, Boston was a more closely governed town and remained a creature of the provincial government. In fact, Boston retained its 1630 mandate and remained subordinate, in legal terms and governance, to the Massachusetts government until 1822 when it received a city charter. It may have been the center of New England's universe throughout the entire colonial era, but it was still a Massachusetts town. Its civic functions were *public,* that is, subject to the tax-paying population's role as a public corporation. Hence, every civic function from the fire watch to night patrols, the supervision of the poor, the control of transients, price controls, and fair weight laws were under the purview of the town meeting, the popular-based body that chose its selectmen, warders, constables, and all other municipal functionaries.

New York and Philadelphia operated differently. For a start, unlike the New England town-dominant model, the middle colonies subdivided into a mixed system of boroughs, shires, and townships in Pennsylvania and manors, counties, and townships in New York. Moreover, chartered towns and cities such as New York City and Philadelphia allowed for considerable autonomy and encouraged private enterprise and more flexibility in municipal affairs. Civic functions such as poor relief and public works were privatized, and each city enjoyed more independence from its senior provincial government than did Boston from the Massachusetts General Court. The populations of both New York City and Philadelphia grew faster than Boston's after the middle of the eighteenth century. In 1730, Philadelphia had a population of about 8,500. That had grown to 28,000 by 1770. New York grew in size from 8,500 to 21,000 in the same period. Boston, meanwhile, had 13,000 inhabitants in 1730 and 15,500 in 1770. In fact, it had grown to over 16,000 in the early 1740s and then lost about 1,000 of its population thereafter. The leveling off of Boston's population mostly resulted from the competition of several other ports in New England and the dispersal of maritime activity.

In the case of Philadelphia and New York, the continued expansion of their economic hinterlands and their roles as ports of entry for immigrants guaranteed growth. Also, there was a distinct absence of competition from other towns in the region for the kinds of maritime industries and warehousing that gave these seaports their cachet. Each enjoyed a regional monopoly that carried their growth into the nineteenth century. Boston did, however, retain one very important role. Although its population sank to about 3 per cent of the New England whole as the region became even more agrarian in the latter half of the eighteenth century, it continued to dominate the region's intellectual, artistic, political, and economic affairs. Thus, a rather odd imbalance developed in the demographics, sociology, and economics of all the northern colonies. While the vast majority of the population was rural, the centers of political authority and the control of regional wealth remained in the three major urban centers of Boston, Philadelphia, and New York City. During New York City's rapid growth, there was an ominous jump in the slave laboring population. By mid century, one in six persons in New York City was a slave or a free black. In 1712 and 1741, racial tensions had already led to riots.

In the period between the Glorious Revolution and the onset of the American Revolution, the middle colonies grew in ways that set the region apart. Geography was important. The climate was not as harsh as New England's and the terrain and soil types favored higher crop yields in some of the river valleys. Conversely, the region's climate did not favor the cash crops that defined very early the social and political future of the Chesapeake and, later on, the Carolinas. Also, as early as the 1620s, the Dutch had settled New York in a way that had no parallel elsewhere in mainland British America. William Penn's pragmatic adjustments in Pennsylvania and similar developments in the Jerseys and Delaware set off those colonies as historically unique.

Often, the distinctiveness of each colony seems reflected in the personalities of its famous sons and daughters. The regions produced leaders who personified the cultures in which they thrived, such as the Calvinist Mathers or the merchant Hancocks in New England, the planter Byrds and Jeffersons in Virginia, and the eclectic Ben Franklin in pluralistic Pennsylvania. In any age, in any place, people like Franklin are rare. Philadelphia was his home, and the city and province and, by extension, the United States are the beneficiaries of his reputation. When he died in 1790, he received what amounted to a state funeral that attracted 20,000 people, allegedly the largest crowd ever assembled in eighteenth century America. He is, with George Washington, the most popularly revered American of the revolutionary generation. By middle age, his wit, intelligence, scientific and technical prowess, political savvy, and statesmanship had made him an international celebrity. He was front and center during the Revolution, as a delegate to the Continental Congress, a signatory to the Declaration of Independence and the United States Constitution, a treaty negotiator during the War for Independence, and ambassador to France. In all his roles, he was a voice of reassurance to Americans. His restless curiosity was driven by a rich mental capacity and by common sense. He appealed alike to both ordinary people with his folksy aphorisms and French intellectuals and statesmen with his sociability and learning. American preoccupation with him continues in a steady flow of popular and academic publications. His story has become so well known to Americans that it appears at times to be mythical or apocryphal, but his experiences, his deeds, his ubiquitous presence, and his long influential life support his reputation. His character has a timeless appeal. He was by no means typical because no one else of that generation was so multitalented and eclectic. And yet it is hard to imagine a more suitable eighteenth century environment, other than a colonial port city, where a cosmopolitan mind could thrive amid the day-to-day affairs of provincial society. He identified himself as a "printer," his first calling and an indicator of his modest origins. He was born and raised in the narrow streets and lanes of Boston. His father was a soap boiler and tallow maker, and Franklin began his working life in the small factory when he was 10 years old. He was apprenticed as a printer and moved to Philadelphia when he was 17. By then, he had been exposed to and had read Bunyan, Plutarch, Locke, Shaftesbury, Xenophon, and others in the canon of the well-educated person of the period. He delved into languages with an enthusiasm that exemplified his personality.

On the basis of his talents and energy, he became a prominent figure in Philadelphia's and Pennsylvania's public, intellectual, and political life. He started a lending library and was constant in advancing civic projects and forming clubs for readings and intellectual exchange. He tried to organize the intercolonial union at Albany, New York in 1754 and thereafter was immersed in public affairs at the provincial and imperial levels. He was among the most cosmopolitan people of the age but was also the most "American" in the eyes of the French and Britons he encountered and impressed. Although the late colonial and revolutionary periods produced a generation of philosophically inclined and socially polished activists, such as John Adams, Thomas Jefferson, Alexander Hamilton, and James Madison, no American of those generations possessed the social acumen or range of interests of Franklin. For all his habit of self-promotion, he attracted attention with his thought and action and was perhaps the best-rounded American in an age of American originals.

Assembly Politics in the Eighteenth Century

Colonists had long assumed that they practiced a transatlantic version of the "mixed" English political system, that is, with a governor as chief executive with responsibility for appointments and the administration of the law. Councils advised the governor and were linked to the assembly as a legislative "upper chamber." The assembly, or "lower house" or "house of representatives" was an elected body that heard petitions, raised taxes, made law, and generally reflected the will of the electorate. These practices, in theory, seemed to echo the Monarch, Lords, and Commons of the British system. Indeed, from the earliest application of charter instructions and the evolution of representative bodies, colonists in North America had adapted English civil law and institutions to meet their needs. Rights of residence, poor laws, marriage and inheritance laws, criminal law and a wide range of social, cultural, and political habits had applied order to the settlement of the North American mainland in the seventeenth century. In spite of having been imitated and admired over time, however, English customs and politics were never entirely appropriate to colonial conditions.

For a start, there was a great deal more social and economic flexibility in the colonial societies than in the British Isles. Property ownership reached levels that were impossible in Britain. Colonial assemblies diverged from being simple imitations of the British House of Commons because they were more inclusive. Even if the electorate varied in size and composition from one colony to the other, all were accessible. One need think only of the huge numbers of small-scale but taxpaying farmers in the colonies who had direct access to the political system to see the sharp differences between the political sociology of the British Isles and of the thirteen colonies. British electoral and legislative practices were considered the most open and accessible in Europe, but tradition, continuity, and landed interests kept the system fairly static in terms of representation. For all its successes in popular terms, Parliament was "unreformed" in the eighteenth century. It was top heavy with elites, and the electorate was tiny.

In the colonies, even allowing for variations from one jurisdiction to the next, widespread electorates, more open access to sit in assemblies, and direct local participation created a more supple relationship between the engines of government and the governed. While appearing to imitate the British system, the assemblies reflected their own environments. The early religious requirements in some places, for voting or for holding office, had disappeared, and charters had been modified or replaced. In Virginia or Maryland, for example, and especially in Pennsylvania, company or proprietary charters, originally restrictive, had yielded to necessity by allowing wider participation in politics. In many jurisdictions, competitive elections were the order of the day, but perhaps the most important quality of colonial politics lay in the relationship between governors and assemblies. In the eight royal colonies, governors were appointed by the Monarch and usually supported by influential patrons in Parliament. Their instructions indicated authority that was more theory than real. Governors could and did veto legislation and had the authority to appoint tax assessors, judges and justices of the peace, customs agents, administrative assistants, deputies, and many other minor officers.

On paper these rights or "privileges" implied considerable influence over local affairs. However, all along, and especially in the eighteenth century as colonial assemblies reached functional maturity, the independence of governors was eroded by legislated rules and funding for appointments. Moreover, assembly representatives tended to serve for much longer terms than governors, a level of continuity that often overwhelmed incoming governors. Many governors saw their appointments as short-term opportunities for gain. Quite often, however, their patrons went broke or fell out of favor, or the governor himself was hounded or obstructed to the point of frustration and departure. Proprietary and royal governors lasted on average for only three years. The governor's role, although central to the political life of each colony, was increasingly dependent on assembly support.

Dozens of royal, company, and proprietary governors circulated through the colonies from 1607 until the Declaration of Independence in 1776. There were, among them, a few long-serving executives who defied the statistical odds of survival. In Virginia, for example, William Berkeley served for a total of 27 years in two separate stints and, for the most part, encountered less assembly trouble than most, although the revolt of Nathanial Bacon in 1676 might count as a lifetime's worth of trouble. Berkeley's endurance was rare. Colonial Virginia used up 39 other governors over the other 143 years of its existence. By the 1760s, eight of the thirteen colonies were under royal charters, nominally controlled by the Crown and its appointed governor. Of the other five chartered colonies, Rhode Island and Connecticut had retained the status of their 1660s charters, which had merely required royal "approval," while Pennsylvania, Maryland, and Delaware were still under proprietary control. While the Crown, that is, Parliament and the Monarch in concert, had charter control over eight colonies, it had not settled or ever operated any colonial government other than in a legal sense. Royal charters had been superimposed upon failed or suspended charters or been applied to existing settlements lacking charters.

Political culture in the colonies reflected the elitism of the planters of the Chesapeake or Carolina tidewater, the pluralistic dynamics of Pennsylvania or New York, or the town-based imperatives of New England. Everywhere, however, the assemblies increasingly had authority after the beginning of the eighteenth century. The unsettled politics revealed by the Dominion of New England's problems and by Bacon's and Leisler's rebellions seemed to be over. Assemblies developed over time into popular and potent political agencies, and governors normally respected them. If they did not, they suffered the consequences, as shown in the famous John Peter Zenger libel case in 1730s New York.

THE ZENGER AFFAIR

By the 1730s, New York's political system resembled the assembly, council, and gubernatorial arrangement of the other colonies, but its governors and assembly had often engaged in hostile exchanges. Historian Patricia Bonomi has called colonial New Yorkers "a factious people," and the colony's politics underscore her judgement. The Zenger affair needs to be understood in that light. The issue pulled a tactless and optimistic governor, trying to exercise his presumptive authority, into a factional political dispute that spilled out into the public realm and into the courts. The case also shows how colonial political activists understood English Whig opposition theory. New York's governor, from 1732 to 1736, was William Cosby (1690–1736) who also had control in New Jersey under a joint governorship. In 1733, he overstepped the limits of his office in a costly misjudgement.

An assembly group led by New York–born James Delancey (1703–1760) supported Cosby in hopes of getting plum positions for their favorites. In 1733, Cosby suspended Chief Justice of New York Lewis Morris (1671–1746) and replaced him with Delancey himself. Like Delancey, Morris was a native New Yorker; he resisted the move on the grounds of a corruption of the "time honored traditions" of the British constitution and parliamentary practices. Morris understood the routine patronage that prevailed in Parliament and in American assemblies and brought out a newspaper against Delancey and Cosby, the *New-York Weekly Journal.* It was printed by Zenger who also, under contemporary standards, was deemed the de facto publisher. The *Journal* heaped opprobrium on Governor Cosby, Delancey, and the members of the council. New York was polarized. In his editorials, Morris employed the well-crafted essays of *Cato's Letters* of 1720–1723 by the English radicals John Trenchard and Thomas Gordon. In that way, Morris associated his enemies with the "court" politics and royal privileges of earlier discredited English practices. But Morris and Zenger went too far for Governor Cosby. Zenger was arrested in early 1734 and charged with seditious libel, for defaming a royally appointed governor. He was held incommunicado for ten months by a vengeful Cosby administration before he went on trial before a jury. The prosecution would not concede the possibility of truth in the *Journal's* editorials, but a superb defense by Zenger's lawyer, the nearly 80-year-old Philadelphian Andrew Hamilton, carried the day. He convinced the jury that Zenger—and Morris, of course—had published accurate criticisms and had not libeled the governor. Hamilton rounded out his defense by claiming that the issue went beyond Zenger or New York but was in defense of British liberties. Zenger was acquitted.

The jury's decision demonstrated that freedom to criticize a royal appointee in New York and, by implication, elsewhere was legal. The Morris attacks condoned the principle of opposition to impropriety as a legally sanctioned right. Governors were not above the will of the assembly and were not immune to the opinions of assembly factions. Cronyism remained a part of the British parliamentary system and did not disappear from the workings of colonial assemblies and their American republican successors, but the Zenger trial put it on watch.

On another level, the trial demonstrated that the colonial assemblies only *appeared* to be miniature versions of Parliament. In the American colonies, a stricter separation between legislature and executive prevailed, and, even when there was open collaboration, there was a line that no governor could cross. The legitimacy of opposition, not only against governors but also against other assembly interests, was confirmed in the Zenger case. In the wake of the acquittal, Morris formed a "popular" party and continued his attacks on Cosby and his Delancey supporters. The "Morrisites" pushed for electoral and executive reforms including fixed dates for elections; courts established by acts of the assembly; and judges appointed on "good behavior," that is, subject to removal for abusing the appointment in any way rather than indefinitely, at the "pleasure" of the governors. This was a clear rebuff of Cosby's firing of Morris. The Morrisites also sought to reform municipal politics, calling for annual elections of mayors, sheriffs, and other public officials. In a clear appeal to popular sentiment, Morris pushed for representation by population in the New York Assembly. Cosby died of tuberculosis in 1736, shortly after the trial. By 1737, Morris's party controlled the lower house in the assembly.

Thereafter, Morris served as governor of New Jersey, and his role in politics was somewhat reversed. He squabbled constantly with the New Jersey Assembly. As for James Delancey, he returned to provincial politics and, until his death in 1760, was a committed supporter of assembly rights. His son, James Delancey, Jr. was also active in New York politics until the imperial crisis, when his loyalist sympathies obliged him to move to England in 1774. While these political convolutions had popular objectives, it is worth noting that Morris and Delancey, the principal players in this case, were each members of New York's landed elites. Popular politics in British America were still guided by men with means.

The Zenger affair was a singular example of the power of the printed word in newspaper format. Newspapers, almost always weeklies, had been a colonial staple since the early eighteenth century, replacing late seventeenth century occasional news bulletins. The first colonial newspaper to run continuously was the Boston *News-Letter* of 1704. By the 1770s, there were 37 newspapers, including a daily, operating in the colonies. Every colony enjoyed the news, advertising, and various social and domestic features that newspapers contained. Newspapers carried the news from Britain and Europe and published royal announcements, shipping news, pleas for the return of runaway slaves, and considerable classified advertising. Zenger's *Weekly Journal,* the Boston *Post-Boy,* Franklin's *Pennsylvania Gazette,* the South Carolina *Gazette,* and many others can still be read as windows into the everyday colonial world. Newspapers would become organs of political opinion during the imperial crisis of the 1760s and 1770s, and, along with the great pamphlet literature of that era, they stoked the fires of resistance and rebellion.

SUGGESTED READINGS

On the importance of regions in American history, see Edward L. Ayers, Patricia Limerick, Stephen Nissenbaum, and Peter Onuf, eds., *All over the Map: Rethinking American Regions* (Baltimore: Johns Hopkins University Press, 1996) and especially Meinig, *Atlantic America: 1492–1800,* cited in the "General Reference Bibliography" section. Allan Kulikoff, *From British Peasants to Colonial American Farmers* (Chapel Hill: University of North Carolina Press, 2000) is an intelligent approach to environmental adaptation over time and deals with the colonial social landscape in a useful way. On the relationship of cultural, ethnic, and social conditions and immigration to regional variation in mainland North America, see David Hackett Fischer, *Albion's Seed: Four British Folkways in America* (New York: Oxford University Press, 1989). Jack P. Greene, *Pursuits of Happiness: The Social Development of Early Modern British Colonies and the Formation of American Culture* (Chapel Hill: University of North Carolina Press, 1988) deals with regional development in a somewhat different way from Fischer's models, but the two studies together are important contributions to regional comparison and contrast. Another way of understanding regional diversity is through the economic models and statistical analysis of Alice Hanson Jones, *Wealth of a Nation to Be: The American Colonies on the Eve of the Revolution* (New York: Columbia University Press, 1980). A generalized approach to the roles of women and families can be found in Carol Berkin, *First Generations: Women in Colonial America* (New York: Hill and Wang, 1996). The late 1960s and early 1970s produced a stream of monographs of "community." These local studies retain their relevance in understanding New England society: See Richard Bushman, *From Puritan to Yankee: Character and the Social Order in Connecticut, 1690–1765* (Cambridge, MA: Harvard University Press, 1967); Edward Cook, *Fathers of the Towns: Leadership and Community Structure in Eighteenth-Century New England* (Baltimore: Johns Hopkins University Press, 1976); Michael Zuckerman, *Peaceable Kingdoms: New England Towns in the Eighteenth Century* (New York: Knopf, 1970); Philip Greven, *Four Generations: Population, Land, and Family in Colonial Andover, Massachusetts* (Ithaca, NY: Cornell University Press, 1970); and Lockridge, *The New England Town,* cited in Chapter 4. Daniel Vickers, *Farmers and Fisherman: Two Centuries of Work in Essex County, Massachusetts, 1630–1830* (Chapel Hill: University of North Carolina Press, 1994) is a vivid, sensitive study of the working lives of New Englanders and Laurel Ulrich, *Good Wives: Image and Reality in the Lives of Women in Northern New England, 1650–1750* (New York: Vintage, 1991) is an exemplary illustration of the value of gender-focused study. On New York and the middle colonies, see Patricia Bonomi, *A Factious People: Politics and*

Society in Colonial New York (New York: Columbia University Press, 1971); Sung Bok Kim, *Landlord and Tenant in Colonial New York: Manorial Society, 1664–1775* (Chapel Hill: University of North Carolina Press, 1978); Alan Tully, *William Penn's Legacy: Politics and Social Structure in Provincial Pennsylvania, 1726–1755* (Baltimore: Johns Hopkins University Press, 1977). The same author's *Forming American Politics: Ideals, Interests, and Institutions in Colonial New York and Pennsylvania* (Baltimore: Johns Hopkins University Press, 1994) is the most comprehensive study available on the politics of any colonial region. See also Leonard W. Labaree, ed., *The Autobiography of Benjamin Franklin* (New Haven: Yale University Press, 1962). Gary B. Nash, *The Urban Crucible: Social Change, Political Consciousness, and the Origins of the American Revolution* (Cambridge, MA: Harvard University Press, 1979) remains the best comparative study of America's seaports and their regional significance.

CHAPTER 8

* * * * * ★ * ★ * * * * *

The Regions of Colonial America: Society and Politics in Eighteenth Century Chesapeake and the South

The Chesapeake Society produced a unique bourgeois aristocracy with more than its share of great and noble men; they were, however, men of intellect, not intellectuals.

—Carl Bridenbaugh, *Myths and Realities: Societies of the Colonial South* (1951; repr., New York: Atheneum, 1968), 53.

The Chesapeake and South: The Historian's Region

The northern reaches of the slave societies began abruptly south of where the Pennsylvania and Delaware borders touched Virginia and Maryland. One of the timeless references in American geography is the "Mason-Dixon Line" named for the English surveyors Charles Mason and Jeremiah Dixon. In the 1760s, they were commissioned to define the southern boundary of Pennsylvania and the northern boundaries of Maryland, Delaware, and parts of what is now the state of West Virginia. Then and for generations to follow, the line came to denote the division between two distinct American realities, "the North" and "the South," terms loaded with historical and cultural meaning. South of the line, there was little of the ethnic mélange of the middle colonies and nothing like the homogeneous white settlements of New England. In the 1760s, a northern colonial or European traveler arriving from the north might reasonably assume he or she was entering another country. And even Pennsylvanians, so close to the plantation regime geographically, were distant from it culturally, politically, and economically. That is not to say that Europeans, Pennsylvanians, or New Englanders were unaware of or shocked by slavery, but the appearance of large numbers of slaves in work gangs or in slave quarters was evidence of the sharp contrasts between various British communities in America. By 1770, 40 per cent of the population south of the Mason-Dixon line was black and enslaved. A tiny 3 per cent of the black population was legally free, and, although the number of free blacks was higher in some places than in others, it was never more than negligible. In New England, in 1770, about 2.5 per cent of the population was black, and the percentage declined to 2 per cent over the next decade. Ten per cent of the black population was free. Rhode Island had the largest percentage of slaves in New England at 6.5 per cent. Corresponding figures for the middle colonies showed that 6 per cent of the population was black. There were clusters of slaves in New York City and Philadelphia and smaller concentrations in Boston and Newport. Slavery was legal in all the northern colonies, but the rural north was emphatically white.

What made the transition from north to south so striking was the immediacy of the change. Even in northern Virginia and along the eastern Maryland shore, the human landscape was visibly different from that a few miles away in Pennsylvania and Delaware. In 1770, Delaware's black population was 5.2 per cent of the whole; in Pennsylvania, it was 2.4 per cent. By contrast, in Maryland, the percentage of blacks in the population was 31.5 per cent, and, in Virginia, 42 per cent. Delaware is sometimes lumped in with the southern region because it retained constitutional slavery until the Civil War, but, in most respects, it shared the economic and social characteristics of the middle colonies. In the Chesapeake, the land distribution and uses created a century earlier, as much as the climate, had led to an agriculture that was skewed toward tobacco but that also encouraged mixed farming. Grain and livestock farming was done in tandem with tobacco growing on some of the larger estates. The image of slave labor in the Chesapeake being devoted to tobacco needs to be modified. A significant minority of slaves were employed in raising edible crops and livestock. Smaller white family farms scattered throughout the region produced another stratum of agricultural activity.

Beyond the Chesapeake, the effects of slavery were revealed most starkly in the tidewater areas of the lower south, especially in the so-called low country of South Carolina. Slaves constituted 60 per cent of South Carolina's total population by mid century, and, in some tidewater areas, blacks outnumbered whites by three to one. In neighboring North Carolina, the overall black-white ratios differed from those in South Carolina and Virginia due in part to the fact that the North Carolina backcountry had been filling in with white farmer migrants after the 1750s. By 1770, the colony's slave population was contained mostly in the tidewater areas where there were slave majorities in some parishes. The least populated and newest of the southern slave societies was Georgia, whose 1752 royal charter had opened the floodgates to plantation culture and the importation of large numbers of slaves. In a zone that ran north to south along the coast from the Chesapeake to Spanish Florida, the black to white ratios of tidewater regions created societies unique in the mainland colonies. Although there was nothing comparable to the 9 to 1 ratios of the British West Indies, the density of slave numbers along the southern mainland coastline was remarkable. That was countered by another demographic trend in the lower south during the eighteenth century, the populating of the frontier backcountry by white farmers and immigrants.

Two economies, two societies, and two cultures developed in each of the southern colonies: a tidewater community dominated by large estates and black majorities and a western zone running to the Appalachian foothills that was dominated by small-scale farming and white majorities. The latter, in some ways, resembled northern agrarian settlements. The only southern colony without a backcountry was Maryland. Virginia's backcountry was not as open to commoner settlement as was the case elsewhere because planters had moved into the piedmont with their slaves and precluded large-scale popular migration. For the most part, however, the southern backcountry was less racially mixed the farther west one traveled to the point where most of it was exclusively white. Also, some of the smaller communities in the hills and valleys of the backcountry consisted of extended kinship groups of as few as several to dozens of related families.

The idea of a southern region is a useful way to look at the effects of climate, geography, and economics on British America's history. But it was less coherent as a region than was New England, for example, and bore some of the marks of the heterogeneity of the middle colonies with race adding a distinct variable. If slavery was a common denominator in some respects, it was practiced differently from place to place. Black-white or slave-master relations varied between individual plantations and farms and between the South Carolina low country and the older Chesapeake environment where native born African Americans were becoming the majority in the black population. Slaves in the north, especially in places like New York City, lived in economic and social surroundings that were in striking contrast to those in rural

Chesapeake or the lower south. There, location, crop types, climate, and the size of plantations and farms meant that slaves and whites dealt with each other and the institution in ways that gave slavery and slave societies greater complexity than the simple terms "slavery" or "slave" imply.

Did the Chesapeake and the lower south constitute a self-conscious region? Perhaps, if we read backwards from the Civil War and see the sectional politics and constitutional issues of the antebellum era as originating in the colonial development of a single "South." What split the new republic north from south, from the post-Revolution period to the Civil War in 1861, was a series of confrontations that arose from a post-Revolution ideology of sectional integrity. If, on the other hand, we choose to see the southern colonies as they saw themselves in the eighteenth century, we will find disparity rather than commonality. However, every planter in Virginia understood that his counterpart in South Carolina was closer to him in social and cultural ways, not to mention economic status and behavior, than any New England merchant was even if the issue of wider rather than colony attachments did not arise in any significant way until after the Seven Years' War and the Crown's reforms.

Those reforms, seen by colonists as impositions, drew the colonies together politically and, at the same time, made each aware of its unique social and cultural qualities. Virginia, South Carolina, Maryland, or any colonial jurisdiction was "home" to its residents and not some historian's "region." Southerners, like northerners, were existentially bound to their respective localities because of the immediacy of day-to-day affairs in rural environments where communication and travel were slow and difficult. There was also an attachment to the colony because it represented political authority at the local level. Finally, the one common bond was with the British Empire as the overarching constitutional and economic guarantor and, of course, the vessel of colonists' cultural heritage.

CLASS AND RACE IN THE CHESAPEAKE

In the 100 years between Bacon's Rebellion and the Declaration of Independence, the ruling classes of Virginia and Maryland consolidated and perpetuated the power and status they had begun to shape in the middle of the seventeenth century. But while the planter oligarchy at the very top of the Chesapeake pyramid maintained its wealth and authority, the society it controlled underwent a profound reshaping. In the middle of the seventeenth century, about one-third of the white population of the Chesapeake was in some form of indentured servitude, but, on the eve of the Revolution, only 1.8 per cent of the white population was indentured. In Virginia and Maryland, the black population in 1650 was about 700, about 3 per cent of the total population. By 1770, blacks constituted 38 per cent of the Chesapeake's population. Slaves had replaced poor dependent whites at the base of the pyramid and had also become the base of the class structure.

The slaveholding planters of Virginia and Maryland were united in their assumptions about race and in the ethics of legislated chattel bondage, but the generalization stopped there. Not all slaveholders were equal. Some, such as the Carters, owned thousands of acres of land and produced tons of tobacco annually with the labor of hundreds of slaves. In the older tidewater region, where huge tracts of land had been acquired with ease in the seventeenth century, large estates flourished, maintained by gangs of slaves. In the piedmont, on the other hand, the median number of slaves per planter was in the 2 to 6 range according to the location of their parishes. The upper end of this slaveholding system produced landholders such as the Carters and the Byrds and political leaders such as Washington, Jefferson, Madison, Mason, Lee, and Randolph. However, many whites in the Chesapeake and the piedmont were small-scale planters, ran successful mixed farms, or lived with their families on marginal homesteads. In a landscape of scattered rural populations, the acreages of white farmers were large compared to those in New England. But 200 acres in Virginia brought no more prosperity to the white farmer there than did 50 acres to a subsistence farmer in New England. The average New England farmer, as part of a corporate community, the town, enjoyed more political status than did his counterpart in the Chesapeake.

In the middle of the eighteenth century, the rural landscape of the Chesapeake was an untidy mix of cultivated fields and rough, unoccupied, difficult terrain and scattered hamlets and plantations. It appeared, in places, to be undeveloped if compared to the ordered contiguous farms in southern New England or the Hudson and Delaware River valleys to the north. In the Chesapeake, after 150 years of settlement, large swaths of arable land had been returned to a pristine state, their soils having been exhausted by repeated tobacco plantings. These areas were often abandoned to woods, thickets, brush, and inaccessible meadows. Yet the area was heavily populated by colonial standards. In 1770, the combined populations of Maryland and Virginia reached nearly 650,000 whites and blacks, and, although the Virginia population was beginning to distribute itself to the south and west, the older tidewater area was still home to several hundred thousand people.

The Chesapeake's rivers and creeks formed a navigable web, providing access to hamlets, farm clusters, and wharves. The larger plantations were often self-contained and had their own blacksmiths, tanners, millers, carpenters, carters, and other tradesmen, most of whom were skilled slaves. Otherwise, the society convened around small docks, crossroad taverns, retailers, and churches and at county courthouses for business, politics, and socializing. Legal and political affairs were conducted at the county and parish level. The established Church of England (Anglican) parish vestry, made up of leading non-ordained residents, controlled church and tithing affairs and, over time, exercised considerable political influence. Where native populations had once thronged, their remnants, in some tribes reduced to several dozen or even fewer survivors, had been pushed to the social and economic margins. They had become nearly invisible in the older settled parts of the Chesapeake.

Slavery determined the community's *raison d'être* to the extent that the slave had raised all whites, rich and poor alike, to a level of simple racial superiority regardless of any political or social inequality among whites. Over time, the racial solidarity of whites was enhanced as the numbers and proportions of blacks rose. As noted earlier, historians still debate the origins of slavery in the British American colonies. Did it derive from preconceptions about cultural, biological, or behavioral inferiority? Did it simply emerge as an opportunistic appropriation of a labor supply that was legally outside Christian mandates? Was it a belated imitation of the Iberian or Dutch practices? Was it a slow and gradual application of laws that were convenient and that, in the end, fixed the black person as worthy of bondage *only*? By the 1770s, the very existence of decades of slavery served tautologically to explain its permanence. Its origins were of little concern to the majority of mid-to-late-eighteenth century slaveholders who, if they considered the roots of slavery at all, did not question the need to maintain it. Their explanation for slavery, if one were needed, was that slaves were sociologically where they should be. They were simple, dependent, and incapable of any other status. Most whites, slaveholders or non-slaveholders, saw the male field hand, the dutiful house servant, or mammy as docile or lazy. That perception fed into the basic premise of the black's inferiority.

The slave was managed by psychological intimidation, for example, the threat of being sold or of having a spouse or child sold; by the threat or actuality of corporal punishment; and by a persistent degradation in the day-to-day confrontations between the ruler and the ruled. In a refreshing development, historians have in recent decades attempted to study American slavery from the perspective of the slave, despite the regrettable absence of any eighteenth century records left behind *by* slaves. Statistics, laws, court cases, and planters' accounts supply what evidence we have. Still, historians argue that, despite legal and tactical control by the master, slaves preserved a social and emotional self-respect while functioning as profit-producing chattels. Slavery was a coerced condition, but, within the slave community, music, religion, and persistent optimism tended to blunt the worst of the oppression. Where families existed, intimacy and emotional comfort offered a degree of security.

Perhaps the most revisionist thesis in the new and expansive historiography of slavery suggests that slaves and slaveholders accommodated each other in a relationship of necessity. Certain "favors" were granted the slave, such as the possession of a small vegetable patch, the celebration of holidays when a pig or steer might be roasted, and the encouragement of collective singing and dancing. In many cases masters tolerated the inefficiencies of slave labor, the apparent incompetence or laziness that was in its way a form of slow sabotage of the planter's assets. Thus, in many cases, slaves determined the pace and style of field work and tobacco processing. Marriages were allowed by some planters as a brake on slave restlessness. On larger holdings, there was a laddered structure within the common class of slaves, where loyalty, hard work, seniority, and skill made it possible for some slaves, male and female, to occupy higher status jobs in the slave labor force. There is some evidence, however, that slave foremen or house slaves were resented and even distrusted by the mass of field hands. We should note that those plantations with scores of slaves and perhaps two or three generations of whites and blacks on the same property resembled comprehensive communities. The "community" demanded a variety of services and skills beyond tobacco culture, most of which had to be provided by slaves.

Those generalized observations are useful in a broad sense, but they hide the complicated and perhaps impenetrable variety of settings, human personalities, time, and place. We need to be careful not to view New World slavery as a single undifferentiated phenomenon. As American slavery differed in legal and sociological terms from the Latin American and West Indian systems, it also varied from British colony to British colony over time and even in master-slave relations. There was not a uniform system of slave labor or slave experience in the thirteen colonies or, for that matter, throughout the western hemisphere. All slaves can be understood to have shared a common status, in legal terms and in the incontrovertible reality of being held, firmly or softly, as an item of human property or, as one of the codes put it, "real estate." Beyond that, however, the experiences of slaves differed as their circumstances differed. There were more African-born slaves in the lower south than in the Chesapeake. Over half the slaves in the Chesapeake by the 1750s were American born, a figure not reached in South Carolina and Georgia until after the Revolution.

There was not even a common plantation model nor a slave personality or condition that can be usefully stereotyped, except in the legal sense. Laws in all jurisdictions specified the rights of slaveholders and the status of the slave as property. The moral issue was buried beneath a white cloak of assumptions concerning white superiority, benevolence, and paternalism. After legalization had taken hold in the late seventeenth century, the complex labor regimes and master-slave relations followed. Slavery had not come with the English to America and was not created in a flash of settler invention. It evolved, quickly, in fact, and, by the middle of the eighteenth century, had become morally and legally defined. For a start, the condition, the life, really, of any slave should be seen in light of the unnatural status and identity of the individual. The relationship of slave to master and to the institution itself complicated the picture further. What did slavery do to whites, either those who owned and worked slaves or those who did not but who saw the slave as the social mudsill of the community? How did the institution work? What mechanisms maintained it over generations and allowed it to grow? Was it significantly different in the Carolina low country from in the Chesapeake or the piedmont? Did larger plantations with large numbers of slaves create a greater separation between whites and blacks than the more intimate smaller holdings?

SLAVERY AT THE END OF ITS FIRST CENTURY

According to most colonists, even if slaves adopted Christianity, their faith did not extend to them moral equality or, in a peculiar twist, access to a white hereafter. Marriages among slaves were tolerated because they helped stabilize behavior, but those marriages could not be sanctioned in civil or ecclesiastical terms. The earliest perceptions of the heathen African, the "other," had been folded into the economic, legal, and sociological development of chattel bondage and had marched hand in hand with the institution's refinement over time. There were other common assumptions across the regions. The "single drop" principle, that is, the existence of any African heredity, however much removed, applied as readily in Massachusetts as it did in South Carolina. "Mulattoes" or "octoroons" and even people with the slightest trace of African ancestry were regarded as black. Any "passing" for white was always risky. The earlier laws regarding miscegenation had made heredity the central definition of status. Also, while the slave was property, he or she was *human* property. Thus, the property was capable of volition, of acting in emotional, intellectual, or physical ways. In that case, owners punished their properties according to the degree of the breech of condoned behavior. A slaveholder with one family of slaves in New York was as legally authorized to strike or scar a miscreant or separate children or spouses from that miscreant as was a planter in South Carolina who owned dozens of slaves.

Yet there were significant differences. In New England, most slaveholders, a tiny proportion of the population to begin with, kept one or two slaves as household help or as laborers. New York, with a slave population that was 14 per cent of the whole, was the only northern colony in the latter part of the colonial period with owners who used slaves extensively. From the

Dutch era to the Revolution and beyond, New York slaves worked not only on the New York City wharves but also in the fields of the great landowners in the Hudson Valley. There, as in other northern districts, the slave enjoyed a bit more freedom than did the throngs who worked the tobacco, rice, indigo, and other crops in twelve-month rotations.

Down time was especially frequent in urban settings, where slaves were often hired out or allowed to work for others for their own gain in otherwise slack periods. Thus, there was a more fluid and often integrated pattern of white-black relations in the seaports. Even that did not result in more toleration but rather led to unease among whites, especially in New York, where free blacks or unsupervised slaves were often seen as a threat to public safety. Rumors of conspiracies were more common in New York than in the south and, as we shall see, led to two horrific attacks on blacks in 1712 and 1741. In the Chesapeake and lower south, as the slave regime took deeper root and the slave population boomed, there were similar fears of the possibility of wide-ranging, sweeping, destructive uprisings. The Stono Rebellion of 1739 served as a reminder to later eighteenth century Carolinians that insurrection was possible. The recognition that slaves were capable of conspiring, organizing, and acting violently against the masters and their system indicates a great dilemma, or rather a paradox. If white colonists, slaveholders or non-slaveholders, believed that nature, sociology, logic, and necessity had placed slaves where they should be, what did the slaves' defiance, revolt, plotting, and permanent resentment say about the ethical and legal absolutes of slaveholding rights? For the most part, slaveholders saw what slaves most often presented to them: submission understood as contentment.

All slaves in the British American colonies were trapped by legal devices that forbade manumission. And slaves who ran away had nowhere to go. Any people of color spotted "abroad" were subject to the authority of any white person suspicious of their being escaped or escaping slaves. Without a fixed community of free blacks in the backcountry or beyond, there was no viable sanctuary for the escapee. The British American system was unique in New World slavery because it was a closed system. The Spanish and Portuguese allowed many routes to freedom. Slavery there was more physically demanding, and slave life expectancy was short by North American standards. However, there were ways to achieve moral and practical release from bondage in the Iberian systems. In Brazil, in particular, there was a very complex set of gradations of status among Africans and a complex hierarchy among the many permutations of color that emerged from the high and constant rates of miscegenation. Comparative studies of various American slave regimes have suggested that, although the Brazilian system was physically harsher than the North American British system, it appeared more flexible and open.

Few Virginia planters would consider turning slaves loose if the plantation failed or if the planter had no heirs, but, in Brazil, the erratic mining and sugar economies often resulted in failed investments, and, at times, scores of slaves were simply let go. If the fortunes of the planter or mining speculator improved, shiploads of new African slaves could be had. Slavery in Brazil's harsh and volatile environment was based on strictly racist terms, but it was a flexible racism that allowed for mobility within the system and the possibility of legal freedom and escape into the few but large independent black communities, the *quilombos*. A substantial part of Brazil's slave population appeared to retain African cultural traits even after many years in the system, contrary to the process of acculturation that went on in most of North America. It is perhaps a small consolation to the generations of Brazilian slaves, but the newest African arrival or fifth generation mulatto slave in Brazil had a moral status that was conspicuously denied the North American slave or, for that matter, the small population of freed blacks in British America.

The fluidity of the Brazilian system resulted in some telling numbers. There were one million slaves in Brazil in the 1770s, but there were also about 400,000 free blacks, nearly one-third of the "colored" population. Those estimates by historian Herbert Klein can be set against his British American figures for the same period, when a slave population of 575,000 dwarfed the estimated 32,000 free blacks. The ratio of free blacks to slaves in the British West Indies was even lower, and the ratios in the French and Dutch systems were similar to those found in the British colonies. As noted earlier, in the eighteenth century Spanish slave societies of the Caribbean and of mainland Central and South America, "free colored" people outnumbered slave populations. The British did away with slavery in their colonies in 1834, and, after American independence, the northern states in the United States eliminated slavery gradually.

The French Caribbean was rocked by the uprisings of freed blacks and slaves in Saint-Domingue after 1791 and the creation of a black republic, the Empire of Haiti, in 1804. In an interesting twist, because of the enormous boom in the Cuban sugar economy in the first half of the nineteenth century, the proportion of free to enslaved blacks in Haiti was smaller than it was in the Spanish Caribbean, where there was a free black majority. In Cuba, the slave population reached nearly 370,000 in 1861 when the "free colored" population sat at 232,000. In Spanish Puerto Rico, on the other hand, free colored people still outnumbered slaves by a six to one ratio. In Brazil, the trend led to majorities of freed colored peoples by the 1860s. By contrast, in the southern slave states of the United States in 1860, free blacks amounted to just over 6 per cent of the total black population. This was one of the more portentous of the United States' inheritances from the colonial period. By the eve of the Revolution, the institution of slavery had been so thoroughly stitched into the colonial fabric that it carried its participants into and beyond independence. It was then woven into the constitution and the new Republic. Such was the durability of the institution that historian Peter Kolchin claims pithily, "by going to war [the Civil War] for the preservation of slavery, [the South] ... took the only action that could foreseeably have led to its speedy and complete abolition" (*American Slavery, 1619–1877* [New York: Hill and Wang, 1993], 199).

Cotton eventually replaced tobacco, rice, and indigo in the early nineteenth century, and slavery followed the new nation, the United States, over the Appalachians and into the rich soils that stretched to the Mississippi. The wealthy, with larger estates, ruled over more slaves than their colonial predecessors, but the white-black, master-slave relationship was retained and enhanced. The slave laws were refined, the planters continued to dominate politics, and the doctrine of racial sovereignty became hardened logic.

One of the major features of American slavery in the 1850s was that the slave population was itself now American. The late twentieth century terms "Afro American" or "African American" would apply to virtually all slaves in mid nineteenth century America. In the eighteenth century, thousands of new slaves arrived in the colonies each year, the majority landing at Charleston, but the rates of natural increase in the slave population had already begun to change the balance from African to African American. In 1700, the African born among the slave population in Virginia was 50 per cent. In 1770, it was 9 per cent. In South Carolina, it was also 50 per cent in 1700, but the Africans in the slave population rose to 66 per cent by 1740, a sign of the rapid growth in the Carolina economy and the hunger for imported black bodies to supply the labor. Thereafter, natural increase rates rose even as thousands of Africans entered the colony, but the percentage of Africans in South Carolina's slave population was still 35 per cent in 1770 and remained as high as a quarter of the whole in the early nineteenth century.

The emergence of the slave family became a defining feature in the Americanization of the African. There had been slave families from the earliest days, but those seventeenth century relationships, sanctioned by the owners, were the exception to the male-dominated populations. During most of the era of the slave trade, inventories sometimes listed children, but, in most cases, these were working-age adolescents. Female slaves were a minority in the transatlantic slave cargoes. Usually, one-quarter to one-third of slave arrivals at American ports in the late seventeenth and eighteenth centuries were females. Slave women in the British colonies did much the same kinds of field work as males. There was enough procreation even with unbalanced sex ratios to eventually lead to a male-female near equivalence in the African American population. The birth rates after the first few decades of the eighteenth century meant that slave imports into the

Chesapeake declined. Children now abounded on most estates, and a truly African American family network was certainly in place in most Chesapeake neighborhoods by the 1770s. The African influence on the slave community in the Carolina tidewater, sustained by steady importation, created a slave population (and an environment, really) that was different from that of the Chesapeake. In coastal South Carolina, for example, slaves were usually on larger holdings, and their communities were comprised of a mixture of young and old, of single slaves and married or cohabiting slaves, and of newly arrived Africans along with African Americans.

SLAVE LABOR

Indigo was a significant cash crop and was second to rice in export value in the South Carolina and Georgia low country. Those two staples, along with the tobacco of the Chesapeake and northern North Carolina, were the main cash crops produced by slaves. Rice production, like tobacco cultivation, took up the bulk of the year. It began with heavy work in the crudely engineered, diked fields of low lying swampy areas and with building sluices for flooding and draining water during the growing cycle of the rice plant. The mature rice had to be cut with sickles, threshed, separated, screened, and, as with tobacco, packed into barrels for shipment. Indigo was a late and unusual addition to the economy of South Carolina. Its viability was demonstrated in the experiments of Elizabeth (Eliza) Pinckney (1722–1793) who realized its potential while managing her father's plantation. After her husband died in 1758, Eliza became a prominent planter in her own right. She was part of the Pinckney dynasty that included her husband Charles and her sons Charles Junior and Thomas. The family had a long-term role in southern and national politics from the Revolution to the Civil War. Indigo launched the Pinckney fortune and that of many others after the middle of the eighteenth century. The plant produced a bloom whose blue dye was recovered in an ingenious but grueling process. As with any field plant, indigo demanded constant attention as it grew. Then it had to be pulled, soaked, fermented, and mixed with limewater and beaten with paddles. After that, it was re-fermented, turned into a dye paste, and shaped into cubes for shipment. It was in great demand in fashionable circles in Britain and commercially profitable throughout the Atlantic world for its use in everyday dyeing.

The cash crop economies had common labor practices. The field hand working sun up to sun down, six days a week, 300 days a year remains one of the enduring images of slavery. We now know that planters cynically accepted limits to what could be wrung out of a slave. There is some evidence that slaves determined the amount of work they were prepared to do, and it is likely that an unspoken acknowledgement of reciprocal needs prevailed. Still, crops had to be sown and then harvested when the conditions were right. The tight schedules for processing and shipping put great demands on the slave's labor and time, and no amount of "accommodation" could diminish the physical demands on agricultural slaves or the numbing repetition of routine field work. For efficiency's sake, planters with large enough acreages and numbers of slaves adopted the "task system" over gang labor. In this system, individuals were assigned specific tasks and allowed free time when these were completed. It was an astute division of labor, a form of "piecework." Moreover, larger estates offered opportunities for occupation as carpenters or blacksmiths or housework.

Most slaves worked together in small groups. Planters with large numbers of slaves usually had their holdings divided into several operations and distributed their slaves accordingly. For example, Robert "King" Carter owned 390 slaves when he died in 1732, but they lived in smaller groupings and usually worked on 48 different holdings. On the eve of the Revolution, the extended Carter family had 2,000 slaves distributed among the family branches, working on many estates spread over several Virginia counties. Thomas Jefferson kept 45 slaves at his home estate, Monticello, but employed another 140 in six other holdings. The enterprising Jonathan Bryan managed to acquire some 32,000 acres of land, and he owned 250 slaves on farms in both Georgia and South Carolina. For most slaves, in any size of operation, the hoe, the axe, and the shovel were daily and perpetual companions. An estimated 50 per cent of slaves in the mainland colonies worked on mixed farms, growing corn, raising livestock, making cider, and doing all the chores that went with mixed farming. In areas where there was an emphasis on cash crops, the majority of slaves were assigned to tobacco or rice or indigo production.

Thus, the mainland North American system differed from that of the British West Indies, where 90 per cent of slaves worked in the sugar fields; indeed, about 75 per cent of all slaves in all of the western hemisphere were engaged in the production of sugar. Everywhere it occurred, stoop labor wore down the hardiest worker, but most North American planters kept their older, worn-out slaves on a form of retirement benefit. There were retired slaves throughout the system whose food, clothing, and shelter were maintained. Over time, some planters came to own not only adult working slaves but the parents *and* the children of those slaves. Propriety, authority, economic need, and social psychology were joined by paternalism as part of the planter's *modus vivendi*.

THE SLAVES' WORLD

What was it like to *be* a slave, to be born to the condition and slowly, through childhood, become aware of it; to be consigned to it in Africa or en route to America; or to be abruptly faced with it upon arrival in the colonies? What was it like to be given a name, not by parents but by a master who thought that classical names like Nero, Caesar, Cato, Cleopatra, or Venus suited his chattels? The few fragments of evidence from slaves themselves are not helpful. The most illustrious eighteenth century account by a slave, Oloudah Equiano's *Life*, set in the mid-eighteenth century and published in 1789, has been questioned for its authenticity. In any case, Equiano claimed noble birth, hardly the status of the millions who were dragged from Africa and had no chance to experience his fabled odyssey. Later accounts, such as Frederick Douglass's brilliant autobiographical *Narrative* (1845), can be read back into the eighteenth century, but these are too few and too subjective to serve as comprehensive evidence of the slave's consciousness. We are left with fragments of slave observations recorded by white planters and travelers, and consequently, because the planter's record is the more common source, with the master's own version of slave personality, behavior, and morality. In the end, those accounts, and there are thousands of them extant, tell us about the white writer's frame of reference more than they help us to see inside the slave consciousness.

For example, what is one to make of William Bartram's 1776 observations of a group of slaves in Georgia felling trees for the lumber market: "The regular heavy strokes of their gleaming axes re-echoed in the deep forests; at the same time, contented and joyful, the sooty sons of Afric forgetting their bondage, in chorus sung the virtues and beneficence of their master in songs of their own composition" (*Travels of William Bartram* [New York: Dover Publications, 1928], 257). It is not clear what Bartram, a botanist and traveler, was seeing. He assumed that the slaves were so happy they *forgot* that they were slaves. They celebrated their master's "virtues" in an odd reverse on the origins of the blues. Yet one might infer that they did have a beneficent master and allow that their happiness was relative to what their condition might have been with another master and other tasks. We don't know. What we can say is that this particular white observer saw what many others did: seemingly contented slaves happy to be under a benevolent master. We, however, might see the slaves as enjoying a measure of escapism.

Most white views of slaves were more prosaic than Bartram's notes might suggest, even the views of people such as Johann Martin Bolzius, who doubted that a Christian could own a slave "in good conscience." Bolzius was a minister to a community of German Lutherans that had been settled in

Ebenezer, Georgia in the 1730s by the Georgia trustees. He was opposed to the introduction of legalized slavery to Georgia, and, in the 1750s, he offered this banal response to the query of a German correspondent who asked if slaves were as "false, malicious, and terrible as they are described":

> A faithful and sincere Negro [by which he meant slave] is a very rare thing, but they do exist, particularly with masters who know how to treat them reasonably and in a Christian way. Foolish masters sometimes make disloyal and malicious Negroes.... Eternal slavery to them as to all people is an unbearable yoke, and very harsh treatment as regards food and work exasperates them greatly.
>
> *Reliable Answers to Some Submitted Questions Concerning the Land Carolina*, in *The William and Mary Quarterly*, 3rd ser., 14, no. 2 (1957): 233).

To maintain discipline and develop "good" slaves, masters were encouraged to reinforce the slave's sense of dependence, inferiority, and fear of physical violence. Without the legally sanctioned power to punish, no master, even the most humane, could have maintained his authority. Slavery could not have existed without the means to punish. If slaves were not literally aware of the laws, they knew of them from personal experience, stories, observation, and gossip. Slaves witnessed routine whippings and enforced family breakups and understood the reach of the master's power. A 1712 South Carolina law, for example, stipulated that, if a slave showed any violence toward a "Christian or white person," he should be whipped for the first offence, branded the second time, and put to death if it happened a third time. Furthermore, according to the same code, if a white person was injured or maimed by a slave, the latter was to be put to death immediately (with impunity). As prescribed by law, recovered runaways were whipped for a first offence, branded the second time, had their ears cut off for a third offense, and castrated if they tried escaping a fourth time. The slave was subject to a range of penalties for failing to toe the line by defying the orders of a master or overseer, by running away, or by resisting or assaulting those in authority.

MASTERS

Even the most caring of masters admitted to using force to control slave conduct. William Byrd II (1674–1744) of Virginia has left in his diary, correspondence, and other writings the most comprehensive set of views and experiences of a great planter of the first half of the eighteenth century. He was a man of considerable status even among his peers. He was educated in England, but returned to Virginia after he inherited his father's land and slaves in 1704. An obligation of his class was to maintain social propriety and to do his civic duty in local and colony-wide affairs. Byrd offers an interesting insight into the ambiguities of controlling and punishing his slaves and white servants while striving for their "faithfulness." His daily diary notes were candid enough to suggest that he kept the entries not for posterity or publication but for personal reference. His criticisms of his wife, for example, and his occasional references to their lovemaking ("I rogered my wife with vigour") as well as his personal opinions on neighbors and associates were clearly intended to be private. Each day he read Greek or Latin or Hebrew for his intellectual health and "danced," as he put it, for recreational practice and exercise. As a manager of a large tobacco enterprise, he was in touch always with "my people." He makes few references to his field hands, leaving the control of them to his white overseers, but he regularly recorded his dealings with his house slaves.

Byrd comes across as a thoughtful, even sensitive person who expressed a paternalistic concern for his "people." Yet he regularly had slaves whipped for crimes as trivial as stubbornness or carelessness or sexual impropriety and was not beyond recording his own outbursts of rage when he responded to minor infractions. Byrd's notes reveal the real source of the slave's lamentable state, the permanent threat of punishment for minor deviations or even serious mistakes. It is not enough to note that white servants and white minors were also subject to corporal punishment or denial of privileges; the slave had no way of leaving a master or acquiring a different status. Although the extreme punishments for violence or running away reveal the heavy hand of authority, it was the more frequent and routinely administered lesser punishments that kept the slave on edge. The slave lived in an atmosphere of punishment and reward, with the latter being mostly the absence of the former or, at best, some perquisites such as additional leisure, permission to visit friends or relatives on other estates, a small plot to garden, or an extra chicken to eat. Freedom, the ultimate reward, was denied.

Like others of his class, Byrd admitted to living with a moral and social dilemma: he thought slavery, and especially the growing Atlantic slave trade, morally wrong. Yet he saw no way of abandoning either. As to the importation of larger numbers of Africans, Byrd feared that this would lead to a culture "not unlike Jamaica," as he put it. By his time, the importation of slaves into Virginia was less a factor than it was in the Carolina low country. Still, slavery had become more than controlled labor, and, even by the 1730s, he saw that there would be no place for slaves to go even if the practice could be ended. In economic terms, planters like Byrd could lament the inefficiencies of slave labor on the one hand but justify it on the other by citing the problems with white agricultural servant labor. As for white servants, who would choose to work in Byrd's tobacco fields when land might be available elsewhere? Owning slaves, Byrd thought, encouraged sloth and criminality among local poor whites, whose understanding of menial labor was now associated with slavery. Byrd understood that he was a product and a beneficiary of the system. His political status and the luxuries he enjoyed were derived from it. On another level, during the eighteenth century and far away and irrelevant to Byrd's stressful relations with inefficient slaves, northern Christians saw slavery as *theft*. Such was the view of Puritan Samuel Sewall of Boston, a merchant and civic official of the late seventeenth and early eighteenth century, and, much later, of John Woolman, a Pennsylvania Quaker. Abolitionists were scarce in colonial America, but Sewall's *The Selling of Joseph* (1700) and Woolman's *Some Considerations on Keeping Negroes* (1754–1762) shared the thesis that slavery was a form of stealing humans, which of course it was, from the seizing of blacks in Africa to the possession of the progeny of slaves. The view of slavery as theft had been offered as early as 1688 by immigrant Mennonites, a Protestant sect that established itself in Pennsylvania. That scattering of antislavery sentiment indicates the absence of serious abolitionism in colonial British America.

RESISTANCE

Slaves resisted the institution in many ways, often using the subtle sabotage of feigning illness, slowing the pace of work, or damaging tools and equipment. As noted, the ultimate resistance was striking or killing a white person or running away and being caught. Byrd and his peers lived in fear of slave revolt, the violent, deadly rising up of large numbers of slaves. Indeed, although those kinds of uprisings were not common in the slave colonies, the perceived threat of them was a preoccupation of whites all the way to the Civil War. As noted, New York City's slaves enjoyed a more liberal social setting. The city was open to gatherings of free and enslaved blacks. In 1712, an organized protest with violent overtones approaching riot conditions resulted in vicious reprisals, and 21 blacks were killed. Later, in 1741, a series of fires in the city led to rumors that a mixed group of free blacks and white laborers were inciting riot. The authorities reacted with brutal and gruesome public punishments intended as a deterrent: 18 blacks and 4 whites were hanged, and 13 blacks were burned alive. There was paranoia at work in both those cases and in the way South Carolinians behaved in the uncovered "plot" in Charleston in 1740, which resulted in 50 blacks being hanged. That was in the shadow of the Stono Rebellion of 1739, the most serious uprising in the colonial period. Several dozen slaves presumably headed toward Spanish territory to the south were routed at Stono by planter militias but not before 30 whites and 44 blacks had been killed. Slave codes in South Carolina had allowed for some freedom of movement for slaves, but these were tightened in the aftermath of Stono.

THE PLANTER CULTURE OF THE CHESAPEAKE AND THE SOUTH

For the most part, the planter elites in the Chesapeake and the northern reaches of tidewater North Carolina were not as wealthy as the elites of the South Carolina and Georgia tidewater, the so-called low country. Despite the presence of families like the Byrds and Carters, the majority of Virginia and Maryland planters were more economically constrained. By 1770, only 30 per cent of Virginia slaveholders had more than 20 slaves, while, in South Carolina, nearly 75 per cent of plantations had work forces of 20 or more slaves, and over 50 per cent had over 50 slaves. The top echelon of South Carolina slaveholders had created a world that differed in several ways from that of the Chesapeake. In the far south, the wealthiest planters were as often absent from their holdings as they were present, and a resident, hired overseer, or manager was more common there than in the Chesapeake. The oppressive heat and fear of disease obliged the planters to retreat from the plantation to coastal Charleston or Savannah or even northward to the salubrious environs of coastal Rhode Island and New York or wherever natural spring water spas could be found. The trip north had to be made by sea and took anywhere from a few days to two weeks in often uncomfortable conditions. Despite the rigors of the trip, by the 1770s several hundred planters made their way north each year. Most, however, stayed in Charleston and built airy townhouses for their comfort.

There was nothing like Charleston in the Chesapeake. In fact, when one considers the universal agrarianism of the south, Charleston stands as an exotic urban exception and a rather sophisticated community. By the end of the 1760s, it had a population of 10,000 and was the region's great *entrepôt*. It hummed with maritime activity and was the financial, judicial, and political heart of the region. It was the point of entry for thousands of African slaves and the site of regular slave markets. It is worth noting that, in the middle of the eighteenth century, there was not a single courthouse in South Carolina beyond Charleston. Half the Church of England (Anglican) parishes in the colony lacked a resident minister. The hinterland was largely vacant or, at best, housed small clusters of white settlers. Charleston, however, rivaled the northern cities in importance. The planter elites created a world of social clubs, theater, and music schools and were proud of the town's residential and public architecture. There was an assumption of collective importance among the great planters, and, though they were not especially given to higher education or to having their children sent off to northern or British schools, they did aspire to refinement and conspicuous consumption. The social and cultural displays in Charleston and in the plantation estates of the very wealthy belied the region's relatively short history and, to British eyes, the overall crudity of the colony. In a few decades a small elite class of local grandees had created a centralized polity and the trappings of civilization to go with it. Wealth and leisure gave an aristocratic sheen to the planter culture of the lower south.

The Carolina gentry created in Charleston a form of domestic imperialism in which a single locale determined the colony's affairs. The luster of Charleston might compare with the urban dynamics of Boston, New York, or Philadelphia, but the wider influence of those cities was tempered in each case by well-populated and politically active hinterlands. In the suburbs of Charleston, however, there was not much other than great plantations where slaves outnumbered whites, regions with little or no social or logistical infrastructure and no meaningful political life. West of the great plantations lay a great stretch of sparsely populated, white-dominated settlements and beyond that was the backcountry. This was a different setting from the Chesapeake where the gentry spilled out across the region rather than concentrating itself in anything like Charleston and its environs.

For a start, most Chesapeake planters were full-time residents on their estates. Their social lives, as gleaned from diaries, commonplace books, and travelers' observations, indicate an entrenched and affluent culture with enough access to credit, if they needed it, to display neighborliness, conviviality, dinners, dances, and assorted social gatherings. The latter were often specifically all-male or all-female affairs, but married couples attended some dances and dinners. There was no urban culture in the Chesapeake. Baltimore, Maryland was the only town in the region on the eve of the Revolution with a population of more than 4,000, but it was hardly urban. Williamsburg, Virginia's capital since 1698, was barely more than a large village. On the surface, the Chesapeake's slaveholding elites seemed more parochial than those in the lower south, but, in fact, their domestic networks fostered a presumption of privilege to go with their civic responsibilities. And they were powerful in local politics and fully integrated as a ruling class within the colony.

Virginia's gentry were inclined to higher education and formal classical studies as much to demonstrate their civility as to refine their minds. There was a graduated scale of slaveholding and a small but widely distributed class of craftsmen, merchants, and small farmers, all of whom endowed the Chesapeake with an energetic village and county culture. Although society appeared less cosmopolitan than that found in Charleston, it managed to produce Thomas Jefferson, George Washington, James Madison, Richard Henry Lee, George Mason, Patrick Henry, and many others who shaped the political culture of late colonial America. Among South Carolina's planter hierarchy, families such as the Laurens, Pinckneys, and Rutledges made political contributions important to American political leadership and identity, if perhaps less decisive than those of the Virginia cadres. The most distinctive feature of the Chesapeake intelligentsia was that it had few, if any, leisured intellectuals. The thinkers and writers of the region were, first and foremost, planters whose dependency on slave labor fed a remarkable traffic in slave imports in the eighteenth century.

The Atlantic Slave Trade

To this day, the scale and scope of the Atlantic slave trade has the power to give us pause. Thanks to the diligent researches of a generation of historians poring over the records, we have reliable estimates of the astonishing volume of humanity that flowed from Africa into the western hemisphere. A recent and excellent summary and analysis of available data by the historian Herbert Klein calculates that, from 1451 to 1871, a total of 10.2 million African slaves were accounted for on ships' lists, over 98 per cent of whom were landed in the western hemisphere (fewer than 200,000 went to Europe and the Atlantic islands). The vast majority of the 10.2 million were taken to the British, French, and Spanish Caribbean and to Brazil, the major recipient, which imported over 4 million slaves over a three-century span that lasted into the second half of the nineteenth century. Reliable mortality rates for the transit from the interior to the shipping ports on the African coast are not available. The so-called middle passage, that part of the Africa-America-Europe Atlantic triangle that ran from Africa to the Americas, took another toll. The total number of Africans captured, sold, and shipped as slaves might have run as high as 15 million people. Over half the total number of listed slaves, some 5.7 million, arrived in the Americas during the eighteenth century. Two-thirds or more of those were carried on British ships, some of which were owned and registered in the colonies. The Spanish and Portuguese also used the British maritime network. By the eighteenth century, many of the ships were customized, and British and colonial merchants maintained profit levels with careful investment and management. Over the long term, from the seventeenth to the early nineteenth centuries, a mere 5 per cent of the total Atlantic slave trade, some 400,000 slaves, ended up at North American ports. That number became four million by 1860.

As early as the first Portuguese contacts of the fifteenth century, Europeans had gone to Africa to trade and to buy human beings rather than to claim and settle territory. During the seventeenth and eighteenth century, European traders seldom ventured more than 50 miles into the interior but rather established forts, compounds, and assembly points on the West African coast for the buying, sorting, and shipping of slaves. These ports or depots, numbering over 20 by the late eighteenth century, ran in a great tropical arc from Senegambia in the north to Angola in the south, from about 20 degrees north latitude to about 20 degrees south. The millions who passed through these ports were drawn from as far as 600 miles inland, transported by an elaborate network of agents and traders that, from the earliest European enterprises, had created a booming industry in capturing, kidnapping, and transferring people from African villages to the plantations, farms, and mines of the Americas. African and Muslim traders and European agents and buyers operated a complex system of supply, demand, and profit. The Portuguese shipped slaves not only from West Africa but also from Mozambique on the east coast.

Every slave who ended up in the Americas began the experience in violence, being either taken in war or by kidnappers. The weeks or months of transit from the African interior to their unknown destinations began a process of complete alienation. Slaves would be gathered together in "coffles," groups of victims marching in line and shackled together at the hands, feet, or neck. The initial shock of capture or seizure was followed by a harrowing journey under the most dreadful conditions. Regular beatings, exhaustion, hunger, pain, demoralization, and despair accompanied these hapless trains of human victims as they walked to the coast. There, another kind of humiliation greeted them as they were penned, priced, bartered for, and branded by the purchasers before being stacked by the hundreds, like cordwood, on ships that, in some cases, had been belatedly redesigned for the commerce.

The horrors of the middle passage can hardly be exaggerated. Any humane treatment by captors, transporters, or guards was minimal and predicated, for the most part, on the need to preserve what was now a commodity. Slaves spent weeks on hard deck floors in individual spaces that were barely the width of the human body. Simple latrine and feeding procedures were conducted in cramped, fetid, claustrophobic rooms among people who were shackled most of the time. Seasickness and dysentery could despoil the quarters for days on end. Mortality rates were high, in the 10 to 20 per cent range for slaves and sailors alike. The latter were induced into the trade for the lucrative pay that followed a successful deposit of slaves. Slaves died from infections, especially from gastrointestinal disorders, but there were also suicides and many slaves lapsed into anomie, torpor, and despair. It has been noted that conditions were bad on many of the passenger vessels taking

European settlers to the Americas. Cramped quarters, inferior food, and outbreaks of disease wreaked havoc on the eighteenth century immigrant, as Mittelberger's German travelers experienced. But the conditions on the hundreds of slave ships that traversed the Atlantic in the eighteenth century were a lot worse, and worse yet was the fate that awaited the African in America. The process of alienation was not complete until the disoriented, frightened, and weakened slave was introduced to the dockside and port auctions that determined his or her price and eventual owners. Then, a process of acculturation or "seasoning" followed until the slave, male, female, adult, or youth, was locked into the slave community.

Spiritually, the slave could trust in the hereafter, either as an animist or Christian, and, as the eighteenth century wore on, Christianity became increasingly important. The earlier exclusion of blacks from a Christian connection gradually gave way to white acceptance of Christianity for black people as irresistible. It became a way of accommodating the slave's spiritual needs while affording an outlet for slave emotion—a control mechanism in the minds of many planters. Although blacks could be Christians, they remained outside the white church organizations and congregations. The Great Awakening of the 1730s and 1740s hinted at a measure of integration, but, in the end, black Christianity was left to develop its own segregated but vital devotion, worship, and outlook.

And how much did a human commodity cost? The price of slaves was at all times subject to the ebb and flow of supply and demand. From the earliest days of Portuguese involvement in Africa, currency was the least of the exchange mediums. Every imaginable material had value in the trade. Rum, guns, metal tools and cooking objects, bars of iron, costume jewelry, and textiles were used to buy slaves from African intermediaries. The cost of those items cannot always be converted to currency values. In America, by contrast, a field hand in late seventeenth century Virginia could be worth as much as 20 to 30 pounds sterling (or the equivalent in tobacco) to the merchant who delivered him on the dock or the planter who bought him from another planter. Age, health, gender, and aptitude determined the worth of a slave, but the prices did follow the market. By the end of the colonial period, a "valued" slave cost about 50 pounds sterling to buy, and the price rose even higher after the Revolution. What exactly was 30 to 50 pounds sterling in coin, bills of credit, or barter goods (cattle, tobacco, wheat, or any other exchange commodity)? It was roughly the average *annual* value of the product of a family farm in New England, Pennsylvania, or the southern backcountry. Slaves were expensive and were held as profit-generating labor first, investments second, and dependents third. And they were always prisoners.

The Southern Backcountry

The Appalachian chain was the great barrier between British communities to the east and the French and large native communities of the Ohio Valley's fertile lands to the west. The French paid no heed to the fact that many British colonial charters had included trans–Appalachian lands in the original grants. Where the Appalachian chain lowered in elevation and created a series of accessible and habitable valleys, there was some penetration of the west by British colonists. By the 1740s, Virginians had found their way above the fall line and had taken their settlements into the valleys that ran north to south. Agreements with natives regarding hunting in the Shenandoah Valley encouraged more westbound migration by white farmers. Virginia migrants ran into settlers coming south out of Pennsylvania, and an important extension of British settlement was underway. Wagon roads and settlers had reached 100 miles from tidewater by the 1750s.

From the Pennsylvania and Virginia backcountry, a massive, wedge-shaped landmass ran south for 600 miles to beyond the Savannah River into Spanish territory. The fall line in Virginia was between 50 and 100 miles from the Chesapeake shoreline. In Georgia and South Carolina, on the other hand, the distance from the Atlantic shore to the fall line ran to nearly 250 miles, and the backcountry beyond the tidewater plantations was between 150 and 200 miles wide. "Backcountry" is a tricky term that is best understood as it was in the eighteenth century: habitable space somewhat distant or remote from the main areas of settlement. The term "frontier" applies here too but does not do justice to the isolation, distances, and distinct cultures that formed in the southern backcountry in the eighteenth century. There was always a "frontier" in colonial settlement. What usually defined it was simply the farthest reach of settlement. It was a moving line.

On the eve of the Revolution, there were 250,000 people living in a zone that included the far western reaches of the Chesapeake and of the Carolinas and Georgia. The area had filled within the space of two generations, accelerating in the generation before 1776. The migrants were a mixture of Pennsylvanian and other middle colony people and European newcomers. They came as families, extended kin groups, and even as ethnic or sectarian communities, seeking opportunities that were either not available in Britain or Germany or less accessible in the colonial north and east. Migration to the backcountry often meant continued migration through it. Residential persistence was not as high as in older settled regions. For example, some 75 per cent of families in southern New England remained in their locations for more than 10 years. In the southern backcountry, the 10-year persistence rate was only 45 per cent in some areas and as low as 25 per cent in others. Most settlements were exclusively or predominantly white. By the early 1770s, some farmers in the backcountry who were better off than the majority employed slaves or white servants, but the area was dominated by white homesteaders in nuclear families, clans, or religious communities. Indeed, in the Carolinas and Georgia, the *majority* of each colony's white population was settled in the backcountry.

In the early stages, settlers survived on the barest household necessities in crude habitations that afforded only meager comforts. Sustenance was maintained by hunting, planting grains and fruits, and raising pigs, cattle, and chickens. Livestock, some grains, timber, skins, and furs provided a means of exchange and export, but transportation was difficult. Although population density increased in the 1760s and 1770s, most communities and settlements remained isolated from each other. If education was less than important to the tidewater elites, it was even further from the priorities of the Scots, Irish, Scotch-Irish, English, and German settlers of the hills and valleys of the backcountry. Formal legal matters were administered irregularly by circuit magistrates, but most business was conducted in local, informal, and extra-legal personal encounters. Nuclear families were usually large, and households of five to eight children prevailed. Travelers reported upwards of ten children in some of the cabins they visited. Having large numbers of children strained some settlers' resources, but, as was the case in much of rural preindustrial North America, children also provided labor for the family unit. Frequent pregnancies took their toll on the health of backcountry women and compounded the physical demands on the farm wife. Most backcountry women were physically worn down by the end of their childbearing years.

Often, the pressures of subsistence in marginal soils and irregular landforms meant that the family unit struggled simply to keep up with its needs. The image of the rugged frontiersman and the busy, dutiful wife is not an entirely false one, but the more accurate image is of a rough, dirty, dangerous existence. An atmosphere of tedium was compounded by loneliness and anxieties over frequent and deadly encounters with natives, who themselves were constantly threatened and abused. In some parts of the Carolinas, there was also the threat of roving bands of thieves. Another image, that of the violence and inbreeding of illiterate "hillbillies" survived into the twentieth century. But again that was no more the norm than was the idealized image of a population of intrepid Daniel Boones. The great majority of the first two generations of backcountry peoples lived tough lives to be sure, but exhausting manual labor on the farm, in the woods, or on the rivers was the lot of 90 per cent of *all* colonial Americans. Different conditions did prevail in the foothills and mountain valleys of the west, but life still came down to the search for a measure of self-sufficiency and the slow, gradual route to security.

By mid century, the older settled parts of the frontier in western Maryland and Virginia, the area that has been called "Greater Pennsylvania," seemed more like an extension of the older tidewater societies than the raw developments that occurred farther south. In the Carolinas, migrants came in a steady flow of humanity that made its way along the Great Philadelphia Wagon Road that ran down the eastern side of the Appalachians from Pennsylvania through the Shenandoah Valley and all the way to the tip of British settlement in South Carolina and Georgia. North Carolina was the fastest growing province in British America after 1750 because its backcountry was accessible and expansive. As noted, the multitude was a mixed lot, made up of ethnic groupings, Protestant sects, and immigrants and American-born settlers of various ages, family sizes, personalities, and competences. For the most part, the settlements were dominated by farm families, but the backcountry also attracted a rich mélange of lawyers; ex-soldiers; land and mercantile speculators; artisans; preachers; teachers; restless hunters; trappers; political, legal, and business entrepreneurs; and even criminals.

Over time, crossroads merchants, taverns, and rudimentary towns appeared. The Germans were noted for being the best farmers and settled in cooperative farming communities. According to contemporaries, the Scotch-Irish and other British settlers appeared to be less efficient farmers than the Germans. Moravians and the Reformed Church groups were especially noted for their ability to succeed. The Germans understood that the best way to bring forested land into production was to fell the trees, burn off the branches, and pull out stumps in a concerted way. The Scotch-Irish, on the other hand, usually "girdled" the trees, that is, choked the trunk near the base, allowing it to die and fall down in a few years. They then farmed around the stumps. The Germans, not surprisingly, usually enjoyed larger yields from a more varied crop selection.

Small surpluses made their way up the wagon roads, down the rivers, and across country to markets. Skins and iron ore, corn, wheat, flax, salted beef, and live cattle and hogs were delivered to the tidewater, assuring adequate food supply. The backcountry farms gradually adopted standard farm economies with gardens, orchards, livestock, grains, and sufficient materials for homespun clothing. Here and there, weavers, blacksmiths, masons, and various craftsmen appeared in neighborhoods with the first wave of settlers, but they usually arrived after some permanent households were established.

There was poverty, and some of it was persistent. In the absence of public poor relief or where no extended family or kinship or communal help was available, the loss of a husband and father meant that widows and orphans often fell into destitution. The inventories noted in southern backcountry wills and deeds reveal lower standards of material comfort than those existing in older eastern districts. Bedding, clothing, and simple domestic implements were passed on to survivors. Diets gradually improved, in caloric value and variety, for all in the backcountry although pork and corn in its many guises, as bread, meal, and whisky, dominated the culinary norms in the region.

What drew migrants was land and autonomy. From Virginia south, western lands were legally available, most commonly through the leasing or buying of plots at rates that were more manageable than the prices to the north and east. Despite the large stretches of unoccupied, unusable land, some backcountry neighborhoods eventually became crowded, so, by the late eighteenth century, people began to push across the Appalachians through the valleys, passes, and gaps into what would be Kentucky, Tennessee, Alabama, and beyond. Before that, however, the northern reaches of the southern backcountry in Virginia were filled in by the 1750s and settlers spilled over into French-claimed territory in the Ohio Valley. In the Pennsylvania backcountry, the pressure had already sent settlers curving west and then south into the Carolinas. The demography of late colonial British America has to be understood in the light of an ever-expanding stream of people moving inland from the Atlantic shore and heading west, with northern and southern extensions. The Maine frontier, to the northeast, an entirely separate zone absorbed much of New England's land seekers.

BACKCOUNTRY CULTURE

A distinct culture developed in the southern backcountry. Few of the people in the scattered settlements recorded their thoughts or experiences, but some travelers' accounts, the notes and diaries of literate planter-politicians' and clergymen, as well as court records help illuminate some of its features. One of the most vivid and detailed observations of southern backcountry society in the 1760s is the journal of Charles Woodmason (ca.1720–ca.1776), an English-born immigrant to South Carolina. He was both a small planter and a merchant before returning to England in 1761 to take orders in the Church of England. Upon returning to South Carolina, he first settled into the good life in Charleston then abruptly took off in 1766 for the backcountry on a church mission that became a tiring and mostly frustrating experience. He combined attempts to bring a small measure of English civility and Christian engagement to societies that he found generally to be in a "state of nature." Woodmason was a missionary not to the natives in the backcountry but to the region's British subjects. His commentary betrays his prejudices, his indignation and even shock at what he observed, but his descriptions are memorable. What he saw was very far removed from the Charleston he had left and even farther from the London he knew, and although we might see him as a disappointed missionary and snob, this intelligent and observant man did catch a great deal of the flavor of the South Carolina backcountry.

Because South Carolina was nominally Anglican, his journal bubbles with irritations over the lack of Anglican commitment and the ever-present "vile" Presbyterians. He laments the slovenly habits of the people but offers us vivid verbal pictures of them, albeit from his often jaundiced view. He was not the first reformist visitor to make notes on the backcountry, but his commentary, allowing for its judgemental tone, is a lively, comprehensive view of a society in the process of formation. He could be as sympathetic to the poverty and filth he witnessed as he was ready to condemn the same people for their lapsed or unformed habits and devotions. He offers glimpses of the terrain, the climate, and the material conditions that underscored the hard lives of the people he chose for his ministry. While he was often critical of the inhabitants, he also chastised the Charleston elites so far away for their failure to provide the backcountry with permanent church facilities, legal infrastructure, and decent political representation. In one journal entry, he noted that in "intolerable" heat some locals struggled to attend one of his services: "Many of these people walk 10 or 12 Miles with their Children in the burning Sun—Ought such to be without the Word of God, when so earnest, so desirous of hearing it and becoming Good Christians" (*The Carolina Backcountry on the Eve of Revolution*, 60).

He then goes on to make both a political and ecclesiastical attack on the South Carolina legislators in Charleston, "so rich, so luxurious, [so] polite a People... [who] look on poor White People in a Meaner Light than their Black Slaves, and care less for them" (60). He noted that, rather than support the established church, the South Carolina government had spent 30,000 pounds sterling to bring into the colony "5 or 6000 Ignorant, mean, worthless, beggarly [Scotch] Irish Presbyterians, the Scum of the Earth, and Refuse of Mankind" (60). If he found immigrant Presbyterians distasteful, he was also appalled by the crudities of the nominal Anglicans. Commenting on one congregation, he noted that not one of them "had a Bible or Common Prayer [book]" nor could one of them recite the Lord's Prayer. Indifference or illiteracy or both confronted him in many places, and he noted, ruefully, that it would take "much Time and Pains to New Model and form the Carriage and Manners, as well as the Morals of these *wild people*" (61, emphasis added).

As to "morals," Woodmason's unrealistic expectations were often at odds with reality, and, in a much quoted and vivid passage, his breathless indignation shows:

It would be (as I once observ'd before) a Great Novelty to a Londoner to see one of these Congregations—The Men with only

a thin Shirt and pair of Breeches or Trousers on—barelegged
and barefooted—The Women bareheaded, barelegged and bare-
foot with only a thin Shift and under Petticoat—Yet I cannot
break [them?] of this—for the heat of the Weather admits not
of any [but] thin Cloathing—I can hardly bear the Weight of
my Whig and Gown, during Service. The Young Women have
a most uncommon Practise, which I cannot break them off. They
draw their Shift as tight as possible to the Body, and pin it close,
to shew the roundness of their Breasts, and slender Waists (for
they are generally finely shaped) and draw their Petticoat close
to their Hips to shew the fineness of their Limbs—so that they
might as well be in Puri Naturalibus—Indeed Nakedness is not
censurable or indecent here, and they expose themselves often
quite Naked, without Ceremony—Rubbing themselves and their
Hair with Bears Oil and tying it up behind in a Bunch like the
Indians—being hardly one degree removed from them—In few
Years, I hope to bring about a Reformation, as I already have done
in several Parts of the Country. (61)

He noted that, in the vast majority of weddings he ministered, the
brides were pregnant, and the prevalence of venereal disease shocked him.
He might have found similar conditions in some sections of the London he
loved or in other urban slums, but his memory of London was idealized. He
might have found pregnant brides in rural New England or Pennsylvania too.
On the other hand, although the behaviors of the backcountry people clearly
displeased him, he was sympathetic to the ways they adapted to the demands
of frontier life. Most were resourceful and tough minded. Simple household
materials, from cooking utensils to clothing and bedding, were scarce in some
areas, and brick, glass, and finished lumber were not always available. By the
1760s, marketable timber, livestock, and skins provided income for many, and
traffic in goods in and out of the backcountry improved, even on primitive
wagon roads. Otherwise people relied on their own homespun clothing and
whatever exchanges that could be made with neighbors, crossroads merchants,
and transient traders for footwear, tools, and weapons. As to the latter, from
Pennsylvania to South Carolina, backcountry hunters, traders, and militiamen had need of gunsmiths, gunpowder supplies, and the lead and implements for making shot. Most gunsmiths in the backcountry were part-time
farmers or storekeepers, as was the case throughout the older colonial communities. The environment encouraged interesting innovations in gun design,
such as the modified smoothbore musket design created by lengthening and
"rifling" (grooving) barrels for greater range. The so-called Pennsylvania long

rifle (or "Kentucky rifle") of the late eighteenth century was a backcountry original drawn from decades of adaptation.

Charles Woodmason was alert to the fact that, in the southern interior, settlement preceded authority. This was particularly the case in South Carolina's backcountry where entire communities sprang up without adequate legal or policing means and where isolation and distances attracted bandits. In 1771, a few years after leaving the backcountry, Woodmason wrote a report to the Bishop of London describing the anarchy and terror in parts of the region during the late 1760s. He noted that "Here Vile and Impudent fellows, would come to a Planters House, and Tye him—Lye with his Wife before his Face—Ravish Virgins, before Eyes of their Parents, a dozen fellows in succession" (256). The report goes on to describe kidnappings, torture, and the general preying on merchants and pedlars. Some of these backcountry gangs were bold enough to come out of the hills, to the "Lower Settlements" and steal slaves, rustle horses and cattle, and threaten the peace wherever they went, having "Confederates in ev'ry Colony" (258). Woodmason notes sarcastically that, when some thieves robbed a member of the council in the "Lower Settlements" the government began to take notice. Here, Woodmason touched on an issue that festered in the backcountry of both Carolinas for several years in the 1760s and 1770s. North Carolina's small farmers complained about the lack of fairness, or regulation, in the justice system. They complained of corruption, class discrimination, and the lack of adequate assembly representation. The South Carolina backcountry vigilante groups used the term "Regulators," as did the North Carolinians, but their concerns were a bit different. The Regulators, as we shall see, added complexity to the imperial crisis in the colonies in the 1760s. At the local level, they wanted law and order and got it, as Woodmason notes, but only after the wave of crime came home to the colony's middle and upper classes. After 1769, courthouses and prisons and the support for them came to the backcountry of South Carolina, but, by then, important regional and class divisions between the backcountry and the tidewater were firmly in place.

Charles Woodmason's mission was undertaken in the late 1760s, after the Seven Years' War, when colonial protests over Parliament's reforms were growing. He was concerned with the weakness of the Anglican establishment in the aftermath of both the Great Awakening and the revivals that had recently swept through the colonies, but he was also a critical observer of the rising political tensions in the 1760s. He often berated the South Carolina Assembly's anti-imperial behavior as hypocritical because it was ignoring its own people in the backcountry. Woodmason could be tender, sarcastic, astute, and hostile by turn, especially as he railed against the Charleston elite. He had a flair for the ironic and was a decent satirist. He made keen notes on geography and society wherever he went. In the end, however, the difficulties he encountered defeated him. He consoled himself in the tone of the martyr, as follows:

> Thus You have a Journal of two Years—In which [I] have rode near Six thousand Miles, almost on one Horse. Wore my Self to a Skeleton and endured all the Extremities of Hunger, Thirst, Cold, and Heat. Have baptized near 1200 Children—Given 200 or more Discourses—Rais'd almost 30 Congregations—Set on foot the building of sundry Chapels Distributed Books, Medicines, Garden Seed, Turnip, Clover, Timothy Burnet, and other Grass Seeds—with Fish Hooks—Small working Tools and variety of Implements to set the Poor at Work, and promote Industry to the amount of at least One hundred Pounds Sterling: Roads are making—Boats building—Bridges framing, and other useful Works begun thro' my Means, as will not only be of public Utility, but make the Country side wear a New face, and the People become New Creatures. And I will venture to attest that these small, weak Endeavours of mine to serve the Community, has (or will) be of more Service to the Colony, than ever Mr. Whitfield's [sic] Orphan House was, or will be. (259)

As he recounts his odyssey, the crusading Woodmason puts a positive face on an experience that at times thoroughly depressed him. The reference at the end is to George Whitefield (1714–1770), who, twenty years earlier, spearheaded a faith-based, cross-sectarian, born-again revival in the south. Here was the bane of Woodmason's experience in the backcountry and later in his sojourn in tidewater Maryland: the Great Awakening had revealed some insecurity not only in the Anglican Church but also in conservative worship and church orders everywhere. Woodmason had discovered a very important development in 1760s America, a booming multiethnic medley of peoples and nonconforming sects in the backcountry and their convergence into a culture unlike that in any other part of British America.

SUGGESTED READINGS

Some of the general studies that have influenced this chapter include Carl Bridenbaugh, *Myths and Realities: Societies of the Colonial South* (New York: Atheneum, 1968), a short personalized survey of the region. It is written in a style that is seldom seen today in scholarly monographs; it is conversational and openly judgemental, but it is recommended as an introduction to the region's social character and has the merit of subdividing the Chesapeake, the backcountry, and the tidewater south. Other recommended studies are David Hackett Fischer, *Albion's Seed: Four British Folkways in America*, cited in Chapter 7; Kathleen Brown, *Good Wives, Nasty Wenches, and Anxious Patriarchs: Gender, Race, and Power in Colonial Virginia* (Chapel Hill: University of North Carolina Press, 1996); David Hackett Fischer and James C. Kelly, *Bound Away: Virginia and the Westward Movement* (Charlottesville: University Press of Virginia, 2000); Allan Kulikoff, *From British Peasants to Colonial American Farmers* (Chapel Hill: University of North Carolina Press, 2000); the relevant chapters in Kirsten Fischer and Eric Hinderaker, eds., *Colonial American History* (Oxford: Blackwell, 2002) and Alice Hanson Jones, *Wealth of a Nation to Be: The American Colonies on the Eve of the Revolution* (New York: Columbia University Press, 1980). The backcountry has received recent and welcome attention and Bridenbaugh's *Myths and Realities* can be compared to David Crass, ed., *The Southern Colonial Backcountry* (Knoxville: University of Tennessee Press, 1998), a welcome interdisciplinary anthology with a superb bibliography and Eric Hindraker and Peter C. Mancall, *At the Edge of Empire: The Backcountry in British North America* (Baltimore: Johns Hopkins University Press, 2003). Louis B. Wright and Marion Tinling, eds., *The Secret Diary of William Byrd of Westover, 1709–1712*, 2 vols. (Richmond, VA: Dietz Press, 1941) is a useful edition of one of Virginia's great diaries and Kenneth Lockridge, *The Diary and Life of William Byrd II of Virginia, 1674–1744* (Chapel Hill: University of North Carolina Press, 1987) advances the value of Byrd's writings. Richard J. Hooker, ed., *The Carolina Backcountry on the Eve of the Revolution: The Journal and Other Writings of Charles Woodmason, Anglican Itinerant* (Chapel Hill: University of North Carolina Press, 1953) should be read by anyone who seeks to recapture the flavor of eighteenth century frontier life.

The social and cultural history of the southern colonies has not attracted as much attention as that of the New England colonies. Slavery, on the other hand, as a distinct historiographical field continues to inspire much scholarly attention. This chapter made extensive use of Ira Berlin, *Many Thousands Gone: The First Two Centuries of Slavery in North America* (Cambridge, MA: Harvard University Press, 1998) and Philip D. Morgan, *Slave Counterpoint:*

Black Culture in the Eighteenth-Century Chesapeake and Lowcountry (Chapel Hill: University of North Carolina Press, 1998). Those two studies take broad and comparative approaches and represent the most recent scholarship. Betty Wood, *Slavery in Colonial America, 1619–1776* (Lanham, MD: Rowman and Littlefield, 2005) is a brief (86 page) and sensitive survey. The early chapters in Peter Kolchin, *American Slavery, 1619–1877* (New York: Hill and Wang, 1993) are also useful. Two excellent theoretical studies are Orlando Patterson, *Slavery and Social Death, a Comparative Study* (Cambridge, MA: Harvard University Press, 1982) and Winthrop Jordan, *White Over Black: American Attitudes toward the Negro, 1550–1812* (Chapel Hill: University of North Carolina Press, 1968). The best survey of slavery in the rest of the Americas is Herbert S. Klein, *African Slavery in Latin America and the Caribbean* (New York: Oxford University Press, 1986). Studies that focus on slavery within particular colonies include Peter H. Wood, *Black Majority: Negroes in South Carolina from 1670 through the Stono Rebellion* (New York: Norton, 1974) and Edmund Morgan, *American Slavery, American Freedom: The Ordeal of Colonial Virginia* (New York: Norton, 1975). The latter is an especially stimulating approach to the deeper influences of slavery on the social, political, and cultural history of the Chesapeake. See also Allan Kulikoff, *Tobacco and Slaves: The Development of Southern Cultures in the Chesapeake, 1680–1800* (Chapel Hill: University of North Carolina Press, 1986). The slave trade is usually seen as a separate branch of America's slavery history. A superb summary of recent scholarship is Herbert S. Klein, *The Atlantic Slave Trade* (New York: Cambridge University Press, 1999). This book's "Bibliographic Essay" is recommended. Klein's book updates the earlier work of Philip Curtin, *The Atlantic Slave Trade: A Census* (Madison: University of Wisconsin Press, 1969). See also Emma Christopher, *Slave Ship Sailors and their Captive Cargoes* (Cambridge, UK: Cambridge University Press, 2006) and Marcus Rediker, *The Slave Ship: A Human History* (New York: Viking, 2007) for more intimate views on the slaves' experience in transit. An excellent "coffee-table" book that includes contributions by many leading scholars in the field is *Captive Passage: The Transatlantic Slave Trade and the Making of the Americas* (Washington, DC: Smithsonian, 2002).

CHAPTER 9

★ ★ ★ ★ ★ ★ ★ ★ ★ ★ ★ ★ ★

Christian America and the Great Awakening

Congress shall make no law respecting an establishment of religion, or prohibiting the free exercise thereof....

—The first part of the First Amendment to the United States Constitution (1791).

The stirring phrases that precede the free speech clause of the Bill of Rights of 1791 reflected established colonial practices. Eighteenth century Americans understood *their* "religion" to mean the Christian religion and if, over time, "free exercise" would eventually include the entire range of the world's religions, in 1791 "free exercise" was understood to apply to Christian sects. Colonial America was too vast, its peoples too spatially and socially mobile, its growth too rapid, its doors too open, and its jurisdictions too diverse to allow any Christian variant to dominate the whole completely. By the middle of the eighteenth century, an assortment of sects, subsets, new strains, and long-established ecclesiastical organizations thrived in America. The Reformation had sent Protestantism along paths of adaptation, experimentation, and change, and while the Church of Rome, the "universal" or Catholic Church, held fast to a global standard of its doctrines, Protestant sects grew in complexity. As the latter became increasingly vernacular over time, that is, Dutch for the Dutch, English for the English, and so on, the Catholic Church retained one very important organizational feature, the global authority of the pope and the hierarchy that assumed to manage the church's affairs throughout the world. There were various orders within the Church of Rome, the Franciscans and Jesuits, for example, but Catholicism's practices, authority, and the style of its missions were less flexible than those of the Protestant denominations. It was not until the nineteenth century that the exclusive use of Latin in the mass was eased. In 1750, there were only 30 Catholic churches in only five colonies out of nearly 1,500 churches throughout the thirteen British mainland colonies. Those 1,500 churches, or congregations, represented several major Protestant denominations and some smaller sects or subdivisions:

Anglican (Church of England) After the Congregationalist Church of New England, this was the second largest church organization in the colonies in 1750, although both the Baptists and Presbyterians surpassed it in size by the 1780s. After its sixteenth century Tudor separation from Rome, the Church of England retained some of the cosmetics and functions of the Catholic Church, such as structured and ritualized worship, elaborate church furnishings, and a hierarchical organization. The Monarch was the head of the church and archbishops, bishops, and clergy at the parish-congregational level ran its affairs. So-called high church Anglicanism was too conservative for many and gave rise to a reform movement in England that attempted to "purify" the church in the Elizabethan era. The term "Puritan" was coined to describe these reformers, and, in the seventeenth century, Puritans became part of the English diaspora that went to America. They founded Massachusetts and shaped the Christian face of New England in a way that stunted the Church of England's prospects to dominate colonial America, if, in fact, that had been possible. From the founding of Jamestown in 1607, Anglican services in America adopted a form of worship that was plain and closer to the Puritan than the "high church" style. There was an immediate modification in church governance so that the vestry was controlled by lay people who controlled the clergy in the absence of a strong bishopric. The vestry distributed charity or poor relief, which was a responsibility of the civil authorities, the town meeting, in New England. In nearly all jurisdictions, there was never enough clergy for the church's plans. Woodmason's South Carolina backcountry was not so much the exception as an extreme version of what the church faced everywhere: sectarian competition and weak or even absent administration. This held true even where the Anglican Church was made the established church, as it was in Virginia, part of New York, Maryland, the Carolinas, and Georgia. British missionary programs for white colonists, the Society for the Promotion of Christian Knowledge (1698) and the Society for the Propagation of the Gospel in Foreign Parts (1701) helped in the modest spread of the Anglican Church in America, especially in the Chesapeake and the lower south. In important and ironic ways, however, the Church of England's relations with its colonial outposts did as much to foster nonconformity as to advance the interests of the church. When the Anglican Church in America dropped its affiliation with the Church of England after independence in 1784, it became the *Episcopalian* Church, a wholly American organization. In Canada, the Anglican Church remains strong in part because loyalists took it there after the Revolution and because the Church of England promoted itself in the creation of later Canadian colonies.

Congregational Church (Puritan) This was the product of the Puritan mission to reform the Church of England in America. In the process, it created what became a powerful new ecclesiastical authority in New England. The initial Calvinist thrust of the Puritan crusade left its mark on the way spiritual and social communalism survived in colonial and revolutionary New England. Congregationalism was partly a top-down organization; the Cambridge Platform of 1648 in Massachusetts gave elders the power to limit who could speak in church, and the 1708 Saybrook Platform in Connecticut acknowledged the principle of "consociation" or the forming of standing councils to ordain ministers and discipline members. However, the Congregational establishment coexisted with local prerogatives, and, although worship, ethical values, and theological discipline were somewhat standardized, local congregations retained considerable control over their day-to-day affairs. A "Puritan ethic" of communalism and spiritual conformity survived well into the eighteenth century, even as other denominations arrived and settled. What changed in Puritan New England was the erosion of the predestination doctrine and its replacement with the prospect of salvation for all. The image of the stern, repressive, and repressed Puritan New Englander should really be replaced by the reality of a sober-minded, neighborly, community-oriented individual surrounded by a culture that took its heaven and hell alternatives seriously and that retained the greatest of the Congregationalist legacies, the town as the fount of civil and social order. But Puritan Congregationalism was fixed in its region. There were more Congregational churches (that is, a greater number of congregations) in British America in 1750 than there were churches of any other denomination, but 98 per cent of them were in New England.

Presbyterian Church Presbyterianism was born in the Scottish Reformation of the sixteenth century and molded in the fiery Calvinism of John Knox and his followers, the founders of the powerful Church of Scotland (the "Kirk"). Presbyterian congregations grew in Northern Ireland as Scots occupied the Ulster counties in the seventeenth and eighteenth centuries. Presbyterian doctrines and manners were close to those of Puritan Calvinism in practice and sentiment, but the "synod" as an assembly of congregations and "presbyters," that is elders and lay officials, differed in important ways from the Puritan models. In Connecticut, for example, Congregationalists tended to become affiliated with the Presbyterian Church because of a preference for the synod. The steady influx of Scots and Scotch-Irish settlers into the middle and southern parts of the mainland colonies boosted the church's numbers in America and greatly expanded its reach. In the eighteenth century, it became an important cultural and social force in the middle colonies and the backcountry and with the Baptist Church passed the Anglican Church in numbers of churches and adherents. The association of Presbyterianism with ethnic and cultural nonconformity is a bit ironic given its favored style of worship and sermonizing, which was often stern. The authoritarian structure of the synod model tended to make the church hierarchical. The Great Awakening's impact on America hit the Presbyterian Church as it did others by challenging its centralizing and formal doctrines, but Presbyterianism survived as a formidable social and political force in Christian America.

Baptist This popular product of the Reformation was considered radical as much for its flexibility as for its theology. Its individual congregations applied methods and models of worship and devotion that ranged from predestination to free will. The scriptures were taken literally, and the baptism of adults seeking redemption was a hallmark of its ethos. The great success of the Baptist movement derived from the autonomy enjoyed by its many individual congregations. From two small congregations in seventeenth century Rhode Island to the explosive rise in the sect's popularity in the eighteenth century, the Baptist Church was the fastest growing denomination in the colonies. By the 1780s, it had passed the Anglican Church in number of congregations and was third in numbers of adherents behind Congregationalists and Presbyterians. Its adaptability, its apparent accessibility, and a basic egalitarian premise made the Baptist movement appealing and dynamic. It was open to novelty and innovation and was immensely popular in the backcountry. For all its popular appeal, the Baptist network respected the need to ordain and support educated ministers. Baptists received a charter for Rhode Island College (later Brown University) in 1764. In many ways, the Baptists became the quintessential revivalist movement during the Great Awakening of the

1730–1750 period. They encouraged itinerancy and benefited from the "born again" credo that marked the revivals.

Lutheran From small Swedish and German roots in the early seventeenth century, this denomination barely survived into the eighteenth century. It then blossomed into a significant force in the middle colonies. German and Swiss immigrants sustained it, and its pietistic, faith-based approach fed into the Great Awakening's redemptive themes. There were over 200 Lutheran congregations in the colonies by the 1770s.

Dutch Reformed The Dutch Reformed Church is one of the oldest Protestant Church organizations in America. There were nine active congregations in New Netherland when the English took it in 1664, and they were tolerated by the Anglican establishment. The Dutch Reformed Church flourished in the middle colonies under the auspices of the Amsterdam Classis, the clerical supervisors of overseas congregations. There were over 100 functioning congregations on the eve of the Revolution. As in other denominations, however, there was internal fissure in the Dutch Reform Church in the eighteenth century. On one hand were traditionalist congregations that maintained ceremonial services and worship with a great deal of emphasis on theology. This was in some contrast to other Dutch Reform congregations, largely rural and often remote, that emphasized spontaneity and open expressions of faith rather than mandatory adherence to doctrine.

German Reformed For most of the eighteenth century, the German Reformed Church operated under the ecclesiastical aegis of the Amsterdam Classis. This arrangement was more a convenience than a demonstration of affinity with the Dutch. The two groups were separated by the locations of their ethnic-based settlements. The German variant appeared first in New York in the first decade of the century, and, as the numbers of German immigrants rose, the church grew to embrace nearly 200 congregations by the 1770s. Perhaps a third of all Rhineland immigrants belonged to the German Reformed Church.

Quakers (Society of Friends) In its earliest manifestations in England, the Society of Friends was among the most radical of sects. Its founder, George Fox (1624–1691) is quoted as saying, "When the Lord sent me forth into the world he forbade me to put off my hat to any, high or low." Its rise in the seventeenth century to a vibrant global movement is a measure of the tenacity and deep spirituality of its membership and its martyrs, who were persecuted in the British Isles and New England. The movement's founder, George Fox, was hounded, ridiculed, and jailed for his radicalism. Quakers threatened the order and authority of the established Church of England and its Puritan offshoot in New England because of their claim to an "inner light," an individual communion with God. This assertion defied the usual sermonizing of most Protestant services and the liturgical thrust of Anglican public worship. The very term Quaker refers to the appearance of "quaking" or trembling that accompanied the believers' experience of the "inner light." In place of conventional church settings, Quakers held "meetings" to discuss spiritual matters in the absence of a trained or ordained ministry. Their focus on family and business led to tight communities and successful economic enterprise, in trade, land development, farming, and merchandizing.

Quakers were pacifists and many were abolitionists, among them the passionate and articulate John Woolman (1720–1772) who traveled the colonies and went to England to denounce slavery. His essay *Some Considerations on the Keeping of Negroes* (noted in Chapter 8) is a humane treatise on the damage slavery inflicted on slaves and slaveholders alike. Woolman's *Journal* is one of the great literary works of the American eighteenth century and should be better known. It captures the social and political lives of a variety of people in various colonies and reveals a very sensitive personality concerned with slavery, poverty, and inequality. Perhaps more than any other branch of British Protestantism, Quakers opposed any link between church and state. Although the proprietary Quaker governments in West Jersey in 1674 and Pennsylvania in 1681 might appear to violate that principle, they accepted all denominations. One of their main influences on general government policy was insisting on fair and peaceful relations with natives. Quaker influence declined throughout the eighteenth century as their dominance yielded to a rich profusion of sects. They were a potent force in Pennsylvania's economy, however, and even as they became a minority by the middle of the eighteenth century, they remained among the most efficient international merchants of the age.

The intimacy of the meeting house and the emphasis on individual rights, the love of family, and the supreme importance of children in society were among the chief characteristics of Quaker culture. None of that obviated the need for formality, and the Philadelphia Yearly Meeting brought Quakers together annually to discuss and debate issues that were central to their interests. Yet, even in the Society of Friends, there was occasional schism. In the 1690s, for example, an important Quaker, George Keith, was rejected by the Quaker leadership for his criticisms of the church's apparent openness He defected to the Anglicans and "took orders" (priesthood) in that church. From time to time, there were other dissenters who found the "inner light" principle too loose and who sought a more rigid scriptural relationship between man and the divine.

Other important Protestant sects thrived in the fluid Christian atmosphere of the eighteenth century. *Mennonites,* for example, led by Daniel Francis Pastorius took their name from an early Protestant, Menno Simons, and settled in Pennsylvania within two years of Penn's charter. As noted, they were perhaps the earliest antislavery activists and in a 1688 resolution likened slavery to theft. They formed cooperative settlements and argued for strict church-state separation while blending Calvinist predestination theory with Quaker pacifism in their theology. The more conservative branch of Mennonites, the *Amish,* strove for simplicity and communalism in their tightly knit settlements. Minor German Baptist sects, *Dunkards* and the *Ephrata Society,* set up in the 1720s and 1730s in the middle colonies along with another exotic German offshoot, the *Schwenkfelders,* in Pennsylvania. *Shakers* were relatively late arrivals, showing up in 1774 during the imperial crisis. The eponymous Dunkers were pacifists who took their name from their immersion practices. The quiet, reflective Ephrata Society members promoted chastity. *Methodists* were an invigorating Anglican faction with an enthusiastic and informal approach to worship. They supported an itinerant ministry.

One of the most enterprising of the many smaller sects was the *Moravians,* the "United Brethren." They landed in Georgia in 1735 on a mission to convert natives and won the approval of the great Methodist, John Wesley. The Moravians founded Bethlehem in Pennsylvania and another short-lived commune of the same name in the North Carolina backcountry. They were industrious and among the most successful Christian sects in dealings with natives, respecting them and often choosing to live among them for the sake of conversion. Their persistent use of the German language added to the checkerboard of ethnic and religious habits especially in the middle colonies and the backcountry. Because religion, family, and community were vital everyday associations for colonists, belonging to a denomination and a congregation formed part of one's sense of place and purpose. Spatial mobility allowed for internal migrations within and across political, geographical, and sectarian boundaries, but the establishment of permanent communities was always the goal of the Christian in America.

It is a commonplace to see seventeenth century Puritans as dissenters seeking freedom of religious expression. That view is only partly correct and only so in its English variant. Once established, the Puritans of Massachusetts applied a rigorous exclusivity. The term given to the Puritan Church establishment, "Congregational," should not be confused with the lower case word "congregation," which simply meant the regular members and attendees of any denomination. Groups such as Quakers and Baptists persistently challenged the Congregational domain, and internal differences were evident throughout. However, as Anne Hutchinson and Roger Williams demonstrated early on, tensions inside the Calvinist communities eventually gave way to official moderation. Moreover, the Massachusetts Royal Charter of 1691 opened the door to other denominations to reflect the modest but legal levels of religious tolerance that prevailed in England in the wake of the Glorious Revolution. In 1650, all but two of the 59 churches in all of New England had been Congregational. By 1750, there were 7 Anglican congregations in Rhode Island and Baptist churches outnumbered Congregational churches by 30 to 12. Even in Massachusetts by mid century, the number of Presbyterian, Anglican, Baptist, and other congregations comprised about 20 per cent of all churches. While advocates of the holy commonwealth such as Cotton Mather had kept alive the corporate and theological values of earlier Puritanism, it was clear that even the most closed of Christian communities was now open to other denominations.

In Virginia, the Anglican Church maintained official status from the start, but there was a persistent lack of parsons to fill the needs of the expanding population. The same thing happened in the Carolinas and Georgia later on in the century and all the way to the Revolution. In the 1630s, the creation of a Catholic refuge was part of the rationale for founding Maryland, but the need to fill the colony with settlers meant that almost immediately Anglicans and even Puritans moved in. The kaleidoscopic ethnic and sectarian future of the middle colonies was evident in the way those colonies came about. English New York was intended to have an official Anglican Church superimposed on existing Dutch sects, but, in a short time, a plethora of Protestant strains called New York home. Quaker proprietors in West Jersey, Pennsylvania, and Delaware were intended to favor Quakers, but hardly had the doors opened when Europe's army of Christian sects moved in and Quaker authority receded. In 1687, long before Charles Woodmason gasped at the jumble of sects in the Carolina backcountry, Catholic Governor of New York Thomas Dongan reported a bewildering congeries of "opinions" that included Anglicans, Dutch Lutherans, Dutch Reformed, French Calvinists, Roman Catholics, "Singing" and "Ranting" Quakers, Sabbatarians, Anti-Sabbatarians, Anabaptists, Independents, and Jews.

In most places, in the early decades of the eighteenth century church, attendance was strong, but membership in some denominations was eroding. One estimate shows that fewer than 70 per cent of colonists were affiliated, a figure that varied with each region, being higher in New England and the tidewater and among certain sects, Quakers and Congregationalists, for example. In any case, the civil authority of the church hierarchies was weak. There were no bishops in Anglican America, and the various Church of England missionary programs, the Presbyterian Synod (a form of central authority), Congregational "consociations," or any formal institutional organization found it difficult to enforce common standards, even though they maintained a thread of coherence through their far-flung congregations. In the late seventeenth and early eighteenth century, Philadelphia was a hub of sectarian variation and organizations, for example, the Philadelphia Yearly Meeting (Quaker), the Synod of Philadelphia (Presbyterian), the Philadelphia Baptist Association, and, in the 1740s, the German Reformed (Calvinist) and the Lutheran Ministerium of Philadelphia. Throughout the colonies, local clergy exercised varying degrees of political and social influence, although the lay vestries in the south usually outranked Anglican ministers in local affairs.

Table 9.1 Numbers of Church Congregations by Denomination, 1660–1780

DENOMINATION	1660	1700	1740	1750	1780
Congregationalist	75	146	423	465	749
Anglican	41	111	246	289	406
Presbyterian	5	28	160	233	495
Baptist	4	33	96	132	457
Lutheran	4	7	95	138	240
Dutch Reformed	13	26	78	79	127
German Reformed			51	90	201
Quakers			100*		
Roman Catholic	12	22	27	30	56

* Quakers used the term "meeting house" rather than "church" or congregation, and the number is approximate.

In 1750 there were 5 Jewish congregations in the colonies, one each in Rhode Island, New York, Pennsylvania, South Carolina, and Georgia.

Source: Adapted from Edwin S. Gaustad and Philip Barlow, *The New Historical Atlas of Religions in America* (New York: Oxford University Press, 2001), Part 1, *passim;* and Thomas L. Purvis, *Colonial America to 1763* (New York: Facts on File, 1999), 178–186.

Diaries, letters, and commonplace books are useful sources for gauging the spiritual behavior and commitment of individuals and groups, and, although statistics are useful in counting numbers of churches and attendees, it is difficult to measure the sentiments of every group in every part of the colonies. What can be said with certainty is the obvious, that institutional Christianity in the middle and late eighteenth century comprised a great number of sects across a wide geography and a varied social landscape.

The Great Awakening

The series of revivals that rippled through the colonies in the 1730s and 1740s were almost immediately referred to as "awakenings." What was *awakened* was renewed spiritual vigor in and across the spectrum of sects, denominations, regions, and classes, a rumbling energy that aroused opposition and denunciations from conservative and established Christian authorities. The duration of the Awakening and the huge numbers of people touched by it certainly warrant the adjective "great." What began in the 1730s has come down to us as the *first* Great Awakening, reaching its peak in the 1730s and 1740s but lingering for decades as a social and spiritual phenomenon. The revivals were characterized by an emphasis on emotion—that strong and personal feeling occasioned by a declared faith in God and the palpable acceptance of Christ over the "reasoning" that was common in scriptural analysis, conventional sermonizing, and clerical authority. The movement was further shaped by the personalities of the "awakeners," many of whom were unordained itinerants. Passionate oratory and a heavy emphasis on individual reform, the act of being "born again," linked the work of the many itinerants into a movement. When attacking what they saw as complacent Christianity, the awakeners' use of the phrase "out of Christ" is a telling insight into the basic message of the Awakening and the root of its appeal. To the masses, the message drew on the first tenet of Luther's reforming ideal, that "the word of God cannot be received and honored by any works, but by faith alone." Certainly existing Lutheran and Baptist congregations were already attuned to the message that salvation was best achieved by faith rather than by reasoned appeal to moral conduct and behavior, or status, or priestly authority, or by "works." According to Luther, the ultimate authority was scripture, which was accessible to all.

The Awakening needs first to be seen in the light of sectarian pluralism. Also, within the conventional groupings of Anglicans, Congregationalists, Presbyterians, Baptists, and so on, there were breakaway minorities, degrees of intensity, and outright failure to keep congregations in step with formal doctrines. The more open approach to Christian life practiced by Baptists in most cases did not exclude firm Calvinists from being Baptists. In other words, single definitions of denominational attitudes and practices do not work. Presbyterians in Pennsylvania shared much with Presbyterians in South Carolina's backcountry, but it would be folly to see a backcountry congregation responding in the same way as Pennsylvanians to the Synod's credos. A second and important root of the American Awakening is the European influence, first in the way immigrants brought new and occasionally flexible ideas and practices with them and second in the fact that revivals had, by the first quarter of the century, begun to influence most Protestant communities. George Whitefield, the name most associated with the Awakening in America, the very model of active, faith-based revivalism, was English. Not only that but he had been raised in the Anglican community and influenced by John Wesley's Methodist alternative, a movement in England that was a clear prelude to transatlantic revivalism. Whitefield made twice as many "tours" of Scotland as he did of America.

Theodorus Frelinghuysen (1691–ca.1747) was a German-born Dutch Reformed pastor who came to America in his late twenties and was a seminal figure in the Awakening in the middle colonies. Another strain of revivalism came from William Tennent (1673–1764), a Scotch-Irish Presbyterian, and his sons Gilbert (1703–1764) and William (1705–1777). These and other preachers remind us that the Awakening was driven by the tenacity and innovations of dozens of itinerants who either preceded Whitefield's appearance in America or followed in his path. Not only itinerants but some conventional clergy incorporated a "born again" message into their sermons and lessons. The Awakening benefited from the advance publicity its major speakers received, especially in Whitefield's case. The appearance of several thousand people to hear an open-air sermon by Whitefield was a polished, organized affair.

The contemporary explanation for the duration and reach of the Awakening was that even the most active of Christian organizations and the healthiest congregations needed to find ways to rejuvenate their spiritual lives. In New England, for example, the standard sermons from many Congregationalist pulpits were increasingly sociological. Lectures on behavior became commonplace. It was not simply that American Protestantism had lost its fervor but rather that it was stuck in routines. The Awakening is important because it applied a fresh activism to congregational culture and is best understood as a reform movement rather than a revolutionary one. It was encouraged by zealots and fundamentalists whose egalitarian and often informal approaches shook the complacency of many churches. It is important to note that, for all its appearance of promoting alternative ways of worship, the Awakening did not destroy the existing church organizations.

What it did was modify the authority of many clergymen and encourage more emotion and enthusiasm in much of the population. It could also be divisive and split some congregations between conservatives and liberals. The itinerants were capable of dividing the massive Congregationalist and Presbyterian organizations into "New Light" and "Old Light" (conservative) factions. Perhaps the best way to consider the Awakening is to note its origins within the churches themselves. In America, the early signs of revivalism occurred at the local level.

By the 1720s, there were signs of dissatisfaction with the conservatism and pedantry of some clergy in all denominations. In the more doctrinal organizations and congregations, the guilt of "original sin" was being challenged by the perceived ability of individuals to wash away the sin with an enthusiastic faith—one emphasizing the heart over the mind and the "born again" principle. The stage was set, in fact, for an eruption of evangelicalism. For example, the Presbyterian Church authority was seen by some to be the source of dull and somber sermonizing; Dutch and German Reformed authorities resisted giving services in English, and the absence of American-trained Presbyterian ministers was resented by many in the Presbyterian orbit. A revival in New Jersey in the late 1720s, known as the "refreshings," was an early sign. It involved the collaboration of Theodorus Frelinghuysen of the Dutch Reformed Church and William Tennent, the Presbyterian. These two immigrant ministers promoted unusual policies. Each preached messages of spiritual rejuvenation, and they went so far as to exchange pulpits. They kept this up for years and together inspired similar revivals in the neighborhood.

Gilbert Tennent, the eldest of William's four sons, became the most prominent revivalist in the middle colonies. He was intense, vibrant, and disruptive, creating a serious breach in the Presbyterian Church that lasted for many years. Long before the arrival of Whitefield, the Tennents aroused a great deal of enthusiasm for reform and itinerancy. Preachers moving through settled areas on horseback—swaying audiences with new and animated versions of redemption and conversion—worried conservative Presbyterians, Baptists, and others. Gilbert Tennent was especially disruptive to the Presbyterian Synod with his loud, fearsome, and animated sermons. He was, like most Awakeners, a human dynamo, and he gave the renowned Whitefield some pointers on sermonizing. Although the movement fueled by the Tennents eventually eased and its proponents became more moderate, the Awakening left a permanent impression on religion and culture in the middle colonies. The Tennent-inspired "Log College" of 1735 was established to train revivalist ministers and was the seed for the later College of New Jersey (ultimately Princeton University). There is also no doubt that Gilbert Tennent's seminal tract *The Danger of an Unconverted Ministry* (1740) put the matter of revivalism on a long-term logical plane.

His premise was straightforward: what hope was there for the restoration of faith in common people if the preachers themselves had not been "born again"?

Ironically, in stodgy New England, the Awakening was abetted by the region's leading Congregationalist, Jonathan Edwards (1703–1758). Edwards was a senior, dominant churchman with a pedigree. His father-in-law had been a leader in mainstream Congregationalism in Massachusetts. In addition to being the minister of the prestigious Northampton church in the Connecticut River Valley, Edwards was a respected intellectual whose theological and philosophical works and published sermons are among the most sophisticated writing produced in colonial America. He was educated at Yale, where he studied Isaac Newton and John Locke and the leading thinkers of the early Enlightenment. His comfortable acquaintance with and acceptance of both rationalism and theology are notable. However, he was at heart a committed Puritan with a streak of Calvinism in him. He adopted the Awakening's theme of emotional engagement as a way to boost the flagging spirit of the older Congregationalism. In 1737, he published *A Faithful Narrative of the Surprising Work of God* in which he describes the effects of revivalism as "God's Work" in that God had intervened in the declining commitments of churchgoers to bolster their faith. He depicts the rush of conversions of 1735 in highly stylized awe-inspired prose and reports that

> souls did, as it were, come by flocks to Jesus Christ. From day to day, for many months together, might be seen evident instances of sinners brought out of darkness into marvelous light, and delivered out of a horrible pit, and from the miry clay, and set upon a rock, with a new song of praise in their mouths.

Works, vol. 3 (New Haven: Yale University Press, 1970), 233–235.

Edwards certainly helped pave the way for Whitefield's New England tour of 1740–1741. While he was more conservative than Whitefield and the others, his famous "Sinners in the Hands of an Angry God" sermon, which he delivered at Enfield, Connecticut in 1741, is one of the most cited examples of the Awakening style. It threatens and terrifies the listener with vivid images of doom and then invites the weak and "unconverted" in the throng to be "saved" by an "awakening." The audience at Enfield was bombarded by Edwards's description of God's power and His anger. They were told that their complacency fed God's wrath. The sermon opened with phrases such as "unconverted men walk over a pit of Hell on a rotten covering" and that "God [is] under no obligation...to keep any natural man out of hell for one moment." Edwards then raised the bar with some graphic images:

The use of this awful subject may be for awakening unconverted persons in this congregation. This that you have heard is the case of every one of you that are out of Christ—That world of misery, that lake of burning brimstone, is extended abroad under you...there is nothing between you and hell but the air; it is only the power and mere pleasure of God that holds you up....[But there] are black clouds of God's wrath hanging directly over your heads...[and the] God that holds you over the pit of hell, much as one holds a spider, or some loathsome insect over the fire, abhors you and is dreadfully provoked: his wrath towards you burns like fire....It is *everlasting* wrath....There will be no end to this exquisite horrible misery.

Works of Jonathan Edwards, 2 vols. (London: Ball, Arnold and Company, 1840), 9–11.

After a long series of repetitions concerning God's displeasure and his power to cast all into "the flames of hell," many in Edwards's shaken audience were convulsed in fear, crying, and trembling. Then, in a bright and helpful shift of tone, the congregation is offered the door to salvation. Edwards tells them that

now you have an extraordinary opportunity, a day wherein Christ has thrown the door of mercy wide open, and stands in calling, and crying with a loud voice to poor sinners; a day wherein many are flocking to him...with love to him who has loved them, and washed them for their sins in his own blood, and rejoicing in hope of the glory of God. How awful is it to be left behind at such a day! To see so many others feasting, while you are pining and perishing!...Therefore let everyone who is out of Christ, now awake....(11–12)

Sin thus becomes more like lapsed commitment than a crime, but "good works" (the Arminian strain) will not keep people from hell. *Sin* is used here to denote the failure to be "born again," as Edwards puts it in the language of the Awakening. This message emphasizes one's personal responsibility to reach a deeper engagement with the Christian meaning of life, a commitment achieved by faith over reason. Edwards saw enthusiasm as a way to enhance his old style Puritanism and his insistence on the older respect for "visible saints." He used Awakening styles and themes in the hope of restoring a conservative platform, an approach that caught up with him eventually when he lost his Northampton position for being too inflexible, too conservative. "Sinners in the Hands of an Angry God" is the work most commonly associated today with Jonathan Edwards, but it was neither typical of his body of work nor the clearest guide to his thought. While he looms large in the history of the Great Awakening, he is an important figure in the maturing intellectual culture of the colonies. He ended up as a missionary to the Stockbridge natives whose successors fought for the patriots in the War for Independence. He died from the effects of a smallpox inoculation at the College of New Jersey after a very brief stint as its president.

If the power of the Awakening spirit aroused passions in the audiences it was aimed at, it also affected some of the preachers. The behavior of James Davenport (1716–1757) was so wild at times that he alienated many of the itinerants and other revivalist clergy and eventually compromised the Awakening by revealing its potential for excess. Davenport was a Yale graduate with a deep New England ancestry that included the founder of New Haven colony. His conversion to revivalism was sudden. He was seduced by Whitefield's charisma in the late 1730s and traveled with him on his 1740 tour. Once he had taken up the evangelical torch, Davenport went on a binge of ranting, passionate, and lengthy sermons that sometimes lasted for hours and sent some of his audience into hysteria. His behavior was erratic and strange. He might, for example, arouse an audience to near riot and then wander off, singing to himself. In 1742, he broke a Connecticut law against itinerancy but was released from custody because he was *non compos mentis* (not legally of sound mind) and simply went about his haphazard ways. He was clearly a delusional neurotic who may have had a nervous breakdown as a youth.

In the space of a few years, he had become a public nuisance and a threat to civil order. The more zealous of his followers became riotous and dangerous at his urging. He was arrested in Boston in 1742 after a particularly noisy demonstration in the streets. He was found not guilty because of his mental state but deported from Massachusetts under militia escort and spent the rest of his life apparently in sober reflection, dying at age 41. Davenport is important in the brief history of the Great Awakening because he embodied its extremism. He caused very serious reactions that underscored the limitations of intense Christian arousal. Still, the Awakening left a mark. It permanently weakened the local authority of conventional clergy by undermining the social framework of institutional Christianity. It weakened the influence of the Congregational Church ministers in Massachusetts and the Anglican establishment in Virginia, and it put great pressure on any residual church-state relations. Its emphasis on the power of individual faith to achieve salvation is perhaps the greatest of its legacies. Although it used Calvinist themes to attack the religion of "good works," it was, in the end, an attempt to revive or apply a pure form of Luther's principle of the primary importance of individual faith.

Of the prominent Awakeners who turned America on its head for a few years in the 1730s and 1740s the most important was George Whitefield. He was the touchstone for all the revivalists. His collaboration or simple association was as important to the Tennents as it was to Jonathan Edwards and, at the other end of the spectrum, to the likes of James Davenport. The great English-born revivalist-itinerant was born an Anglican, raised in a tavern, graduated from Oxford, and, by the mid-1730s, was an accomplished orator who could deliver spellbinding sermons. He knew Charles and John Wesley and picked up on the evangelizing spirit of those two innovative Anglican priests. He followed them to Georgia in 1738 and began his American career there. Whitefield and John Wesley shared similar ideas on faith conversion and itinerancy, but Wesley had no success in the primitive precincts of Oglethorpe's Georgia, so he went back to England and began to preach in the open air. He traveled extensively for a half century in an English version of the Awakening, covering 250,000 miles and delivering as many as 40,000 sermons, a measure of his energy and vision. Wesley was hounded, insulted, and had his life threatened, but he left behind a great legacy, Methodism, an originally pejorative term for his small group of Anglican followers, which grew in importance over time in England and America. His brother Charles also has a legacy that can be found in hymnbooks everywhere in the Protestant world; he wrote over 6,000 devotional songs.

The Wesleys and Whitefield crossed paths several times over the next few decades, and, although Whitefield had a notable career in Britain, it was America that made his reputation as an evangelist thundering forth in Calvinist tones. His renown as a verbal master with a strong musical voice endures. He carried the forceful message of regeneration everywhere he went, but he was also a social and educational reformer, starting schools and opening an orphanage. He shared with others an odd ambiguity regarding slavery; he spoke out against it but actually owned a few slaves. His own itinerary over the years, on both sides of the Atlantic, stacked up some extraordinary statistics. Like the Wesleys, he was indefatigable. He made seven strenuous tours of America, gave thousands of lectures in his lifetime, and appealed to the educated and untutored alike. Inevitably he made enemies, especially in New England where "Old Light" conservative clergy and politicians saw him as simply disruptive. He even fell out with John Wesley, who accused him of becoming too Calvinistic. That charge was not altogether unfair, but Whitefield persevered in his promotion of liberty of conscience in matters of faith. For all the attractiveness of his ideas and methods, a major reason for Whitefield's success and his overall influence was his style. He was theatrical. He was a natural on stage whose gestures, tone, and vocabulary carried his message with great effect. Samuel Johnson thought him one of the most persuasive speakers of his generation, and the great London actor, David Garrick, considered him the most impressive performer he had seen. Benjamin Franklin's well-known appraisal of an open-air service he attended in Philadelphia in 1739 is apt:

> The multitudes of all sects and denominations that attended his sermons were enormous [because of] the extraordinary influence of his oratory on his hearers and how much they admired and respected him, notwithstanding his common abuse of them [for their sins]....I happened soon...to attend one of his sermons, in the course of which I perceived he intended to finish with a collection, and I silently resolved he should get nothing from me....As he proceeded, I began to soften [and I gave him my coppers]....Another stroke of his oratory made me ashamed [and I gave him silver]...and he finished so admirably that I emptied my pocket wholly into the collector's dish, gold and all.

> *The Autobiography and Other Writings* (New York: Signet Classic, 2001), 116–117.

The shrewd and frugal Franklin's testimony is persuasive. Whitefield was not only effective in delivering the revivalist message, but, as noted, his campaigns were superbly organized by advance parties of advertisers and promoters and accompanied by an entourage of helpers. He raised large sums of money and was a prolific writer and publisher. He remained a transatlantic purveyor of the revivalist message up to his death in New England in 1770.

By then the apogee of the Great Awakening had passed, and Whitefield had been contained by the New England clergy that had offered him their pulpits a generation earlier. If the Old Lights, in modified form, had recovered somewhat in New England and the middle colonies, the Awakening continued to flourish in parts of the lower south, especially in the backcountry. If we think of the Great Awakening as the first great trans-colonial social event, we should note that it also revealed regional differences that were there to begin with and persisted beyond the era. Its causes and effects were as varied as the peoples whom it touched. The common thread of "faith over reason" meant something to Baptists in South Carolina but something else to Congregationalists in Massachusetts. By the 1750s, in the north, there was a counter-revival that attacked the angry God of the itinerants. A more beneficent God, the God that looked kindly upon all men and allowed for redemption of the soul for good works and morality, without the need for emotional displays of faith, had crept into sermons. In 1750, Charles Chauncy of Boston's First Church wrote a manuscript that he called "pudding" to keep its explosive contents secret. Between 1782 and 1785, he published some of these musings, and his *The Benevolence of the Deity* (1784) can be read as a counter to the revivalists' "wrathful" God. In other words, there were other ways to redemption, but, by the 1750s, the Awakening had made its mark. It had thrust Christian commitment back into the mainstream of colonial life. It had also left behind a set of colleges.

Before the Awakening only three had been established in the mainland colonies: Harvard (Congregational) in 1636 in Massachusetts, the College of William and Mary (Anglican) in 1693 in Virginia, and Yale (Congregational) in 1701 in Connecticut. These were joined by The College of New Jersey (Presbyterian) in 1746, which later evolved into Princeton University; Rhode Island College (Baptist) in 1764, which would become Brown University; Queen's College in New Jersey (Dutch Reformed) in 1766, which would become Rutgers; and Dartmouth College in New Hampshire (Congregational) in 1769. The designations were real and intended to promote the cause of the founding denominations and produce well-educated clergy. These schools were not as focused on theological training as their origins might suggest, but offered mostly liberal arts instruction. Benjamin Franklin's Philadelphia Academy, which opened in 1751, was nonsectarian and later became the basis of the University of Pennsylvania. King's College in New York City was established in 1754 under an Anglican administration but was effectively nonsectarian. It closed during the War for Independence and reopened in the 1780s as Columbia College. Public universities were slower to develop and appeared later, during and after the Revolution.

As for Whitefield, he remained an Anglican, albeit of the Methodist persuasion. And therein is one of the central characteristics of the Great Awakening. It was not begun by or confined to radical unaffiliated evangelicals. It was, for the most part, a self-conscious attempt to reinvigorate the Christian experience and restore all peoples' enthusiasm for the Christian ethic. Formal institutionalized Christianity survived the Awakening, but it would now have to compete for the souls of Americans with evangelical, faith-based, and emotional Christian practices everywhere.

SUGGESTED READINGS

Christianity was central to the lives of colonists and the authorized King James Bible (1611) was their standard scriptural reference. It is as important as any other literary source for considering the spiritual and indeed intellectual universe of eighteenth century colonists. This chapter referred to a variety of general studies but also made specific use of E.S. Gaustad and Philip Barlow, *New Historical Atlas of Religion in America* (New York: Oxford University Press, 2001); Jon Butler, *Becoming America: The Revolution before 1776* (Cambridge, MA: Harvard University Press, 2000), Chapter 5; Patricia Bonomi, *Under the Cope of Heaven: Religion, Society, and Politics in Colonial America* (New York: Oxford University Press, 2003). Bonomi's book is richly documented and includes some 57 pages of notes for just over 220 pages of text. Chapters 6–8 of Richard Hofstadter's *America at 1750: A Social Portrait* (New York: Knopf, 1971) provide a brilliant brief survey of the status of Christianity in the middle decades of the eighteenth century and include a fine chapter on the Great Awakening. For more detail, see Frank Lambert, *"Pedlar in Divinity": George Whitefield and the Transatlantic Revivals, 1737–1770* (Princeton, NJ: Princeton University Press, 1994); Darrett B. Rutman, ed., *The Great Awakening: Event and Exegesis* (New York: Wiley, 1970), and the stimulating thesis in Bonomi's *Under the Cope of Heaven*, cited above, on the intersection of religion and politics.

Time Line

1756–1763	The Seven Years' War (in North America, the French and Indian War, 1754–1763).
1763	The Royal Proclamation.
1765	The Stamp Act and the Stamp Act Congress.
1766	The Declaratory Act.
1767	The Townshend duties.
1773	The Boston Tea Party.
1774	The Coercive Acts and the Quebec Act.
September 1774	First Continental Congress.
1775	The Battle of Lexington and Concord.
May 1775	Second Continental Congress.
1776	The Declaration of Independence.

CHAPTER 10

* * * * * ★ * ★ * * * * *

The New Empire
and the
Revolt of the
Colonies,
1748–1776

Q. What was the temper of America towards Great Britain before the year 1763?

A. The best in the world. They submitted willingly to the government of the Crown, and paid, in all their courts, obedience to acts of parliament....

Q. And what is their temper now?

A. O, very much altered.

—Benjamin Franklin, testifying before the House of Commons in 1766.

A New Empire?

In the middle of the eighteenth century, colonists were engaged in Christian revivals and settling new frontiers. They enjoyed a measure of political stability and the prospects of continuing economic improvement. As for the Crown, during and after the 1740–1748 war, it began to reassess the empire's objectives. In 1748, Lord Halifax was made president of the Board of Trade, which had been established in 1696 as the "Lords Commissioners of Trade and Foreign

Plantations." The board was nominally responsible for colonial affairs. For Halifax, the appointment was a step toward political advancement, and he took it seriously. In 1749, he established a settlement in Nova Scotia that bore his name. He encouraged Virginia's Ohio Company to move people into the Ohio country. His purpose was to increase trade and tighten the administration of it. He managed to have the board appoint governors. The neglect of colonial affairs was ending, and his busy approach was a portent of changing imperial outlook. Halifax and others noted the rise in value of the empire's American trade and saw the potential for more revenue from duties and an expanded market for British goods. As it was, the balance of trade between the colonies and Britain was widening, in the mother country's favor. Colonial merchants and assemblies in the 1750s were aware of the issue.

Table 10.1 Selected Average Annual Values of British Imports and Exports, 1699–1774

(Figures are in 1000s of pounds sterling.)

IMPORTED FROM AMERICA (INCLUDING THE WEST INDIES) AND AFRICA	
1699–1701	1,107 (19 per cent of all British imports)
1752–1754	2,684 (33 per cent of all British imports)
1772–1774	4,769 (37 per cent of all British imports)

EXPORTED TO AMERICA (INCLUDING THE WEST INDIES) AND AFRICA	
1699–1701	539 (12 per cent of all British exports)
1752–1754	1,707 (33 per cent of all British exports)
1772–1774	4,176 (42 per cent of all British exports)

IMPORTED BY ENGLAND AND SCOTLAND [*] FROM THE MAINLAND COLONIES OF BRITISH AMERICA		
1700	395	no figures for Scotland
1750	814	160 by Scotland
1770	1,015	224 by Scotland
1774 [**]	1,373	253 by Scotland (136 of it from Virginia)

IMPORTED BY THE THIRTEEN MAINLAND COLONIES FROM ENGLAND		
1700	344	no figures for Scotland
1750	1,313	160 from Scotland
1770 [***]	1,925	482 from Scotland
1774	2,590	473 from Scotland

[*]   Note that figures for Scotland were kept separate to the end of the Revolution.

[**]   The imports into England reached 1,920 in 1775 and fell to 103 in 1776. With the start of the Revolutionary War, imports dropped immediately. In 1777, they amounted to a paltry value recorded as 12 thousand pounds sterling.

[***]   Between 1768 and 1770, imports into the colonies fell by nearly half because of the non-importation movements in the colonies.

Source: Adapted from McCusker John and Russell Menard, *The Economy of British America, 1607–1789* (1985), 41 and *Historical Statistics of the United States, Colonial Times to 1970* (Washington DC: Bureau of the Census, 1975), Part 2, Section Z, pp. 1176–1177.

The second set of figures shows a steady and wide disparity in colonial exports to Britain against the imports from Britain. Between 1750 and 1770, the gap widened. British exports to the colonies were running at twice the value of colonial exports to Britain.

The climax of the episodic Franco-British wars in North America began in the forests of the upper Ohio Valley in the 1750s. Following the Treaty of Aix-la-Chapelle, the French resumed their policy of securing native alliances west of the Appalachians and, in the early 1750s, began erecting forts in the upper Ohio Valley. By then, settlers from Pennsylvania and Virginia were trickling into the area. The flow quickened after 1747 when the recently formed Ohio Company began selling plots to eager farmers and investors. In 1752, a trading post at Pickawillany was attacked by the French. The Crown urged northern colonial governments to secure native alliances, principally with the Six Nations. At the same time, the keen and usually pre-scient Benjamin Franklin helped organize a conference at Albany. He invited the colonial governments to send delegates to discuss collective security and a political and military confederation. The Albany Congress of 1754 was a failure. Only New York, Pennsylvania, Maryland, and the New England colonies attended, and there was no enthusiasm for any union that included an executive authority. Moreover, the Crown saw no merit in its awkward design. Neither was the Crown in the mood to yield to the French theory that the Ohio River and the Mississippi systems were exclusively French and that British legitimacy was limited to the eastern watershed of the Appalachians.

In 1750, Lewis Burwell, who was briefly the governor of Virginia, made the case for the Crown, the Virginia Assembly, and settlers, in a pithy bit of theory. He noted

> [t]hat, notwithstanding the Grants of the Kings of England, France, or Spain, the Property of these *uninhabited* Parts of the World must be founded upon prior Occupancy according to the Law of Nature;...it is the Seating and Cultivating of the soil and not the bare traveling through a Territory that constitutes [the] Right [to it].
>
> Quoted in Lawrence Henry Gipson, *The British Empire Before the American Revolution*, vol. 4 (Caldwell, ID: Caxton Printers, 1936), 226 (emphasis added).

Burwell's concept of empire and territory fit perfectly into the British history of settlement. It did not suit the French version. The latter had traded and traveled in the region and, for the most part, kept up good relations with the natives, but they had not established permanent communities beyond the strip along the St. Lawrence and the surrendered Acadian colony. The natives in the zones around the expanding British colonies increasingly feared British encroachment, and that threat as much as anything drew them closer to the non-colonizing French. The expansion of French trading posts in the southern Great Lakes region indicated a vigorous French territorial policy. It meant that the inexorable press of westbound British American colonists would confront determined French and native resistance.

In 1754, the French erected Fort Duquesne at the confluence of the Ohio, Allegheny, and Monongahela Rivers, the present site of Pittsburgh.

They preempted Robert Dinwiddie, the lieutenant governor of Virginia, who had wanted to build a British fort at that site. Dinwiddie dispatched the young George Washington (1732–1799), a colonel in the Virginia militia, in charge of 150 militiamen to remove the French. After building a makeshift fort and stalling a larger French contingent, the eager Washington was forced to withdraw. Then General Edward Braddock, the commander in chief of British forces in America, with 1,400 British Army regulars and nearly 500 militiamen under Washington, crossed into the upper Ohio Valley in 1755. They were routed at the Battle of the Wilderness by French and native forces of about half their number and, with serious losses, were sent packing. Braddock was killed. This disaster was followed by Massachusetts Governor William Shirley's failed campaign against the French at Niagara. Before he was removed as governor and sent to a new post in the West Indies, Shirley warned all who would listen that colonial militias were not reliable. That became a common complaint of nearly every Crown military and political observer during and after the war. As befit their civilian and part-time status, most militiamen saw their service in short-term, local, contractual terms. To the British, they were simply undisciplined and uncommitted to the empire. The colonists saw the British Army and especially its officers as arrogant and intrusive. There is some truth to both views, but, in most cases, militiamen did perform well and the British regular army displayed patience and cooperation with the local militias. But the biases stuck, later compounding or flavoring mutual antagonisms over political and jurisdictional matters.

In the short term, those issues were shelved because the French and Indian phase of the Seven Years' War had just begun in earnest. It began slowly and then erupted into years of skirmishes and small raids along with several major campaigns and formal European-style battles. It was fought by permutations of regulars, militias, and natives. New York's Sir William Johnson had managed to keep the Six Nations people allied to the British during King George's War, and he maintained the connection into the 1750s. With 3,500 militiamen and 400 natives, he secured the frontier at Lake George in September of 1755. On the Atlantic coast, the British Army destroyed Acadian settlements in the Bay of Fundy and began the removal of some 6,000 French-speaking Acadians who, it was thought, might favor French interests if the war were to reach them. The exiled Acadians, sadly, should have been protected by the British Empire under the terms of the 1713 Treaty of Utrecht. This was essentially a pogrom, as ruthless in its conduct as the British Army's earlier purges in the Scottish Highlands after the Battle of Culloden. Ironically, the so-called Highland Clearances, which began at the end of the eighteenth century, sent thousands of Gaelic-speaking Scots into Nova Scotia, especially into Cape Breton.

In 1756, the French captured the British-held island of Minorca in the Mediterranean, and another European war was underway, one that, in a very short time, became a world war. The scale, scope, and consequences of this war surpassed those of the earlier imperial conflicts of the eighteenth century. A British-Prussian-Hanoverian coalition faced a French alliance that included Austria, Russia, Sweden, Saxony, and, eventually, Spain. The alliances were important but this was clearly a Franco-British struggle for supremacy in Europe, America, and Asia. In Britain, when Prime Minister Thomas Pelham, the Duke of Newcastle's ministry failed, William Pitt "The Elder" and later Earl of Chatham was restored to prominence in Parliament as secretary of state with practical control over the war effort. More than any other politician, Pitt set the course of the war. He encouraged a massive investment in shipbuilding and military recruitment and drove the Treasury into increasing debt with his policy of all-out war. He subsidized Britain's allies in Europe and the colonial governments in America. The war touched most of Europe's global empires, including the coveted Indian subcontinent. In 1757, Britain scored a great victory in Bengal when Robert Clive's East India Company army defeated the French and their allies at the Battle of Plassey. This encounter ranks with the fall of Quebec as a decisive event of the Seven Years' War.

In 1756, France sent the Marquis de Montcalm to America with an army of several thousand regulars. He soon embarrassed his British counterpart, Lord Loudoun, in a series of encounters that included the capitulation of British forts at Oswego and Fort William Henry. In those encounters, the French had difficulty controlling their native allies, whose concepts of war were often at odds with those of the European combatants. Montcalm or any other European commander balked at the killing of prisoners, but at Oswego and William Henry many British prisoners were killed by natives who slipped out of French control. The war in America was at times marked by an untidy mix of regular army, native, and colonial militia objectives and conduct.

Loudoun was ordered to attack Louisbourg rather than Quebec, but the campaign was stalled in the face of French naval reinforcements. Then, a storm at Halifax, where Loudoun had assembled his invasion force, curtailed the endeavor. Before he was replaced, Loudoun added his voice to the complaints against colonial governments for their tepid support. In the wake of a string of setbacks, Pitt advanced his program of subsidies and military reinforcements in Europe and America. Over the course of the war, the British sent 25,000 troops to the colonial theater and had as many as 15,000 in the field at any time. The British Army, the so-called American Army, consisted of some 5 per cent colonials and another 5 per cent European "foreigners."

The number of militiamen who saw combat is difficult to estimate because the musters would go home after the completion of a campaign or sortie.

The new British commander in America was James Abercromby (1706–1781) whose 12,000-strong force was defeated by Montcalm, with fewer numbers, at Ticonderoga in 1758. The bleak British prospects brightened that same year, however, when, in a strategic and symbolic victory, Generals Jeffery Amherst and James Wolfe with nearly 10,000 men and a fleet of 40 warships, captured Louisbourg to open up the Gulf of St. Lawrence. Only 500 or so of that victorious army were colonial militiamen. The British took Fort Frontenac at the east end of Lake Ontario, another vital point on French Canada's defensive perimeter. Abercromby was dismissed and replaced by Amherst, and, following Pitt's advice, the British launched an ambitious and expensive three-way assault on the heartland of New France, at Niagara, the Lake Champlain corridor, and Quebec. By July 1759, Amherst had taken Crown Point on Lake Champlain and William Johnson, with help from the Iroquois, had captured Niagara.

General Wolfe laid siege to Quebec, pounding it with artillery. He landed 9,000 troops and confronted Montcalm above the town on the Plains of Abraham and defeated him in the most decisive event of the war in America. Both Montcalm and Wolfe died at Quebec, reminding us that, in the eighteenth century, senior officers and even commanders were directly involved in combat. Montcalm is remembered for his tactical abilities, civility, and courage. Wolfe is still celebrated as the conqueror of Canada and the military genius who brought the war to an end. But the war's outcome was, in many ways, the result of Pitt's emphatic policy of full-scale and fully funded war. Montreal fell in 1760, and, when Detroit was taken, the full impact of British victory began to be felt. Spain foolishly lent its support to the French in 1761, and the British seized Spanish Havana to go with the occupation of French Martinique, Guadelupe, and St. Lucia. In Asia, they captured Manila. France pressed for peace talks and thanked Spain for its belated efforts. It ceded to Spain the remaining French claims west of the Mississippi and the port of New Orleans.

The Treaty of Paris of February 1763 formalized the extent of the British victory. With no apparent sense of distress, France abandoned its American claims and left over 50,000 French subjects along the St. Lawrence in the hands of the British. The French exchanged the British West Indian islands it had taken during the war, including St. Vincent, Dominica, and Tobago, in return for its own sugar-producing islands. British control of Bengal was confirmed, and, in Europe, France evacuated Hanover. Britain returned Cuba to Spain and abandoned its Honduras forts in exchange for East and West Florida. The political map of North America had been thoroughly redrawn. After 150 years, France's North American Empire was gone, but Britain's triumph came with serious challenges. How was the empire to deal with a resident French population to the north of the thirteen colonies and with the administration of a massive new territory with large native populations? Perhaps more pressing was the need to pay for Pitt's bold but expensive war. The national debt had doubled, and a major reform of imperial policy in America was in the offing even as the Treaty of Paris was being signed.

The Royal Proclamation and Pontiac's Rebellion

George II died in 1760 and was succeeded by his 22-year-old grandson George III (1738–1820), who reigned from 1760 to 1820. He had been tutored by the Earl of Bute who apparently left the king with an elevated sense of his policy-making role. The strong-willed George III nevertheless had to adjust to the realities of the "constitutional monarchy," the need to consult and cooperate with Parliament's factions and majorities. He became as important as any other figure in the era of the American Revolution, beginning with his adamant dismissal of colonial opposition to the new post-1763 empire. Colonial pamphleteers attacked him relentlessly for his failure to restrain what they saw as Parliament's unsavory legislation. Throughout the 1760s and early 1770s, the king acted in concert with Parliament and even advised it on some matters. He rejected any idea that the colonial assemblies, individually or in concert, had rights that superseded or even matched the Crown's authority.

In October 1763, the "Royal Proclamation" was issued as a strategy for dealing with the territories acquired after France's departure. The order was "royal" but was in fact the work of the cabinet and privy council. The first draft, drawn up by the Board of Trade under Lord Shelburne, called for a line to be drawn along the spines of the various Appalachian ranges, reserving land to the west for natives. An area for white settlement in the upper Ohio was at first allowed and then rescinded. Another area was to be set aside for natives on the eastern side of the Appalachians. The plan also called for the creation of new provinces in Quebec to the north and in East and West Florida. When Lord Hillsborough replaced Shelburne in September, the plan was tightened to omit the clause that allowed for limited white settlement west of the Appalachians, and it ordered any whites who had settled there in the upper Ohio to leave. Meanwhile, the so-called Delaware Prophet, Pontiac, launched an all-out war against traders, settlers, and the British military west of the mountains. Forts and trading posts fell in a shocking series of attacks, and the prolonged native siege of Detroit indicated the power that Pontiac had unleashed. The uprising was slowly suppressed, a peace treaty was agreed to, and military order was established in the upper Ohio. But Pontiac's ability to raise thousands of natives in concert was a sobering jolt to the British administrators in America and in London and a warning of the potential difficulties of uncontrolled western settlement.

The proclamation created a furor in the colonies. At first, the prohibition was thought to be temporary, but, when it was retained and made more restrictive, colonists reacted with anger. The clearing out of the French had surely made the Ohio Valley British and accessible to colonists, so the closing of the territory to settlement was now seen as a betrayal. The reasons for the proclamation were, of course, a lot more complicated than its apparent insensitivity to colonial ambitions. It incorporated a strategy for development that reflected the 1748 suggestion by Lord Halifax of the Board of Trade that the Crown should adopt a more direct role in colonial affairs. It was intended to appease a restless native population to the west and keep whites from provoking more frontier violence. It was also concerned with the future of the newly acquired Floridas and especially of Quebec, which was allowed to keep its language and legal and religious customs in 1763. These rights were affirmed with more formality in the Quebec Act of 1774. The proclamation was an adjustment to changed circumstances. It made perfect sense to the king, his cabinet, and Parliament. To the colonists, however, it looked very much like a general revocation of older charter claims to the regions west of the Appalachians.

Map 10.1 The Proclamation Line of 1763

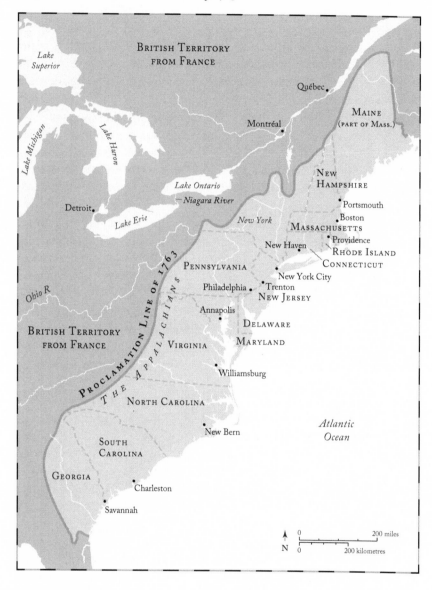

Source: Eric Nellis, *The Long Road to Change: America's Revolution, 1750–1820* (Peterborough,
    ON: Broadview, 2007), 52.

Backcountry Problems

With the war over and British restraints on western expansion taking effect, a series of long-simmering disorders boiled over on the eastern slopes of the Appalachians. In Pennsylvania and in the Carolinas especially, the backcountry population was growing fast. It was also becoming alienated from eastern power bases. It rose up to redress long-held grievances. The backcountry that the missionary Charles Woodmason described was an accurate assessment of South Carolina in the late 1760s. A wave of white banditry hit the settlements in the aftermath of the Cherokee War of 1760–1761. In the absence of courts or adequate policing, an association of concerned settlers, the "Regulators," conducted a campaign of vigilantism that lasted for three years. Although their principal targets were the criminal gangs, the Regulators also issued a public "remonstrance" in late 1767. They noted that, because they were unprotected and because the "Back Parts of this Province hath been infested with an infernal Gang of Villains," they had acted out of necessity as a police force with widespread public support. They had finally controlled theft, rape, and general pillage, the document continued, but it cited deeper political issues and grievances. The backcountry people were, they claimed, "unrelieved [ignored] by Government" because "the present Constitution of this Province is very defective, and become a Burden, rather than being beneficial to the Back-Inhabitants."

The remonstrance is a comprehensive and articulate critique of the tidewater oligarchy that ran the colony. As the protest notes, "We are *Free-men*— British subjects—Not Born *Slaves*," but "unequally represented in Assembly," in fact, grossly "underrepresented." The neglect that the petitioners identified covered everything from the absence of courts, jails, and constables to problems with transients and paupers. As Woodmason had noted, there was a woeful lack of parish ministers and of schools. The tone of the appeal is sober and reasonable; it is a political protest not against the British but against the wealth of the tidewater gentry for the political imbalance it encouraged. Given that slavery was rare in the backcountry, a racist theme runs through the complaint: "it is to this Great Disproportion of Representatives on our Part, that our Interests have been so long neglected, and the Back Country disregarded. But it is the Number of the Free Men, not Black Slaves, that constitute the Strength and Riches of a State."

The Regulators made their point and better representation and administrative improvements followed. The authorities also saw the sense in not prosecuting the vigilantes for their extralegal actions. However, an interesting problem had been exposed, the existence of internal discord, class conflict, and regional disparity. Settlement may have preceded law into the backcountry, but a system of law was apparently needed. The South Carolina Regulators had been led by the "better sorts" of the backcountry, the more articulate community leadership, but the movement was guided by clear class, communal, and circumstantial solidarity. A widespread reaction to a crime wave had brought the South Carolina backcountry together. Its cultural, political, and geographical distance from tidewater society made some of its people less likely to support the aims of the tidewater gentry when the latter opposed Britain's reforms. Considerable numbers of backcountry people became loyalists as much to resist tidewater power as to support Parliament's constitutional sovereignty.

There was also a Regulator movement in North Carolina. In 1768, a group of North Carolina backcountry men came together to protest tidewater negligence in that province. In this case, the North Carolina Regulators actually threatened the North Carolina government with rebellion. Their opposition to the government continued until 1771, when Governor William Tryon took 1,200 militiamen into the backcountry and, at the Battle of Alamance Creek, defeated a force of some 2,000 Regulators, many of whom were armed only with axes, hoes, and other farm implements. Under an earlier act of the North Carolina legislature, the Regulators were subject to charges of treason, and seven of their leaders were executed in the aftermath, including one on the battlefield. Over 6,000 backcountry settlers were then forced to swear loyalty to the North Carolina government as part of its campaign to stamp out dissent.

In some ways, the Carolina Regulator protests echoed an earlier east-west confrontation in the Pennsylvania backcountry in 1763–1764. For years, residents in western Pennsylvania had been under threat from natives affiliated with the French, a condition that continued through the French and Indian War. Their pleas and requests for better security were largely ignored by the Pennsylvania Assembly, which had inherited the Quaker policy of peaceful relations with natives. As Pontiac's Rebellion intensified, some backcountry men from Paxton and Donegal in Pennsylvania murdered some friendly Conestoga natives near Lancaster. The assembly ordered the arrest of the so-called Paxton Boys, who marched on Philadelphia with a large following. Only the intercession of Benjamin Franklin prevented an armed confrontation. The Paxton protesters issued a "Declaration of the Injured Frontier Inhabitants" and demanded a harsher and better funded native policy. In a subsequent appeal, their spokesmen requested better representation in the provincial assembly. As with the Regulators, ideological dissent with racist undertones marked the Paxton Boys' behavior. While backcountry concerns were couched in the language of political rights, the actions of the Paxtons and Regulators revealed that significant social disparities were fueling their regional concerns.

The Reforms

Within months of the Royal Proclamation of 1763, on April 5, 1764, Parliament passed the American Revenue Act, better known as the Sugar Act. It revised the duties on sugar, coffee, tea, wine, and other imports and expanded the jurisdiction of vice-admiralty courts. Foreign rum and French wines were banned. After experiencing decades of the somewhat lax enforcement of the Navigation Acts, the new duties and the announced intention to tighten up customs control caught colonial merchants and politicians by surprise. Merchant anger was compounded by the fact that there had been no consultation with any of the colonial governments. But merchant consternation did not end there. Chancellor of the Exchequer George Grenville had gone a step further with the Sugar Act and assigned the revenues, estimated at 45,000 pounds sterling a year, to the Treasury. Several colonial assemblies protested, claiming that monies raised by duties had always been used to enhance or administer trade and had never been used simply to provide revenue to the Crown. In a long address to the Boston Town Meeting on May 24, 1764, Richard Dana responded to the act on behalf of the town, stating very clearly a local assumption about British constitutional rights:

> [The Sugar Act] strikes at our British Privileges which as we have never forfeited them we hold in common with our Fellow Subjects who are Natives of Britain: If Taxes are laid upon us in any shape without ever having a Legal Representation where they are laid, are we not reduced from the Character of Free Subjects to the miserable state of tributary slaves.
>
> *Report of the Record Commissioners: Boston Town Records, 1758 to 1769* (Boston: Rockwell and Churchill, 1886), 122.

The principle of "no taxation without representation" is sharply noted in that remark. It became the central theme of colonial response to British policy in the 1760s. Merchants dominated the leadership of the Boston Town Meeting, and Dana was summarizing a concern that had been stewing for some time.

The 1764 Sugar Act was largely a revision of the last major detail of the Navigation Acts, the 1733 Molasses Act, which had been routinely circumvented. William Pitt's 1760 order to customs collectors in America to apply more vigorous enforcement was, in part, a wartime measure, but it indicated a more thorough revision of customs practices. The collectors now applied to the Massachusetts courts for "writs of assistance," a legal means for searching for violators of the act. The Massachusetts-born James Otis (1725–1783) had been appointed as a prosecutor (deputy "advocate general) in the vice-admiralty court. In 1761, he denounced the "writs," arguing that "an act against the Constitution is void." Otis suggested that Parliament could not make laws that were "against natural equity," by which he meant specifically that Parliament was denying colonial Americans their constitutional rights by having courts issue general search warrants (the "writs").

There was nothing new in the issuing of writs in the British Empire. They had already been used in Massachusetts in 1751. But Otis turned the issue into a systematic questioning of Crown policy, which he articulated forcefully in his 1764 pamphlet, *The Rights of the British Colonies Asserted and Proved*. There he argued that the British Empire was a single commonwealth and that there should be *formal* representation of colonial constituents in the House of Commons. Although that idea was rejected as impractical a year later at the Stamp Act Congress in New York, his basic objection (the absence of a consent mechanism) was taken up by the protests that followed. He was front and center throughout the mounting political crisis of the 1760s but receded in importance after suffering a blow to the head in 1769, after which his behavior became erratic. He was judged to be mentally ill, and the protests, resistance, war, and the independence that followed passed him by as other dissenters and pamphleteers took over. In a bizarre twist, he died following a lightning strike in the year colonial independence was attained—1783.

A pattern of parliamentary action and colonial reaction had been established as early as 1764. Grenville ordered a vice-admiralty court to be held at Halifax, Nova Scotia to adjudicate customs matters and avoid the favoritism that often went on in the thirteen older colonial courts. From the Crown's perspective, the colonial mentality of casual disrespect for the Navigation Acts had reached the point at which it cost the Crown four times as much to administer its customs service than it received in duties. Putting the court in Halifax became a festering affront to colonial miscreants who assumed, reasonably enough, a right to be heard in their own courts. The Currency Act of 1764 added to the widening dissent in the colonies. This act forbade the issuance of paper money as legal tender in the colonies. It was specifically targeted at Virginia, which had been printing money during the war, in effect creating its own currency with local relative value. The Crown had earlier, in 1751, prohibited the New England colonies from issuing paper money. Colonial currencies had commonly been issued as paper to go with the hard currency ("specie") that made its way into local economies. These currencies, along with bills of credit, barter, and commodity exchange (tobacco, pelts, or grain) were the monetary mechanisms in local economies. Specie was typically gold or silver coinage from any source. The volume of specie in the colonies was, on average, about 20 per cent of the money in circulation.

All colonial paper issues were convertible to pounds sterling, the British Empire's standard currency medium. However, the means of defining the exchange rate at the colony level annoyed the British Exchequer because it implied a local fiscal autonomy that ran counter to the Crown's ideas of regulatory conformity.

The Currency Act was deflationary and hit hard at all colonial economies, coming as it did on the heels of a postwar recession. The act sparked an interesting response from Massachusetts. A week after the Boston Town Meeting issued its attack on the Sugar Act, the Massachusetts House of Representatives put together a Committee of Correspondence to communicate with other colonial assemblies. A precedent for serious intercolonial collaboration was set. Then, at the beginning of 1765, the British military commander in America, Thomas Gage, asked Parliament to order local communities to pay for the quartering of regular army personnel. The Quartering Act, which was attached to the annual Mutiny Act for the British Army, obliged colonial authorities to provide billeting, firewood, candles, and other materials for British troops stationed in their communities. In New York City, where Gage was headquartered, British troops and the newly formed "Sons of Liberty" fought in the streets. The New York Assembly at first refused to comply with the requisitions, but it capitulated under Parliament's threat to nullify subsequent New York legislation.

The Stamp Act Crisis

When Parliament passed the Stamp Act on March 22, 1765, it did so in a soured atmosphere. The act immediately raised the core question of whether Parliament had the constitutional authority to tax *in* the colonies for the Crown's use. It stands as a watershed event in imperial relations. The preamble announced "An act for granting and applying certain stamp duties, and other duties, in the British colonies and plantations in America, towards further defraying the expences of defending, protecting, and securing the same." It applied a surcharge to hundreds of items by way of a compulsory affixed stamp. Grenville hoped to soften the impact by employing colonists as collectors for the Crown, a tactic that immediately backfired. The price of the stamps was as low as a few pence for a posted notice to 10 pounds sterling for notices of government appointments. It included everything from playing cards to newspapers, books and almanacs, ships' papers, retail licenses, and marriage and fiscal contracts. It introduced each particular category with the words "For every skin or piece of vellum or parchment, or sheet or piece of paper, on which shall be ingrossed, written or printed [the details]"

(*Prologue to Revolution: Sources and Documents on the Stamp Act Crisis, 1764–1766*, ed. Edmund S. Morgan [Chapel Hill: University of North Carolina Press, 1959], 35–36). Lawyers, publishers and merchants were notably affected. The Sugar Act had clearly intended its revenues to go to the Crown for the Crown's use, but those revenues were to come from duties and excises. The Stamp Act tax was altogether different. This was a novel, direct tax on colonists, passed into law by Parliament and intended to raise money in the colonies for the Crown's use. It was, by any reckoning, a tax and not a duty on trade items. Ostensibly, it was to help cover the costs of the British Army stationed in America. That was not how it was perceived in America.

Angry artisans, retailers, laborers, and seamen in New York and Boston, aided and abetted by merchants and politicians, organized themselves under the banner of the Sons of Liberty. The implementation of the act was delayed to November 1765, and, by that summer, the Sons of Liberty had forced the resignation and withdrawal of nearly all the appointed collectors in the major ports. In Boston, mobs seized and burned vice-admiralty court records and vandalized the home of the currency comptroller. The looting of the home of Massachusetts Chief Justice Thomas Hutchinson (1711–1780), a descendent of Anne Hutchinson and later a prominent loyalist, was the most overt and the most publicized of all the demonstrations. The high-profile Hutchinson had been targeted because he had made a point of defending the legality of the Stamp Act, even though he thought it was ill advised.

Daniel Dulany (1722–1797), a Maryland lawyer, anticipated the problems that British taxing policy would cause in his essay *Considerations on the Propriety of Imposing Taxes in the British Colonies*. He even questioned the legitimacy of the Stamp tax but did not press the issue further. Like many others who questioned British policy, Dulany remained loyal to the Crown. He later opposed independence. Otherwise, Patrick Henry (1736–1799) presented his famous Stamp Act Resolves (the Virginia Resolves of 1765) to the Virginia House of Burgesses in May. These were predicated on a vivid but treasonous threat, which warned George III that, if he executed Parliament's tax, he would end up like Julius Caesar or Charles I. The Virginia House of Burgesses adopted all the resolves except the last two, which were turned down as being too incendiary. But these were published anyway in various colonial journals, and they kept alive the idea that only colonists or their actual representatives could impose taxes on themselves.

Patrick Henry had earlier attacked the Crown for interfering in Virginia's affairs. The "parson's cause" of 1763 was, on the face of it, a minor issue. The Virginia clergy had been traditionally paid in tobacco, but in the 1750s, when the price of tobacco fell, the colony decided to pay the clergy in clearly depreciated currency. The clergy, who were unpopular in any case, sued, and the Crown upheld their plea. In the subsequent court case, Patrick Henry successfully attacked the Crown's decision by arguing that it had no right to disavow Virginia's legal right in the case. Two years before his 1765 Stamp Act comments Henry had already called the king a "tyrant."

Virginia slaveholders, Boston brewers, New York Sons of Liberty, and Pennsylvania farmers, along with a great cross-section of colonists in all colonies, could agree on one thing, at least, that there should be no taxes levied on them without their representatives' consent. A trans-colonial movement was underway, and the Stamp Act Congress convened in New York in October 1765, attended by representatives from nine colonies, three of which were represented informally. The congress thus comprised a minority of the colonial governments. Still, it was the first collective colonial meeting to deal with a common issue, and its resolutions comprised a groundbreaking statement of shared political principles.

The earlier street violence had abated when the Stamp Act Congress convened. There was a great deal of pamphlet literature being circulated, but the atmosphere was one of sober reflection. The congress considered all the issues that troubled the delegates but laid a special emphasis on the Stamp tax and issued a firm statement of what was a generally held view, that no taxes could be imposed without the consent of those being taxed. In the 1765 "Declaration of Rights of the Stamp Act Congress," the term "His Majesty's liege subjects" was a sincere announcement that colonists were in and for the British Empire. Indeed, the declaration emphasized the fact that "his Majesty's subjects in these colonies owe the same allegiance to the Crown of Great Britain that is owing from his subjects born within the realm, and all due subordination to that august body, the Parliament of Great Britain." The main thrust of the declaration is a model of clarity:

> That … no taxes should be imposed upon … [the colonists], but with their own consent, given personally, or by their representatives. That the people of these colonies are not, and from their local circumstances cannot be represented in the House of Commons in Great Britain. That the only representatives of the people of these colonies are persons chosen therein, by themselves; and that no taxes have ever been or can be constitutionally imposed on them but by their respective legislatures [and that it is] inconsistent with the principles and spirit of the British Constitution, for the people of Great Britain to grant to His Majesty the property of the colonies.

Otis's earlier appeal for *actual* representation was dismissed by the Stamp Act Congress as being impractical, and Parliament operated on the assumption that every member of Parliament *virtually* represented every person in the empire. The cordial tone of the 1765 Declaration is worth noting because it would give way over time to a more rancorous one.

The Stamp Act Congress brought John Dickinson (1732–1808) of the Pennsylvania delegation into prominence. He was by temperament a moderate, even conservative person. He simultaneously sought harmony with the Crown and supported the non-importation movement. He was also an eloquent pamphleteer who argued, quite logically, that the Stamp Act would be detrimental to the British economy. As late as 1774, he wrote a conciliatory "petition to the king." He annoyed militant New Englanders in the first and second continental congresses in 1774 and 1775 with his appeals for caution. By 1775, however, he stated clearly that colonists had a right to resort to force if their constitutional status was threatened. He voted against the Declaration of Independence but served in the war to attain it. He fought against separation until he saw its inevitability. He is an example of the many colonial leaders who made the transition from British subject to independent republican over a twenty-year span.

With no choice, given its failure to apply it, Parliament withdrew the Stamp Act in 1766. The American resistance had actually moved many in the House of Commons to oppose the tax. Grenville had wanted to use military force, but Pitt and others saw some sense in the colonists' opposition. British merchants were terrified about a possible collapse of trade. The debate over the responsibility for the war's costs was patently irresolvable. Benjamin Franklin testified that Pennsylvania had spent what seems like an exaggerated sum of 500,000 pounds sterling during the war to protect the empire's interests but had received only 60,000 pounds sterling from the Crown in compensation. The Crown's view was that the empire collectively had defended Pennsylvania during the war and that any costs it incurred were fair. Indeed, the repeal of the Stamp Act brought only short-lived joy to the colonists. Parliament passed the Declaratory Act on the same day as the repeal, March 18, 1766. Its thesis was that Parliament "had, hath, and of right ought to have, full power and authority to make laws and statutes of sufficient force and validity to bind the colonies and peoples of America, subjects of the Crown of Great Britain, in all cases whatsoever." The core phrase, "in all cases whatsoever" was ignored or downplayed in the colonies, but colonists would be reminded of its potent claim over the next few years. More than any other statement or action, the Declaratory Act was an unequivocal assertion of the Crown's unilateral sovereignty.

The Empire's New Approach

Charles Townshend became chancellor of the exchequer in late 1766 and, by the summer of 1767, had set Parliament and the colonies on yet another collision course. Although he considered colonial reasoning regarding taxation as specious, he wanted to avoid convoluted dealings with colonial governments and launched a revenue program that was patently *external*. Heavy import duties were applied to a range of goods, including tea. The returns, estimated at 40,000 pounds sterling a year, were to pay for the upkeep of troops still stationed in the colonies and to fund a tighter administration of "justice," as the Revenue Act's preamble put it. That meant that superior courts had the authority to issue writs of assistance, a slap in the face of James Otis. An American Board of Commissioners of the Customs was set up at Boston to report directly to the British Treasury. More vice-admiralty courts were to be established. If anyone had doubted Parliament's commitment to ending "salutary neglect" and pursuing its longer-term policies for America, the message in 1767 was a firm corrective. There was an immediate response in Boston, New York, Newport, and elsewhere, and a new non-importation movement began. At the start of 1768, the Massachusetts House of Representatives issued a "circular letter" to the other twelve colonies, condemning the Townshend duties and their enforcement mechanisms. The Crown, through its royal governors, denounced the circular letter as sedition. The recurring threat of the unilateral royal suspension of dissenting assemblies was looking more and more like the suppression of opinion.

Meanwhile, the erstwhile brewer Samuel Adams (1722–1803) was deeply involved in local politics and public affairs and was a committed opponent of British policy. He had previously taken part in the Stamp Act opposition. His importance lay in his ability to mesh the interests of the artisan and working class with the constitutional refinements of his cousin John Adams's essays and pamphlets and also with the commercial interests of one of Boston's richest merchants, John Hancock. Boston was alive with a dissent that embraced the activism of Samuel Adams, the thoughtful ruminations of John Adams, and the commercial fears of John Hancock. Samuel Adams was in the thick of things, arousing Bostonians of all classes and circumstances.

Frustrated customs officials were harassed to the point that they requested military protection. When two regiments of British regulars were stationed in Boston in the fall of 1768, the mood in the town became caustic. As far as imperial relations went, the Townshend duties were proving to be as divisive as any earlier issue in the imperial imbroglio. On the other hand, they did have the effect of pulling the colonies closer together politically, which was not, ironically, part of Townshend's grand plan to control trade and revenues. In 1767, Parliament passed the New York Restraining Act, which shut down the New York Assembly until it complied with the 1765 Quartering Act. John Dickinson reappeared as a voice of caution. The first of his reasoned *Letters from a Farmer in Pennsylvania to the Inhabitants of the British Colonies* (1767–1768) summarized a simple logic in the colonies' situation: "The cause of one is the cause of all."

By 1769, the non-importation movement was evident everywhere except in New Hampshire. Virginia's political leaders were now prominent in the resistance to the Townshend duties. In May, with the prompting of such notables as George Washington, George Mason, Patrick Henry, and Richard Henry Lee, the Virginia House of Burgesses passed a resolution, the "Virginia Resolves of 1769" (not to be confused with Patrick Henry's 1765 resolves).

These 1769 Virginia Resolves inspired the "Association," a pact to boycott all goods subject to duty, including slaves. As the boycotts spread, the value of imports from Britain fell by as much as half during 1768–1769 and into 1770. Townshend had died in September 1767, a few months after his controversial duties had gone into effect. Now there was growing displeasure in Britain because of non-importation and, under pressure, Parliament annulled the duties in April 1770. The duty on tea was retained, but the repeal of the other duties calmed most critics in the colonies. Nevertheless, there were politically charged public disorders in New York and Boston during 1770. In New York, persistent opposition to the Quartering Act by both the New York Assembly and the Sons of Liberty led to armed confrontations in the streets, which included the use of bayonets by British troops. No one was killed, but the wounding of several protesters testified to the strain that garrisoned soldiers put on an unhappy populace. The Quartering Act, as it turned out, was allowed to expire.

In Boston, one confrontation between civilians and soldiers had deadly results. Taunting, pushing, and oral threats were now common. In the wake of a fistfight between a worker and a soldier on March 5, 1770, gangs of locals roamed Boston's streets, ignored by local constables. Inevitably, near the Province House, they were challenged by an on-duty British soldier, and their threatening mood led to reinforcements being called. A squad of 10 British regulars was confronted by an animated mob of about 60 men. Shots were fired, and three rioters were killed and another two mortally wounded. Six of the eight soldiers charged with murder were found not guilty by a civil court. The other two were convicted of manslaughter and had brands burned into their hands as punishment. The fact that Lieutenant Governor Thomas Hutchinson was persuaded to send the Boston garrison to islands in Boston harbor likely kept the "Massacre" from escalating into widespread riot-ing. Nevertheless, the five "martyrs" were celebrated in a pamphlet, *A Short Narrative of the Horrid Massacre in Boston,* a provocative attempt by Samuel Adams and others, including merchants, to keep the radical cause on the boil. Paul Revere's engraving for the cover depicted a line of British soldiers firing a volley at point blank range into a crowd of unarmed civilians. It remains one of the most enduring visual images of the revolutionary era. The "Boston Massacre" would later be revived as a symbol of British barbarism, but, in the short term, it receded into the margins as a calmer mood followed the repeal of the Townshend duties.

That mood did not last. In June 1772, a royal customs schooner, the *Gaspee,* ran aground near Providence, Rhode Island. Several boatloads of locals scattered the crew and burned the ship to the waterline. The local Crown officials who investigated recommended that any persons charged with the crime should be sent to England for trial. This was grim news that troubled even moderates because it suggested a further whittling away of local judicial control. The problem was compounded when it was learned that the newly appointed (1770) Governor of Massachusetts Thomas Hutchinson was to receive his salary from the king and not from the Massachusetts assembly. The "power of the purse" was an important mechanism for the assemblies. The disclosure led to an act of extreme provocation by Samuel Adams and his supporters. He convinced the Boston Town Meeting to authorize the first Committee of Correspondence, which would circulate general opposi-tion materials and views throughout the colonies. The idea was to exchange local concerns and information on imperial matters that might affect any or all of them. This gave pause to some radicals. They were worried that the committees might urge collective action on *all* constitutional matters. The line between opposition to Crown policy or specific acts and a denial of its *ultimate* authority was still a fuzzy one. In any case, the question in the colo-nies of which legislative agency, colonial assembly, or Parliament had supe-rior authority in local affairs still needed an answer. There was no debate on that point in Britain's Parliament, which had made its position clear in the Declaratory Act. By the middle of 1773, committees of correspondence had been established in all the colonies save North Carolina and Pennsylvania. Acting under the aegis of their respective assemblies, the committees packed more punch than the issue-specific Stamp Act Congress, the Sons of Liberty, or the non-importation associations. Condoned by assemblies, they were approaching the status of a collective political opposition.

Politics and Tea

More than anything, Charles Townshend's 1767 Revenue Act had exacerbated existing problems and intensified the issue of rights. From a question of taxing authority and purpose, the conflict had moved into the very marrow of colonial life. In questioning the Townshend duties and the methods for their collection and administration, colonial political leaders had begun to question their place in the Empire. If the Crown could take *Gaspee* suspects to London for trial, pay the salaries and expenses of Crown-appointed colonial governors, and station troops permanently in the colonies, all without consultation, what lay ahead? Colonial intellectuals rummaged through their classics to find comparable examples of despotism and tyranny. By 1773, over the course of ten years, two new realities had emerged. The first was that the colonial assumption of the empire's principal objective, to protect, nurture, and respect the colonies with a minimum of interference, might be mistaken. The imperial authorities, on the other hand, had now a sharper sense of the colonies' presumptions and had countered by reminding them that they were constitutionally dependent outlands. Collectively, the colonies were providers and consumers. Each one had been "created" by the Crown and so remained subordinate to it. The paradox was that the colonists were British subjects, with rights equal to those of all other British subjects, distinguished only by their local circumstances. However, as equals they were also equally subject to Parliament's power and so satisfied Edmund Burke's "virtual representation" logic. The question, in the end, for colonists was not the constitutionality of Parliament's authority but the constitutionality of its actions. In 1773, the Tea Act further complicated the question.

The near bankrupt East India Company had a stockpile of 17 million pounds of tea in England. Parliament was eager to help, given the number of stockholders in the Commons. It passed the Tea Act, which retained a tax on the tea but reduced the import duty. The act allowed the East India Company to sell directly to selected consignees in America, bypassing middlemen in both Britain and the colonies and thus lowering the end price to the consumer and promising increased consumption. The company sent half a million pounds of tea to Boston, New York, Philadelphia, and Charleston. When the Boston shipment was held up because of customs technicalities, the town's radicals had time to organize, and they dumped 342 chests of tea into Boston Harbor. A merchant-organized body of men worked all night at their happy task. Samuel Adams had led a gathering of 8,000 Bostonians earlier in the day to add a theatrical touch to the "destruction of the tea." The "Tea Party" (as it came to be known in the nineteenth century) had much to do with merchant initiatives, but the financial and competition issues were easily politicized, especially in Boston in 1773. In other ports, such as New York and Philadelphia, the consignees were intimidated and most resigned. In Boston, Governor Hutchinson and other conservatives were exposed for their favoritism. Hutchinson was already considered a pariah by people like James Otis and Samuel Adams, and he alienated the larger community when it was revealed that his sons and a nephew had been favored with consignee licenses. His position as governor was now untenable, and he went into exile to London in 1774.

In March 1774, Parliament met to consider the king's desire to punish Massachusetts, not over the tea dumping so much as for its earlier and apparently permanent defiance of Crown initiatives. Some, like Pitt and Edmund Burke, wanted to take a softer tack, but George III wanted harsher action and Parliament obliged, with explosive results. The throngs who attended and endorsed the dumping of the tea and, by extension, the entire Massachusetts community were all guilty of treason, according to the king. The Massachusetts General Court was culpable because it appeared to have condoned the vandals' actions. Between March 25 and June 2, 1774, an angry Parliament passed the four Coercive Acts:

Boston Port Bill This act prohibited routine shipping in Boston Harbor. It allowed military supplies to be unloaded along with food and fuel for civilian use under customs supervision. Customs officers were to be located in Salem, and Boston's port would be closed to commercial traffic until the East India Company and the customs service were somehow reimbursed for the loss of the tea.

Administration of Justice Act This complex act was designed to protect Crown officials from the antipathy of local courts. For example, if any official acting legally on behalf of the Crown was charged with a capital crime, the royal governor could have the case removed to Britain for trial.

Massachusetts Government Act This act, passed on May 20, was at the heart of what the Parliament and the king meant by "coercion." It gave the royal governor extensive powers to appoint public officials, including sheriffs and lower court judges; to approve or disapprove assembly and town meetings (to stifle the radicals); and to govern the province. Without actually writing into law the cancellation of the 1691 Massachusetts charter, this act effectively suspended it. Moreover, on May 13, General Thomas Gage was appointed royal governor suggesting the likelihood of martial law.

Quartering Act: The June 2 act applied to all colonies, but its main target was Massachusetts.

On the same day the Massachusetts Government Act was passed, May 20, 1774, Parliament passed a separate piece of legislation, the *Quebec Act.* It hearkened back to the Royal Proclamation of 1763. At first blush, the 1774 act was a tightening of government in Quebec, which had been administered in an ad hoc way since 1763. But it went further. It expanded the territory of the new Province of Quebec all the way south to the Ohio River and west to the Mississippi. It formally, and with a touch of finality, closed off the west to the northern colonies by using the boundary line set in the proclamation as Quebec's eastern boundary. Moreover, it assigned most taxing rights in the new territory to Parliament. Any future legislative system was to be controlled by a Crown-appointed council. It guaranteed Quebecers the use of the French language and the rights to their Catholic institutions and practices. If this was the future, it was a scary one for the thirteen colonies. Also, an immense area south of the Ohio and west to the Mississippi was made an "Indian Reservation" under Crown control. The whole of the west was now closed off to any expansion of the various colonies.

A major crisis loomed. The Quebec Act was lumped in with the Coercive Acts by colonists as one of the "Intolerable Acts." The committees of correspondence now rose in importance in the electric atmosphere of 1774. Boston's calls for boycotts were superseded by a more ambitious plan from Rhode Island and New York for an intercolonial meeting to discuss issues and frame a response to Parliament. Members of the disbanded Massachusetts legislature then recommended that a congress be held in Philadelphia. By the end of August, every colony except Georgia had chosen delegates by one formal means or another, and the first Continental Congress met on September 5 in Philadelphia's Carpenters Hall.

The First Continental Congress

The first thing to note about the first Continental Congress is that there was initially no clear consensus on how to deal with the crisis. Each colony was given one vote, regardless of the number of delegates it sent to Philadelphia, and, during the proceedings, conservative and radical delegates turned the discussions into debates. But the delegates' options were narrowing. The general hope of "reconciliation" was a forlorn one, and British intransigence had made the polite appeals of the Stamp Act Congress a distant memory. The discussions became focused when Paul Revere delivered to the Congress a package of proposals from

Suffolk, the county in which Boston was located. These succinct recommenda-tions, known as the "Suffolk Resolves," were serious rejections of the Crown's constitutional sovereignty. First, the resolves denied the constitutionality of the Coercive Acts. Second, the people of Massachusetts were urged to compose a new government, collect taxes, and withhold any that were normally due to the Crown until the acts were repealed. The third resolve was the familiar one of con-certed economic sanctions. The fourth was daring, the result of a passionate reac-tion to the Intolerable Acts. The people of Massachusetts, with the support of the collective, were to arm themselves and coordinate their local militias for action. The moderates reacted with fear, and, although most of them disapproved of most of the Crown's actions and supported a concerted protest, few were prepared to wage war against the Crown or reject its ultimate constitutional supremacy.

The Suffolk Resolves proposed armed resistance to the Crown. No one doubted that the Crown would see the resolves as insurrection. Joseph Galloway of the Pennsylvania delegation prepared a "plan" that he hoped would allay the radicals and find favor with the king and Parliament. His elaborate and novel proposal rested on a simple premise of each colony retaining authority over its internal affairs while designing a supra-colonial federation. There would be a "union" between the colonies, as a collective, and Britain. The empire had entered a new era, and the events of the last 10 years had convinced even the most conservative politician in America that the world of 1763 could not be fully restored. The most aggressive opponents of British policy had moved on from a basically conservative desire to resume the status quo of the 1750s to becoming unshakable disputants of British sovereignty. Galloway's plan was, in fact, an attempt not only to reconcile the colonies with British policy but also to blunt the developing movement toward a radical versus conservative schism in each colony. His elaborate plan rested on the model of a federated council made up with equal representation from each colony and a president appointed by the king with veto powers. The president and council would serve as a "branch" of Parliament, and acts or regulations dealing with America could originate in either the "union" or Parliament but would require the consent of each. Galloway's plan was almost adopted by the Congress, losing by a 6–5 vote, but, in a telling decision, the radicals had the motion expunged from the min-utes. In any case, Galloway's plan was likely unacceptable to either Parliament or colonial assemblies. It did, however, indicate the apprehensions of much of the colonial population, and, if its design was imaginative, it nevertheless was impractical in the circumstances. The Congress concluded with a biting declaration of colonial rights. It predictably denounced the Crown's post-1763 revenue policies and identified 13 acts of Parliament that violated assumed colonial constitutional rights. The delegates agreed to reconvene on May 10, 1775 if their proposals were not dealt with.

No one was contemplating separation. Indeed, the colonies were not far enough along in their collectivism to think of anything beyond expressing a common front for locally held concerns. However, the common front was hardening. John Dickinson's 1767 thesis regarding the proposed punishment of New York, "the cause of one is the cause of all," was starting to look like the only way to view the wider potential of the Crown's actions in the Coercive Acts. When Patrick Henry declared, "I am not a Virginian but an American" at the first Continental Congress in the fall of 1774, he saw the Coercive Acts as an action against all the colonies. Of course, Henry was a Virginian in the sense that it was a sovereign entity in the way of John Adams's suggestion that the colonies were not part of Great Britain but that "Massachusetts is a realm, New York is a realm [and all colonies are similarly realms]" under the sovereign authority and under the protective cloak of the king. Meanwhile, appeals to the Crown continued. James Wilson of Pennsylvania, Thomas Jefferson of Virginia, and John Adams of Massachusetts each published pamphlets that stressed the unique circumstances of the colonies. They were not ready to go further than to suggest that the king's somewhat ambiguous role as protector of colonial prerogatives was in limbo.

By the fall of 1774 words were taking a back seat to actions. Militiamen were congregating in the Boston area and General Gage was fortifying the town's approaches. The towns of Massachusetts were taking the Continental Congress's instructions about armed preparations seriously. When Parliament considered the declarations of the Continental Congress, there was some minority support in Britain for using the Continental Congress as a mechanism for dealing with the impasse. There was even a hint of understanding from the otherwise intolerant George III, but the majority in Parliament had already declared Massachusetts to be in a state of rebellion. The use of trade as a political weapon reached a climax during the winter of 1774–1775 when, in all colonies, the non-importation hardliners in the Continental Association agreed to enforce the boycotts in their communities. Parliament then passed the New England Restraining Act, which forbade New Englanders from trading with foreign nations, and, later, it extended the proscription to include all the other colonies engaged in the Continental Association.

Armed Resistance

The likelihood of sanctioned military action by colonial militias increased because the prospects for moderation were dying in both Parliament and the Continental Congress. In February, an illegal Massachusetts Provincial Congress gave out directions to the population to prepare for war. Earlier, in

January 1775, Lord Dartmouth, the secretary of state for the colonies, sent a letter to General Gage ordering him to enforce the Coercive Acts with vigor and to stifle any militia preparations. Gage did not get those instructions until April. Meanwhile, the Massachusetts countryside was buzzing with expectation. In Virginia, Patrick Henry gave his famous "give me liberty or give me death" speech to the House of Burgesses in anticipation of New England's confrontation with the British Army. A month later, on April 19, 1775, war broke out in Massachusetts.

Lexington and Concord are towns immediately to the west of Boston. Taken together, the names are among the most immediately recognizable in the Revolution's glossary of events and symbols. The site of the first formal military confrontation between the citizen soldiers of Massachusetts and the British Army is now the Minute Man National Historical Park and is located on Liberty Street in Concord. National historical parks are public, secular shrines. The naming of the site after the "ready in a minute" militiamen celebrates the New England militiamen who fought at Lexington and Concord. The legendary events are wrapped in the stirring and dramatic ride of Paul Revere to warn the assembled militias. He likely did not utter the lines the "British are coming" and was actually captured before he got to Concord, but his motivation and actions and those of the civilian soldiers who fought there are what matter. The wonderful metaphor the "shot heard around the World" was not coined until July 4, 1837, during the commemoration of a monument at Concord.

General Gage sent 700 regulars (on what was considered a police action) to Concord, twenty miles from Boston, to destroy the military materials that reportedly were being gathered by the "rebels." After brushing aside a hesitant resistance at Lexington, the British force proceeded to Concord, took down a liberty pole (by then an ideological colonial emblem of resistance), and destroyed some equipment. Within hours, it was under attack from a very large number of militiamen, and the British commander, Lieutenant Colonel Smith, chose to march back to Boston. En route, he was attacked from all sides by large numbers of militiamen. Eventually, an estimated 4,000 militiamen were engaged that day. Smith's orderly retreat turned into a panicked rush and only reinforcements at Lexington prevented a complete rout. Even so, the numbers of British casualties were shocking. Nearly 300 British troops were killed, wounded, or missing, compared with fewer than 100 Americans. The British made it back to the safety of Charlestown, adjacent to Boston, but an undeclared war had begun.

There was excitement in New England with the news of a victory over what was now clearly understood to be a callous British government. On May 10, the second Continental Congress met in Philadelphia's state house, which would later be enshrined as "Independence Hall" after it provided the venue for the signing of the Declaration of Independence. In June, John Adams recommended that the militia forces surrounding Boston be designated as the core of a proposed Continental Army. An organizational plan was devised, and George Washington was the unanimous choice as commander in chief. Meanwhile, the Battle of Bunker Hill and Breed's Hill in Charlestown, Massachusetts on June 17 sent more shock waves through the British leadership. Again, a large militia army inflicted stunning casualties on the British, who, although they claimed victory at the end of a bloody day, could see that control of Boston was unattainable. If that were the case, Massachusetts and perhaps all of New England were out of reach of the Crown. Gage, in what was immediately understood as a token decision, had earlier declared martial law and offered amnesty to all rebels except John Hancock and Samuel Adams. If the announcements had any effect at all, they served to spur on the rebels and add to the propaganda war that was forming around the events. Two weeks after Bunker Hill, when Washington arrived in Massachusetts to take command, the militia army was over 14,000 strong. A civil war was underway, even if the British chose to see it as a rebellion. The Continental Congress now had a military arm, the Continental Army, and militias were being raised in all colonies at the local level. At the same time, there was no unanimity on the direction resistance should take. The earlier debates on the way to resist or cope with British policy had divided the colonial population. The division would ripen into "loyalist" and "patriot" convictions in a war that was not a *declared war* until after the Declaration of Independence but was in fact underway after the spring of 1775.

Colonial Identity and the Declaration of Independence

The meaning of the conflict was difficult to grasp for even the most outraged colonist. Was there a way to resolve the impasse and avoid further bloodshed? Far to the right of the radical members of the Continental Congress and most colonial assemblies was a substantial part of the population that was apprehensive of any outcome that released the Crown from its role in America. No one wanted martial law or war, but no conservative wanted power to reside exclusively in the hands of what many saw as a dangerous minority of local politicians and demagogues. No radical could abide the future of a hegemonic Parliament. What to do? The outbreak of war had brought the issues into sharp focus. Sober observers were horrified at the prospects of more war. Had the opposition to the Crown gone too far? A test came in July 1775, mere weeks after the extraordinary violence at Bunker Hill. John Dickinson, with the formal approval of the Continental Congress, composed an appeal to George III that repeated the common theme of colonial affection and historical association with the Monarchy and specifically with George. The petition, best remembered as the "Olive Branch Petition," asked the king to call a halt to military action and set an agenda for reconciliation. Perhaps Dickinson knew how this appeal would be greeted and perhaps Congress saw it as a public relations exercise because, after all, as far as the British were concerned, the colonists had forced the fighting on the British Army and the Crown needed to suppress the uprising. In any case, Congress went ahead with war plans even as the petition was on its way to London.

At the same time, Dickinson and Thomas Jefferson produced another resolution, a "Declaration of the Causes and Necessities of Taking Up Arms," which skirted the issue of independence but made it clear that now that arms had been taken up, colonists would resist to the death rather than submit to Parliament's strategies. Congress adopted the declaration. It broke for recess at the beginning of August but had begun to act like a federated union of the colonies. It appointed officers to negotiate with native tribes and set up a post office to expedite the flow of political, military, and civil instructions across the thirteen colonies. As for the "Olive Branch," when it reached the king, he refused to acknowledge it and added the royal imprimatur to Parliament's announcement that the colonies were in a state of rebellion. The Continental Congress ended its vacation on September 12 with Georgia in attendance. Members learned the fate of the Olive Branch Petition and the king's announcement in December. It was clear to the most sanguine colonial observer that there was little or no hope for a satisfactory and peaceful resolution to the conflict.

The experiences and the education of Americans since the Seven Years' War had led to some very basic revisions in their sense of identity. As they were drawn into the conflict, they had protested and then resisted as Britons. John Adams, Patrick Henry, the Carolina Regulators, and the New England minutemen *were* British. They had appealed their cases as Britons. They were also parochial members of local societies. The crises of the 1760s and 1770s had not made them "American" so much as it had blurred and then eroded their affections for Britain. Their local affinities, with town or province for example, rose higher than their imperial connections. At least that was the case for most. It is sad, perhaps, to note that Joseph Galloway wanted badly to return to America after its independence but was denied access and Thomas Hutchinson's great desire in exile was to be buried in Massachusetts. Still, the 100,000 or so loyalists who left for Canada, the West Indies, or Britain after independence represent the largest exodus of refugees in the history of the Americas. Most remained Virginians or New Yorkers or Carolinians even in exile. But the population as a whole had come a long way from the emphatic claim to British citizenship in Dickinson's Stamp Act Congress pronouncements.

For the colonists, the war that had begun at Lexington-Concord would be difficult to fight, but, in the heady atmosphere of the fall of 1775, an ambitious Congress authorized two expeditions against Canada. Having noted an earlier success at Fort Ticonderoga on Lake Champlain, the Congress hoped to "liberate" Quebec. The campaign failed, and, during 1776 and 1777, the fortunes of Washington's armies and the various militias declined, before successes in 1777 at home and French intervention turned the tide of the war. By then, independence had been declared, and the war was no longer just a matter of defending property and principles. It had become a struggle to prevent the restoration of some form of Crown sovereignty. The year 1776 began with an ideological bang. In January, Thomas Paine, an English populist radical who had been in Philadelphia for less than two years, published *Common Sense*. Its success can be measured in two ways: in the sales within a very short time of an estimated 120,000 copies and in its marvelous mix of direct, logical advice and comprehendible political theory. Its themes were straightforward: the colonies had passed Great Britain in quality of life and in the optimism of their political institutions. The point of no return had passed, in any case. Britain was decadent and redundant. Paine's attack on the "Royal Brute," George III, was typical of the common language used to illustrate elaborate issues. For Paine, the universal democrat, the cause in America would serve "mankind," but, for the moment, it appeared to Congress that the colonies had *no choice* but to continue to pursue the process of separation.

Even as Paine added "common sense" to the pamphlet wars, there was a rising tide of support for independence in Congress and in many colonial assemblies. A convention in North Carolina in April advised its delegation in Philadelphia to seek a declaration of independence. Virginia did the same. Richard Henry Lee struck the memorable phrase that the colonies *were* "free and independent States" (each an independent sovereignty). But, given the exigencies of war, no colony was in a position to make a unilateral declaration of independence. Independence had to be declared by all thirteen colonies in concert. Congress put together a committee consisting of Thomas Jefferson, Benjamin Franklin, John Adams, Robert Livingston of New York, and Roger Sherman of Connecticut. Jefferson was given the job of writing up a draft of the resolution, and Franklin was its main editor. The 1,333-word document is first and foremost a manifesto. It is identified more formally in its preamble as "The unanimous Declaration of the thirteen united States of America." Its tone is reasonable. It states the causes and inevitability of separation.

Its audience is the colonial population, the British public, and the international community, and it makes a formal statement to Parliament and the king. It is also a call to arms already taken up—a logical, stylistic, and quite firm justification for the end of British rule. It addresses the king in the third person and refers to Parliament only obliquely, by implication. It opens with a ruminative discourse on the natural rights of colonists and lays out its case in a series of deterministic phrases:

> We hold these truths to be self-evident, that all men are created equal, that they are endowed by their Creator with certain unalienable Rights, that among these are Life, Liberty and the pursuit of Happiness.—That to secure these rights, Governments are instituted among Men, deriving their just powers from the consent of the governed,—That whenever any Form of Government becomes destructive of these ends, it is the Right of the People to alter or abolish it, and to institute new Government, laying its foundation on such principles and organizing its powers in such Form, as to them shall seem most likely to effect their Safety and Happiness.

There follows a list of 27 violations of colonial rights. That is, that the *contract* between governed and government (the colonists' consent, as defined in the clause cited above) had been nullified by the king's complicity in Parliament's unconstitutional behavior. The 27 violations referred to specific acts and actions of the Crown, the sum of which had made any association with the empire impossible. Allowing for exaggeration, the complaints trace the troubled history of the post-1763 era. The colonies had rejected Parliament's authority in several ways before the Declaration of Independence, but here the king's abnegation of his protective role is used as the unavoidable cause for separation. Finally, the declaration concludes with a stirring paragraph that combines courage and hope. Courage in that the signatories were guilty of treason if the war effort failed. And hope that the world would understand the logic of separation. The peroration is decisive:

> We [the representatives in Congress],... in the Name, and by the Authority of the good People of these Colonies solemnly publish and declare, That these United Colonies are, and of Right out to be Free and Independent States [a direct use of Richard Henry Lee's earlier phrase]; that they are Absolved from all Allegiance to the British Crown....

The term "all men are created equal" has bedeviled analysis since 1776. In a society where slaves, natives, women, and loyalists were patently not equal, the phrase is a philosophical abstraction on natural law or refers to the equality between colonial assemblies and other legislative bodies. It remains a controversial issue. Also, Jefferson's claim that the Declaration of Independence is made in the "Name" and "by the Authority" of the people slides around the opposition to independence that included as much as one-third of the population in 1776.

It is misleading to see the declaration as making the colonies independent or, in fact, as defining the Revolution. It took a long and bloody war to gain independence and more than independence to complete the Revolution. How many colonial leaders in 1776 could have envisioned the 1787 Constitution of the United States? The Revolution represents more than the sentiments and objectives laid out in the Declaration of Independence. The American Revolution was an experiment in redefining what was there already, a set of regional and local authorities with long histories. The first stage of that experiment began in the war and then occupied the peace that followed. It led to the creation of a new federal nation-state, a constitutional republic. Although social change was slower in coming than political change, the way was open to a future that took a great deal of its colonial conditions with it: slavery, regionalism, localism, and territorial presumptions. The objectives of the Declaration of Independence had still to be worked out, but, in July 1776, a start to the formal end of the colonial phase of American history was made.

SUGGESTED READINGS

On the Seven Years' War see Fred Anderson, *The Crucible of War: The Seven Years' War and the Fate of Empire in British North America, 1754–1766* (New York: Knopf, 2000) and *The War That Made America: A Short History of the French and Indian War* (New York: Viking Press, 2005). Together, these books serve as descriptive and analytical overviews of the war as a military and political event. See also Walter Borneman, *The French and Indian War: Deciding the Fate of North America* (New York: HarperCollins, 2006) and Stephen Brumwell, *Redcoats: The British Soldier and War in the Americas, 1755–1763* (Cambridge: Cambridge University Press, 2002). Although his histories are no longer used in academic analyses of the Anglo-French struggle in North America, Francis Parkman's huge body of work, composed in the second half of the nineteenth century, is worth our notice. The research is impressive but so too is Parkman's lyrical and graphic narratives. See, for example, his *A Half Century of Conflict* (1892). The most accessible survey of pre-Revolutionary pamphlets and manifestoes is Bernard Bailyn, *The Ideological Origins of the American Revolution*, enlarged ed. (Cambridge, MA: Harvard University Press, 1992). Robert M. Calhoon, *The Loyalists in Revolutionary America, 1760–1781* (New York: Harcourt Brace, 1973) deals with the complexities of the loyalists' problems in a readable, comprehensive way. William H. Nelson, *The American Tory* (Oxford: Clarendon Press, 1961) stands up well 50 years after its publication. The growing resistance to British imperial reforms is handled with great insight by Pauline Maier, *From Resistance to Revolution: Colonial Radicals and the Development of America Opposition to Britain, 1765–1776* (New York: Norton, 1991). Edmund Morgan and Helen Morgan, *The Stamp Act Crisis: Prologue to Revolution* (Chapel Hill: University of North Carolina Press, 1953) is still the definitive introduction to the crisis that sewed ideological resistance into colonial attitudes. Jane Merritt, *At the Crossroads: Indians and Empires on the Mid-Atlantic Frontier, 1700–1763* (Chapel Hill: University of North Carolina Press, 2004) includes useful commentary on the impact on native populations of the Seven Years' War and the imperial crisis. The early chapters in Eric Nellis, *The Long Road to Change: America's Revolution, 1750–1820* (Toronto: Broadview Press, 2007) review much of the content of this chapter.

General Reference Bibliography

* * * * * ★ * ★ * * * * *

See also the Suggested Readings after each chapter.

Documents

There are several useful collections of transcribed published contemporary documents, the best of which are Jack P. Greene, *Settlements to Society, 1607–1763: A Documentary History of Colonial America* (New York: Norton, 1975) and *Colonies to Nation, 1763–1789: A Documentary History of the American Revolution* (New York: Norton, 1975). There are many published diaries, correspondences, memoirs, and travelogues in circulation. The diaries of Samuel Sewall and William Byrd II in various editions are among the most commonly consulted and the *Autobiography* of Benjamin Franklin is never out of print. The diaries and historical narratives of New England's founders, such as John Winthrop and William Bradford and many others, are available in print. Colonial Americans were fond of writing histories even as they were making history, and from John Smith in the 1620s to Thomas Hutchinson in the 1750s there is a rich seam of contemporary thought and expression. I have been especially influenced by travelogues. An older but fascinating collection of sometimes obscure travelers' memories is Newton D. Mereness, ed., *Travels in the American Colonies* (1916; repr., New York: Antiquarian Press, 1961). Richard J. Hooker, ed., *The Carolina Backcountry on the Eve of the Revolution: The Journal and Other Writings of Charles Woodmason, Anglican Itinerant* (Chapel Hill: University of North Carolina Press, 1953) is one of the most compelling in the genre. Familiar travelogues are Peter Kalm, *Travels in North America,* translated by Johann Reinhold Forster (Barre, MA: Imprint Society, 1972); Albert Bushnell Hart, ed., *Hamilton's Itinerarium* (St. Louis: W.K. Bixby, 1907); Mark Van Doren, ed., *The Travels of William Bartram* (New York: Dover, 1928); and Andrew Burnaby, *Travels Through the Middle Settlements in North America* (Ithaca, NY: Cornell University Press, 1960 [imprint of 1775 edition]). An interesting northern colonial view of the late colonial south is Daniel Coquillette and Neil York, eds., *Portrait of a Patriot: The Major Political and Legal Papers of Josiah Quincy Junior,* vol. 3, *The Southern Journal* (Boston: The Colonial Society of Massachusetts, 2007). The nineteenth century publications of colonial legislative and other official papers and records are available in most large academic libraries. The Internet has made available extensive sources of private, public, and official documents from the colonial period. The Library of Congress site (http://catalog.loc.gov/) and the Avalon Project site at Yale University (http://avalon.law.yale.edu/default.asp) suggest the depth and range of documents that are available online. Each of the thirteen original states has archival collections that are being digitalized and made available, and state historical societies are doing the same with their collections of private diaries, notebooks, and correspondence. Kelly Schrum, et al., *U.S. History Matters: A Student Guide to U.S. History Online,* 2nd ed. (Boston: Bedford /St. Martins, 2009) is an up-to-date reference on Internet sources.

Survey Texts

D.W. Meinig, *The Shaping of America: A Geographical Perspective on 500 Years of History,* vol. 1, *Atlantic America, 1492–1800* (New Haven: Yale University Press, 1986) is historical geography at its best and offers original ways of understanding settlement patterns. It is highly recommended. Richard Middleton, *Colonial America: A History, 1565–1776,* 3rd ed. (Oxford: Blackwell, 2002) is comprehensive, well documented, and has a superb bibliography, as has Peter C. Hoffer, *The Brave New World: A History of Early America* (Baltimore: Johns Hopkins University Press, 2006). Gary B. Nash, *Red, White, and Black: The Peoples of Early North America,* 5th ed. (Upper Saddle River, NJ: Prentice Hall, 2006) works as a conventional survey text, but the themes of racial and ethnic interplay give it a unique quality. It is also very well written. R.C. Simmons, *The American Colonies: From Settlement to Independence* (New York: Norton, 1976) is dense and dependable. Paul Lucas, *American Odyssey, 1607–1789* (Englewood Cliffs, NJ: Prentice Hall, 1984) is a well-organized text with a very good bibliography. Alan Taylor's award-winning *American Colonies: The Settling of North America* (New York: Penguin, 2002) approaches the subject from a comparative and regional perspective and reminds us that the various European empires in America were shaped by the cultures, landscapes, and aims of the founding nations. Although the book's organization is a bit unconventional, it effectively fuses regional, chronological, cultural, and ethnographic issues. A useful if now dated bibliography for the subject is David L. Ammerman and Philip D. Morgan, *Books about Early America: 2001 Titles* (Williamsburg, VA: Institute of Early American History and Culture, 1989). The early chapters in Douglas P. Egerton et al., *The Atlantic World: A History, 1400–1888* (Wheeling, IL: Harlan Davidson, 2007) show a wider scope of the ways early American history is now studied. For examples of the detailed studies produced by early twentieth century historians, see Lawrence Henry Gipson, *The British Empire Before the American Revolution*, 15 vols. (Caldwell, ID: Caxton Printers, 1936–1970) and Charles McLean Andrews, *The Colonial Period of American History*, 4 vols. (New Haven: Yale University Press, 1934–1938).

General Reference

Jeffrey Morris and Richard B. Morris, eds., *Encyclopedia of American History*, 7th ed. (New York: Harper Collins, 1996) is indispensable as a reference and is efficiently organized. See also Thomas L. Purvis, *Almanacs of American Life: Colonial America to 1763* (New York: Facts on File, 1999), which is a very useful compilation of important data. Thomas C. Cochran and Wayne Andrews, eds., *Concise Dictionary of American History* (New York: Scribner's, 1962) is an older but dependable source, arranged alphabetically by topic and event. *Historical Statistics of the United States, Colonial Times to 1970* (Washington, DC: Bureau of the Census, 1975) is especially useful for colonial trade and population data. Biographical information is included in the Morris and Cochran volumes cited above but the *American National Biography*, 25 vols. (New York: Oxford University Press, 1999–2002) is the obvious starting place for any biographical information and comment. The single volume *Concise Dictionary of American Biography* (New York: Scribner's, 1980) can be consulted for abbreviated biographies of the prominent colonial personages. The biographical literature on important colonial Americans is vast, and the lives of personalities such as Benjamin Franklin, John Winthrop, Cotton Mather, and many others continue to attract scholars.

Specific References

On colonial agriculture, the work of Percy Bidwell and John Falconer, *History of Agriculture in the Northern United States, 1620–1860* (1925; repr., New York: Peter Smith, 1941) and Lewis C. Gray, *History of Agriculture in the Southern United States to 1860* (Washington, DC: Carnegie Institution, 1933) stand up well even after three generations of monograph scholarship. There is a growing scholarly interest in the "material culture" of the colonists, and an excellent starting point is James Deetz, *In Small Things Forgotten: An Archeology of Early American Life,* rev. and expanded ed. (New York: Anchor Books, 1996). Two very useful introductions to "lifestyles" can be found in the dated and chatty but well-researched Alice Morse Earle, *Home Life in Colonial Days* (New York: The Macmillan Company, 1898) and in David Freeman Hawke, *Everyday Life in Early America* (New York: Harper and Row, 1988), which is largely about seventeenth century conditions.

Two recommended treatments of colonial economic history are John J. McCusker and Russell R. Menard, *The Economy of British America 1607–1789* (Chapel Hill: University of North Carolina Press, 1985) and John McCusker and Kenneth Morgan, eds., *The Early Modern Atlantic Economy* (Cambridge: Cambridge University Press, 2000). The latter is an anthology of recent scholarship and works well as a general reference. An important and much-cited work on the early modern world economy is Immanuel Wallerstein, *The Modern World-System,* vol. 2, *Mercantilism and the Consolidation of the European World Economy, 1600–1750* (New York: Academic Press, 1980). Bruce Trigger et al., eds., *The Cambridge History of the Native Peoples of the Americas,* 3 vols. (New York: Cambridge University Press, 1996–2000) is a mine of scholarly reference and interpretation. African American subjects and chronologies can be found in Alton Hornsby, *Chronology of African American History* (Detroit: Gale, 1997) a volume that includes material not found in most general reference works. See also the Suggested Readings for Chapter 8.

The population data for colonial America is dealt with in *Historical Statistics* cited previously. For native populations, see William M. Denevan, *The Native Populations of the Americas in 1492,* 2nd ed. (Madison, WI: University of Wisconsin Press, 1992). An impressive summary of slave populations in the western hemisphere is appended to Orlando Patterson, *Slavery and Social Death: A Comparative Study* (Cambridge, MA: Harvard University Press, 1982). See also the early chapters of Herbert S. Klein, *A Population History of the United States* (Cambridge: Cambridge University Press, 2004) for concise estimates and demographic analysis. For Europe, see Massimo Livi Bacci, *The Population of Europe* (Malden, MA: Blackwell, 1999). There are useful essays on early modern British demographics in Michael

Anderson, ed., *British Population History* (Cambridge: Cambridge University Press, 1996). See also E.A. Wrigley's seminal *Population and History* (New York: McGraw Hill, 1969), which remains valuable as an introduction to demographic method and theory.

The best reference for the religious history of the colonies is E.S. Gaustad and Philip Barlow, *New Historical Atlas of Religion in America* (New York: Oxford University Press, 2001), which combines regional, cultural, and chronological references with sectarian data. The best general reference to the interplay of time and geography is Geoffrey Barraclough, ed., *The Times Atlas of World History*, rev. ed. (Maplewood, NJ: Hammond, 1984). The graphics and cartography in this well-organized volume are accompanied by excellent text. That volume can be complemented by Herman Kinder and Werner Hilgemann, *The Penguin Atlas of World History*, vol. 1, *From the Beginning to the eve of the French Revolution* (Harmondsworth, UK: Penguin, 1974), which contains a thorough annotated chronology to go with its superb maps; it is especially useful in sorting out the political and dynastic complexities of early modern Europe and for its clear treatment of American and African history. Colin McEvedy, *The Penguin Atlas of African History* (London: Penguin, 1980) has clearly delineated material on medieval and early modern African history. Kenneth T. Jackson, ed., *Atlas of American History*, rev. ed. (New York: Charles Scribner's Sons, 1984) has a useful, brief, and detailed set of maps for the colonial period. A model of the genre is R. Cole Harris, ed., *Historical Atlas of Canada*, vol. 1 (Toronto: University of Toronto Press, 1987). N.J.G. Pounds, *An Historical Geography of Europe* (Cambridge: Cambridge University Press, 1990) has the virtue of being descriptive and interpretive. Alva Curtis Wilgus, *Historical Atlas of Latin America* (New York: Cooper Square Publishing, 1969) has not been updated but is generally reliable. A very specific but useful compilation is David Henige, *Colonial Governors from the Fifteenth Century to the Present* (Madison, WI: University of Wisconsin Press, 1970). This volume identifies every governor who served in the American colonies.

Anthologies

The best way to keep abreast of the trends in research and themes in early American history is to review current and past articles in the journal *The William and Mary Quarterly*. A superb recent anthology is Daniel Vickers, ed., *A Companion to Colonial America* (Malden, MA: Blackwell, 2003). See also Jack P. Greene and J.R. Pole, *Colonial British America: Essays in the New History of the Early Modern Era* (Baltimore: Johns Hopkins University Press, 1984). Karen O. Kupperman, ed., *Major Problems in American Colonial History:*

Documents and Essays, 2nd ed. (Boston: Houghton Mifflin, 2000) matches excerpts of recent scholarly essays with relevant document selections. A broader context is offered in Alison Games and Adam Rothman, eds., *Major Problems in Atlantic History: Documents and Essays* (Boston: Houghton Mifflin, 2008). Also useful are the early sections of Richard D. Brown, ed., *Major Problems in the Era of the American Revolution*, 2nd ed. (Boston: Houghton Mifflin, 2000); it is in the same series as the Kupperman and Games volumes. In a field that is consistently being revised, Gad Heuman and James Walvin, eds., *The Slavery Reader* (London: Routledge, 2003) is a welcome resource. James Marten, ed., *Children in Colonial America* (New York: New York University Press, 2007) opens up another layer of scholarship in colonial historiography.

Index

* * * * * ★ ★ ★ * * * * *